W9-APG-512

Water Conflict

*Economics, Politics, Law and
Palestinian-Israeli
Water Resources*

Water Conflict

Economics, Politics, Law and Palestinian-Israeli Water Resources

Sharif S. Elmusa

Institute for Palestine Studies
Washington, DC

The Institute for Palestine Studies, founded in Beirut in 1963, is an independent nonprofit Arab research and publication center, not affiliated with any political organization or government. The opinions expressed in this publication do not necessarily reflect those of the Institute.

Library of Congress Cataloging-in-Publication Data

Elmusa, Sharif S.
  Water Conflict: economics, politics, law and Palestinian-Israeli water resources / Sharif S. Elmusa.
    p.   cm.
Includes bibliographic references (p.) and index.
  ISBN 0-88728-268-7.
  1. West Bank/Gaza Strip—Water resources. 2. West Bank/Gaza Strip—Water policy.—Israel.   3. West Bank/Gaza Strip—Economics of water—Israel.   4. West Bank/Gaza Strip—Proposals for resolution—Israel.
I. Title
Library of Congress Catalog Number: 97-75290

Printed in the United States of America

In memory of

Abd al-Karim
Abd al-Rahim
and Salih

*My cousins and playmates
who drowned in 1961 in the Jordan River*

Acknowledgments

Writing this book was an exhilarating journey. I had the luck and the burden of starting it in the midst of the peace talks (1992–93) and being asked to join the Palestinian delegation in Washington as an "advisor," because at that time the Palestinians from outside the Israeli-occupied territories of the West Bank and Gaza Strip were not permitted to join as "members." Although the negotiations seemed in perpetual deadlock in the "land and water working group," my involvement in them was highly motivating for me as an author. The credit for that goes to the members of the negotiating team, in particular to Dr. Haidar 'Abd al-Shafi, then the head of the delegation and the grand man of Palestine, and to Saud Amery, Akram Haniyya, Penny Johnson, Camille Mansour, and Raja Shehada.

I would like to thank many colleagues at the Applied Research Institute of Jerusalem (ARIJ), where I subsequently spent a year as senior Fulbright fellow, for their warmth and generosity, and for sharing with me their expertise: Jad Isaac, ARIJ's executive director, and Muhammad Abu Amiriyya, Yusuf Abu As'ad, Nina Beebe, Ibrahim al-Dajani, Nadia al-Dajani, Ahamd Hammad, Rujis Qumsiyya, Violet Qumsiyya, and Walid Sabbah. During my Fulbright year I also spent time at the University of Jordan's Center for Strategic Studies in Amman. I must acknowledge the most generous welcome by Mustafa Hamarneh, the Center's executive director, and Nahla Khalaf, the chief manager. I also wish to extend my gratitude for the sharing of expertise and help in locating sources to Hussein al-Musa and Ibrahim Yaghi (both members of the University of Jordan's faculty in the Department of Agriculture) and to Elias Salama, former head of the university's Center for Water Research.

My special thanks go to the staff of the Palestinian Hydrology Group, especially to 'Abd al-Rahman al-Tamimi and Ayman al-Rabi, for their friendship, continuous exchange of views, and the stream of reports and studies they provided me throughout the duration of this project. Other Palestinian water specialists to whom this work is indebted are Amjad Aliewi, 'Abd al-Karim As'ad, Karen Assaf, Hisham Awartani, Shehada al-Dajani, Rami 'Abd al-Hadi, Fadil Ka'wash, Nadir al-Khatib, Tahir Nasir al-Din, Mustafa Nusayba, Issam Shawwa, and Hisham Zarour. They all were most generous with opinion and material. Thanks as well to Mahmud El-Ja'afari, from the Department of Economics at al-Quds (Jerusalem) University, for his friendship and for giving me unrestricted access to his database and econometric research on the agricultural sector and trade of the West Bank and Gaza.

There are others I wish to acknowledge. Tony Allan (School of Oriental and African Studies, University of London), Shawki Barghouti (World Bank), Joseph Dellapenna (Villanova University), Usaid El-Hanbali (World Bank), and Fredric Hof (Armitage Associates, Washington). They all read the manuscript or parts thereof and offered suggestions that improved the text in vital ways. A. Duewer, from the U.S. Department of Agriculture, kindly spent many hours discussing with me the animal feed requirements for meat and dairy. Thomas Naff (University of Pennsylvania) is to be thanked for his generous help with finding sources in the database of the Associates for Middle East Research Water Project (AMER), which he founded before water in the region became a "hot" topic. I must express my gratitude to Idit Avidan and Dan Bitan, of the Truman Institute (Hebrew University), who gracefully kept me abreast on the Institute's research and publications. David Nygaard, the former head of the Ford Foundation's Cairo Office, was most encouraging and went beyond the bounds of duty supplying me with the occasional article or book. Finally, Gary Garrison, Fulbright program officer for the Middle East, and Lee Perez, U.S. Information and Cultural Affairs Consul (East Jerusalem), were most caring in the handling of the Fulbright business and always made me feel they were there to help if needed.

I owe a great debt to former and present members of the staff of the Institute for Palestine Studies, Washington, D.C.: Mary Anderson, Bill Donnelly, Heather Henyon, Inez Kerch, Mark Mecheler, Urvi Mehta, Paul Perry, and Oliver Wilcox. In numerous ways they provided support and broke the tedium of my long hours in the "carrel" in front of the computer's slate screen. In particular, I want to thank Philip Mattar, the executive director of IPS, for his calm and persistent prodding for me to finish and for the many soul-searching conversations concerning the "Palestinian condition." My thanks also to Linda Butler, managing editor of the *Journal of Palestine Studies*, for her rigorous editing of my articles that were published in *JPS*, parts of which also appear in this book. Michele Kjorlien, the encyclopedic author of the chronology and documents sections and assistant editor of *JPS*, always found the time to leave in my mailbox a copy of the latest news item on water. I am most grateful for her help.

I wish to express my immeasurable gratitude to Eric Hooglund, a distinguished scholar of the Middle East, for his superb editing and smoothing of what was a tough-going manuscript and for maintaining his enthusiasm despite the manuscript's interminable length and the profusion of tables and numbers. Without editors, authors would be exposed. I was delighted when told that the proofreader of the book would be Ida Audeh, who copyedited another book of mine and who seems to possess a knack for spotting errors, remembering inconsistencies, and finding the exact word.

Who knows what impels us to do what we do in life? In the Arabic language segment of the national high school test we were asked to write about what "a young Arab man standing by the Jordan River" would tell the river. That was in 1965, a year after Israel's massive diversion of the water from Lake Tiberias which produced an uproar in the Arab world. All I am certain of was that I wrote two pages of lyrical prose, interspersed with some factual material. The factual material I owed to my junior high school social studies teacher, Tawfiq Mar'i. That teacher believed in maps as an essential tool of learning. I still can recall that he let my own modest map of "The Euphrates and the Tigris Rivers and Their Irrigation Projects" hang for an entire semester on the beige wall of my home room in the school of the refugee camp of al-Nuway'ma, near Jericho (the camp since has been razed and a stone's throw away from the site rose the Israeli settlement of No'oma).

He believed, too, that maps were not enough and that geography must be studied on the ground. On one of several trips he organized, he took us to see the tunnel that was under construction for the diversion of the East Ghor (now King Abd Allah) Canal from the Yarmuk River, near the village of al-'Adasiyya. As a bonus, we were able to savor a panoramic view of the spectacular gorge through which the river coursed. Whether these incidents or others like them have had anything to do with my becoming a student of water is immaterial; but I would like to think of this book as a tribute to that dedicated teacher.

Friends and family members on both sides of the Atlantic have been indispensable for the stability of my vision in the midst of the often destabilizing realities in the Middle East. Of the friends, I shall mention Ibrahim Ali, Nabeel Audeh, Fateh Azzam, Lamis Jarrar, May Jayyusi, Lena Jayyusi, Sam'an Khoury, Mary McKone, Lee O'Brien, Mary Sebold, Lynn Simarski (who took my picture for the book), Sami Suleiman, and Anita Vitullo; and of my family members, my sisters, Bahiyya, Suad, and Subhiyya, and brothers, Afif, Ahmad, and Ibrahim. This leaves out other friends and nearly half of the siblings, an incentive for further writing.

My everlasting debt, of course, is to my wife, Judith Tucker, who subsidized the writing of this book in every which way and who was willing to sacrifice her time from writing her own book on the family and Islamic law in eighteenth-century Palestine and Syria. Karmah, my daughter, and Layth, my son, both kept this whole enterprise in perspective by wondering aloud often why instead I wasn't writing a thriller or a best seller.

Contents

3

Water Economics in the West Bank and Gaza 135

4

The Matrix of the Israeli-Palestinian Water Conflict 213

5

Toward Equitable Utilization and Joint Management 289

List of Illustrations

Tables

Maps

Figures

List of Abbreviations

AMER	Associates for Middle East Research
ANERA	American Near East Refugee Aid
ARIJ	Applied Research Institute-Jerusalem
ASIR	Arab Scientific Institute for Research and Technology
BUNT	Ben-Gurion University and Tahal
CF	Conversion Factor
DMZ	Demilitarized Zone
DOP	Declaration of Principles
EU	European Union
FAO	Food and Agriculture Organization
fc	fecal coliform
GDP	Gross Domestic Product
GNP	Gross National Product
HIID	Harvard Institute for International Development
IDA	International Development Association
IDF	Israeli Defense Forces
ILA	International Law Association
ILC	International Law Commission
IWE	Irrigation water equivalent
JD	Jordanian dinar
JNF	Jewish National Fund

JSET	Joint Supervision and Enforcement Teams
JWC	Joint Water Committee
JWU	Jerusalem Water Undertaking
M&I	Municipal and industrial
MVPW	Marginal value product of water
MWGW	Multilateral Working Group on Water
NIS	New Israeli shekel
NRA	Natural Resources Authority
PA	Palestinian Authority
PHG	Palestinian Hydrology Group
R&D	Research and Development
SAR	Sodium adsorption ratio
TDS	Total dissolved solids
UNDP	United Nations Development Program
UNRWA	United Nations Relief and Works Agency
USAID	United States Agency for International Development
WBDP	West Bank Data Base Project

List of Equivalents

Length
centimeter	0.39 inch
meter	3.28 feet, or
	1.09 yards
kilometer	0.62 mile

Area
square meter	1.20 square yards, or
	10.76 square feet
dunum	1,000 square meters, or
	0.10 hectare, or
	0.247 acre
square kilometer	0.386 square mile

Volume
cubic meter	1,000 liters, or
	35.3 cubic feet, or
	1.3 cubic yards, or
	264.2 gallons

Other volume
1,000 cubic meters	0.81 acre-foot
acre-foot	1234 cubic meters
100 cubic meters per year	274 liters per day
	72.4 gallons per day
100 liters per day	36.5 cubic meters per year

100 gallons per day	138.1 cubic meters per year
1 million cubic meters per year	.032 cubic meters per second
1 cubic meter per second per year	31.54 million cubic meters

Abbreviations

bmc = billion cubic meters
cm = centimeter
m = meter
mg/l = milligram per liter
ml = milliliter
mm = millimeter
m^3 = cubic meter
km = kilometer
sq km = square kilometer
sq m = square meter
mcmy = million cubic meters per year.

Introduction

Water is a unique, omnipresent resource. It appears in solid, liquid, and gaseous forms and plays a part in all physical and biological processes: "Life is animated water," wrote Russian biologist Vladimir Vernadsky about a century ago.[1] Water best is studied by tracking the pathways of the hydrologic or water cycle. In the "pristine," or natural hydrologic cycle, precipitation—rain, snow, and dew—that falls on the land travels through different pathways. Some of it evaporates directly under the impact of thermal energy. Some precipitation infiltrates the soil, where it gets absorbed by plants, from which it transpires, and/or percolates deep into water-bearing rock strata (aquifers). Other precipitation forms flood or storm "runoff" and is "stored" in wadis (or streams) or in rivers and lakes.

Human intervention alters the pristine cycle, creating a combined natural-social water cycle. According to the law of conservation of matter, the amount of water in the new cycle remains the same as that of the natural cycle, but its pathways multiply and its properties are modified. Humans tap water from rivers, lakes, springs, and wells. They harness it for many purposes: household (drinking, cleaning, gardening); municipal (parks, commercial); and industrial. Water use often contaminates the used water, rendering it a source of disease for humans and animals

1. Cited in Hillel, 1991, p. 32.

1

and of further pollution to the water storage units to which it returns.

Moreover, because humans divide the world into political units, water stored in rivers or aquifers may pass from one unit to another or may constitute boundaries between them. Those watercourses that pass from one polity to another are dubbed "consecutive" or "serial," whereas those that form boundaries are called "boundary" or "contiguous." Either way, they are considered by international water law to constitute common international watercourses.[2] The commonality of the water resources and their scarcity, especially in the Middle East, have rendered them a source of conflict among the riparians that share them.

This book examines the political economy of the water conflict between Israelis and Palestinians and suggests how it may be resolved equitably and cooperatively. The water conflict is a key ingredient of the wider political feud between the two sides, and its resolution is essential for a final peace accord. It also may be that progress on accommodation between the two sides would bolster the effort to bring about a resolution of the water dispute. Since 1993, the Israelis and Palestinians have signed three landmark agreements. The Declaration of Principles (DOP), negotiated in Oslo and signed in Washington on 13 September 1993, specified the terms of reference for a resolution of the conflict and arrangements for an interim phase for Palestinian self-government to end no later than September 1998.[3] The Cairo Agreement of 4 May 1994—known as "Gaza-Jericho First"—established the Palestinian Authority (PA) in Jericho and parts of Gaza.[4] Finally, the Taba Agreement, signed in Washington on 28 September 1995, extended the PA's limited jurisdiction to the population centers of the rest of the West Bank.[5] The water-related provisions of the preceding accords are included in the Appendix.

Despite these agreements, reconciliation remains a long way off because the critical issues that drive the conflict have been

2. For example, the Draft Articles of the forty-sixth session of the United Nations' International Law Commission (ILC) define an international water resource as a "watercourse, parts of which are situated in different states." See text in International Law Commission, 1994.

3. Text available in *Journal of Palestine Studies*, 1993, pp. 115–21.

4. Text of the main parts of the agreement is available in the *Journal of Palestine Studies*, 1994, pp. 103–118.

5. The full text of this very long agreement (300-plus pages) is available in Israel, Ministry of Foreign Affairs, 1995.

deferred for settlement until the final status negotiations about the West Bank and Gaza, and by implication, about Israel. These deferred issues include refugees, Jerusalem, Israeli settlements in the West Bank and Gaza, boundaries, security, and water. Although the final status talks are scheduled for completion by May 1999, schedules have not been adhered to during the interim phase, and whether this deadline will prove to be an exception is far from certain.

Insofar as water is concerned, the agreements have stipulated broad principles for resolving the conflict, notably equitable utilization and joint management of the common water resources as well as makeshift arrangements for the interim period. The arrangements include a small increase of water supply to the Palestinians, preservation of the status quo ante of water supply for the Israeli settlements in the West Bank and Gaza, and giving the Palestinians a partial role in the management of water in the West Bank in the areas under the jurisdiction of the PA and full powers in those areas under its jurisdiction in Gaza. On the whole, these arrangements do not alter tangibly the pre-existing situation. Thus, the conflict over water is likely to continue until the end of the century, if not beyond—whenever the final status negotiations are completed.[6] The interim arrangements will be referred to in this text when necessary.

The Israeli-Palestinian water conflict is but one of several such disputes in the Middle East, an area not noted for its water abundance. Virtually all the major, common international water basins in the region are contested: the Nile, the Euphrates and the Tigris, and the Jordan. In all of them, the central bone of contention is the allocation of water rights among the riparians. Increasingly, though, concern has grown over water quality and contamination in upstream areas.

Attempts have been made to settle some of these disputes, and pacts have been reached. In the Nile basin, for example, Egypt and Sudan agreed in 1959 on a formula to divide the water impounded in Lake Nasser behind the Aswan High Dam.[7] In the Jordan basin, there was in 1955 the Johnston Plan, named after

6. I have analyzed the interim water agreements and their implications for the final status in Elmusa, 1996, pp. 51–54.

7. For details of this pact and the process of negotiations, see Waterbury, 1979, pp. 63–115.

special American ambassador Eric Johnston, who mediated the water feud between the Arab countries and Israel. This plan is discussed at length in the last two chapters of the book. On 26 October 1994, Israel and Jordan signed a peace treaty that includes what amounts to a water agreement specifying water allocations for the two states from segments of the Jordan and Yarmuk rivers common to both of them.

The preceding accords, however, address only fragments of the overall disputes. The Egypt-Sudan pact leaves out seven other riparians, notably Ethiopia, where much of the Nile's water originates, and does not address the maintenance of water quality. The treaty between Israel and Jordan does not include the three other riparians (Lebanon, Palestine, and Syria), but it does accent the protection of water quality and specifies measures to be taken for that purpose. Further, in the Euphrates-Tigris basin Iraq, Syria, and Turkey have yet to settle their differences over water. Thus, much remains to be done to understand and resolve the water feuds in the Middle East. Lacking resolution, these disputes only can fester and add one more element to the chronic instability there. Indeed, the pressure on the fixed water resources is expected to mount owing to population and income growth, relentless urbanization, and worsening pollution.

Perhaps in recognition of such a prospect, interest has surged since the mid-1980s in Middle Eastern water. On the diplomatic level, one of the five international Multilateral Working Groups, which complement the bilateral tracks, has been devoted solely to water.[8] Among analysts, the surge of interest is evident from the steady output of articles and books on the topic. The growing literature has sharpened greatly our understanding of the conflict over these resources and underscored the need for careful management. Political scientists have given accounts of the history of several of the conflicts. They have attempted to identify the conditions of conflict formation and those that promote and/or inhibit resolution. In particular, they have noted the scarcity (in both the economic and common sense of the word) and maldistribution of international common water resources, overall relations and power

---

8. Thirty-five countries have participated in these groups, including China, the European Union countries, Russia, and the United States, in addition to Arab countries and Israel. Lebanon and Syria have stayed away from this track, conditioning their participation on progress in the bilateral talks.

distribution among riparians, and the riparians' perception of water.[9] Economists, whose research on the water sector still lags behind the work of political scientists, have made estimates of the economic value of water and highlighted the prevalence of economic inefficiency in the use of the meager water resources. They have proposed economic incentives such as taxation, pricing, and marketing to improve efficiency.[10] From work on water in other parts of the world, the environmental critique has compelled people to rethink water resources in a systemic manner—to go beyond the standard view of water as only a technical input for social and economic development while ignoring its other roles in areas like soil water-logging and salinity or disease-bearing vectors—and consider the management of water resources in terms of watersheds or basins, rather than of discrete segments. It suggests that one needs to treat as productive that water which contributes to biomass production in general and to rainfed agriculture in particular, not just that water which is extracted artificially, and to be concerned with the welfare of future generations (through the notion of sustainability).[11] Finally, as a guide to resolving water conflicts, international law organizations have formulated the doctrine of equitable utilization or apportionment of common international water resources and called for undertaking joint management of such resources.[12]

Yet, despite the surge of interest and progress in understanding the issues, many areas remain in need of in-depth examination. For example, a 1993 symposium on "Water in the Arab World" held at Harvard University named more than a dozen such topics.[13]

9. See Frey, 1992; Homer-Dixon, 1991; Lowi, 1993; Naff and Matson, 1984; United States Army Corps of Engineers, 1991; Waterbury, 1979; and Wolf, 1992.

10. See Bowen and Young, 1985; Fishelson, 1994; Kislev, 1990; Kutcher, 1980; Whittington and Haynes, 1980; and World Bank, 1988 and 1994.

11. For example, Biswas, 1993; Falkenmark, 1984 and 1986; Hillel, 1991; Postel, 1996; and *World Resources Report*, various issues.

12. See, for example, Barberis, 1991; Hayton and Utton, 1989; and Lipper, 1967.

13. Rogers and Lydon, 1994, pp. xvi–xviii. Among the topics are case studies and empirical research at the country and regional levels; economic value and productivity of water in various uses; availability of food in world markets and the risk of dependence on imported food; consequences and practical aspects of a shift away from agriculture if such a shift is judged to be needed; comparative regional management; desalination; and a host of technical matters related to natural water systems, notably groundwater.

In the area of water conflicts, systematic assessments of these conflicts are lacking. Such assessments need to include all the riparians, or at least the key members, of each basin. They would have to assess the disputants' contributions to water quantity and quality; their other available natural-source supplies; their capabilities of developing alternative resources; their sectoral water allocations; their water-related economic policies; and their future needs or demands. In addition, they would need to explore how the doctrine of equitable apportionment may be applied to the basin at hand. Nor could they be complete without exploring the management tasks that can be taken up jointly and their economic and political ramifications.

This book seeks to carry out precisely this kind of assessment for the Israeli-Palestinian dispute. Despite the rapidly accumulating literature on the topic, a rounded and sustained exposé still is lacking. Two publications that appeared during the writing of this book, however, deserve special mention. One is a report prepared by a Palestinian water team under the auspices of the United Nations Development Program (UNDP).[14] It contains a résumé of the water resources and conditions in the West Bank and Gaza and identifies a hierarchy of tasks that Palestinian water managers face, but it says virtually nothing about the conflict with Israel. The second is a book published by the Canadian International Development Research Center that reviews some of the questions covered in the present study but focuses on Israel.[15]

What might be term the "matrix" of the Israeli-Palestinian water conflict consists of two broad categories: transboundary and occupation-related issues. The transboundary issues pertain to the common water resources and are similar to those in other disputes, namely the maldistribution of water rights and joint management. The common water resources are essentially those in the Israeli and Palestinian territory west of the Jordan River and the Jordan River basin. The occupation-related issues consist of the consequences for the Palestinians of water supply to the Israeli settlers; Israel's takeover of the management of water resources and sectors in the West Bank and Gaza; and the land-water nexus, or the ability of one side to control one resource because of the control of the other resource.

14. The Water Resources Action Program Task Force, 1994.
15. Lonergan and Brooks, 1994.

Among the foregoing issues, the maldistribution of water rights between the Israelis and Palestinians lies at the core of the conflict. The other issues have to a large extent been spawned by Israel's desire to maintain and enforce its water privilege. The maldistribution brought about substandard water use and services for the Palestinians and a stark water gap between them and the Israelis. This book investigates the water gap in its myriad manifestations: levels of extraction and consumption, quality and coverage of the services, sectoral allocations, prices and economics in general, and overall objectives that inform Israel's allocation policies. I examine as well the administrative and legal apparatus employed by Israel to accomplish its goals. Throughout, expert and official opinion that has been employed in Israel to rationalize these injurious policies and practices is brought under close scrutiny.

The examination of the water gap and Israeli policies, by definition, requires a comparative approach. Thus, although the stress is on water conditions in the West Bank and Gaza, water extraction, use, and its institutional aspects in Israel and the Israeli settlements also are outlined. To bring the water gap and institutional means that maintain it into sharper relief, occasional comparisons also are drawn between the West Bank and Jordan as well, for the West Bank should have the same level of use and institutional development as water-short Jordan, of which the West Bank was a part before its seizure by Israel in 1967.

Apart from analyzing the water conflict, the book explores how it can be resolved on the basis of equity and mutuality. It will be argued that the best guide for an equitable resolution is to be found in international water law, in particular the doctrine of equitable utilization or apportionment. The core of the doctrine is a list of factors that it stipulates must be weighed to ensure fairness. These factors include the natural attributes of the water resources, prior use, social and economic needs, and the relative capability to tap alternative water resources. The intention is not to give a blueprint for reallocation of water rights or a definitive figure—these are only possible on the basis of mutually accepted data. Rather, it will be demonstrated that equitable utilization entitles the Palestinians to a much larger share of the common resources than they presently obtain. On a more general plane, the doctrine of equitable utilization and the factors it posits seldom have been clarified conceptually in any other water dispute, and the comments offered in the Israeli-Palestinian context should have relevance for other disputed water basins.

The second transboundary issue that the text tackles is the future management of the groundwater and surface water resources common to both sides. International law and modern water management principles advocate that common resources be managed jointly as unified basins. However, there is little experience by way of successful joint management models for emulation, especially of groundwater. I argue that successful management first must recognize and then resolve the tension between ecological demands and the political and economic constraints that conspire against unified management. This is illustrated through identification of several types of joint management tasks (e.g., verification and protection of water quality) and measures needed to implement them. Central to the management of scarce water resources is the efficiency of their use. The stress of the present study is on economic, not technical, efficiency, although the technical aspect is not overlooked. The target of the investigation is agriculture, which is the chief water-consuming sector. Farm budgets and sectoral data are used to evaluate the efficiency of water use for various crops in Palestinian irrigated and rainfed agriculture. I also draw on studies by Israeli economists to illustrate the levels of efficiency in the Israeli irrigated sector. Although future Palestinian management of their own water sector is not a focus of the book, possible policies to promote efficiency, especially pricing and markets, are assessed. Last, I draw attention to the need for raising the efficiency of water use in the rainfed sector, which uses relatively large amounts of water that seldom are included in the accounts of countries' water-use budgets.

This text also is intended to be a primary source of information on the water sector of the West Bank and Gaza. Assembling this information, however, was particularly demanding because the hydrological systems of the West Bank and Gaza are different, and data pertaining to each were available in different sources. The inclusion of the water sector in Israel and Israeli settlements presented additional demands.

The collected data had to be organized, cross-checked, sorted out, and, as much as possible, traced to its original source in order to verify the reliability of the figures and ensure proper crediting. This last task in particular proved especially time consuming because the past few years have witnessed a proliferation of data sources and guesswork verging on chaos; proper crediting fared poorly in the process. Only a lifelong fascination with those ancient Arab scholars who roamed the Arabian Desert on their beasts to authenticate a word of the Arabic language or a saying of the Prophet Muhammad made me persist, although my purpose is in no way as lofty as theirs, nor my harvest as worthy.

A chief reason for the proliferation of data sources and guesswork is that Israel, which since 1967 has held a virtual monopoly over data collection and dissemination in the West Bank and Gaza and much of the Jordan basin, has viewed the data as something to be kept secret. Israel is not the only party to value secrecy. Syria also seldom furnishes information on its water resources and uses; but that country is not as pivotally located in the basin, at least not since 1967, and it is removed from the groundwater resources under consideration. Only Jordan has been more forthcoming with respect to information about its water sector, perhaps because most of the surveys and studies were undertaken by international firms in the form of foreign aid, and also because that country has been in general more open to researchers than have its neighbors. It thus is to Jordan that we are indebted for the first comprehensive study of the natural groundwater system of the West Bank (1963–65 by the British firm Rofe and Raffety[16]), as well as for a continuous, publicly available record of the flows of the Yarmuk and the Jordan rivers (up until 1967) in its territory.

To be sure, Israeli water-related institutions offer information and studies on the water sector. They have supplied an uninterrupted set of figures on sectoral use from the early 1950s onward.[17] Other types of data, however, leave much to be desired. Recharge and flow of the various sources often appear as averages rather than as time-series figures, and without the supporting primary or raw data and technical reasoning. Thus, it is difficult for the investigator to assess the reliability of the information. Further, Israel publishes only occasional, cryptic fragments on water budgets by source of extraction. Withholding data is acknowledged, for example, in the following excerpt from the 1990 report to the World Bank by Tahal, the firm that has been the semiofficial water planning body:

16. Rofe and Raffety Consulting Engineers, 1965a and 1965b.
17. Israel, Central Bureau of Statistics, *Statistical Abstract*, various issues.

Restrictions imposed by security and privacy regulations limit the publication and dissemination of water resources data at the detailed level of single users and single abstraction structures.[18]

It is hard to fathom how publishing water data endangers a state's security or violates privacy when the water resources are state-owned, as they are in Israel. It is even harder to accept such rationalization for censoring information on the water sector in the West Bank and Gaza. At any rate, the secrecy has engendered skepticism—as if another source of mistrust was needed between the two sides—about the reliability of the officially published data.

Two precedents in the Israeli-Palestinian conflict illustrate the reason for skepticism, even if it proves groundless. Before the establishment of the State of Israel, the Zionist movement tried to persuade the British and other powers of the day that Palestine had enough water to absorb a large number of Jewish immigrants. In the process, an argument ensued between experts sympathetic to Zionist goals and M. G. Ionides, a British engineer who conducted in 1939 the first comprehensive survey of the eastern Jordan valley, on the available quantities of water. For example, W. G. Lowdermilk, an American soil conservation engineer enlisted by the Jewish Agency, wrote in 1944 that "After studying these figures [the Ionides report], I am inclined to agree with the Palestinian [Jewish] experts who consider them an underestimate."[19] Later on, Ionides rejoined: "Their [Lowdermilk's and others'] estimates of water supply are inflated."[20] As it turned out, the high estimates were inaccurate. "Some ten years ago," wrote Ze'ev Schiff in 1962, "Israel still lived under the illusion that she had a water potential of 3,200 million cbm [mcmy]. This estimate was then reduced to 2,400 [million] cbm," a figure that subsequently was lowered even further.[21]

More recently, Israeli estimates of the groundwater of the eastern basin of the mountain aquifer have been very contradictory. For example, Tahal, Israel's water planning company, consistently

18. Ben Gurion University of the Negev with Tahal (hereafter BUNT), 1994; and Tahal, 1990, p. 8.12.
19. Cited in *Friends of the Middle East*, 1964, p. 3.
20. Ionides, 1946, p. 274.
21. Cited in *Friends of the Middle East*, 1964, p. 3. Karmon, 1971, p. 120, also makes the same point.

put the potential of this basin at 100 million cubic meters per year (mcmy) or less.[22] However, this potential has been listed in the Taba Agreement at 172 mcmy (Annex III, Article 40, Schedule 10). The relatively large discrepancy in the numbers gives cause for skepticism concerning Israeli-furnished data until they are verified mutually.

Even in the absence of political passions, data disagreements and discrepancies still can be present, because, as the U.S. Office of Technology Assessment notes, "To some extent, all measurements of the elements of the hydrologic cycle are estimates."[23] Specialists also may come up with different results, depending on their models, assumptions, and periods of the study, as we shall see amply in the text. In addition, the mountain aquifer may not be understood fully, and it appears that Israel has not conducted an extensive survey like that of Rofe and Raffety during the Jordanian period. However, these technical uncertainties differ from the guesswork that results from the suppression of data.

In the final analysis, the manner in which data are used depends on the purpose of the investigation. The data assembled in this text, in my opinion, are sufficient for illustrating the issues and constructing the arguments. I have made a special effort to present the data in a transparent fashion and to identify discrepancies, disagreements, and gaps so that the reader can make up his or her mind independently and not be bound by my interpretations. Resolution of the water conflict between Israelis and Palestinians, however, requires opening the records of raw information for Palestinian specialists and researchers and establishing mutually agreed upon baseline data.

The text is organized as follows. Chapter 1 is devoted mainly to delineation of the quantities and spatial distribution of the natural water resources as well as the topographic, climatic, and hydrogeological factors that determine them. The water resources are divided into two categories: groundwater aquifers and surface water in numerous streams and, most importantly, in the Jordan River basin.

Chapter 2 examines the use, distribution, and quality of municipal water in the West Bank and Gaza. The main theme is the

22. Tahal Consulting Engineers, 1990, p. 2.8. See also table 1 in this monograph; the table is based on another report to the World Bank produced by BUNT.

23. Office of Technology Assessment, 1988, p. 50.

backwardness of the water sector as manifested in the low-level and intermittent supply, the unavailability of piped water to a significant minority of the West Bank population, the dilapidated water distribution network in the cities and towns, and the substandard water quality, notably in Gaza. I examine in detail the underlying Israeli policies, especially the severe restrictions on access and the low level of investment. The chapter also highlights developments pertaining to the water infrastructure since the signing of the DOP, in particular provisions in the Taba Agreement and efforts by the international "donors."

Chapter 3 consists of three parts: the economics of water use in households and agriculture; an "extended" water use balance; and demand projections. In the economics section, I present preliminary estimates of the marginal value product of water (MVPW) in irrigated and rainfed agriculture and compare the latter with those of Jordan and Israel. A main argument in the chapter is that the relatively low income of the Palestinians does not explain the existing low level of use and that there exists a latent, unsatisfied water demand in both the municipal and agricultural sectors. The proposed "extended" water balance goes beyond the conventional ones by accounting for water in the rainfed sector (irrigation water equivalent, or IWE) and that used to produce food and agricultural exports and imports (or "requisite" water). Last, water projections that have been made by several analysts are contrasted and compared, and the problems that confront attempts to make such projections are indicated.

Chapter 4 is the core of the book. It brings together the three previous chapters and offers elaborate analyses of the content, or issues, of the dispute. I outline the water conditions in Israel and the Israeli settlements, then compare and contrast them with those of the Palestinians as described in the preceding two chapters. The issues include the quantitative gaps in water withdrawals, per capita use, pricing, and irrigated land areas. I also cover the Israeli takeover of the management of the Palestinian water sector and the laws (military orders) Israel enacted to implement its policies. In this connection, I highlight the arrested development of Palestinian water-related institutions and management capabilities, as well as the draconian laws applied by Israel to the Palestinian water sector in contrast to its own egalitarian laws. The land-water nexus, as defined above, also is introduced in the chapter as an issue.

A final topic, although not an issue per se, that is addressed is the perception of water by the Israelis and Palestinians. A principal argument that I seek to make is that the suggestion of some scholars that water is perceived ideologically through its association with agriculture in Israel may have been true in the past; however, today the material foundations of such a perception virtually have disappeared owing to the demographic and economic transformations within Israel. At the same time, a morally grounded perception of water that views it as a symbol of Israel's policy of dispossession has developed among the Palestinians. I hope that the discussion of the land-water nexus and the ideological perception of water imparts to the study of the water conflict an historical and intellectual perspective that, besides relieving the ennui of number-weary readers, helps them to appreciate some of the antagonists' thoughts and feelings about water that underlie the technical matters.

The first four chapters deal with conflict. Chapter 5 is concerned with how the conflict might be resolved equitably and cooperatively. It provides ideas on what the principles of equitable apportionment of water rights and joint management of the common water resources entail. The emphasis is, first, on the conceptual interpretation of the factors of international law's doctrine of equitable utilization and how it applies in the Israeli-Palestinian context; and, second, on joint management tasks and the economic and political constraints that confront their implementation. In the course of the narrative, the hydrostrategic factors that promote conflict and cooperation will be highlighted.

Although the Israeli-Palestinian water conflict may be less significant than the other disputes in the Middle East, studying it is important because it is probably the most complex of all issues. It involves not only the conventional questions of maldistribution but also a set of further issues stemming from Israel's occupation of the West Bank and Gaza. Moreover, the level of water scarcity, measured in available natural fresh water per person, is lower than in any of the other basins: Assuming that the current Israeli municipal and industrial consumption rate of 120 cm per person remains constant, between 2020 and 2040 all the natural fresh water available for the Palestinians and Israelis will be sufficient only for household and industrial consumption. The scarcity is aggravated by the high level of hydrological interdependence of the Israelis and Palestinians, in the sense that the water of the contested resources constitutes the bulk of the water available to both sides. In contrast, in the Euphrates-Tigris basin, at least one of the riparians, Turkey, gets most of its water from out-of-basin resources. A final aspect of the Israeli-Palestinian water dispute that renders it knottier than the others is that it combines groundwater and surface water, whereas the other conflicts center primarily around surface water. Groundwater is less functionally versatile (e.g., it cannot be used to generate hydropower) and hence offers less tradable "goods" in a bargaining situation. It is harder to manage jointly than surface water because of the difficulty of monitoring and regulating its flow and because aquifers underlie extensive terrain and their protection requires regulating numerous activities, from waste water disposal, landfills, and chemical use in agriculture to underground storage of gasoline. These features—multiplicity of the issues and categories of contested resources, the exceptional scarcity of natural fresh water, and the high degree of hydrological interdependence—may make the Israeli-Palestinian dispute appear unique and not of universal interest. Nevertheless, it could be thought of as a "general" conflict because it does encompass a wider range of issues and problems than the "typical" conflict, if there is such a category. If this tangled dispute can be settled equitably, then its resolution may give hope and example that the others, too, are amenable to resolution.

1

The Natural Water Resources

T he natural water resources of geographic Palestine—
Israel, the West Bank, and the Gaza Strip—consist of
groundwater and surface water; they are listed in table 1.1.
The storage figures are averages and will be examined together with other natural and hydropolitical properties separately for each individual resource. The flow of the Jordan
River is for the entire river system, not just the portion that
occurs in geographic Palestine. In all, they amount to 1,600–
1,800 million cubic meters per year (mcmy).

The groundwater is found mainly in the mountain,
coastal, and Galilee aquifers. There are also two smaller
aquifers: the Carmel (after Mount Carmel, or Karmil in
Arabic) and the 'Araba. The chief surface water source is
the Jordan River, to which the West Bank and Israel are
the smallest contributors among the riparians. A much
smaller quantity of surface water is also available in numerous wadis, many of which flow only during the rainy
season. They commence at the main watershed, which
meanders across Israel and the West Bank in a north-south
direction, and terminate either in the Mediterranean Sea
or the Jordan River and Dead Sea.

In addition to the above resources, a tremendous nonrenewable (fossil) aquifer underlies the Negev Desert. The
aquifer may contain a total of 70 billion cubic meters (bcm)
of water, occurring at depths of 800 meters (m) or more.
Its water is brackish but suitable for irrigation, and some
respected Israeli scientists and economists have advocated

TABLE 1.1 Water Resources in Geographic Palestine

(In mcmy)

Source	Potential
Renewable aquifers	
Mountain	
Eastern	100
Northeastern	140
Western	360
Coastal	340[a]
Galilee	
Eastern	55(?)[b]
Western	155
Carmel	70
'Araba (Arava)	25[c]
Surface water	
Jordan River basin	1,300[d]
Floodwater	90
Nonrenewable aquifer	
Negev Desert	70,000

SOURCES: Principally, BUNT, 1994; Issar and Nativ, 1988; and Tahal, 1990.
NOTES:
[a]Includes the portion of the aquifer underlying Gaza.
[b]This figure consists of the potential of one aquifer and the currently exploited volume, not the potential, of another aquifer. Thus, the figure is an underestimate.
[c]Could be overexploited at 60 mcmy for an interim period.
[d]This is the total potentially exploitable water of the Jordan River system, not the contribution of Israel and the West Bank.

its gradual mining for the benefit of the Negev (to which water currently is transferred from the Jordan basin in the north) and even of the coastal plain.[1] Although the aquifer probably is located entirely within Israel, accounting for its water potential is important in the process of dividing the water resources between the Israelis and Palestinians. However, its natural attributes will not be examined in this book.

PHYSICAL ATTRIBUTES

The properties, volume, and distribution of natural water resources are shaped by the physical attributes of the country, its geomor-

1. Issar, et al., 1972; and Issar and Nativ, 1988.

phology, geology, and climate. An outline of these attributes is hence a necessary background for understanding the properties of the water resources themselves. Although the outline covers geographic Palestine, the focus is on the West Bank and Gaza.

Topography

Geographic Palestine is bounded by the Mediterranean in the west, Lebanon in the north, Syria and Jordan in the east, and Egypt in the south (see map 1.1). Its total area is 27,024 square kilometers (sq km), of which 26,320 sq km are land mass and 704 sq km inland water.[2] It was carved out of the Ottoman province of Syria, which encompassed most of the Fertile Crescent, as a result of agreements between Britain and France after they conquered the region and evicted the Ottomans in World War I. Britain assumed control of Palestine in 1918, and subsequently the League of Nations recognized the territory as a British Mandate in 1922. British rule lasted until 1948. In that year, the State of Israel was created in Palestine amidst the flight of an estimated 750,000 Palestinians who became refugees. Geographic Palestine hence was divided into Israel, the West Bank (which became part of Jordan in 1950), and the Gaza Strip, which was placed under Egyptian administration. As a consequence of the June 1967 war between Israel and the Arab countries, Israel captured both the West Bank and Gaza, in addition to the Egyptian Sinai Peninsula (from which it withdrew in phases between 1974 and 1982) and the Golan Heights in Syria.

The West Bank is a small landlocked territory bounded by Jordan in the east and Israel on the other three sides. It has a land mass area of 5,545 sq km.[3] Gaza, which officially is called the Gaza Strip, is literally a strip of land situated along the Mediterranean Sea. It is tucked into the southwestern corner of the coast of geographic Palestine, bordering the Sinai Peninsula. Its area is estimated at 365 sq km; its width varies from 7 to 12 km; and its length is about 45 km.[4] Thus, the combined area of the West Bank and Gaza totals 5,910 sq km, or less than 22 percent of the total

2. *Government of Palestine*, 1946, vol. 1, p. 103.
3. Rofe and Raffety, 1965b, p. 4.
4. The area of the original Gaza district of geographic Palestine was 13,689 sq km; see *Government of Palestine*, 1946, vol. 1, p. 104.

MAP 1.1 Topography of Geographic Palestine

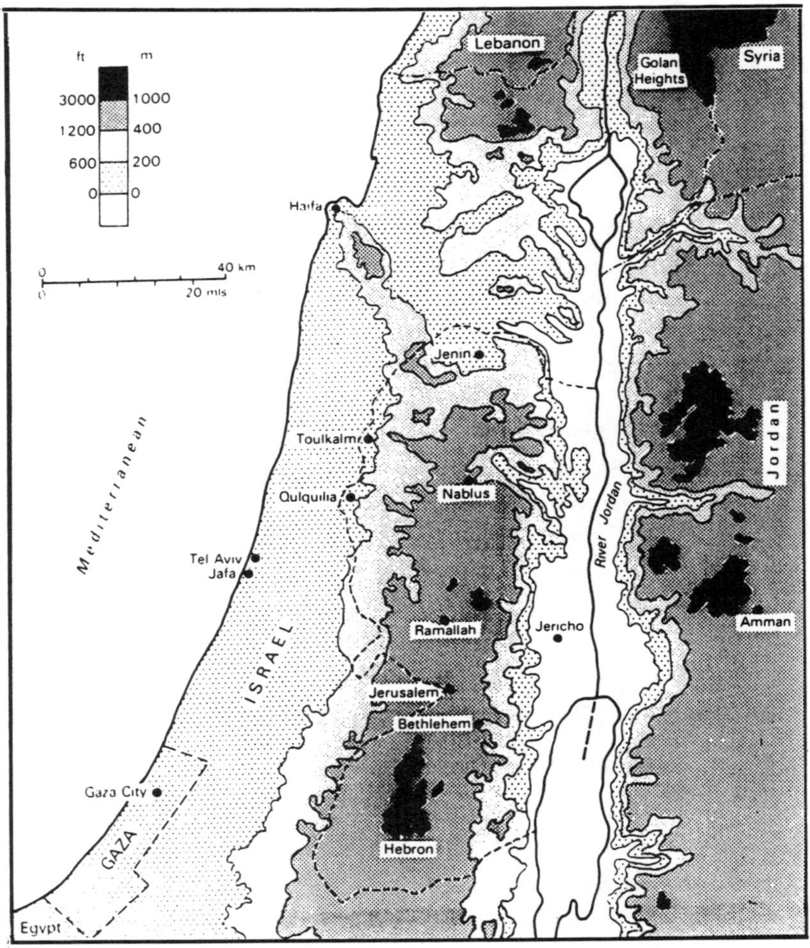

SOURCE: Adapted from Kluwer Academic Publishers, *Geo Journal* 21, no. 4 (1990): 350.

area of geographic Palestine. In contrast, Israel's land mass area is 20,255 sq km.[5]

Geographic Palestine can be divided broadly into the following regions: the coastal or maritime plain, inland plains, Mount

5. The aggregate area of Israel, the West Bank, and Gaza does not match exactly that of pre-1948 geographic Palestine. The reason for the discrepancy is that the boundaries of Israel are those that resulted from the 1949 armistice agreements, which were signed by the Arab states and Israel after the 1948 war. The armistice boundaries did not coincide in all cases with the boundaries of geographic Palestine.

Carmel, the central West Bank range, the Galilee Mountains, the Jordan Rift Valley, and the Negev Desert. A brief mention will be made first of those regions within Israel, followed by a finer geomorphological description of the West Bank and Gaza. The coastal plain runs parallel to the Mediterranean from the border with Egypt in the south (where Gaza is located) to the border with Lebanon in the north, interrupted in the north by Cape Carmel and Haifa Bay. A mostly irrigable terrain, it is about 270 km long and 40 km wide in the south, decreasing to about 5 km wide at the border with Lebanon. This plain overlies one of the main aquifers in the country, the coastal aquifer. The major interior plain is Marj ibn 'Amir (Jerzeel), wedged between the central range and the Lower Galilee Mountains.[6] The maritime and interior plains contain the bulk of the irrigable land in geographic Palestine.

Mount Carmel has a triangular plan, the base stretching along the coast and the apex protruding into the Jerzeel Valley. Its highest elevation is 546 meters above mean sea level (subsequently, sea level). The Galilee Mountains extend into Lebanon in the north and are delimited by the Jordan Rift in the east. In the west they meet the coastal plain and in the south the interior of Marj ibn 'Amir and the Jalud (Harod) Valley. They are cleaved by the Majd al-Kurum (ha-Kerem) gorge and the Amud stream into Upper (north) and Lower (south) Galilee. The highest peak in the former is Mount Jarmaq (Meron), which, at 1,208 m above sea level, is the highest in geographic Palestine as well. The highest elevation in Lower Galilee occurs at Mount Qamun, 598 m above sea level. In general, the mountains are suitable for rainfed (or rain-watered) agriculture because they receive sufficient rainfall.

The Negev is a vast, nearly triangular desert in the south of the country, covering an area close to 12,500 sq km, or slightly less than half the total area of geographic Palestine. It overlies the tremendous, nonrenewable (or fossil) aquifer cited earlier. Some of the land in the northern Negev is irrigable, although crops require large quantities of water because of very high daytime temperatures.

6. In British documents during the Mandate this plain appears as a composite of two parts, the Esdaraelon Plain in the west and the Jerzeel Valley in the east. See, for example, *Government of Palestine*, 1946, vol. 1, p. 103. For the identification of the properties of the Marj ibn 'Amir (Jerzeel) Plain, see *Encyclopaedia Palaestina*, 1984, vol. 4, p. 189; Karmon, 1971, appended map; and Orni and Efrat, 1973, pp. 82 and 94–97.

The West Bank can be divided into five regions: the central range, eastern foothills, western foothills, semicoastal (Tulkarm-Qalqilya), and the Jordan Rift Valley. The central range extends along a nearly north-south axis across the entire length of the West Bank.[7] It includes a series of mountains named after the major cities, Nablus, Jerusalem, and Hebron (from north to south).[8] The Nablus (Samarian) Mountains vary in height between 300 and 400 m in the northern hills of the Jinin area to 800 m in the middle segment.[9] They are generally greener, less rugged, and traversed by more wadis than the Hebron and Jerusalem mountains. The Jerusalem Mountains resemble a saddle, being higher in the eastern than in the western segment. Their width ranges between 24 and 40 km, and their height exceeds 1,000 m. In the south extend the Hebron Mountains, 20 to 45 km long and varying from 700 m to more than 1,000 m above sea level.

The foothills slope gently to the west and sharply to the east because the distance to the Mediterranean is greater than to the Jordan River and because of the precipitous fall in altitude in the Jordan Valley. The valley itself is a narrow depression, mostly below sea level, on both sides of the Jordan River from its origins at the foothills of Mount Hermon to where it terminates in the Dead Sea;[10] it will be described in detail in conjunction with the Jordan basin.

The central hills receive the highest levels of rainfall in the West Bank (see map 1.2), and their rocks consist of highly porous limestone and dolomite that allow water to percolate underground. They contain the main groundwater divide (anticline) and comprise the primary replenishment area of the mountain aquifer. The surface watershed is found along their peaks, reaching the Galilee Mountains in the north. Two groups of wadis flow from this watershed, one westward toward the Mediterranean and the other

7. The central hills, together with their extension in Israel, and the Galilee mountains comprise 38 percent of the combined area of geographic Palestine; see Abd al-Salam, 1990, p. 173.
8. Orni and Efrat, 1973, p. 54, give a more refined geomorphological classification, but the major divisions suffice for the present purpose.
9. In Israeli sources the Nablus Mountains are considered part of the Samarian Mountains. However, Abid, 1990, p. 101, argues that there are no "real natural boundaries" between the Jerusalem and Nablus Mountains, although they are distinguished by "some features."
10. In Jordan, the agricultural area south of the Dead Sea also is subsumed under the Jordan Valley.

MAP 1.2 Annual Rainfall in Geographic Palestine (in mm)

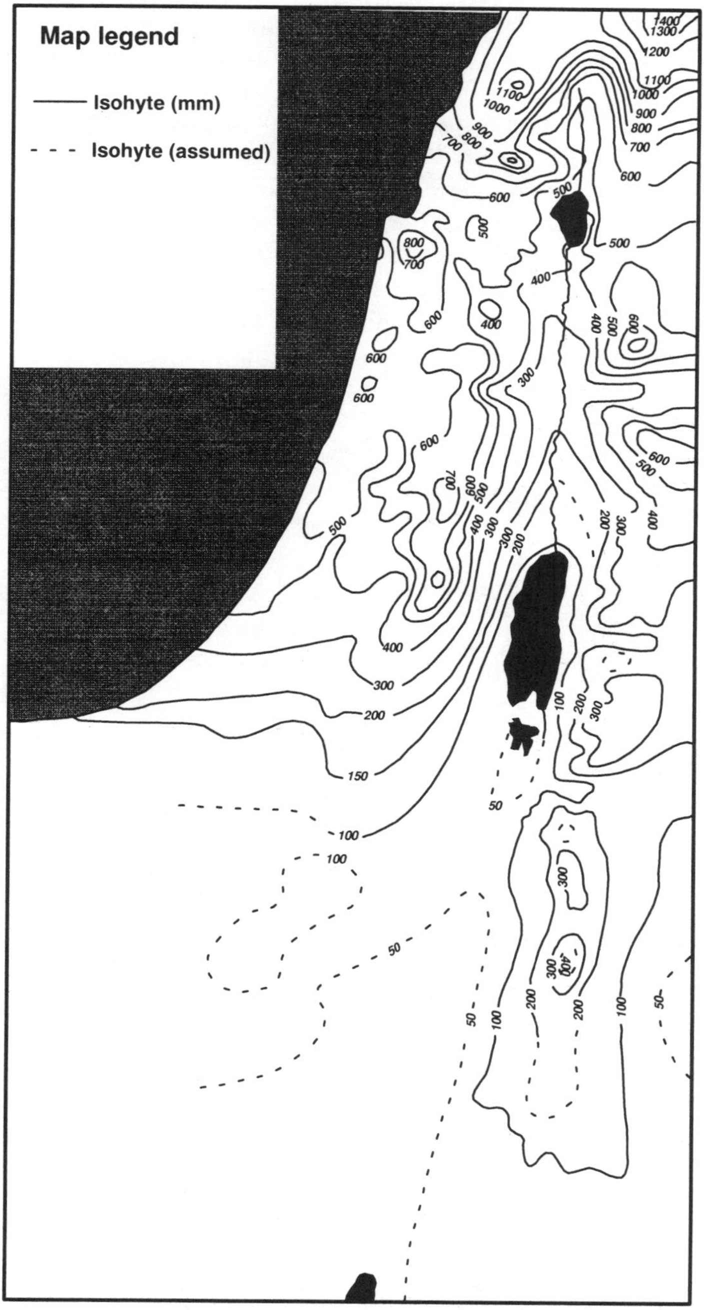

Map legend

——— Isohyte (mm)

- - - Isohyte (assumed)

SOURCE: Orni and Etrat, *Geography of Israel* (Philadelphia: Jewish Publication of America, 1973).

eastward toward the Jordan basin.[11] The central hills are thus the topographical backbone and the dominant hydrological region of the West Bank and, to a considerable extent, of geographic Palestine.

Gaza is a flat terrain inclining imperceptibly westward, with elevations ranging from 20 m to more than 80 m above sea level. The soils of the shoreline consist of highly permeable sand and sand dunes. In the eastern part of the shore, the dunes cover ridges of sandstone—locally called *kurkar*—which may have resulted from the hardening of the sand dunes themselves. In some interior areas, for instance in and around Wadi Gaza, sand also tops clay-like sand, silt, and loess, or sands finer than those of dunes deposited by wind or water. The sequence of porous and impermeable layers "traps" the water, acting in a sense like a plant pot. This mechanism renders the relatively poor soils most favorable for growing crops, especially citrus.[12]

Rainfall and Evapotranspiration

The climate of geographic Palestine is Mediterranean. Winter, the season of precipitation, is short and cool. Summer is long, hot, and dry, leaving the soil of much cultivable land with a moisture deficit for most of the year and making irrigation mandatory for successful farming. The main form of precipitation is rain. In Jerusalem, for instance, the number of snow days averages only two per year, and in Jericho and Gaza none. Dew is most prevalent along the coast, notably in the south at Gaza where humidity is high and land at night is cooler than the sea, a combination favorable to condensation. Nevertheless, the contribution of dew to the water budget is as negligible as that of snowfall. Thus, it can be said with little error that precipitation in the form of rain is the origin of groundwater and surface water (apart from the Jordan River system) in both the West Bank and Gaza.[13]

A chief characteristic of rainfall that is decisive for water planning and agricultural development is its "variability." Rainfall

11. Abd al-Salam, 1990, pp. 172–6; Abid, 1990, pp. 99–103, and 114; Benvenisti and Khayat, 1988, p. 25; and Orni and Efrat, 1973, pp. 53–105.
12. Abid, 1990, pp. 49–50, 55 and 124–31; Orni and Efrat, 1973, pp. 35–45; and Schwarz, 1982, pp. 95.
13. Abd al-Salam, 1990, p. 199; and Orni and Efrat, 1973, pp. 44 and 147.

fluctuates sharply, both within a season and from year to year, as well as among regions. Commonly, the rainy season falls between October and the end of April, with December and January being the wettest months. Perhaps more than two-thirds of the annual rainfall occurs between November and February. The average number of rain days (i.e., when rainfall exceeds 1 mm) is approximately 50–60 in the Upper Galilee, 25 in the Jordan Valley, and 30–40 in Gaza.[14]

The winter rain can be advantageous to crops because of lower evaporation. A 400–500 mm of average annual rainfall (subsequently all rainfall figures are average and annual) in geographic Palestine may be the equivalent of 600–700 mm in a place like Arizona, which has summer rain.[15] However, the concentration of rainfall within a single season has its drawbacks. This can be illustrated by the example of Jerusalem and London, both of which receive the same amount of rainfall, about 550 mm per annum.[16] Yet, because London averages about 300 rain days, the amount of biomass it can support is much greater than Jerusalem, which averages only 50 rain days. The disadvantage of seasonal concentration is aggravated by the intensity of rainfall, or its further concentration in a number of days within the season. In the more arid regions in particular, the entire year's rainfall can occur in a few downpours. Consequently, these regions suffer from both aridity and damaging floods.

Moreover, rainfall varies from year to year. In Nablus, for example, maximum rainfall might be three times as much as the minimum and in Jericho 3.3 times as much.[17] Generally, interannual variability of rainfall increases as the level of rainfall decreases.[18] The yearly fluctuation results in droughts, which sometimes last for several years. Droughts greatly reduce replenishment of aquifers and surface watercourses and have particularly deleterious effects on rainfed agriculture. The drought in the late 1980s, for example, did not end until 1991–92. Analyses of long-term rainfall records for Jerusalem indicate that in the century from the mid–1860s to the early 1970s, the city experienced a precipitation pattern of three "wet" seasons, two "average" seasons, and two

14. Katsnelson, 1985, sheet 13, p, 19; and Orni and Efrat, 1973, p. 147.
15. Hillel, 1991, p. 96.
16. Orni and Efrat, 1973, p. 147.
17. Abd al-Salam, 1990, p. 197.
18. Katsnelson, 1985, sheet 13, p. 19.

TABLE 1.2 Spatial Variation of Annual Rainfall in Geographic Palestine

(In millimeters)

Region	Coast	Hills	Jordan Valley
North	650	1,000	500
Middle North	550	650	300
Middle South	470	500	80
South	380	470	70
Far South	150	50	50

SOURCES: Abd al-Salam, 1990, p. 196; and Orni and Efrat, 1973, p. 145.

"dry" seasons.[19] However, it cannot be assumed that future rainfall variations will follow this pattern.

The second type of rainfall variation is spatial. Broadly, rainfall tends to decrease (1) from north to south, (2) from higher to lower altitudes, and (3) from areas with greater exposure to rain-bearing winds to areas exposed to downwind (see table 1.2).[20] The first pattern can be observed in the sharp drop of rainfall along the coastal plain, from 650 mm in the north to 150 mm in the extreme south, and the even sharper decline along the hills and in the Jordan Valley. The decrease from higher to lower altitude, the second pattern, is exemplified by the greater amount of rainfall in the hills than on the coast, and on the coast than in the Jordan Valley. The third pattern is evident from the difference in rainfall between the western and the eastern foothills, as will be discussed below.

The West Bank includes three climatic zones: arid (desert) in the Jordan Valley and eastern foothills; semiarid in the western foothills and semicoastal area; and subhumid in the central hills, the main exception being large parts of the Nablus Mountains. Gaza is semiarid in the north and arid in the south.[21] Rainfall in

19. Rofe and Raffety, 1965b, p. 1; and Schwarz, 1982, p. 85. Rofe and Raffety's analysis is for the period 1884–1957, while that mentioned in Schwarz is longer, 1861–62 to 1975–76; both, however, reveal similar patterns.

20. Katsnelson, 1985, sheet 12, p. 18.

21. Goldraich, 1977–78, p. 31. This classification is based on rainfall and potential, not actual, evapotranspiration (or the evapotranspiration that would occur if the soil moisture remained sufficient for use by vegetation throughout the year). As a general guide, McGinnies, 1983, p. 4, proposes that in Mediterranean climates precipitation from 0 to 150 mm might represent arid (desert) conditions, 150 mm to 400 mm semiarid (steppe), and from

the West Bank averages between 600 and 800 mm in the central range, 500–600 mm in the western foothills, 250–400 mm in the eastern foothills, and 50–200 mm in the Jordan Valley.[22] Thus, rainfall is greater in the western foothills than in the eastern, which are a "rain shadow," and reaches its lowest level in the Jordan Valley and Dead Sea areas.[23] Overall, rainfall in the West Bank may range between 400 and 600 mm,[24] or a total average of approximately 2,800 mcmy. Compared to many areas of the Middle East, these are respectable levels.

In Gaza, rainfall ranges between 350 and 400 mm in the north and 150–200 mm in the south, which is consistent with the overall pattern of rainfall decline from north to south.[25] The overall average is 275 mm, representing a total in the order of 100 mcmy.[26] Accordingly, the combined rainfall over the West Bank and Gaza is 2,900 mcmy.[27]

A large quantity of the rainfall evapotranspires, another portion percolates deep underground as aquifer recharge, and a small fraction runs off on the surface. Here, only evapotranspiration is discussed; runoff and aquifer recharge are examined in subsequent sections. The available data on evapotranspiration are extremely

---

300 mm to 500 mm subhumid (savannaral). These levels are 100 mm less than in arid climates with summer rainfall.

22. Benvenisti and Khayat, 1988, p. 25.

23. The central hills receive more rain than other areas because the air temperature falls as it ascends their slopes, and more condensation occurs. The greater rainfall on the western foothills derives from their facing the rain-bearing westerly winds, as opposed to the eastern foothills which are "rain shadows" owing to their exposure to downwind. The Jordan Valley's modest rainfall results from it being a rain shadow as well as having an exceptionally low altitude.

24. ASIR, 1986, p. 5; al-Tamimi, 1988, p. 22. ASIR's figure is 550– 600 mm, and al-Tamimi's 400–600 mm; but neither state how they obtained those estimates. Rofe and Raffety, 1965b, p. 2, table 2, gives a figure as low as 384 mm or a total of 2,130 mcmy, based on records for a 13-year period (1952–53 to 1964–65). The latter may be an underestimate.

25. Bruins and Tuinhof, 1991, p. 7; al-Khudari, 1992; and Schwarz, 1982, p. 95. Bruins and Tuinhof base their figures on records provided by Mekorot for the period 1951–80; theirs are the higher ranges, 400 in the north to 200 in the south. Khudari uses the same figures as Bruins and Tuinhof.

26. Bruins and Tuinhof, 1991, p. 11.

27. The *Center for Engineering Analysis*, 1992a, p. 25, gives higher figures of 2,900 mcmy in the West Bank and 130 mcmy in Gaza, or a total of 3,030 mcmy.

thin because collecting such data is a demanding technical task.[28] In Israel, 60–70 percent of precipitation evaporates, 50–60 percent of it immediately.[29] Evapotranspiration in the West Bank may average 1,900 mm annually in the western foothills and 2,600 mm per year along the Dead Sea shores.[30] The only aggregate figure available comes from the rough estimates of Rofe and Raffety for the period 1963–65.[31] It indicates that about two-thirds of rainfall, or 1,900 mcmy, evapotranspires. In Gaza, evapotranspiration may amount to 75 percent of the rainfall, or about 70 mcmy. Accordingly, aggregate evapotranspiration in the West Bank and Gaza may approach 2,000 mcmy, or more than two-thirds of the total rainfall.

GROUNDWATER

The renewable water resources of the West Bank, Gaza, and Israel are interconnected and, for the most part, qualify as common international resources. They belong to two basins: the Jordan River and the Mediterranean Sea. However, for technical and hydropolitical reasons, it is more convenient to examine them under the headings of groundwater and surface water; the latter includes water from runoff, but mainly from the Jordan basin.

Groundwater is the main source of water in geographic Palestine. This contrasts with the water balance in many other Middle East countries, where the principal source of water is rivers.[32] Technically, groundwater is subsurface water present in the saturated layers below the water table. The definition thus excludes the subsurface water between the water table and ground surface, which

28. Estimation of actual evapotranspiration is difficult owing to a multitude of variables (temperature, wind, soil type, vegetation, etc.) that influence it. Sometimes it is estimated as a residual of rainfall and aquifer recharge, where aquifer recharge is estimated from spring flow and discharge into seas or rivers.

29. Orni and Efrat, 1973, p. 148.

30. Schwarz, 1982, p. 86.

31. Rofe and Raffety, 1965b, p. 45.

32. The only states in the region that obtain the major proportion of water from aquifers are Israel (75 percent) and Lebanon (65 percent); in Jordan the breakdown is almost even. Groundwater represents only 17 percent of Syria's water supply and only 2 percent of Iraq's. See further Kolars, 1992, p. 105.

does not yield water to a well placed above it.[33] Such water constitutes the soil moisture and is subject to the forces of evapotranspiration. Groundwater is stored in and transmitted through the pores, fractures, and openings of rock strata. When the rock strata are able to transmit and yield significant amounts of water to springs and wells, they are called aquifers.[34] Aquifers are of two types: confined and unconfined. Unconfined aquifers are bounded by the water table and also are termed "water-table aquifers." Roughly speaking, they can be thought of as underground lakes. Confined aquifers, or artesian aquifers, are overlain by impermeable layers, such as marl, chert, and clay.[35] In a sense, a confined aquifer resembles an underground water pipe. The aquifer systems in geographic Palestine may be grouped into three: the mountain, the coastal, and the rest of the aquifers (Galilee, Carmel and 'Araba; see map 1.3). The focus, as above, is on the two key groundwater basins, the mountain and coastal aquifers.

The Mountain Aquifer

The mountain aquifer consists of three main basins, each of which is divided into subbasins (see map 1.4). The main basins (the term basin will be used interchangeably with aquifer) are the western, the northeastern (subsequently, northern), and the eastern. The boundaries between the three basins and the direction of water flow in them are determined by the axes of the principal water divides, especially the dominant Jerusalem (Judean) anticline, which traverses the West Bank from north to south, bending to the southwest in the Negev and northeast in Israel.[36] As a result of

33. Because the water in that zone, called the "aeration" zone, is at less than atmospheric pressure.

34. The term "significant" is, of course, relative; some authors, e.g., Fetter, 1988, p. 101, use the term "reasonable."

35. Confined aquifers sometimes are divided into aquifuge, or absolutely impermeable unit; aquitard, or a unit of low permeability; and aquiclude, a unit of low permeability that forms an upper or lower boundary of an underground water flow system. Increasingly, however, the terms "confining layer" and "leaky confining layer" are being used instead. See further Fetter, 1988, p. 101.

36. When the bedrock folds into an arch like shape, the fold is called anticline; when it dips inward, the fold is a syncline. An example of the latter is the broad Nablus-Bayt Qad syncline in the Jinin subseries. (Bayt Qad is a village to the east of Jinin and northeast of Nablus.)

MAP 1.3 Groundwater Basins in Geographic Palestine

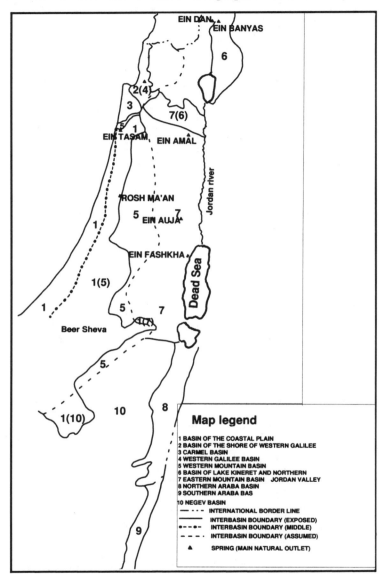

SOURCE: Adapted from Y. Bachmat, 1974.

MAP 1.4 Mountain and Coastal Aquifers in Geographic Palestine

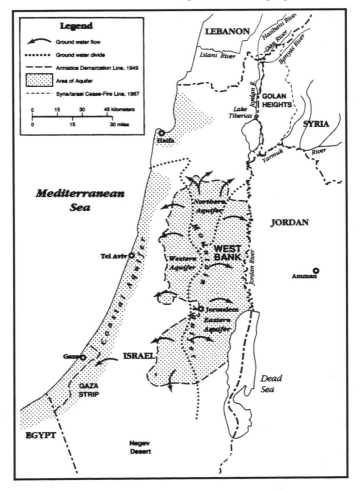

SOURCE: © The Jerusalem Fund and printed in The Center for Policy Analysis on Palestine, *Beyond Rhetoric: Perspectives on a Negotiated Settlement in Palestine, Part Two* (Washington: Author, 1996), p. 24.

erosion over geologic time, the groundwater divide does not coincide with the surface water divide.[37] In the western basin, the water flows west toward the Mediterranean; in the northern, northward and northeastward into the Baysan (Bet She'an) Plain in the Jordan Valley and into the plain of Jerzeel; and in the eastern, eastward and southeastward toward the Jordan River, Dead Sea, and Wadi

37. See Orni and Efrat, 1973, p. 62, for a more detailed explanation of this phenomenon.

'Araba. The natural drains are primarily springs that issue forth not in the central hills themselves but mainly in the lowlands of the western and eastern foothills, the coastal plain, the Jordan and Baysan valleys, and the western shore of the Dead Sea. Springs occur when the water table meets the ground surface in topographically low spots (depression springs), when permeable rocks overlie rocks of low permeability (contact springs), and when geologic faulting places an impermeable rock next to an aquifer (fault springs).[38]

The eastern, northern, and western aquifers are present in several complex geologic formations. A broad outline of their properties is exhibited in table 1.3.[39] The basin incidence of the formations is illustrated in table 1.4, and stratification is sketched in figure 1.1.

The Western Aquifer

The western aquifer drains the Ajlun (Judea) group of the upper and lower Cenomanian ages, separated by a middle Cenomanian confining layer of marls and chalks. The upper Cenomanian commonly is overlain by confining layers of the Balqa (Mount Scopus) group, of the Senonian-Paleocene. The rocks of the Ajlun (Judea) group are porous dolomite and limestone and possess high aquifer value. Although these kinds of rocks are hard and resistant to surface erosion, having a large component of calcium carbonate renders them susceptible to dissolution in a weak solution of carbon oxide, which is present in raindrops. The process of dissolution is called karstification (after the Karst region in Slovenia, where the process first was identified). With the percolation of water deep underground, karstification leads to the creation of interconnected

38. There are also sinkhole springs, which occur when a cavern with subterranean water is connected to a shaft, and fracture springs, which occur when a faulted permeable fault zone is present in low permeability rocks; see Fetter, 1988, pp. 231–32.

39. Rofe and Raffety, 1965a and idem, 1965b, contain a synthesis of the geology of the West Bank; Abid, 1990, and *Encyclopedia Judaica*, 1971, vol. 9, pp. 194–220, provide geological descriptions of geographic Palestine. There are also older formations besides those in table 1.2. The Kurnub (after the Kurnub region in Wadi al-Huthayra, Beersheba) sandstone and marl from the Albian age is found in the western basin. There are formations from the Jurassic age, the aquiferous properties of which are not well understood as they occur at great depths.

TABLE 1.3 Hydrogeologic Characteristics of Major Rock Formations in the West Bank and Gaza

Formation	Age	Thickness (meter)	Rock type	Aquifer/ confining layer
West Bank				
Ajlun[a] (Judea)	Upper & Lower Cenomanian	400–900[b]	Dolomite, limestone	Aquifer
Balqa[a] (Mt. Scopus)	Senonian-Paleocene	150–250	Chalk, chert, marl	Confining
Jinin[c] (Avdat)	Eocene	200–500	Limestone, chalk	Aquifer, semi-confining
Lisan and Samra[d]	Pleistocene-Neogene	1–400	Marl, gravel, conglomerate	Aquifer
Gaza				
Kurkar[e]	Pleistocene	5–180	Sand, sandstone, clay marl, lime	Aquifer, confining, semi-confining

(Continued)

TABLE 1.3 Hydrogeologic Characteristics of Major Rock Formations in the West Bank and Gaza (Continued)

Formation	Age	Thickness (meter)	Rock type	Aquifer/ confining layer
Saqiya	Upper, middle Pliocene	600–800	Clay, marl	Confining
"Fossil"	Lower and upper Cretaceous (?)		Nubian sandstone, limestone (?)	Aquifer

SOURCES: Abid, 1990; *Atlas of Israel*, 1985, p. 9; Bruins and Tuinhof, 1991; Davidson and Hirzallah, 1966; European Community, 1993; Issar and Nativ, 1990, pp. 49–51; Rofe and Raffety, 1965a, 1965b, geologic map and pp. 17–18; Scarpa, 1994; Schwarz, 1982, pp. 87–88, 95–96.

NOTES:

[a]Ajlun and Balqa are Jordanian provinces. Balqa also is called Jabal al-Masharif; Abid, 1990, p. 32. The Ajlun group includes the subgroups Jerusalem, Bethlehem, Hebron, Yatta, and Bayt Kahil.

[b]The upper Cenomanian (or upper Ajlun) is 300–500 meters thick, according to Davidson and Hirzallah, 1966, p. 3.

[c]Jinin also is called Abda, after Khirbat Abada between Hebron and Beersheba; see Abid, 1990, p. 43.

[d]The Lisan—which means "tongue" in Arabic—is named after the tonguelike shape of the peninsula that juts into the eastern shore of the Dead Sea, while Samra—which means "dark" in Arabic—is named after al-Khirba al-Samra, 6 kilometers northeast of Jericho.

[e]Called thus locally.

TABLE 1.4 Properties of the Basins in the Mountain Aquifer

Basin/subbasin	Formation	Recharge area[a] (sq km)
Western		
al-Auja/al-Timsah (Yarqon/Tanninim)	Upper and lower Cenomanian	1,300
Hebron-Beersheba	Upper and lower Cenomanian	300
Northern		
Samarian	Upper and lower Cenomanian	500
Nablus-Jinin	Eocene	
Eastern		
Bardala	Upper and lower Cenomanian	90
Buqaya—Wadi Malih	Upper and lower Cenomanian and Eoecene	66
al-Fari'a	Pleistocene-Neogene	145
Fasayil—al-Auja	Upper and lower Cenomanian	610
Ramallah-Jerusalem		610
Jerusalem Desert	Upper and lower Cenomanian	590
Total		4,211

SOURCES: Abd al-Salam, 1990, p. 196; and Orni and Efrat, 1973, p. 145.
NOTE:
[a]Alternative estimates are considered in the text.

caverns, channels, and passageways. These rocks thus become excellent aquiferous formations. However, the high level of transmissivity[40] allows for rapid propagation of contaminants, making the aquifers prone to pollution, a topic discussed in the next chapter. The Ajlun group outcrops in large sectors of the central hills, where rainfall is also highest. In the western foothills and the coastal region, the western aquifer comprises two overlying aquifers, interbedded with confining marls and chalks.

Available data on other properties are scant. The recharge area of the western basin is estimated at 1,600–1,800 sq km. The exact distribution of this area between the West Bank and Israel is not known. According to one estimate, 1,400 sq km are in the West Bank and 400 sq km are in Israel.[41] Hence, it can be said that

40. According to BUNT, 1994, p. 2.8, the transmissivity of the western aquifer is about 200,000 sq meters per day.
41. Gvirtzman, 1994, p. 211. He also points out the storage area of the

FIGURE 1.1 Cross Section of the Mountain Aquifer

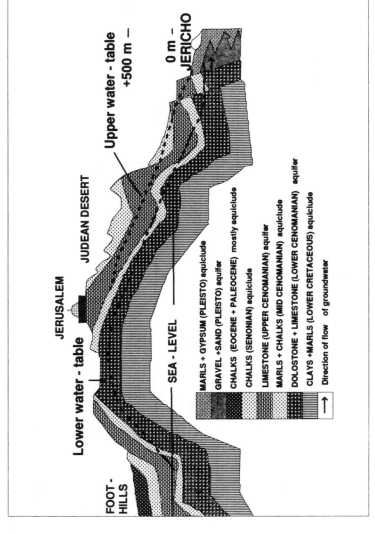

SOURCE: Adapted from Issar, 1990

about 80 percent of the recharge area of the western basin is situated in the West Bank, and 20 percent in Israel. Because the rainfall in the recharge area of the West Bank generally exceeds the rainfall in its counterpart in Israel, the West Bank probably contributes a greater proportion of replenishment than is indicated by its contribution to the area alone.

The proven natural outlets of the western basin are mainly two groups of springs that lie in Israel and a number of very small springs in the West Bank.[42] The first group is Ra's al- 'Ayn (Rosh Ha'ayin), in the central part of the coastal plain, northeast of the town of Petah Tiqva. They are the dominant feeder of the al-Auja (Yarqon) River, which empties into the Mediterranean north of Tel Aviv. The other group is the al-Timsah (Tanninim) in the central coastal plain north of Khudayra (Hadera). This has led Israeli authors to dub the basin the "Yarqon-Tanninim" aquifer.[43] The spring discharge in Israel, however, has been largely "replaced" by that of hundreds of man-made wells. In addition to the springs, an unproven direct outlet to the Mediterranean possibly exists near the al-Timsah springs.[44]

The Northern Aquifer

The northern basin consists of two overlying aquifers, the Samarian and Nablus-Jinin. The Samarian aquifer, like the western basin, drains the Ajlun (Judea) group of the upper and lower Cenomanian ages. It underlies the Nablus-Jinin aquifer that drains the Jinin (Mt. Scopus) group of the Eocene age and is made up of limestone supported in some areas with thick chalk acting as a confining

---

aquifer is 2,500 sq km, all of which is located within Israel. This point is taken up in chapter 5 in the discussion of equitable utilization.

42. The springs in the West Bank usually are classified according to their location with respect to the surface water divide, which, as was mentioned above, does not coincide with that of the groundwater. It is difficult to say how many minor springs exist in this basin itself.

43. It may be worth mentioning that the Hebrew word, *tannin* (singular of *tanninim*), means crocodile as does the Arabic counterpart, *timsah*. A similar word to *tannin* in Arabic is *tinnin*, which means dragon. It has been said that when the English King Richard the Lion-Heart (1157–99) camped near the river during the Crusades, two of his soldiers were eaten by crocodiles. Reportedly, crocodiles were spotted in the river early in the twentieth century; see al-Dabbagh, 1973, p. 34; and Orni and Efrat, 1973, p. 181.

44. Tahal, 1990, p. 2.4.

layer. The two aquifers have varying aquiferous characteristics but are structurally accessible.

The recharge area of the northern basin has been estimated variously at 500 to 590 sq km, depending on whether the Bardala aquifer is included. Another source has estimated the recharge area at 700 sq km, without stating the reasons for this larger estimate.[45] The recharge and storage areas are basically identical, that is, water discharges within the same boundaries of the percolation area, unlike the western or eastern basins. Probably more than 92 percent of those areas (650 sq km) are in the West Bank. An alternative estimate states that 95 percent of the "combined" recharge area of the western and northern basins lies in the West Bank.[46]

The general direction of the flow in the northern basin is north-northeast, following the Nablus-Bayt Qad syncline. The natural outlets of this basin are springs, as in the western basin. The bulk of the discharge occurs in Israel, although this has changed owing to the replacement of springs by wells, as was done in the western basin. A smaller portion of discharge is drained naturally in the West Bank as well. The Nablus-Jinin aquifer is drained through two sets of springs. The first includes the eight springs of Wadi al-Fari'a, near the city of Nablus, and scattered springs in the villages located in the basin. The second set are springs in the Faqqu'a (Gilboa) Mountains along the edge of the Baysan Valley in Israel, consisting of seven springs. In addition to the water from the Nablus-Jinin aquifer, the two sets of springs are believed to drain about 20 mcmy that, for structural reasons, leak from the underlying Samarian aquifer. The Samarian aquifer naturally drains for the most part in Israel, through two dozen springs in the Baysan Valley, four of which are large and the rest minor.[47]

The Eastern Aquifer

The eastern basin covers six subbasins if the Bardala is included (as it is in this book). Four of the aquifers (Bardala, Buqay'a-al-Malih, Fasayil al-Auja, and Jerusalem [Judean] Desert) drain the Ajlun (Judea) group of the upper and lower Cenomanian, while the al-Fari'a aquifer drains local formations such as the Lisan

45. Gvirtzman, 1994, p. 211.
46. Naff, 1991b, p. 4; and U.S. Department of State, n.d.
47. Schwarz, 1982, pp. 89–90.

TABLE 1.5 Recharge of the Subbasins of the Mountain Aquifer
(In mcmy)

Region	Boneh and Baida	Schwarz
Western		
al-Auja—al-Timsah	350–370	335[a]
(Yarqon-Tanninim)		
Hebron-Beersheba	17–21	
Northern		
Samarian	80–95	88–98
Nablus-Jinin	40–50	40–50
Eastern		
Bardala	3–6	
Buqay'a and Muawylih	2–3	1
al-Fari'a	9–15	4
Fasayil—al-Auja	24–40	14–29[b]
Ramallah-Jerusalem	50–70	46–68
Jerusalem Desert	35–40	18–23

SOURCES: Boneh and Baida, 1977–78, p. 39; Schwarz, 1982, pp. 89–91.
NOTES:
[a]235 mcmy from al-Auja and 100 mcmy from al-Timsah.
[b]Schwarz gives a partial account of the spring discharge in this subbasin. I calculated 14–29 mcmy by subtracting all the other flows from the total flow of this basin which he gives as being in the range of 85–125 mcmy.

(Lashon) and Samra groups of the Pleistocene-Neogene ages. The latter formations consist of sands, conglomerates, clays, and marls of variable aquiferous properties. The Lisan is extensively present in the Jordan Valley bordering the river. Estimates of the recharge area of the eastern basin range from 2,111 sq km, or 2,021 sq km if the Bardala aquifer is not included (see table 1.5), to 2,200 sq km.[48] The basin is replenished from the West Bank.[49] It drains in the Jordan Valley and west of the Dead Sea, although an insignificant flow may leak across the southern border of the West Bank

48. Gvirtzman, 1994; and Scarpa, 1994, citing the figure of 2,700 sq km from Arad and Michaeli, 1967. However, Arad and Michaeli actually discuss a different catchment area, which they call the "western catchment of the Dead Sea" (p. 181); the boundaries of this catchment extend from Wadi al-Qilt in the north to the southern tip of the Dead Sea.
49. According to Gvirtzman, 1994, the basin gets 4 mcmy from rainfall and 6 mcmy from the sewage system and pipe leakage in Jerusalem and the vicinity. These are not irrelevant, but he does not include the contribution of sewage and pipe leakage in the other basins. Also, his definition of Jerusalem includes a large sector of the West Bank.

into Israel. The basin is thus essentially a West Bank hydrological unit.

The general direction of flow in the basin is east and southeast toward the Jordan River and the Dead Sea. The natural drains of the eastern basin are springs in the Jordan Valley and along the western shore of the Dead Sea. The springs are distributed as follows:

Subbasin	Springs
Bardala	11–12 springs
al-Buqya'a-al-Malih	Wadi al-Malih
al-Fari'a	3 major springs
Fasayil al-Auja	al-Auja, Samiya, Fasayil
Ramallah-Jerusalem	Jericho springs (3), Wadi al-Qilt, Gihon (in Jerusalem), Fashkha (water leaks from Fasayil al-Auja basin)
Jerusalem Desert	Ghuwayr and Turayba, 'Ayn Jadi, and some small springs near Hebron

Mountain Aquifer Replenishment

Water in a renewable aquifer system consists of annual replenishment and base or "dead" nonrenewable storage.[50] The annual recharge determines the long-range "safe yield" of the aquifer, or the threshold of water abstraction that should not be exceeded if damage to the aquifer is to be avoided. The initial storage, however, enables users some flexibility to maintain a steady level of pumping, so long as it is commensurate with the general trend of replenishment.

Determination of aquifer replenishment and yield is replete with technical difficulties and uncertainties. In the case of the mountain aquifer system, vital physical properties also need further

50. Information on the base storage in the West Bank basins is extremely limited. Yaacov Vardi, 1980, p. 44, gives an estimate of the base storage of the western basin in 1977 as 40,000 mcm base or dead storage and 1,500 mcm operative stock, of which 800 mcm are interannual (assessment of the latter two is difficult and depends on the properties of the aquifer and how deep the users wish to mine it). It is unclear whether the base storage represents the volume within both Israel and the West Bank or just Israel, although the tenor of Vardi's text suggests the latter.

TABLE 1.6 Mountain Aquifer Replenishment

(In mcmy)

Basin	Boneh and Baida[a]	Rofe and Raffety[b]	Schwarz (Tahal)[c]	USG/DS	Taba Agreement
Western	367–391		325–345 (340)		362
Northern	120–145		130–150 (140)		145
Eastern	123–174		85–125 (100)		172
Total	610–710	720[b]	540–620 (580)	850	679

SOURCES: BUNT, 1994, pp. 2.7–2.9; Boneh and Baida, 1977–78, p. 39; Government of Israel and the PLO, September 1995, Annex III, Article 40, Schedule 10; Rofe and Raffety, 1965b, p. 15; Schwarz, 1982, pp. 89–90; Tahal, 1990, pp. 2.4–2.8; and USG/DS (n.d.).
USG/DS = United States Government/Department of State
NOTES:
[a]Based on the residual method (recharge = rainfall − runoff − evapotranspiration).
[b]Based on the residual method. The 720 mcmy is the average of the two years 1963–64 (713 mcmy) and 1964–65 (726 mcmy).
[c]Recharge = sum of spring discharge + minor percolation to the Jordan River.

study. For example, the total void space, an important variable in calculating aquifer yield, is unknown.[51] Also unknown is the extent of downward and upward leakage.[52]

The annual recharge of the mountain aquifer has been estimated in two ways: (1) as a "residual" of rainfall, evapotranspiration, and surface runoff; and (2) as the aggregation of the flow of springs. Various estimates of recharge for the three main components and subcomponents of the aquifer system are provided in table 1.6. The hydrometeorological raw data, time interval, methodology, and assumptions that inform the estimates, with the exception of those of Rofe and Raffety, are not supplied by the authors. Hence, it is difficult to draw any definite inferences about the various numbers; all that can be done is to compare the differences and speculate on possible reasons.

In general, there is agreement among the sources on the average recharge of the northern basin being in the vicinity of 145

51. Formally, the potential yield of an aquifer can be expressed as $y = v \times p \times r$, where y = yield, v = volume of the aquifer, p = porosity as a percentage of void space, and r = recoverable water as a percentage of the total water in the aquifer. See further Scarpa, 1994, p. 403.
52. Ibid.

mcmy. Differences, however, exist in the case of the other two aquifers, notably the eastern. The estimates by Joshua Schwarz are based on the first method of estimation, that is, spring discharge. When he published the estimates, Schwarz was a high-level manager at Tahal, and Tahal's figures are the averages of the bands he uses. Here, Tahal and Schwarz will be used interchangeably. Schwarz's estimates are the lowest of any in table 1.6. For the mountain aquifer as a whole, his upper range is close to the lower limit of Boneh and Baida, whose calculations use the residual method. On the other hand, the State Department's figure significantly exceeds all the others. Although the State Department's figure is conceivable in very wet years, it may be an overestimate if it is meant as an average, a point that the document does not clarify. Rofe and Raffety's figures apply only for two years and may not reflect a long-term trend. The two years were good rain years, and replenishment could have been greater than average.[53] On the whole, there is a close proximity among Boneh and Baida's upper limit and the averages of Rofe and Raffety and the Taba Agreement. Because Schwarz's figures are at variance with all the others and because they are semiofficial, they deserve scrutiny.[54]

For the western basin, Schwarz's *upper* limit is 22 mcmy less than even the *lower* limit of Boneh and Baida, both of whom also worked for Tahal. It is also less than the average that appeared in the Taba Agreement. His figure may be the cumulative effect of several steps. Schwarz gives the historical discharge of Ra's al-'Ayn springs as 235 mcmy, which is 33 mcmy less than the 268 mcmy mentioned by G. S. Blake in his 1947 survey of water resources in Palestine.[55] In addition, whereas Boneh and Baida include a recharge of 17–20 mcmy to the Beersheba-Hebron subbasin, Schwarz does not. Nor does he consider the 2 mcmy or so discharge of the springs of the western watershed. Finally, there is the possibility that, according to Tahal itself, an unproven direct outlet to the Mediterranean exists near Tanninim springs.[56] All this leads

53. Attur and Pike, 1966, p. 15.
54. I use Schwarz's article because it is more explicit about the sources of the estimates than are Tahal's reports.
55. Blake, 1947, p. 29. The discharge as cited by Blake is 8.5 m³/second, which is the equivalent of 268 mcmy. Blake obtained his figure from Rutenberg Engineers. Because Israeli-dug wells subsequently affected the flow of those springs to the point of drying them up, the earlier records are the only ones extant of the spring discharge.
56. Tahal, 1990, p. 2.4.

me to question whether Schwarz underestimated the recharge of the western aquifer, albeit not overly so considering the innumerable technical uncertainties involved.

In the eastern basin, however, there is a tangible discrepancy between Tahal's average of 100 mcmy and the Taba Agreement's 172 mcmy or Boneh and Baida's upper bound of 174 mcmy. In what may be a tacit attempt to explain the discrepancy between its previous numbers and those in the Taba Agreement, Tahal, in a report to the Multilateral Working Group on Water (MWGW), put the aquifer's recharge at 120–180 mcmy and stated that measurements "performed in 1992–1993 rationalized the adoption of an estimate on the higher edge of the range."[57] Questions remain, however. The figures in the Taba Agreement are almost identical to those published in the 1977–78 study by Boneh and Baida. In the years between the appearance of that study and the Taba Agreement, the estimates of Schwarz and Tahal were published. Schwarz's figures appeared in 1982 and subsequently were reiterated in Tahal's 1990 and 1994 reports to the World Bank. During this period, the expansion of, and planning for more, Israeli settlements in the West Bank was in full swing. Could it be that the low estimate was a way of saying that there was no more water to be tapped in the eastern aquifer, thus providing a justification for the restrictions on Palestinian water abstraction from it? Israel did not need such an alibi for the curbs on Palestinian water use in the northern and western basins that flow into its own territory; it could, and did, justify those restrictions on the grounds that the two aquifers already were overdrawn.

It may be that such questioning is much ado about little and that there is no hidden agenda in Tahal's inconsistency. However, if the numbers are to have any credibility, then Israel needs to provide the supporting raw data and technical material on which both the old and new estimates are based.

A point related to the above is the Taba Agreement's promise to the Palestinians in the West Bank of additional water (70–80 mcmy), 60 percent of which is supposed to come from the eastern basin (Annex III, Article 40, Schedule 10). As it turns out, the "extra" water in the eastern aquifer, according to the new estimate, is brackish. Harnessing it requires larger capital outlays than ex-

57. Tahal, 1990, p. 2.16.

tracting fresh water and carries the threat of contamination to the source aquifer because of potential brine seepage.

An aspect of the quantity of the mountain aquifer recharge that also should be highlighted is its fluctuation from year to year. Depending on the source of estimate, it ranges between 520–540 mcmy and 610–710 mcmy, or about 8 percent below or above the average. Such deviation, although not insignificant in a semiarid area, is not too large. The average recharge may be thought of as the safe yield. Nonetheless, the safe yield could plummet further during protracted droughts.

Finally, the bulk of the water in the mountain aquifer is naturally freshwater of drinkable quality. This is what, in part, gives it its key place as a water source. Pollution, however, has found its way to many previously clean parts of the aquifer, as is illustrated in tandem with Palestinian water use in chapter 2.

The Coastal Aquifer

The coastal aquifer underlies the Mediterranean seashore in Israel and Gaza, between Rafah and Mount Carmel.[58] In the literature, the term coastal aquifer often has been used to refer to the segment in Israel, whereas that in Gaza frequently is called the Gaza aquifer. In its two reports to the World Bank, Tahal makes the distinction clear and claims that the two segments are not "significantly" connected and presumably do not qualify as joint resources.[59] This argument, however, is more of a hydropolitical than a hydrogeological one. The fact is that, from a hydrogeological point of view, this is a joint Israeli-Palestinian aquifer, whether because of the continuity of the flow, geological properties, or sources of replenishment, as will become apparent in the following examination. After all, Gaza's borders were drawn as a result of war, not finessed according to hydrology. I will first describe the main features of the aquifer in general, then offer a more detailed account of the Gaza segment in order to clarify further some of these features.

The coastal aquifer is comprised of Pliocene-Pleistocene sand and sandstone, interrupted by wedges of marls and shales. Neogene shales and marls separate it from the underlying formations. The

58. The information about the coastal aquifer is largely from BUNT, 1994, pp. 2.9–2.10; Issar and Nativ, 1990; and Tahal, 1990, pp. 2.5–2.6
59. Tahal, 1990, p. 2.9; and BUNT, 1994, p. 2.12.

aquifer in the main is unconfined, except where the wedges of marls and shales are present. It is about 150 km long and wider in the south (18 km) than in the north (3–10 km). Its approximate area is about 2,200 sq km, more than 1,800 sq km of which is in Israel and the rest in Gaza.

The main natural source of replenishment is infiltration from direct rainfall on the coast and runoff from the streams that head seaward from the watershed in the central range. The average natural replenishment is about 340 mcmy. Apart from natural replenishment, the aquifer receives return water from irrigation and sewage, amounting to 110–120 mcmy, 90 from Israel and 20–30 from Gaza. In addition, Israel injects into it (or artificially recharges it) with about 80 mcmy from 60 wells and 10 spreading basins at the rate of about 80 mcmy. Translated into safe yield, the replenishment amounts to 280 mcmy, with a caveat regarding its fluctuation in order.

The transmissivity of the coastal aquifer is about 1,000–2,000 sq m daily, lower than its mountain aquifer counterpart. As a reservoir, however, the coastal aquifer is the largest of all the aquifers in geographic Palestine, with a storage area of several billion cubic meters. As such, it has been used to regulate the water balance in Israel throughout the year and from one year to the next. It also could have a strategic hydrologic value if water were imported in large quantities.

The coastal aquifer in Gaza (or Gaza aquifer) is present in a rock formation of the *kurkar* group of the Pleistocene age.[60] It is overlain by highly absorbent sand dunes in the western segment of Gaza, extending 4–5 km inland, and narrower in the center than in the north and south. East of the sand dunes there are finer continental deposits. The aquifer is underlain by a confining layer, 400–600 m thick, of clay-like marine deposits and marl that belong to the Saqiya group of the upper and middle Pliocene. The total thickness of the aquifer ranges from 80–100 m in the east to 120–160 m by the shore. It thins out to around 20 m east of Gaza's border. Water in the uppermost layer, which is also the best-quality water, can be pumped at depths ranging from 5 to 80 m.[61] The aquiferous layers are interrupted in some areas by confining and semiconfining layers

60. Schwarz, 1982. This reference provides the basic text on the aquifer.
61. Abid, 1990, pp. 43 and 47–49; European Community, 1993, pp. 1–2 and figure 1.2; and Schwarz, 1982, p. 96.

of marine and continental clays and marls, dividing the aquifer into several overlying subaquifers (A, B, and C in figure 1.2). The three subaquifers extend offshore but, with the exception of the topmost layer (A), lie mainly inland. The lower the subaquifer, the farther it reaches inland: The lowest layer, C, reaches up to 5 km, while layer A reaches only up to 2 km.[62] The layering pattern thus renders each of the subaquifers partly confined and partly unconfined.

The water in the Gaza aquifer flows chiefly east-west, with the downward slope of the rock formations. The natural outlet of the aquifer is the Mediterranean; there are no springs in Gaza. In addition to the sea, water flows into coastal depressions at levels of 1–2 m below sea level; these depressions have been created by chronic over pumping.[63] Gaza's aquifer is replenished from rainfall in Gaza itself. It also receives a flow from the segment of the coastal aquifer in Israel, but this is less than the natural flow because Israel intercepts the flow before it reaches Gaza's border. How much of the flow would reach Gaza without Israel's interception is a disputed matter, as is discussed below.

In addition to the Pleistocene aquifer, an aquiferous layer may exist below the confining Saqiya formation. The layer has been explored only by two stratigraphic wells. The rocks of the layer may be Nubian sandstone or limestone of Cenomanian age. The water of this deep aquifer in Gaza is highly saline, having about 8,000 milligrams of chloride per liter (mg/l), but the salinity decreases to 2,000 mg/l about 30–40 km to the southeast of Gaza. This aquifer probably is not connected to the *kurkar* aquifer above; nor does it drain into the sea because the rocks in the western section change from limestone to confining marls.[64]

The recharge of the coastal aquifer in Gaza comes mainly from rainfall, infiltration from the wadis, flow from Israel, and return water. Because of the absence of springs as natural outlets, recharge has been estimated by the residual method. Replenishment from rainfall has been put variously at 25 mcmy, 40 mcmy, and 47 mcmy (see table 1.7). H. J. Bruins and A. Tuinhof based their figure on field work on the sand dunes in Mozambique, where the

62. Schwarz, 1982, p. 96.
63. European Community, 1993, p. 2.
64. Bruins and Tuinhof, 1991, p. 9, citing Mills and Shata; European Community, 1993, p. 2.

FIGURE 1.2 Cross Section of Gaza Aquifer

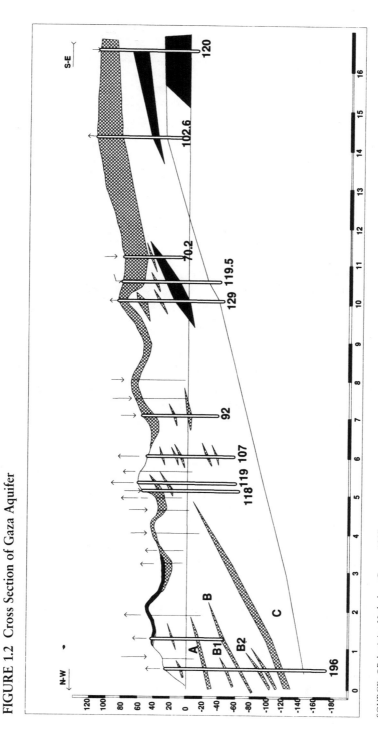

SOURCE: ©Palestinian Hydrology Group, 1997

TABLE 1.7 Coastal Aquifer Replenishment in Gaza
(In mcmy)

	Source			
Author	Rainfall flow	Eastern flow	Return	Total
Bruins and Tuinhof	25			
European Community	47	20	14–25	80–90
Schwarz	40	10–20	20–30	70–90

SOURCE: Bruins and Tuinhof, 1991; European Community, 1993, p. 5 (citing a water balance figure given by the Israeli government); and Schwarz, 1982, pp. 95–96.

recharge rate was found to be 25 percent of rainfall.[65] The groundwater flow from Israel may amount to 10–20 mcmy of saline water. Palestinian specialists, however, have charged that Israel pumped an unspecified amount of water from a string of wells along the eastern Gaza border, a closed military area.[66] In fact, since the 1940s Israel has extracted freshwater at Nir'am in the northeastern corner of the aquifer just outside Gaza, but it has not disclosed the quantities.[67] It also has been reported that this extraction has been of saline water, which would exacerbate the salinity of Gaza's aquifer if it were not intercepted.[68] This may be so, but it must have some utility in Israel and might be of use for Gaza, if not presently then at some future date.

Besides the natural recharge, the aquifer receives perhaps 20–30 mcmy of return water from irrigation and cesspools. Thus, the total recharge of the aquifer amounts to 70–90 mcmy. If, however, the lower value of 25 mcmy of rainfall recharge is used, while maintaining the other values unchanged, the actual recharge would range between 55 and 75 mcmy.[69]

The safe yield cannot be assumed automatically in this case to equal the average recharge, and account must be taken of the special hydrogeology of the aquifer. Because the aquifer empties into the sea, prevention of sea water intrusion dictates that the water table in the aquifer not drop below a certain level. Such a

65. They use a rainfall level in Gaza of 100 mcmy, as indicated earlier.
66. Bruins and Tuinhof, 1991, pp. 9–10.
67. Schwarz, 1982, p. 96.
68. Bruins and Tuinhof, 1991, pp. 9–10.
69. The actual recharge excludes the unspecified flow intercepted by Israel.

level requires that at least 20 mcmy of water be allowed to flow into the sea, reducing the long-term safe yield to 40 mcmy.[70]

An Assortment of Aquifers

Apart from the mountain and coastal aquifers, geographic Palestine's renewable groundwater resources include an assortment of smaller aquifers,[71] especially in the north, in the Galilee and Carmel basins. The Galilee basin is hydrogeologically a continuation of the mountain aquifer. It consists of two basins, the eastern and western.

The water of the eastern basin is present in several mainly basalt aquifers, in the eastern Galilee and the Jordan Valley. It drains into the Jordan basin, notably into Lake Tiberias. Its discharge is subsumed under the Jordan basin's balance in the next section. Israel exploits a small amount of the water from the aquifers themselves, about 8 mcmy. These aquifers can be tapped by wells only from Israel; however, they are still common aquifers by virtue of their drainage into the Jordan River basin.

The western Galilee aquifer drains naturally toward the Mediterranean through two springs, Nu'man (saline) and al-Kabri. It is built of upper Cretaceous (Cenomanian and Turonian) limestone and dolomite formations with karstic characteristics, similar to the mountain aquifer. The annual replenishment is estimated at 115 mcmy. The aquifer can be tapped only from Israel, which exploits it through more than 100 wells and directly from al-Kabri spring.

The Carmel Mountain contains a set of minor aquifers. Their safe yield is about 60 mcmy, about 10 mcmy of which are brackish. On its western coast, there is a small aquifer (7 mcmy) of the Pliocene-Pleistocene age, similar to the composition of the coastal aquifer. Lastly, minor aquifers exist in the Wadi 'Araba area, with an annual replenishment of maybe 25 mcmy, two-thirds of which are brackish. It may be possible to mine up to 60 mcmy from them for a short period. The last three groups, the western Galilee, Car-

70. Schwarz mentioned in 1982 that there were additional reserves in the aquifer that could be mined at the rate of about 20 mcmy for a period of 10 years. One must assume that those reserves by now have been depleted because pumping continually has exceeded the 60 mcmy level, as will be discussed below.

71. The discussion of these aquifers is based mainly on BUNT, 1994, pp. 2.11–2.12.

mel, and 'Araba, do not qualify, hydrogeologically speaking, as international common aquifers because they are fed from and drain inside Israel.

RUNOFF AND WADIS

Surface water is provided by two sources: the Jordan River system (the principal source) and runoff inside the country. Runoff in geographic Palestine represents a small fraction of total rainfall, thanks to the highly absorbent limestone rock formations of the hills and the sandy formations of the coastal regions. The relationship between rainfall and runoff is complex, a function of, among other things, the level, intensity, and duration of rainfall, as well as the topography of the landscape. Runoff gathers in innumerable streams (wadis) that are frequently intermittent; some, however, are perennial because they collect water from springs, in addition to the flood runoff. The spring discharge already has been included in the groundwater balance and will be mentioned in this section only for clarification; it should *not* be double-counted in the overall water balance.

Runoff in the West Bank

The surface watershed in geographic Palestine runs along a north-south axis, as indicated in the discussion of topography. The catchment area of the western basin is much larger than the eastern. Within the West Bank, however, the area of the western basin is approximately 3,000 sq km, larger than the eastern's area of 2,500 sq km.[72] On the whole, despite a large number of wadis in absolute terms, the drainage network is considered "thin"—has a small number of wadis relative to the drainage area—in the south-western part of the western basin, but is somewhat denser in the Judean Desert area of the eastern basin owing to the prevalence of chalk rock.[73]

In the western basin, the wadis generally flow west toward the Mediterranean. They lie partly in the West Bank and partly in

72. Boneh and Baida, 1977–78. Due to the approximate nature of the figures, the sum of the two areas, 5,500 sq km, is slightly less than the total West Bank land mass of 5,545 sq km.

73. Abd al-Salam, 1990, pp. 224–26; Orni and Efrat, 1973, pp. 50–59.

Israel. In the eastern basin, the wadis flow east toward the Jordan Rift and belong to the greater Jordan River, Dead Sea, and Wadi 'Araba basin. In both basins, the large difference in elevation between the central hills, on the one hand, and the coastal area and the Jordan Rift, on the other, causes the water of the wadis to travel at high velocity in the foothills. Thus, during intervals of intense or torrential rainfall, the topography abets in the making of damaging floods.

The stream flows and their drainage areas in the West Bank and Gaza are exhibited in table 1.8. The figures for the main wadis represent averages that do not capture the temporal or spatial flow variations. They are thus of limited value for planning or designing structures for impounding the water. More detailed monitoring and analysis would be required for such tasks. The quantities, it must be underlined, also include spring discharge, limiting their value as data on flood runoff.

The wadis of the western basin in the West Bank develop fully as they approach the Mediterranean, in Israel. The names given to the main catchment areas are those of the streams toward the end of their course. The northern wadis of this basin become rivers, thanks to the additional large base flows from springs. The most important river is the al-Auja (Yarqon), supplied mainly by the springs at Ra's al-'Ayn, as mentioned earlier. Israel's replacement of springs by wells, however, altered this situation, and the al-Auja, for example, has turned essentially into a ditch. Israel impounds water from the wadis inside its borders. The wadis remain intermittent in the West Bank, with a total flood runoff of probably 20–25 mcmy.

In the West Bank, the total discharge of the eastern wadis is greater than that of their western counterparts, even though the drainage area of the latter is greater than that of the former. The reason is that the eastern wadis receive more spring water.[74] The largest of the eastern wadis is al-Fari'a, which is fed by a relatively large number of springs along its course before it enters the Jordan Valley. Its average flood flow ranges between 0.0 and 4.5 mcm[75]

74. The most important springs are al-Fari'a (also known as upper al-Fari'a or Ra's al-Birka), Idlib or Dulib (also known as lower al-Fari'a), al-Sidra, Qadira, and Miska. See *Encyclopedia Palaestina*, 1984, vol. 3, p. 424; and *Shu'un Tanmawiyya*, 1988, p. 17.

75. Boneh and Baida, 1977–78; and Rofe and Raffety, 1965b, p. 6.

TABLE 1.8 Stream Drainage Area and Average Flow in the West Bank and Gaza

Wadi and tributary[a]	Catchment area[a] (sq km)	Average flow (mcmy)
West Bank		
Western		
al-Muqatta' (Qishon)	1,090	
al-Muqatta'	95	0.9
Jamus	32	0.5
al-Khudayra (Hadera)	604	
Abu Nar	159	1.1
Massin	113	0.4
Iskandarun (Alexander)	561	
Zimar	123	4.2
al-Tin	119	0.7
al-Auja (Yarqon)		
Qana	188	1.5
Sarida	331	0.8
Dilib	111	1.2
suqrir (Lachish)		
Zayta	25	1.2
Dahiriyya (Shiqma)		
al-Sammu' (Habsor)		
Nar al-Gharbi	179	2.8
Eastern		
Dead Sea group		
al-Mashash	1,100	7.5
Gaza		
Gaza (Bessor)	3,500	14.0

SOURCES: Abd al-Salam, 1990, pp. 215–17; Benvinisti and Khayat, 1988, p. 3; Boneh and Baida, 1977–78; Center for Engineering and Analysis, 1992b; al-Dabbagh, 1973, pp. 29–37; *Encyclopedia Palaestina*, 1984, vols. 3 and 4; Rofe and Raffety, 1965b, pp. 4–6 and map no. 4.
NOTES:
[a]The catchment areas and flows of the tributaries of the western wadis are those monitored by Rofe and Raffety in 1964–65. This also applies to the eastern wadis, except for al-Fari'a and al-Qilt.

and its average total flow is 5.3 mcmy.[76] The second major wadi is al-Qilt. The wadi carries flood water in addition to the flow of three main springs (Fara, al-Fawwar, and al-Qilt) that emerge through its floor at various points in its course. One of the springs, al-Fawwar, is seasonal with an unusual cyclical flow, while the

76. Calculated from Nuseibeh and Nasser Eddin, 1995.

other two are perennial.[77] The average total flow of the wadi may amount to 7.2 mcmy.

The total average runoff in geographic Palestine may be 140 mcmy, of which 90 mcmy are considered exploitable.[78] How much of this runoff can be tapped from Israel and how much from the West Bank and Gaza is unclear, especially since runoff in the West Bank has been poorly monitored in the past. The available information on the West Bank's runoff is a combination of data from the pre–1967 period collected by Jordan and scattered estimates from Israeli sources. Those data give a total runoff-to-rainfall ratio of 1 to 2.4 percent for the entire West Bank.[79] However, a recent study of the Khudayra (Hadera) catchment area, which falls largely in the northwest of the West Bank, casts doubt about such low ratios. Whereas the average runoff over the same area was estimated by Rofe and Raffety at 0.2 percent of rainfall, the new study estimates it at 4.5 percent.[80] The new study also indicates clearly that the amount of rainfall decisively affects runoff ratio.[81] Nevertheless, the difference between the findings of the two studies is significant, and further research that considers longer historical records is needed to settle more satisfactorily the question of runoff.

To sum up, runoff in the West Bank may average 50 mcmy, with the economically harnessable volume yet to be determined.[82] The average spring discharge in the two basins has been put at 90–110 mcmy.[83]

77. Al-Fawwar spring flows cyclically, bursting out every 20 minutes and gathering in a pool. The reason for this is that the water percolates through the limestone rocks and fills a karstic cave; once the cave is filled, it empties out, and the cycle is repeated ad infinitum. According to local legend, the cycle reflects an ongoing struggle between good and bad demons. When the good demons have the upper hand, the water flows, but when the bad ones dominate, the flow ebbs. See *Jerusalem Post*, 15 May 1994, p. 14.

78. BUNT, 1994, p. 2.14.

79. Boneh and Baida, 1977–78; Rofe and Raffety, 1965b, p. 4; and Schwarz, 1982, p. 86. The ratio of Rofe and Raffety—2.4 percent—is based on runoff measurements in an area covering about 32 percent of the West Bank, while that of Boneh and Baida and Schwarz—1 to 2 percent—comes with no explanation as to how it was obtained.

80. Husary et al., 1995, p. 54.

81. For example, runoff was 3.3 percent at 693 mm of rainfall, 4.6 percent at 816 mm, and 16.2 percent at 1,255 mm; ibid., p. 49.

82. Boneh and Baida, 1977–78, gives the average at 40–50 mcmy; Schwarz, 1982, p. 86, at 30–50 mcmy; and Rofe and Raffety, 1965b, p. 4, at 60–64 mcmy.

83. The first figure is from Boneh and Baida, 1977–78; and the second from Schwarz, 1982, p. 87.

Runoff in Gaza

In Gaza the main runoff shows up in intermittent wadis that originate in Israel and the West Bank. Owing to the absorbent soil and flat terrain, runoff within Gaza itself probably is confined to one-third of the area. The quantity that could be "harvested" has been estimated at 2 to 3.6 percent of the rainfall, or 2 to 3.6 mcmy. These estimates must be viewed as tentative; they are not based on field work or rigorous modeling, and the authors do not say how they arrived at them.[84] The main source of runoff is to be found in three wadis (from north to south): Bayt Hanun, Gaza (Bessor), and al-Sulqa.[85] The largest of the wadis, and the one for which data are available, is Gaza (Bessor). It drains an area of about 3,500 sq km and runs only in winter. The flow of Wadi Gaza at Reim has been estimated to be in the range of 0.5 to 70 mcmy, with a median of 5 mcmy and an average of 14 mcmy.[86] The natural surface flow in Gaza therefore may average 16–18 mcmy. Finally, in Gaza and the West Bank the combined flood runoff may average 56–65 mcmy, and the total combined (that is, including spring flow) may average 131–178 mcmy. How much of this runoff can be economically tapped is yet to be determined.

THE JORDAN RIVER BASIN

The Jordan River flows north-south in a small segment of the great African-Syrian Rift that extends from the Horn of Africa to Mount Amanos in Turkey.[87] It is unique historically, ecologically, and as a source of water supply. It continues to be central to the history, myth, and religion of the Arabs and Jews, and it has been the subject of endless description and writing. Although the interest in this book is in the Jordan River as a water-supply source, it is

84. The lower number is from al-Khatib and Assaf, 1992, p. 9, citing Riad al-Khudari; the higher number is from Bruins and Tuinhof, 1991, p. 14.

85. According to al-Dabbagh, 1973, p. 36, the name Bessor was used by the Canaanites; it is now in common usage in Israeli sources.

86. Schwarz, 1993. See chapter 4 for the quantities of water that Israel impounds from Wadi Gaza.

87. There is a voluminous literature containing geological and geomorphological descriptions of the Jordan River system. The following description relies largely on al-Buhayri, 1991, pp. 85–103; *Encyclopaedia Judaica*, 1971, vol. 8, p. 373, vol. 9, pp. 156–74, vol. 10, pp. 189–97, and vol. 16, pp. 718–20; Orni and Efrat, 1973, pp. 80–105; and Smith, 1966.

necessary to emphasize that its natural and historical features impart to the river system a notable "in-stream" value that needs to be kept in mind in schemes to develop its waters. The in-stream value becomes even more pronounced if one takes into account that the Jordan River is the principal water source of the Dead Sea—itself of distinct natural and historical significance—and substantial modification of the river's flow has a profound impact on the fragile ecology of this inland lake.

The amount of water in the Jordan basin is small compared with the flows of such other great rivers of the Middle East as the Nile, the Euphrates, and the Tigris.[88] Nonetheless, it is vital for Israel, Jordan, the West Bank, and the regions in Lebanon and Syria where the Jordan River and its main tributaries rise. Since 1948, the Jordan basin has been the site of battles and of a protracted water dispute among the Arab riparians and Israel and sometimes among the Arab riparians themselves. Aspects of this dispute will be examined in chapters 4 and 5. Here I delineate the basic hydrogeological features of the system and the contribution of its five riparians. Because the water withdrawals of several of these riparians have significantly altered the natural flows of the system, and because there is no other occasion in the book for addressing water use from the basin as there is from the aquifers, I highlight the locations of diversion and the type of projects built for those purposes. The amounts of withdrawals by the various riparians are given in chapter 5 in tandem with the discussion of the Johnston Plan.

For expository purposes, the basin is divided into four segments: the upper Jordan, Lake Tiberias, the Yarmuk River, and the lower Jordan (a sketch of the basin is shown in map 1.5). The upper Jordan extends between the rise of the river system in the foothills of Mount Hermon—Jabal al-Shaykh, in Arabic—and its entry into Lake Tiberias. The Yarmuk River feeds it from the east soon after its exit from Lake Tiberias. The lower segment stretches between the point confluence of the Yarmuk and the Jordan rivers to the Dead Sea, where the latter empties.

---

88. The Jordan River's discharge (assumed at 1.5 bcmy) is 4.6 percent of the Euphrates' (33 bcmy), 3 percent of the Tigris' (49 bcmy), and 1.8 percent of the Nile's (84 bcmy). The statistics for the Euphrates and the Tigris are from Kolars, 1992, p. 106; for the Nile from Waterbury, 1979, p. 20.

MAP 1.5 Drainage Area of the Jordan Basin

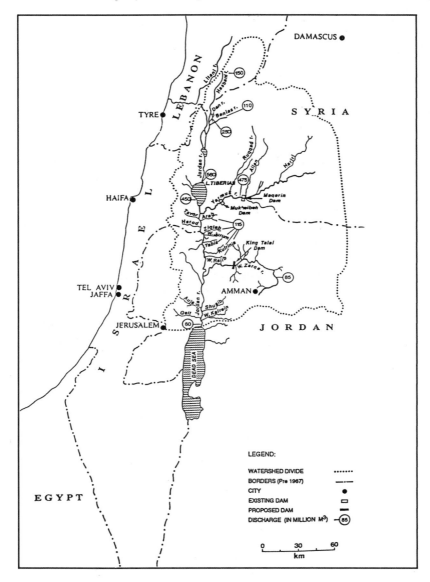

The Upper Jordan

The headwaters of the upper Jordan River consist principally of three rivers: the Banyas (Hermon), Dan (al-Qadi in Arabic), and al-Hasibani (Senir). The three rivers are fed by floodwater and, primarily, by groundwater issuing at their beds. The groundwater comes from the snow melt and rainfall over the aquiferous, limestone rocks—Jurassic and Cretaceous—of Mount Hermon overlooking the edge of the river. It also has been hinted that the groundwater which the springs drain may be part of a large regional aquifer, because the discharge of the springs is greater than the precipitation over the catchment area and because laboratory analysis indicated the occurrence of considerable isotopic exchange among the springs.[89] This thesis, however, has not been confirmed so far. Mount Hermon itself is more than 2,800 m above sea level and receives ample precipitation of 1,200–1,500 mm annually;[90] it is topped by snow virtually all year round. The snow cap lies behind its Arabic name, Jabal al-Shaykh, or "the old man's mountain." The mountain is located equally in both Syria and Lebanon. Israel seized parts of it during the June 1967 war and its 1982 invasion of Lebanon and thus was able to gain control of the Jordan's headwaters.

The al-Hasibani River, the longest of the three tributaries, rises from near the village of Hasibiyya in Lebanon on the western slope of Mount Hermon at more than 900 meters above sea level. It is fed by the springs of al-Hasibani and al-Wazzani. The Banyas River begins its course in Syria adjacent to the village of Banyas at 380 meters above sea level on the southern slopes of Mount Hermon from cave Paneas, believed to have been dedicated to the god Pan in Hellenistic times. The Dan River begins as Spring Dan in Israel near the ancient Biblical *tal* ("hill") of Dan, midway between the other two tributaries and at 260 m above sea level on the lower foot of Mount Hermon.[91] About 6.5 km inside Israel, the al-Hasibani and the Dan rivers meet, and a short distance thereafter their unified channel is joined by the Banyas River, at which point the Jordan River acquires its name.

The Jordan River then descends through the Hula Valley, which is 25 km long (north-south) and 6 to 8 km wide (east-west).[92] In this subbasin, the water used to collect in what was known as Lake Hula and its associated marshlands. The lake's water level measured 70 meters above sea level and its area was 16 sq km,

---

89. Naff and Matson, 1984, p. 19.
90. *Encyclopaedia Judaica*, 1971, vol. 8, pp. 373–74.
91. The elevations are from Smith, 1966, p. 115.
92. The area is 177 sq km; figures from Orni and Efrat, 1973, p. 84.

much smaller than the marshlands' 177 sq km.[93] Israel drained both the lake and the marshlands between 1951 and 1958 to bring the land under cultivation. The river's natural channel also was replaced by two laterally-connected canals.[94] In the Hula Valley, the Jordan River is fed by streams, both ephemeral and perennial, from the eastern and western rims; the most important stream is Burayghith (Ayyun). This feeder issues as a spring in Lebanon, near the village of Marj'yun; it discharges today into the western man-made canal instead of the marshes, as it used to do. About 10 km south of its former exit from Lake Hula, the Jordan River becomes a deep gorge and drops steeply, about 270 m in the 15 km between this point and Lake Tiberias, or the biblical Sea of Galilee (Kinneret).

Between 1949 and 1967, the upper Jordan River fell within Israeli territory from the junction of its headwaters to a point below the northeast corner of Lake Hula. From here to its entry into Lake Tiberias, it was part of a demilitarized zone between Israel and Syria. After Israel's seizure of the Golan Heights, the entire trunk of the upper Jordan came under Israeli control.

Lake Tiberias

Lake Tiberias is the Jordan River's second largest natural reservoir after the Dead Sea, with a volume of 4,000 m³. Its surface area covers approximately 165 sq km; its maximum depth is 44 meters; and its water level, which varies according to rainfall and extraction, is about 212 m below sea level.[95] Its outflow is regulated by four gates at its southern end at Degania (in Israel) that keep its level between 213 and 209 m below sea level. The 4 meter-difference allows for an operational water volume of 670 mcmy.[96] The lake originally may have been rectangular, then gradually alluvial deposits from the river and erosion at the southern tip around the exit imparted to it its current pear like shape. The lake receives most of its freshwater supply from the Jordan River. The remainder

93. Ibid.
94. The first canal is 19.5 km long and the second, to the east of the first, is 16 km long, according to *Encyclopaedia Judaica*, 1971, vol. 8, pp. 1065–67.
95. *Encyclopaedia Judaica*, 1971, vol. 10, p. 1034.
96. Tahal, 1990, p. 2.3.

is rendered by direct rainfall; streams from the Golan on the eastern shore, including four relatively rich ones; and streams from Israel on the western shore. In addition to the freshwater, the lake is fed by brackish-to-saline groups of springs on the lake's western shore, the largest of which is al-Tabigha, and others issuing at its bottom (sublacustrine springs).[97] The flow of the sublacustrine springs is affected by the level of water in the lake—the higher the level, the greater the suppression of the flow and the lower the salinity.[98] On the other hand, the discharge of on-the-shore springs, or at least of the al-Tabigha group, is not affected by the level of the lake.[99]

Lake Tiberias fell within Israel's territory between 1949 and 1967, and the northern half of its eastern shore formed a boundary between Israel and Syria while the other half was a demilitarized zone between the two states. Since 1967, however, Israel has assumed control of the entire shore. Israel has substantially altered the natural water balance of the lake by the diversion since 1964 of sizable amounts of water at al-Tabigha into its National Water Carrier. In that same year, Israel also redirected the course of the largest of the exogenous saline springs into the mainstream of the Jordan River after its exit from the lake.

The Yarmuk River

About 10 km south of its emergence from the lake, the Jordan River is joined from the east by the Yarmuk River, its largest single tributary. The Yarmuk River drains a large area in the southeastern foot of Mount Hermon, the Golan Heights, and Jabal al-Duruz (all in southern Syria) and the northwest of Jordan. The drainage area is largely semiarid and has elevations reaching up to 1,200–1,500 m and a top stratum of volcanic Quaternary rocks.[100] The Yarmuk River is fed by an intricate network of mostly ephemeral streams formed by winter floods; the five main feeders are, clockwise from the north, al-Raqqad, Allan, al-Harir, al-Zaydi (all in Syria), and Shallala (in Jordan). Its main trunk first coincides with al-Zaydi, the major intermittent tributary, before the other streams discharge

97. Several hypotheses have been proposed for the emergence and salinity of these springs; they are discussed in Goldschmidt et al., 1967.
98. *Encyclopaedia Judaica*, 1971, v. 10, p. 1035.
99. Goldschmidt et al., 1967, p. 13.
100. Salameh and Bannayan, 1991, pp. 16–17, and map, p. 16.

into it. It becomes a perennial stream and first receives springwater near the village of Muzayrib (in Syria). From that point onward, it turns into a deep gorge and is supplied with perennial water from an estimated 170 springs issuing at its bed.[101] For about 40 km, the Yarmuk River forms a boundary between Jordan and Syria, then becomes a border zone between Jordan and Israel for about 12 km at its tail end, west of the hot mineral springs of al-Himma (Himmat Ghader). These springs were part of geographic Palestine but during the 1948 war were taken by the Jordanian army, which subsequently handed them to Syria. In 1967, they were captured by Israel together with another larger area of the Yarmuk River extending beyond its point of confluence with the al-Raqqad River.

Since the 1960s, Israel, Jordan, and Syria all have considerably modified the natural water balance of the river. Jordan diverted part of the flow into the East Ghor (now King Abdallah) Canal, which was completed between 1962 and 1988. The canal runs parallel to the lower Jordan up to the margin of the Dead Sea. Syria impounded the water of the Yarmuk River's numerous feeders behind small dams in the 1980s and reportedly is planning more such structures. Israel for many years has diverted water from the Yarmuk River and tripled or quadrupled its extraction after 1967.

The Lower Jordan

Between the point of its confluence with the Yarmuk River and termination in the Dead Sea, the Jordan River covers a straight distance of about 100 km and descends 190 m, which is considered a steep gradient for rivers. It is, or rather used to be, fed by largely seasonal streams that run nearly parallel to each other and gush through the mountain ranges rising on the eastern and western fringes of the rift. The discharge from the eastern streams (all in Jordan) by far exceeds the contribution of the western streams. The largest tributary is the al-Zarqa River (in Jordan), which joins the main stream near the village of Dayr Alla and drains an extensive terrain that reaches into Jordan's heartland and even into the foothills of Jabal al-Duruz in southern Syria.[102] The main western feeders

101. The number of springs is from Abd al-Salam, 1990, p. 222.
102. Salameh and Bannayan, 1991, p. 19, estimate the catchment area of al-Zarqa River at 4,025 sq km. Other wadis from Jordan include (from north to south) al-Arab, Ziqlab, al-Jurum, al-Yabis, and Kufranja.

are the Jalud (Harod) in Israel, which joins the Jordan River in the Baysan Valley, and al-Fariʻa in the West Bank. The water of most of these tributaries is tapped for irrigation, and only a minor amount of their flow directly reaches the Jordan River's channel.

The lower reach of the river is believed to be of a recent geological origin, formed as a result of the retreat of both the Dead Sea and Lake Tiberias during the middle Pleistocene. Until that age the two lakes had constituted a single water body depositing thick layers of Lisan. Geologists also theorize that this segment of the rift was separated from the upper half by lava that flowed down from the Golan Heights and the Huran Plain, then solidified and dammed the Hula Valley north of Lake Tiberias.[103]

A chief characteristic of the lower Jordan are the extraordinary meanders of its lower channel.[104] These meanders make its river length nearly double the straight distance of about 100 km between its debouchure at Lake Tiberias and entry into the Dead Sea. It is as if the lower Jordan is still in the process of finding a permanent course, for, in addition to meandering, it cuts a new channel from time to time owing to the damming of its course from the collapse of its high flood plain.[105] The latter phenomenon was taken into account in the Israel-Jordan water agreement by the inclusion of provisions for the demarcation of borders between the two states along the course of the Jordan (and the Yarmuk) River in the event the courses change in this manner (Annex I [a]. 2.A.3).

The rift on both sides of the lower Jordan is a natural terrace, consisting of three zones: the Zor (Ge'on ha-Yardin), the Katar, and the Ghor (Kikkar). The Zor is a narrow flood plain, only hundreds of meters wide. Owing to heat and humidity, the Zor is covered by dense vegetation, such as ditch reed. It was irrigated before 1967 by water pumped directly from the river on the eastern and western banks.[106] However, cultivation ceased after 1967: on

103. Al-Buhayri, 1991, pp. 88–89; and *Encyclopaedia Judaica*, 1971, vol. 9, p. 156.

104. There are several competing explanations for the phenomenon; some experts attribute it to the fluctuations of the flow, others to the types of deposits borne by the river, and still others to the original formation of the river. See further al-Buhayri, 1991, p. 96.

105. Rivers usually change their courses as a result of such mechanisms as erosion, accretion, or flooding, but the collapse of the flood plain may not be common. The Jordan River's frequency of channel change has decreased in recent years as a result of the decline of its flow.

106. The area on the eastern bank of the Jordan River was estimated at 12,000 dunums in Elmusa, 1994a, p. 82.

the western Zor because of Israel's closure of the area on security grounds; and on the eastern Zor because of the fighting between the Palestinian guerrillas and Israel in the area in the late 1960s. Even without the war, the water of the Jordan became too saline for irrigation mainly because of Israel's diversion of the saline springs on Lake Tiberias' shore into the river's channel.

The Zor is flanked on both sides by a slightly rugged terrain known as the Katar, or badlands, that rises tens of meters above it but lacks a vegetation cover and is unsuitable for growing crops. The badlands are no more than 3 km wide and are fringed by another zone with alluvium deposits formed at the bed of the ancient lake known as the Ghor (the term *ghor*, which means depression in Arabic, locally refers to the entire Jordan Valley). The Ghor contains the principal agricultural land of the Jordan Valley. It is wider, and the irrigable area greater, on the eastern than on the western bank.[107]

The moderate winter and low elevation of the Ghor produce a natural greenhouse effect, which, coupled with irrigation water, impart to it a favorable agroenvironment distinguished by a seasonal comparative advantage, thanks to the absence of competition from other areas. In fact, the irrigated agriculture in the Ghor represents about one-half of the total irrigated land of both Jordan and the West Bank.[108] In Israel, by comparison, the irrigated area in the valley comprises a small fraction, around 10 percent, of the irrigated land, which is found mainly in the coastal plain and in the Negev Desert.[109] The bulk of irrigation water evapotranspires.

The Dead Sea

The final station of the Jordan River is the Dead Sea, which it enters as two channels enclosing a minor delta that forms after the

107. One hypothesis for why this is so is that the water volume and deposits of the eastern tributaries at their conjuncture with the main channel are much greater than those of their western counterpart. This asymmetry pushes the river's course westward. See further al-Buhayri, 1991, pp. 94–95.
108. The total irrigated area in Jordan in 1991 was over 609,000 dunums, of which 328,000 dunums were in the Ghor; see Ghezawi and Khasawneh, 1993, p. 9. The geographic distribution of irrigated land in the West Bank is spelled out in detail in chapter 3; the 50 percent does not include the irrigated area of the Jewish settlements.
109. Israel, Central Bureau of Statistics, *Statistical Abstract*, various years. The 10 percent includes the irrigated land in the Hula Valley.

river bifurcates close to the sea.[110] The Dead Sea is an elongated (north-south) inland lake, and, as described in old travel books, appears like a blue pendant at the end of the river. Its dimensions change according to weather conditions, although the trend in the last three decades has been to shrink, thanks to the diversion of much of the exogenous water supply. As a long-term trend, the water level fluctuated by 12 m over the 100-year period 1865 and 1966.[111] The maximum depth of the Dead Sea is 400 m, length 74–80 km, and width 16–18 km along an altitude above the Jadi (Gedi) springs on the western shore. The water volume in the lake exceeds 140 km³,[112] distributed over an area in the vicinity of 1,000 sq km.[113] The lake narrows in the south at the Lisan Peninsula and then widens again, but large swaths of the southern sector have dried up.

The Dead Sea drains a total area of 40,000 to 47,000 sq km, including that of the Jordan basin.[114] The water supply comes from both exogenous and endogenous sources. The exogenous sources include the Jordan River itself and two groups of ephemeral and perennial streams that gash the mountains framing the lake on its eastern and western rims; the largest of these streams is Wadi al-Mujib on the eastern shore. The chief feeder, however, is the Jordan River, which prior to the massive exploitation provided some 80 percent of the lake's water. The endogenous supply comes from saline springs issuing at the bottom of the sea and rainfall, which is extremely low, averaging 50 mm.

The Dead Sea loses a great deal of water to evaporation, estimated at 1,900 mm annually in Jericho, just to the north. The high evaporation rate, apart from reducing the water level, adds to the lake's already phenomenal salinity. The aggravation of natural water loss by the massive diversion from the Jordan basin led to the retreating of the sea, to the point where its level had fallen to 401 m below sea level by the 1990s. The drought of the 1980s undoubtedly added to the decline, but no one denies the adverse impact of the diversion of the inflow.

110. The description of the Dead Sea is based on al-Buhayri, 1991, pp. 98–103; and Orni and Efrat, 1973, pp. 98–100.

111. Al-Buhayri, 1991, p. 99.

112. Ibid; and *Encyclopaedia Palaestina*, vol. 1, p. 353.

113. The area is given as 1,015 sq km in Orni and Efrat, 1973, p. 98; and as 940 sq km in *Encyclopaedia Judaica*, 1971, vol. 5, p. 1392.

114. The figure of 40,000 is from al-Buhayri, 1991, p. 99; the 47,000 figure is from Smith, 1966, p. 117.

The Dead Sea's water has a salinity of 250,000 mg/l chloride, or nine times greater than that of ocean water, and a density that is 20–30 percent more than the density of freshwater. It is rich in minerals, in addition to salt, and both Jordan and Israel extract potash and bromide for use in photographic emulsions and dyes and as a mild sedative (hence the expression "old bromide").

Until 1967 the southwestern quadrant of the Dead Sea was under Israel's sovereignty and the other three quadrants under Jordan's. Today all of the western half of the sea is under Israeli control, while the eastern half is Jordanian territory. The water scarcity and disputes have skewed the focus in favor of the Jordan River when, ecologically, it would be sounder to think in terms of the Dead Sea basin. Excluding this lake from the picture often obscures the adverse impact of the development of the water resources of the river basin on its integrity.

Advantages and Constraints of the Basin's Geography

The Jordan basin possesses several favorable features for the development of its water resources. The first is the extensive and deep aquiferous layers of the drainage areas of the upper Jordan and Yarmuk rivers, namely, the limestone of Mount Hermon and the Galilee, the basalt of southern Syria, and the limestone and sandstone of northern Jordan. These layers are responsible for the base flow, which makes up more than one-half of the major tributaries and is not as susceptible to rain fluctuations as floodwater. The second feature is the Jordan Rift's steep slope, which makes possible the utilization of gravity in the transportation of water within the parts of the rift, as exemplified by the King Abdallah Canal. Furthermore, the steep gradients create conditions suitable for hydroelectric power generation. Although the small volume of water severely circumscribes the amount of electricity that can be tapped from the river system, especially when compared with today's consumption, the Jordan Valley and the Dead Sea have inspired schemes that could generate significant amounts of hydropower by channeling water from the Mediterranean Sea or Red Sea and harnessing the elevation difference.

On the other hand, the rift adversely affects the utility of the waters of the basin. The extreme temperature of the summer months causes high levels of evaporation, notably in Lake Tiberias, and also the Hula Valley before the lake and the marshlands were drained. Even along the channel itself, the heat and dense vegetation cover in the river's flood plain cause high rates of water loss, albeit partly productive loss, to evapotranspiration. Moreover, although the steep gradients may be advantageous for water diversion and hydropower generation, the high velocity they impart to the water is responsible, particularly during flooding, for extensive soil erosion and occasional crop damage. Finally, the low level of the rift makes out-of-basin water conveyance costly. For example, it has been estimated that about one-fourth of total water production costs in Israel is consumed by energy expenditures, a substantial portion of which is for lifting water from Lake Tiberias.[115] Jordan is likely to face a similar situation as it begins to supply increasing amounts of household water to Amman from the Jordan Valley, and so will the Palestinians if they try to transport water from the eastern basin to the population centers in the hills.

Drainage Areas

Several estimates of the drainage areas are found in the literature about the Jordan basin. They range from a minimum of 16,665 sq km to 19,839 sq km, a difference of nearly 20 percent.[116] This discrepancy is the outcome of cumulative differences in the assessment of the areas of individual catchments. It may be that in the future, cooperation among the riparians, satellite imagery, and computer simulation all can refine the calculations. Table 1.9 shows two estimates of the drainage areas and their distribution among the five riparians; the parenthetical is from Israeli sources and the second from a Jordanian source.[117] It may be that the Israelis have more accurate numbers for the upper and the western catchments, and the Jordanians are more accurate for those southeast of the Yarmuk River.

Even though there is a difference in the gross estimates, the two tallies agree on the spatial pattern of area distribution. They indicate that the drainage area on the eastern side by far exceeds

---

115. Tahal, 1990, p. 9.1.
116. The first figure comes from *Encyclopaedia Judaica*, 1971, vol. 10, p. 192; the second is from Weshah and Elias, 1993, p. 14.
117. The Israeli sources are Karmon, 1971, and Kilot, 1992; the Jordanian source is Weshah and Elias, 1993.

TABLE 1.9 Drainage Area and Riparian Contributions in the Jordan River Basin[a]
(In sq km)

Subbasin	Syria	Jordan	Lebanon	Israel	W. Bank	Total	%
Upper Jordan[b]	1,084[c] (1,045)		664[c] (640)	1,075[c] (1,037)		2,823 (2,722)	14 (15)
Yarmuk	6,217 (6,135)	1,426 (620)				7,643 (6,800)	39 (39)
Lower Jordan							
Eastern rim		6,237 (6,175)				6,237 (6,175)	31 (35)
Western rim				792 (860)	2,344 (1,100)	3,136 (1,960)	16 (11)
Total	7,301 (7,180)	7,663 (6,795)	664 (640)	1,867 (1,942)	2,344 (1,100)	19,839 (17,657)	100 (100)
Percent	37 (41)	39 (38)	3 (4)	9 (11)	12 (6)	100 (100)	

SOURCES: Karmon, 1971, p. 163; Kilot, 1992; Weshah and Elias, 1993, p. 14.
NOTES:
[a]The top figures in each row are from Weshah and Elias and the parenthetical ones are from Kilot.
[b]Includes Lake Tiberias. The catchment area of the lake itself is 1,100 sq km.
[c]Weshah and Elias do not disaggregate the total area; I proportioned it as was done by Kilot, 1992.

that on the western. In particular, they show that the area below and to the east of Lake Tiberias is the most extensive, thanks to the Yarmuk River's sprawling catchments that render it the largest single tributary both in terms of flow and drainage area.

The riparian contribution to the drainage area is nearly identical in the two tallies. Roughly speaking, Syria and Jordan contribute 40 percent each, and the remaining 20 percent is distributed among Israel, Lebanon, and the West Bank. The most noticeable difference in the statistics pertains to the contribution of the West Bank, which is 5 percent higher in the Jordanian than in the Israeli figures. As a result of the 1967 war, Israel may have come to control about 24 percent of the drainage area of the basin, or 2.5 times as much as it did previously.

Water Balance

The various aspects of the flow of the Jordan basin (annual average, range, and division between base flow and runoff) are exhibited in table 1.10. The figures are not meant to be aggregated because they apply for different periods; a second tally with totals is offered shortly. Overall, the table indicates that the headwaters, as an aggregate, render the largest amount of water to the basin, followed by the Yarmuk River, then the eastern streams feeding the lower Jordan River. This pattern is at variance with the drainage area of these components. The difference is particularly marked between the headwaters' sizable share of the flow and their much smaller proportion of the drainage area, mirroring the high level of precipitation over Mount Hermon.

The statistics on the headwaters are from Moshe Brawer, who credits them to Israel's *Hydrological Yearbook*.[118] They are fairly close to other numbers published subsequently by C. G. Smith and a number of Israeli sources.[119] According to them, the largest of the headwaters is the Dan River, which supplies about one-half of the basin's flow. Its discharge is fairly constant seasonally and interannually, and essentially all of it is base flow. The other half of the headwaters' discharge is divided almost equally between those of the Banyas and al-Hasibani rivers. The latter's flow is

118. Brawer, 1968.
119. Smith, 1966; *Encyclopaedia Judaica*, 1971, vol. 10, p. 192; Karmon, 1971, p. 163; and Soffer, 1994.

TABLE 1.10 Indicative Natural Water Flows of the Jordan River System, by Subbasin

Subbasin	Average (mcmy)	Period (years)	Range (mcmy)	Base flow (%)
Upper Jordan				
Headwaters				
Banyas	140	1942–62	81–148[a]	87
Dan	240	1942–62	217–285[a]	~100
al-Hasibani	263	1942–62	64–263[a]	63–70
al-Hula				
Burayghith	8			
Springs	60			
Direct rainfall	90			
Eastern rim	34			
Western rim	12			
Evaporation	–60			
Lake Tiberias				
Fresh side streams	219	1949–68[b]	130–219[a]	
Saline springs[c]	65	?		

Direct rainfall	66		33–89[a]	
Evaporation	−289	1949–68	260–308[a]	
Yarmuk	435	1926–62	269–893[a]	54
Lower Jordan				
Eastern rim of which:	207			67
al-Zarqa	92			50
Western rim	64			
Evaporation	−20			
Jordan River at Allenby Bridge	1,067	1932–52	380–1,600	

SOURCES: al-Bilbasi and Bani Hani, 1990; Brawer, 1968; *Encyclopedia Judaica*, 1971, vol. 10; Karmon, 1971; Miro and Ben Zvi, 1969; Mudallal, 1975; Salameh and Bannayan, 1991; and World Bank, 1988.

NOTES:

[a]The range is during the same period as the average.

[b]Missing from the period is the interval 1955–56 through 1958–59.

[c]The discharge of the saline springs on the western and northwestern shore of the lake averaged approximately 38 mcmy between 1949-50 and 1959-60, according to Glodschmidt et al., 1967, p. 9.

somewhat greater than the former's, but it oscillates more markedly because it includes a large proportion of floodwater. The figures for the Hula Valley, from Yehuda Karmon, are for the pre-drainage period, as is also evident from the high evaporation rate.[120] Although there are no statistics on the range of variation of this valley's water balance, it must fluctuate palpably owing to the significant share of direct runoff.

A fairly "standard" water balance of Lake Tiberias, taken from Karmon, has appeared in several publications.[121] That balance applies for the period 1935–47. The one I offer here was calculated subsequently by P. Miro and A. Ben Zvi for the period 1949–68.[122] The difference between the two lies in their estimate of the inflow from local catchments and of evaporation. In the standard balance the inflow from local catchments is 135 mcmy, of which 70 mcmy are from the fresh streams and 65 mcmy from the saline springs. In Miro and Ben Zvi's balance, the average inflow from the catchment area is more than 210 mcmy, or 75 mcmy more than in the standard. Their balance, however, does not include a breakdown between the flow of the saline springs and fresh water streams. With respect to evaporation, it appears as an average of 270 mcmy in the standard balance and 290 mcmy in Miro and Ben Zvi's study, or a difference of 20 mcmy. Overall, the standard balance nets 55 mcmy less than Miro and Ben Zvi's. In either balance, Lake Tiberias is a net water loser because of its marked evaporation level.

As for the Yarmuk River, its discharge is measured at two stations, near al-Maqarin and al-'Adasiyya, where the river is diverted into the King Abdallah Canal. The record of discharge is relatively long and unbroken. The average measured flow amounted to 435 mcmy for the 37-year period between 1926 and 1962.[123] Different values, some higher and some lower, depending on the time period, have been given in other sources, including a low of 400 mcmy for the period 1950–76.[124] The Yarmuk River's

120. Karmon, 1971, p. 163. Karmon's net balance of 140 mcmy is nearly identical to the one given by Smith (1966), who does not offer a breakdown of the total balance.

121. Karmon, 1971, p. 164.

122. Miro and Ben Zvi, 1969.

123. These figures are from Jordan's former Natural Resources Authority and contained in Mudallal, 1975.

124. Salameh and Bannayan, 1991, p. 18.

flow varies considerably from year to year; for example, a low of 269 mcmy was recorded in 1928 and a high of 893 mcmy—3.3 times as much—in the following year.[125]

The last components of the Jordan River system are the tributaries on the eastern and western sides that feed its lower segment. The eastern feeders are the primary source; their flows are those that appear in Jordan's 1977 National Water Plan.[126] The largest of them is al-Zarqa River, which supplies 93 mcmy on the average, or about 45 percent of their total, half of which is base flow. Overall, the total flow of the eastern tributaries averages more than 200 mcmy, approximately half of which is base flow. The discharge of the western feeders includes the discharge of the Israeli and West Bank streams. The West Bank's streams have not been sufficiently monitored, as mentioned earlier. The key western streams are Wadi Jalud (Harod) in Israel and Wadi al-Fari'a in the West Bank.

The Jordan River's total average flow of 1,067 mcmy is based on the measurements that the Jordanians took at a station by the Allenby (King Hussein) Bridge up until Israel captured the area in 1967. It applies for the period 1932–33 to 1951–52, which was chosen here because it proceeded major water diversionary works. Nonetheless, the 1,067 mcmy is still smaller than the natural average because, although there were no major diversionary works, water was diverted in small amounts at various points in its course. Also, Charles T. Main, the Boston-based engineering firm that formulated a plan for the river's development in 1953, questioned whether the measurements sufficiently reflected the high flood level over the river's banks that made gauging difficult.[127] Estimates of the total flow have varied since that time, from 1,290 mcmy by Charles T. Main itself to 1,550 mcmy. A better assessment of the flows only can be made through the combination of the riparians' records, especially those of Jordan and Israel that together span more than 60 years.

At any rate, the Jordan River's discharge fluctuates because of the variations in the discharge of its tributaries, notably the Yarmuk River. The measurements at Allenby Bridge show a minimum of 380 mcmy in 1932–33 and a maximum of 1,600 mcmy

125. *Encyclopaedia Judaica*, 1971, vol. 10, p. 194.
126. World Bank, 1988.
127. Main, 1953, p. 18.

in 1943–44.[128] Apart from interannual oscillations, the river's flow also varies seasonally. For instance, over the period between 1932–33 and 1958–59, the average flow of the river in September—the month when flow usually is at its lowest level—was less than 50 percent of that in February.[129] After all the diversion projects, however, the lower Jordan has been left with a minuscule amount of 200–300 mcmy, some of which is return irrigation water.

The average flows are only broadly indicative of what can be tapped from the river system. That is because not all the water flowing in a river or a stream can (or should be allowed to) be diverted; a fraction of it must remain in the channels even in the driest years for in-stream use and in order to maintain the integrity of the system. Further, it is ordinarily not cost-effective to design impoundment structures to capture a peak flow that rarely occurs. Effectively, the average that can be impounded is commonly less than the average of the naturally occurring flow. Nonetheless, the tapped average can be increased if the water in years of abundant rain can be used for the artificial recharge of the aquifers and be pumped later on without being lost to evaporation. Among the Jordan River's riparians, Israel is the only party that has had large-scale artificial recharge operations, owing to the large storage area in the coastal aquifer and the integrated water system that enables it to move water from the surface sources to recharge sites. This option is, in theory, available to all the riparians, although only to a very small extent in the West Bank and Gaza, where surface water is limited.

The water of the basin varies in quality; the variations are part natural and part human induced. The water of the Jordan River above Lake Tiberias is fresh (20 mg/l chloride), and so is the water of the Yarmuk River. In between them, a salinity problem appears in Lake Tiberias that also affects the lower Jordan. The lake's chloride content used to reach 350 mg/l chloride or more.[130] The primary cause of the salinity are the saline springs that feed the lake, although evaporation and extraction rates have an impact on the salinity as well. The average chloride content of the three

128. The range in the same period appears differently in *Encyclopaedia Judaica*, 1971, vol. 10, p. 193—a minimum of 287 mcmy for 1932–33 instead of 380, and a maximum of 1,313 mcmy for 1934–35; further, the flow for 1934–35 in Jordanian records is 1,500 mcmy, not 1,313 mcmy.
129. Mudallal, 1975.
130. Tahal, 1990, p. 6.2.

groups of onshore springs was estimated at 1,080 mg/l, 1,810 mg/l, and 17,700 mg/l chloride for the al-Tabigha, Fuliyya, and Tiberias hot springs, respectively.[131] The lake's chloride content is not critical (the standard for drinking water is 250 mg/l chloride); nonetheless, protracted use of such brackish water for irrigation can lead to soil salinization. By diverting the water of the large saline springs, Israel lowered the lake's salinity to about 200 mg/l chloride.[132] However, it transferred the problem, in worse form, to the lower reaches of the river, raising its chloride content to 2,000 mg/l.

The lower Jordan also has been contaminated by the dumping of municipal wastewater into its channel, as well as the dumping of wastes into the Yarmuk, in Israel, Jordan, and, one assumes, Syria. Although there are no data on this aspect of contamination, it is widely acknowledged. In their water agreement, Israel and Jordan declared their intention to clean up the river and keep its water fit for irrigation. They also agreed to desalinate part of the water of the saline springs (see chapter 5).

Riparians' Contributions Reconsidered

The contributions of the five riparians to the flows of the Jordan River system are exhibited in table 1.11. Several approximations and assumptions are made in the table that require clarification. To start with, the flows of the various components are rounded-up averages. In the Hula Valley, the evaporation level is for the natural, not postdrainage, condition. Also, the distribution of evaporation among Israel, Jordan, and the West Bank along the lower Jordan River is approximate, and, at any rate, does not affect the conclusions because the quantities involved are minor. Further, the water balance of Lake Tiberias is the one cited by Miro and Ben Zvi, not the standard one. Use of the standard balance, however, yields similar results. Miro and Ben Zvi do not divide the flow from the local catchments between Israel and Syria (they computed rather than measured it). In the table, it is assumed that this flow, excluding the discharge of the saline springs, comes equally from both states, although Syria's share is probably larger because four water-rich feeders from its territory empty into the lake.

131. Goldschmidt et al., 1967, p. 9.
132. Tahal, 1990, p. 6.2.

TABLE 1.11 Riparians' Contribution to the Flow of the Jordan Basin
(In mcmy)

Subbasin	Average	Syria	Jordan	Lebanon	Israel	W. Bank
Upper Jordan						
Headwaters						
Banyas	125	125				
Dan	250	125		125		
al-Hasibani	125			125		
al-Hula						
Burayghith	10			10		
Springs	60				60	
Direct rainfall	90				90	
Eastern rim	35	35				
Western rim	15				15	
Evaporation	−60				−60	
Lake Tiberias						
Local catchment[a]	210	75			135	
Direct rainfall	65				65	
Evaporation	−290				−290	

Yarmuk	435	320	115			
Lower Jordan						
Eastern rim	210		210			
Western rim	65				30	35
Evaporation	−20		−10		−5	−5
Total	1,325	680	315	260	40	30
(%)	100	51	24	20	3	2
Riparians' Contribution if the Dan were an Israeli river						
Total	1,325	555	315	135	290	30
(%)	100	42	24	10	22	2

SOURCE: Calculated by the author on the basis of table 1.10.
NOTE:
[a]Includes saline springs.

A final, and critical, clarification regarding the Dan River is necessary before assessing the riparians' contributions. Without exception, writings on the Jordan basin treat the Dan River as an Israeli river owing to the location of its entire aboveground channel within Israel. Based on this premise, Israeli geographer Arnon Soffer estimated the contribution of the five riparians as follows: Syria, 42 percent; Jordan, 27 percent; Israel and the West Bank combined, 25 percent; and Lebanon 6 percent.[133] Mahmoud Riyadh, a former Egyptian foreign minister and former secretary general of the Arab League, suggested that the opinion of Arab experts at the time of the Johnston mission was that the contribution of Israel was 25 percent. Moreover, a survey of Middle East water resources by the U.S. Army Corps of Engineers says that about 23 percent of the basin's discharge was from Israel.[134] The consensus on the division of the basin's flow needs revision, because it overlooks where the water of the Dan River comes from before it shows up in Israel. A sizable part of this river's water, like that of the Banyas and al-Hasibani rivers, undoubtedly comes from Mount Hermon, which, it will be recalled, is located equally in Syria and Lebanon. The Dan River, therefore, should be considered a common transboundary water resource, not unlike, say, the Auja (Yarqon) River that rises in Israel but is fed primarily from the mountain aquifer.

In order to revise the contribution of Israel, Lebanon, and Syria, investigations are needed to determine how much of the discharge of the Dan River originates from each of these states because it turns out that their overall relative contribution, notably Israel's, is sensitive to their shares in this river. According to the traditional view of the Dan River, Israel's contribution to the Jordan basin is 22 percent. However, this ratio drops precipitously to only 3 percent if the Dan River were assumed to be entirely fed from Lebanon and Syria. Thus, until there are more precise estimates of where the Dan River's water comes from, it can be stated that Israel contributes to the Jordan basin only several percentage points, not the 20 percent or more that traditionally has been asserted. This brings its contribution close to that of the West Bank—about 2 to 3 percent.

133. Soffer, 1994, p. 109.
134. Riyadh, 1985, p. 13; United States Army Corps of Engineers, 1991, section 2, p. 1.

FIGURE 1.3 Riparian Contribution to the Jordan Basin

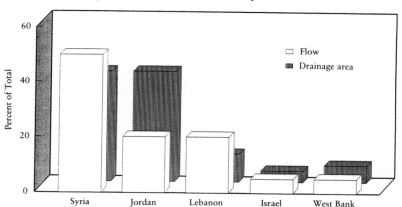

By far, the largest contribution is that of Syria, which, even without the Dan River, exceeds 40 percent of the basin's waters and increases to 50 percent if it is assumed that half of the Dan River's flow originates from its territory. Jordan is the second largest contributor, with about 25 percent of the total flow. Lebanon ranks third; its share doubles from 10 percent without the Dan River to 20 percent with one-half of this river's flow. The relative contributions of the five parties to the drainage area of the basin are summarized in figure 1.3.

2

Control, Supply, and Distribution of Water in the West Bank and Gaza

Traditionally, Palestinians harnessed water resources by various means commensurate with the type of use. For households, they collected rainwater in cisterns and pools during the rainy season or fetched it from springs and rivers. Toward the end of the nineteenth century, a group of German colonists, the "Templars,"[1] introduced the mechanical pump into Palestine.[2] The introduction of the pump helped in the discovery of the coastal aquifer in the 1920s and the mountain aquifer later on and the subsequent rapid spread of artesian wells. The pump, artesian wells, and economic development all led to the diminishment of the relative contribution of the cisterns and pools. Nevertheless, fetching water from springs and other sources has persisted for a significant minority of the population. The bulk of households now are supplied with piped water through municipal networks. This water is pumped from wells and, occasionally, springs. Because Gaza has no springs, its water is supplied from wells only. The water is supplied to the consumers by the municipalities, village councils, or the United Nations Relief and Works Agency ([UNRWA] for the refugee camps), and all

1. Originally, the Templars were a Christian order organized in 1119 to protect European pilgrimage to the Holy Land during the Crusades. Their first residence was near the site of Solomon's Temple, hence their name, the Templars. See Hitti, 1951, p. 601, f. 5.
2. Karmon, 1971, p. 119.

obtain a portion of their water from Mekorot, the parastatal Israeli water company.

For watering crops, farmers have relied either on direct rainfall (rainfed agriculture), especially in the central highlands where rainfall is sufficient for crop cultivation, or on water diverted from springs, rivers, and wells. The wells are largely under private ownership, whereas the springs are communal property.

The access of the Palestinian and Jewish communities to water in geographic Palestine has been a function of their ability to control the resources. As a result of the 1967 war, Israel came to control the entire country and with it the water resources as well. Moreover, through the occupation of the Golan Heights, Israel added to its area of control the headwaters of the Jordan River basin. After its seizure of the West Bank and Gaza, Israel promptly took over the management of the water supply and distribution system in both places. It instituted a severely restrictive policy with respect to Palestinian access to the resources. In Gaza, although Israel introduced similar restrictions, the water supply was limited by natural constraints. The downstream of the water supply—the sewage system and treatment plants—remained at a primitive stage. As a result, water pollution has been rampant in Gaza and has spread slowly in the West Bank. The foregoing themes—Israel's progressive takeover of the water resources and its restrictive policies in the West Bank and Gaza, the state of the Palestinian water supply, water distribution systems and property rights, and water quality—occupy the bulk of this chapter.

Israel's complete control continued until the signing of the Gaza and Taba accords. The Cairo and Taba accords handed the Palestinian Authority (PA) the management of the water sector in the territories under its jurisdiction in Gaza and a more limited role in the West Bank. The Taba Agreement also allocated "additional water" to the Palestinians in both areas during the interim period, but the other restrictions remained in force. Because the PA lacked financial resources and often technical expertise, many of the participants in the MWGW, including the European Union countries, the United States, Japan, the United Nations, and the World Bank, have undertaken projects to improve the water supply and sewage systems in the Palestinian territories. The implications of the Taba Agreement and international assistance will be touched upon in the final section.

CONTROL OF THE WATER RESOURCES

Although the conflict among Israelis and Palestinians and other Arabs has centered on land, water also has been a primary object of contention. As the Zionist movement and later Israel progressively took over Palestinian and Arab territories, they also acquired the associated water resources. The water of the Jordan basin entered into the equation of the Arab-Israeli conflict in the process of splitting up the territory of Ottoman Syria between Britain and France after the defeat of the Ottoman Empire in World War I. Zionist leaders lobbied the two European powers, notably at the 1919 Paris Peace Conference (see chapter 4), to incorporate within what was to become Mandate Palestine the headwaters of the Jordan River as well as segments of the Yarmuk River and the Litani River (in Lebanon), after it bends west toward the Mediterranean. After prolonged negotiations, Britain and France in 1923 drew the boundaries of their mandated territories such that Palestine bounded some of these water sources but not others.[3] Thus, Palestine's borders excluded the Litani River and important segments of the Banyas, al-Hasibani, and the Yarmuk rivers. On the other hand, the boundaries included key components of the basin, notably Lake Tiberias, the largest freshwater reservoir of the basin, and the entire aboveground channel of the Dan River.

Britain and France sought at the time to divide and regulate the use of the Jordan basin's water, which suddenly became a shared resource among Palestine, Syria (which then still included Lebanon), and Transjordan (as present-day Jordan was known until 1950). The most significant water-related agreement between the two powers was the 1920 Anglo-French Convention, which accorded priority of access to the waters of the upper Jordan and Yarmuk rivers to Syria.[4] According to the convention, Palestine was to use the residual or "surplus" water. Another noteworthy development during those years was the granting by Britain in 1926 of a seventy-year concession to Pinhas Rutenberg, a Zionist engineer and activist, for electric hydropower generation on the Jordan River. (Britain earlier had rejected a similar request by an Arab entrepreneur.) Rutenberg, who earlier had created the Palestine Electric Corporation, Ltd., built a power plant just south of the

3. See, for example, Garfinkle, 1994; and Toye, 1989, vol. 3.
4. Toye, 1989, vol. 3, p. 232.

point of confluence of the Yarmuk and Jordan rivers. The facility was destroyed by Jewish forces during the 1948 war when the Arabs captured the station. The terms of the concession allowed Transjordan to develop the Yarmuk water in excess of the station's requirements. In actuality, however, the corporation always claimed that there was no excess water.[5]

The conflict over the Jordan basin intensified in the immediate years after the establishment of Israel in 1948,[6] especially in connection with Israel's endeavor to drain Lake Hula and its marshlands, to which Syria objected on the grounds that the river was an international watercourse; alterations of its natural attributes could be not be done unilaterally but needed the consent of all the riparians; and some of the drainage canals fell in the demilitarized zone (DMZ) between the two states.[7] However, Israel went ahead with the drainage scheme, completing it in 1958. In the meantime, the United States dispatched in 1953 a special ambassador, Eric Johnston, to mediate the conflict over the Jordan basin's water. Another aim of the mediation effort was the resettlement of those among the Palestinian refugees who in 1948 fled to the Jordan Valley. Resettlement was to be induced by granting the refugees land and irrigation water. After two years of shuttle diplomacy, two studies by American engineering firms, and plans and counterplans by the Arabs and Israelis, Johnston formulated what has become known as the Johnston Plan, which was a modified version of a plan proposed by the American engineering firm, Charles T. Main, and known in the literature as the Unified Plan. The Johnston Plan maintained the Anglo-French Convention's assignment of priority of water use in the Jordan River to Syria and Lebanon, extending it to Jordan as well. On the other hand, it accorded priority of use in the Yarmuk River to Syria and Israel. However, the plan went beyond the convention and allotted fixed water quotas from specific segments of the Jordan River system to each of the riparians of the basin. The plan, which was not ratified by the riparians, can be said (for reasons to be explained subsequently) to have served as a form of customary law at least between Jordan and Israel (see chapter 5).

5. Ionides, 1946, p. 277.
6. The account of the Jordan River dispute after 1948 is based on American Friends of the Middle East, 1964; Lowi, 1993; Naff and Matson, 1984; Saliba, 1968; and Stevens, 1965.
7. Saliba, 1968, pp. 26–27.

In 1959, Israel made known its plans for the National Water Carrier, which entailed diverting water from the northwestern corner of Lake Tiberias through a system of canals, tunnels, and pipes to the coastal plain and the Negev Desert, the two areas where most of the irrigable land in Israel is located. The Arab states objected to the diversion scheme for many reasons, including that customary law did not allow out-of-basin transfer before the satisfaction of needs within the basin itself. To stop Israel from implementing its project, they attempted in 1964, after much hesitation and bickering, to divert the waters of the al-Hasibani and Banyas rivers. Clashes ensued, and Israel shelled the construction sites, aborting the diversion attempt. At the same time, Israel was able in that same year to inaugurate its National Water Carrier and begin diverting substantial quantities of water from the basin.

In the 1967 June war, Israel seized the Golan Heights and brought under its dominion all the headwaters of the Jordan River system and a larger stretch of the Yarmuk River than before the war. Its occupation of the West Bank in effect afforded it hegemony over the lower Jordan as well. Furthermore, when it invaded Lebanon in 1978 and retained the "security zone" in the south, it completed its hold over the upper and lower Jordan River as well as the lower reach of the Litani River. Israel since has taken advantage of its new hydrostrategic position and acted as if it was an absolute sovereign in the basin. It has drawn as much water from the Jordan basin as has been possible within the hydrologic constraints (see chapter 4).

The only exceptions to this hegemonic position have been in the upper and middle reaches of the Yarmuk River in Syria and Jordan and the feeders of the lower Jordan River from Jordanian territory. Much of the Yarmuk River's water originates in Syria, which has exercised a measure of autonomy concerning the use of its water. Jordan, a midstream but less powerful riparian than either Israel or Syria, has had little influence in the Yarmuk basin.

Unlike the situation in the Jordan basin, the Palestinians and Israelis are the only parties to the feud over the water resources in geographic Palestine proper. Under the British Mandate, both sides pumped or diverted (from springs) groundwater, using most of it for irrigation. There are no available statistics on water consumption during that period, in part because the wells were not metered. However, the irrigated area can be used as a proxy indicator of the relative water use of the Palestinian and Jewish communities. By the mid-1940s, the irrigated land in the country was roughly 500,000 dunums, about half of it planted with citrus.[8] The citrus areas of both sides were nearly equal, but the Palestinian vegetable area was almost three times larger than that of the Jewish counterpart, suggesting greater use of irrigation water by the Palestinians than by the Jews. This conclusion is at variance with most Israeli literature on water, which leaves the impression that only the Jews had exploited the water resources of Palestine.[9]

As a consequence of the establishment of Israel, the Palestinians lost access to many of the groundwater resources they previously had harnessed, notably the coastal aquifer, but continued to develop the sources on their side of the armistice lines in the West Bank and Gaza. The Israelis maintained access to all the sources to which they formerly had had access and tapped them to the fullest. The Palestinians, still reeling from the 1948 *al-nakba* (disaster), could not drill as many wells or draw as much water from the mountain aquifer. It is unclear how Israel would have responded had they tried to extract greater quantities of water from the mountain aquifer than they actually did, but the stringent controls it imposed after 1967 on Palestinian water use is telling.

Inside Israel itself, the Palestinians who stayed and became Israeli citizens also lost control over their water sources. Under Israeli water law, water is a state property, and ownership of land does not include ownership of water sources underlying or passing through owned lands. Water rights of individuals and communities are defined in terms of quantities without specification as to source. Israeli law contrasts with the pre-existing Ottoman and British laws in Mandate Palestine. Whereas the Israeli law may not have been designed specifically to compromise the Palestinian-Israelis' water resources, it did so in practice. Their water allotment became the responsibility of Mekorot. The control of the water supply by Mekorot, together with a complex institutional apparatus inside Israel generally favoring Jewish citizens, resulted in discriminatory water allocations for Palestinian-Israelis. The discriminatory water allotment contributed to the stagnation of their agriculture, which in turn resulted in the eventual sale of land by Palestinian-Israeli landowners to Jewish land-purchasing institutions.[10]

8. Government of Palestine, 1946, vol. 1, pp. 314, 325–26, 339, and 410.
9. For recent examples, see E. Benvenisti and Gvirtzman, 1993, pp. 557–59; and Hillel, 1994, pp. 147–49.
10. See, for example, Falah, 1990; and Lustick, 1980, pp. 163–71.

Israel's seizure of the West Bank and Gaza in 1967 brought under its control all the water resources in geographic Palestine, including sources to which the Jews had not had access before, such as the eastern basin of the mountain aquifer. As it did in the upper Jordan basin, Israel acted as if it was an absolute sovereign over the water resources of the West Bank and Gaza. Israel modified the pre-existing water legislation in the two regions by issuing a series of military orders, which were the primary means of governing the Palestinians (the Jewish settlers in the territories are effectively subject to Israeli laws). Those orders proclaimed the water resources of the West Bank as "public" property, as in Israel itself, and Israel appointed a water officer in whom it vested sweeping powers over water policy. Israel subsequently (in 1982) sealed its control by granting Mekorot a lease to manage the water sector in the West Bank for 49 years, the period of land lease from the state in Israel.[11] Within the legal framework established by the military orders, the company pursued a dual water policy in the West Bank and Gaza that applied discriminatory standards and measures to the Palestinians as compared with Israeli settlers.

The interim agreements shifted the control of water resources to the PA in the areas under its jurisdiction in Gaza and to the PA and Israel in the corresponding areas of the West Bank. They included provisions for supplying additional water to the Palestinians in both the West Bank and Gaza during the transitional period, but otherwise maintained the whole gamut of the previous restrictions and laws in the West Bank, where the water resources are much more substantial.

The focus in the rest of this chapter is on the types of policies that were pursued by Israel and their impact on the Palestinian water sector. The institutional and legal framework of these policies, as well as water supply for the settlements, are deferred to chapter 4. Relevant provisions of the interim water agreements and their implications for that sector also will be examined.

SUPPLY SOURCES AND RESTRICTIONS

Israeli water policy consisted of restricting Palestinian well-drilling, through overseeing the licensing process and fixing water quotas for operating wells. It also was characterized by a low level of

11. Israel Ministry of Foreign Affairs, 1982b.

investment in the development and maintenance of the water supply and distribution infrastructure and in the extension of sewage services—the indispensable adjunct to a modern water supply network. The combination of curbs on well-drilling and low investment arrested the growth of irrigation water supply. Likewise, municipal water supply remained quantitatively substandard, intermittent, and of inferior quality, particularly in Gaza.

West Bank's Wells

The last official statistical report on the Palestinian wells in the West Bank was published in 1977–78 by the Water Department.[12] After the release of the study, the head of the Water Department was relieved from his job, and no similar information has been released subsequently. However, a sample survey of 60 out of approximately 350 working wells, which was undertaken by Hisham Awartani, provides valuable information and is drawn upon extensively in the present section.[13]

The changes that occurred in the number as well as output of West Bank wells before and after the occupation are exhibited in table 2.1. The table indicates that the vast majority of the drilled and operating wells were developed in the 1950–67 period, when the West Bank was part of Jordan. Only 6 percent of the operating wells in 1990 (not all drilled wells were functional) were drilled under Israeli rule; the rest were from the Jordanian period (70 percent) or the British Mandate (23 percent). The period from the late 1950s to 1970 witnessed the expansion of irrigated agriculture, which was stimulated by the arrival of Palestinian refugees, who supplied labor and farming experience, in the Jordan Valley and the semicoastal areas, as well as by the gradual opening of a produce-export market in the neighboring Arab states. Agricultural expansion needed water, which was supplied by drilled wells. This is particularly evident in the Jordan Valley region, where practically

12. The report contains the names of the wells' owners and the output and grid references of the wells themselves. It is available in several places, including the archives of the "Social History of the Jordan Valley Project" at the Institute for Archeology and Anthropology, Yarmuk University, Jordan. It also has been summarized in a number of publications, including ASIR, 1986; and Awartani, 1991a.

13. Awartani, 1991a.

TABLE 2.1 Number and Output of West Bank Wells, 1967–90

	Number		Output	
Period ending	Drilled	Operating	Total (mcmy)	Average (1,000 cmy)
1967	750	413		
1978	6–7	328[a]	38	116
1990	17	354	58	164

SOURCE: ASIR, 1986, p. 42; Awartani, 1991a, pp. 7–11; and Jordan Valley Authority, 1981.
NOTE:
[a]This figure, from Awartani, includes 14 wells belonging to the Arab Development Society in Jericho that were drilled before 1967, but operated without a license until the late 1980s. These wells seem to have caused confusion in the well count; they were not listed in the 1977–78 report of the Water Department (see text) because they were not licensed. That is why, for example, the number of operating wells appeared as 314 instead of 328 in ASIR, 1986, p. 42. Apart from this, in the 1981 report of the Jordan Valley Authority, 7 of the 314 wells were listed as "not pumping," and one as unreachable, which would reduce the number of operating wells to 320.

no wells had existed by the end of the 1940s;[14] yet by 1967 there were 110 wells in the region (see table 2.2). In contrast, during more than 20 years of Israeli control a total of only 35 (23 new and 12 replacement) Palestinian wells were drilled in the West Bank. Yet, Israel's State Comptroller pointed out, as evidence of

TABLE 2.2 Spatial Distribution of West Bank Wells, 1977 and 1990

	1977–78		1990	
Location	Number	%	Number	%
Jordan Valley	110[a]	31	118[b]	30
Wadi al-Fari'a	23	7	27	8
Jinin	56	18	64	18
Tulkarm and Qalqilya	129[c]	41	141[d]	40
Ramallah, Bethlehem, Hebron	10[e]	3	14[f]	4
Total	328	100	364	100

SOURCES: Same sources as table 2.1
NOTES:
[a]Jericho, 54; al-Auja and Fasayil, 11; Jiftlik, 29; Marj Ni'ma, 8; Bardala, 8.
[b]Jericho, 56; rest of areas, 62.
[c]Tulkarm, 59; Qalqilya, 70.
[d]Tulkarm, 65; Qalqilya, 76.
[e]Ramallah, 3; Bethlehem, 3; Hebron, 4.
[f]Ramallah, 5; Bethlehem, 5; Hebron, 4.

14. Government of Palestine, 1946, vol. 1, pp. 417–18.

efforts to improve the water situation, that "dozens of wells" were drilled in the West Bank after the occupation.[15]

The modest increase in wells drilled was not sufficient to offset those that went out of commission, and the number of working wells declined by 14 percent during the period 1967–90. Some of those were shut outright, including approximately 15 wells in the Jordan Valley area after it was enclosed as a security zone in 1967. Others ceased to function due to technical problems and lack of maintenance or dried up altogether owing to the fall of the water table. Still others became highly saline and unsuitable for irrigation or uneconomical because of low yield and high operation and maintenance costs.[16]

The minuscule number of new wells since 1967 reflected the administrative hurdles that Palestinians wishing to dig wells, notably for irrigation, had to overcome. To obtain a drilling license, applicants had to go through an 18-step approval process that took them through the offices of the Civil Administration, Mekorot, Tahal, and the Israeli Ministry of Agriculture.[17] Whether the complications were deliberate or mere bureaucratic imperatives, they served to discourage potential license seekers. Two well-informed Palestinians sources told me that obtaining a license was singularly difficult; one of them said that the wait for a license, when it was granted, could exceed five years. For example, the Jerusalem Water Undertaking,[18] a water utility in Ramallah, applied for a permit to drill a municipal water well in 1982 but did not obtain it until 1990.[19]

The Israeli Ministry of Foreign Affairs claimed that between 1967 and 1979 it approved 30 out of 80 applications by Palestinians for permits to "prospect" for water.[20] The conclusions of a number of analysts, however, cast doubt about the factuality and meaning of that claim. For example, Meron Benvenisti noted: "According to a strict policy, licenses for drilling [wells] in the West

15. Israel State Comptroller, 1990.
16. Awartani, 1991a, p. 8.
17. United States Department of State (hereafter, USG/DS), n.d.
18. This is the official translation of the Arabic name. The utility was established in 1966 and was empowered to develop new water resources and control all water projects in the Jerusalem district and the then Ramallah subdistrict; see Jerusalem Water Undertaking—Ramallah District, 1991, p. 6.
19. *Al-Nahar,* 7 September 1990.
20. Israel, Ministry of Foreign Affairs, 1982a; United Nations, 1992, p. 56.

Bank are refused."[21] A Palestinian engineer who worked for the Civil Administration was quoted as saying that only 5 percent of all permit applications are approved.[22]

Could it be that the term "prospect" for water, which is used in Israeli official sources in place of the more usual "drill," did not include the "actual digging and operation of wells?"[23] Further, Israel did not specify the type of wells—whether new or replacement—nor that the permits for the replacement wells were granted with the proviso that one or two old wells be closed off for each replacement well.[24]

Of the new wells, only two were for agriculture and the rest for municipal purposes. In his study, Awartani concluded:

> The prohibition imposed on the Arab citizens against drilling new wells was the linchpin of the water policy of the Israeli occupation authorities. Those authorities did not approve the vast majority of the applications for new agricultural wells.[25]

Likewise, Meron Benvenisti observed that it was the policy of the Israeli government that Palestinian agricultural growth be through intensification rather than expansion of the irrigated area.[26]

Permits for municipal wells were granted more frequently than those for irrigation wells, but in some instances they were issued because denying them would have resulted in "seriously impairing water supplies for domestic consumption."[27] In other instances, municipalities were refused permits unless they consented to hook up their system with Israel's network and to supply water to Israeli settlers. A case in point was the Jerusalem Water Undertaking, which linked with Mekorot in the late 1970s.

Licenses for municipal wells, too, seem not to have been exempt from being denied. A number of villages in the Nablus district reportedly were refused drilling permits after "repeated applications" despite the dearth of water supply in the villages themselves and hardships that villagers faced in fetching water from springs.[28]

21. M. Benvenisti, 1984, p. 14; also cited in Dillman, 1989, p. 56.
22. United States, Department of State, n.d.
23. Dillman, 1989, p. 56.
24. Ibid., citing Awartani and Shehadeh.
25. Awartani, 1991a, p. 10.
26. Benvenisti, 1984, p. 14.
27. United Nations, 1980a, p. 12.
28. Rowley, 1990, pp. 46–47.

Israel asserted in the above-cited Foreign Ministry briefing that permits were denied only in the "overexploited" basins. The "over-exploited" aquifers implicitly refer to the northern and western basins of the mountain aquifer, which Israel itself had overtapped. A question remains as to why restrictions were applied to the eastern aquifer even from the very first years of the occupation, and only to Palestinians and not to the settlers. To cite just one specific example, Israel delayed for more than two decades licensing the 14 wells in Jericho of the Arab Development Society, which cares for orphans, even though those wells had been dug before Israel seized the West Bank.[29]

The restrictions on well-drilling have been lifted partially under the Taba Agreement in order to supply part of the additional 70–80 mcmy for the Palestinians during the interim period. The ability of the Palestinians to develop these resources, however, still was tied to Israel's approval and the availability of financial resources, as is discussed at the end of this chapter.

Water Quotas By Surprise

When Jordan had ruled the West Bank, it had not imposed limits on abstraction from wells, and owners made the decision on the basis of agronomy, economics, and the technical requirements of their wells. Israel changed this practice by instituting for each well quotas that were monitored by meters and enforced by levying fines on violators. The Water Department installed meters beginning in 1975 and set a ceiling on abstraction equal to the output of the well in 1976–77 plus 10 percent. The average ceiling in 1990, according to Awartani's sample, was 60,000 to 120,000 m^3 per year, much smaller than the average output of 164,000 m^3 shown in table 2.1. The reason for the difference most likely stemmed from the larger output of municipal wells, which may have been under-represented in Awartani's sample. These same ceilings remained in effect until 1986, when they were lowered gradually in response to the prolonged drought in the 1980s.[30] There was a general compliance with the quotas owing to the fear

29. The information on this licensing delay was given to the author by Shehadeh al-Dajani, the head of the society. Interview, March 1992.
30. Awartani, 1991a.

of fines, the poor conditions of the wells themselves, and a decline in the profitability of agriculture in the 1980s.

Well owners were not informed of the actual purpose of the meters when the devices first were installed for fear that they would protest or draw larger than normal quantities of water. While the method proved effective in limiting water abstraction, it may have had an injurious impact on some farmers. Cropping patterns change and with them water requirements; for farmers who, at the time when the meters initially were installed, had left some land fallow or grown less-water-consuming crops, the quotas only could have hamstrung their ability to realize the potential of their land. Also, the water-use ceiling made it difficult for farmers to switch (for example) from vegetable to fruit cultivation because water requirements per unit area were greater for trees than for vegetables. Nor could the practice have contributed to the building of trust between the "managers" and "managed"; a minimal ingredient of sound management requires not just such trust but also the active participation of the users.

All of this is not to argue against the need for control of licensing or even fixing quotas, but against Israel's extensive use of these instruments to deny Palestinians water they needed and asked for. That these denials were not justified on hydrological grounds is evident in light of the wide water gap between the Palestinians and Israeli settlers in the West Bank (see chapter 4).

The quotas and metering system were kept in place by the Taba accord. Monitoring compliance was to be done by "joint supervision and enforcement teams" (JSET), made up of equal numbers from both sides. Those teams were empowered with free access to all the Palestinian sites and enforcement of compliance whenever violations were detected (Annex III, Article 40, Schedule 9).

The Poor Condition of the Wells

Not only were drilling licenses denied and abstraction quotas fixed, but those wells that were in operation, notably the ones used for irrigation, had serious technical problems. These problems included insufficient depth, motor horsepower, and maintenance. In general, the depth of the wells, save of those supplying municipal water, ranged (according to various estimates) between 60 and

120 m. This meant their water came from the upper Cenomanian, not the more plentiful lower Cenomanian layer that was exploited for the benefit of the Israeli settlers. The shallower depths perhaps suited the economic conditions in the West Bank before the occupation and were dictated by the technological capabilities and hydrological information available at the time.

In some cases, Israel allowed the digging of deeper wells and the deepening of existing ones but vetoed these activities in other cases, leaving the impression that a certain arbitrariness governed such decisions.[31] To illustrate, the Nablus municipality was allowed to deepen one well but for several years (beginning in 1984) was denied permission to deepen another well. The municipality compensated for its water deficit by buying more costly water from Jewish settlements.[32]

The confinement of the wells to the upper layers of the aquifer lowered their yields and made them sensitive to rainfall fluctuations. The deeper layers of the basin also commonly, and up to certain depths, contained fresher water; overpumping from the aquifers by Israel and the deep wells serving the settlements inside the West Bank were believed by Palestinian hydrologists to have increased the salinity of many Palestinian wells. Other adverse impacts that the Israeli settlements had on Palestinian water sources are examined in chapter 4.

Apart from their shallowness, the Palestinian wells generally were poorly equipped. The motors had low horsepower, and the pumps low efficiency and pumping capability. Many pumps operated on diesel fuel, not electricity. Many well owners were partially discouraged from maintaining and upgrading their wells owing to the high price of equipment. The equipment, like essentially all West Bank and Gaza imports, had to be bought from Israel or through Israeli middlemen, which usually entailed payment of taxes at the Israeli level, including tariffs and value added tax, as well as fees for middlemen. In contrast, before the Israeli occupation, no tariffs had been levied on agricultural inputs and equipment. In the first half of the 1980s, a trend of falling net farm incomes added a further disincentive for investment in well improvements.[33]

31. Jerusalem Water Undertaking, 1991; and Rowley, 1990, p. 46.
32. Rowley, 1990, pp. 46–47.
33. World Bank, 1993a, vol. 4, pp. 2–4; although the total value of farm

The limitations on well drilling and pumping and the technical inferiority of wells combined to put a tight lid on the expansion of total well output in the West Bank. It is difficult to draw a comparison between the output of the wells before and after the occupation because the government of Jordan did not monitor or set a ceiling on well abstraction. The limitations on irrigation wells and the slow expansion of municipal wells, however, are evident in their respective production figures. In all, the output of wells for irrigation ranged between 28 and 34 mcmy during the period 1978–92. The fluctuation was a function of the cropped area and rainfall and attendant spring flow. Municipal output grew with the increase in the number of wells, reaching 23 mcmy in 1991, up from 15 mcmy in 1985.[34]

Spatial Distribution and Ownership of Wells

The spatial distribution of West Bank wells in 1977–78 and 1994 is illustrated in table 2.2 and map 2.1. The table reveals that the relative spatial distribution remained stable over time. The majority of the wells were located in 1990 in the semicoastal region followed by the Jordan Valley. The eastern foothills and central range claimed the least percentage of wells. The location of wells generally mirrored the spatial distribution of irrigated agriculture, which absorbed more than 60 percent of the wells' output. Although it was not easy to make a clear-cut distinction between irrigation and municipal wells, in 1990 approximately 326 wells belonged to the former category and 38 wells to the latter.[35] This was a slight increase in the share of municipal wells, reflecting both the curbs on new agricultural wells and drilling of new municipal wells. The distribution of the wells, however, did not match that of output. Because municipal wells commonly had greater output than irrigation wells, the share of the municipal wells of total output was about 20 percent, as opposed to 4 percent of the number of wells. Overall, 62 percent of the wells' water was extracted from the

production increased, net income fell, thanks to high inflation rates, faster increase in the price of inputs than of output, and difficult marketing conditions, notably for citrus.

34. ARIJ, 1994.

35. Awartani, 1991a, p. 19, citing unpublished archival material at Hebrew University.

MAP 2.1 Location of Groundwater Wells in the West Bank

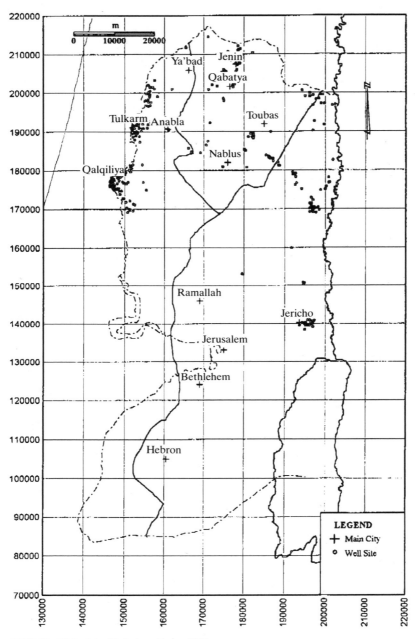

SOURCE: ©Palestinian Hydrology Group, 1996.

western and northern basins while the rest (38 percent) was from the eastern basin.

The property rights in the wells were related to whether the wells served the municipal or agricultural sector. The agricultural wells, with the exception of the 14 semipublic wells of the Arab Development Society and one well that was owned by a cooperative, were privately owned. The private ownership of agricultural wells was the norm when the West Bank was part of Jordan and was not altered under Israel. In contrast to the agricultural wells, the municipal wells were almost all publicly or semipublicly owned.

Gaza's Wells

There are two classes of wells in Gaza: artesian wells with depths of 25 to 90 m, narrow diameters, and fitted with mechanical pumps; and, spread along the coastline, *mawasi*, or shallow wells, whose water traditionally was drawn either by hand pumps or manually with a bucket. The latter wells are between 4 and 20 m deep, wide in diameter, commonly manually-dug, and lined in their upper interior with stone for holding back the sand. The availability of water at such shallow depths is adduced to the presence of an impervious, hard crust locally called *nazzaz*, which probably is formed when floods and heavy rains sink down the clay cover of the sand. Not surprisingly then, the *mawasi* wells are the older type of wells, reportedly dating back to the nineteenth century.[36]

Historical information on Gaza's wells is lacking. It is believed that the number of wells in existence between 1930 and 1950 did not exceed 200 (see table 2.3).[37] Because the bulk of the water was (and continues to be) consumed by the agricultural sector, the number of wells increased as the irrigated area expanded. There were perhaps 416 wells by 1958, and 1,600–1,700 by 1967.[38] The number of wells continued to grow for two decades after the occupation, declined in the late 1980s and early 1990s, then rose again after the PA entered Gaza in 1994. For instance,

36. European Community, 1993, p. 3; Kahan, 1987, p. 24; Orni and Efrat, 1973, p. 43; and Shawwa, 1993. The point about the *mawasi* wells as going back to the nineteenth century was made to the author by Shawwa, Interview, 1993.

37. Rajab, 1991, p. 4.

38. Abu Mayla, 1990, pp. 33–34; Shawwa, 1993; and Israel State Comptroller, 1990. The 416 number is deduced from figures in Abu Mayla.

TABLE 2.3 Number and Output of Gaza's Wells

Year	Number	Output (mcmy)
1950	200	
1958	416	
1967	1,600–1,700	100–120
1989	2,140	86–98
mawasi	300	

SOURCES: Abu Mayla, 1990; Awartani, 1991a; European Community,1993; Khudari, 1992; Rajab, 1991; Schwarz, 1982; and Shawwa, 1993.
Mawasi = shallow wells.

there were 1,850 artesian wells in 1986, compared with 1,700 in 1993.[39] The preceding figures do not include the *mawasi* wells; the reader ought to be careful in studying the wells because some data sources do not include the *mawasi*. There seems to be either inaccuracy in the reporting of the *mawasi* wells or fluctuation in their numbers, perhaps because they are not monitored and are easy to start or put out of commission.[40]

The slight decline in the number of artesian wells may be attributed to Israeli restrictions on drilling, technical reasons, residential expansion, and the deterioration of water quality due to persistent overabstraction from the aquifer. The instruments of restriction were similar to those in the West Bank and covered licensing quotas and fines for violators. They were promulgated in separate military orders. After 1987 licenses were not issued for new wells, only for replacement wells.[41]

Meters for monitoring pumping were installed first on the wells of large farmers; meters for small farmers followed suit.[42] The quotas were based on crop type and land area and were reduced by 10 percent in 1984. No quotas, however, were set for the *mawasi* wells, owing to the insufficiency of their water output, or for municipal wells. The quotas were enforced by the imposition

39. Abu Mayla, 1990, pp. 33–34; Awartani, 1991a, pp. 20–21; European Community, 1993, p. 3; Kahan, 1987, p. 24; and Israel State Comptroller, 1990.
40. The number of *mawasi* wells has been given variously as 350 by Kahan, 1987, p. 24; as 200 in 1988 by Khudari, 1992; as 274 in 1989 by Agriculture Unit (Gaza), 1989; and as 300 in 1993 by European Community, 1993.
41. Makki, 1992.
42. Ibid.

of fines.[43] The fines were progressive, rising with the increase of excess pumping.[44] It appears that there was a general compliance with the quotas. For example, in 1991, 150 wells were reported as violating the quotas.[45]

Nonetheless, abstraction exceeded the replenishment rate. The output of wells has been estimated at 100–120 mcmy in 1967 and 100 mcmy in the early 1980s. Those rates should be taken as averages: Output fluctuated according to weather and cropping patterns. By the end of the 1980s and the early 1990s, the wells' output was in decline, 86–98 mcmy.[46] To this add 2–6 mcmy pumped by Mekorot, primarily for the settlements, and the total well output amounts to 88–104 mcmy.[47] These quantities represent about twice the safe yield. The inference that can be deduced from these statistics is that even if licensing had been more liberal, the room for drilling extra wells practically has been closed: The aquifer has been overexploited for many years and salinity has reached ruinous proportions.

As in the West Bank, the vast majority of the wells catered to agriculture, although there has been a steady rise of supply for municipal use at the expense of irrigation. Of the 1,840 wells operating in 1989, irrigation wells numbered 1,791; the other 49 were municipal wells. However, the number of wells of each category is deceptive as an indicator of the actual contribution to total output. The average output of a municipal well, for instance, was more than 15 times the output of an irrigation well. On average, the 1,791 irrigation wells produced 52 mcmy, whereas the 49 municipal wells produced 22 mcmy, or nearly one-half of the irrigation wells' total output.

Geographically, the wells were distributed as shown in table 2.4. They were concentrated along the coast and in the northern segment of the Gaza Strip. The Gaza city district alone accounted

43. Israel State Comptroller, 1990.
44. Ibid. In 1991 the fines ranged from 10 aguras/m³ (1 NIS = 100 aguras) for violations of 0–25 percent above the quota, and 80 aguras for more than 100 percent. Violations of 25 percent or less were exempted.
45. Ibid; and Awartani 1991a, p. 17.
46. Awartani, 1991a, pp. 20–21; European Community, 1993, p. 3; Khudari, 1992; Schwarz, 1982, p. 99; and Shawwa, 1993.
47. The 2–6 mcmy is from Israeli sources and cited in European Community, 1993, p. 11. Palestinian sources put the settlements' use in the range of 5–20 mcmy; see further Abu Mayla, 1992; Khudari, 1992; and Society for Austro-Arab Relations, 1992, p. 74.

TABLE 2.4 Distribution, Output, and Type of Gaza Wells, 1989[a]

| Location | Irrigation wells | | Municipal wells | | Total |
	Number	Output (mcmy)	Number	Output (mcmy)	(mcmy)
North Gaza[b]	554	18.5	11	3.1	21.6
Gaza city	499	10.9	18	13.5	24.4
Dayr al-Balah[c]	278	6.9	3	0.2	7.1
Khan Yunus[d]	322	9.4	10	4.1	13.5
Rafah	138	6.2		0	6.2
Total	1,791	51.9	49[e]	21.5[f]	73.4

SOURCE: Gaza Water Unit, 1989 (also cited in Awartani, 1991a, pp. 20–21).

NOTES:
[a]Does not include the *mawasi* wells.
[b]Includes Bayt Lahya, Bayt Hanun, and Jabala
[c]Includes Abu Middain, al-Nusayrat, and Dayr al-Balah.
[d]Includes Khan Yunis, Aradi al-Saba', al-Sumayri, Bani Syhayla, 'Abasan, and Khuzza'a.
[e]Includes 7 UNRWA wells.
[f]Includes 0.6 mcmy from UNRWA wells.

for 25 percent of the irrigation wells and a similar percentage of municipal wells. The reason for the concentration of irrigation wells in the north was hydrological: Water was more abundant and of better quality in the north and along the coast than in the south and the interior. The distribution of municipal wells, however, was governed primarily by population distribution.

The irrigation wells commonly were privately owned by landowners; Israel did not alter this form of property right. The municipal wells, on the other hand, were public property. Of the 49 wells, nine belonged to UNRWA, which assists the refugees in the camps; 18 belonged to the municipality of Gaza; and the remaining 23 belonged to other municipalities and village councils.

There have been reports that several hundred wells were dug by private owners immediately after the PA assumed self-government in Gaza and before it consolidated its power, thereby aggravating the problem of overexploitation. No information has been available about these wells and their spatial distribution. In all likelihood, they were irrigation wells because the aquifer's water was no longer suitable for drinking, and, according to the Taba accord, extra municipal water, 10 mcmy, would be purchased from Israel (Annex III, Article 40, Schedule 10).

West Bank's Springs

There were more than 310 springs or spring groups in the West Bank, according to a preliminary survey by the Palestinian Hydrology Group[48] (see map 2.2). Only about one-third of them have been monitored periodically by the Water Department to determine year-round discharge and geophysical and chemical properties.[49] The vast majority of the 310 springs surveyed yielded a small, seasonal discharge and were scattered across the territory of the West Bank, inside or near villages (historically, the presence of springs was often a factor in the choice of village sites). Many of them needed rehabilitation after long neglect or road-building that led to the loss of water and dispersion of the flow.[50]

In 1967 and 1969 Israel declared the headwaters of five spring groups to be "natural reserves," or protected natural areas, and charged fees for entrance to their perimeters. The springs were al-Auja, al-Badan, al-Fashkha, al-Qilt and al-Turba.[51] Whether by accident or design, and with the exception of al-Auja spring, they all fell within enclosed military areas or adjacent to settlement boundaries.[52] The declaration on natural reserves, moreover, was made by the Ministerial Committee for Settlement within a framework of "land acquisition."[53] In effect, "the declaration of a nature reserve signifies the transfer of the area to Israeli control."[54] The exact area of the individual reserves was unknown, but the overall area of the reserves totaled 250,000 dunums in 1983, with an additional 90,000 dunums planned.

A 24-year flow record, from 1970–71 to 1993–94, of 113 springs within the boundaries of the West Bank was kept by the Water Department and has been made public in a monograph

48. Al-Rabi and al-Tamimi, 1989.
49. The number of such wells is 109 according to Palestine Liberation Organization, 1992, p. 23.
50. Al-Rabi and al-Tamimi, 1989.
51. Al-Labadi, 1990, p. 17; the springs were declared thus by Military Order No. 166, 10 November 1967 (al-Fashkha and al-Qilt), and Military Order No. 308, 11 February 1969 (al-Auja, al-Badan, and al-Turba). Their boundaries were defined subsequently by Military Order No. 363, 22 December 1969.
52. M. Benvenisti, 1984, pp. 20, 79, and map 4.
53. M. Benvenisti et al., 1986, p. 165, quoting the Committee.
54. Ibid.

MAP 2.2 Location of Springs in the West Bank

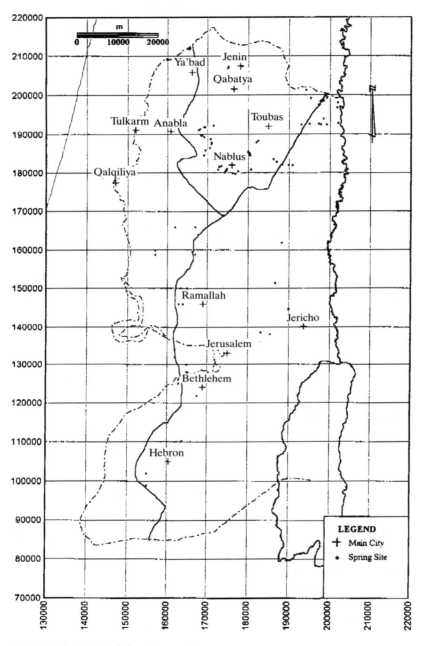

SOURCE: Palestinian Hydrology Group, 1996.

published by the department's two senior hydrologists.[55] Although the accuracy of the record is hard to assess, it seems to be generally consistent with the rainfall pattern. Still, there are apparent inconsistencies that need explanation. For example, the flow of the al-Qilt spring group in 1982–83 was recorded as being 22 mcmy, compared with only 5 mcmy the year before and the year after.[56] No other spring showed such a high level of discharge change during the same interval.

The monitored springs were all freshwater springs, with a chloride content of 20–450 mg/l. The only exception was the geothermal group of Hammam al-Malih, in the northern Jordan Valley, with an average flow of 0.8 mcmy and a salinity of 1,763 mg/l chloride. The nonmonitored springs were small, but they also included the main group of brackish springs along the Dead Sea shore, al-Fashkha, a potential source of brackish water, as indicated below in the discussion of the Taba accord.

The smallest of the monitored springs had an average discharge of only 0.36 m³/day,[57] or the equivalent of 131 m³/year, while the largest, the al-Auja spring (north of Jericho), discharged 9.24 mcmy. A dozen of the springs had a discharge of 1 mcmy or more, as illustrated in table 2.5, an amount sufficient for irrigating 1,500 dunums or providing water for a community of 10,000 people at the rate of 100 m³ each. All the latter springs were located in the eastern basin of the mountain aquifer. The flow of the 113 springs averaged about 53 mcmy, with more than 85 percent contributed by the springs of the eastern basin. (The major springs draining the northeastern and western basins were situated in Israel.) It fluctuated widely, however, chiefly in response to rainfall variations. The fluctuation was seasonal and interannual, with the former being usually more severe than the latter. Many of the springs were dry in the summer months.

The interannual fluctuation of the discharge is exhibited in figure 2.1. The flow's peak was 119 mcmy in 1991 while the trough was 24 mcmy in 1978, the two years with the highest and lowest rainfall, respectively, during the monitoring period. Overall, the fluctuation was sharp, as can be seen from the high value of the standard deviation, 20.6 mcmy, which measured the dispersion of

55. Nuseibeh and Nasser Eddin, 1995.
56. Ibid, p. 28.
57. Ibid., p. ix.

TABLE 2.5 Average Annual Flow of Twelve Largest Springs in the West Bank, 1970–71 to 1993–94

Spring	Catchment	Average flow (mcmy)	Standard deviation (mcmy)
al-Auja	al-Auja/Fasayil	9.24	4.01
al-Qilt[a]	Wadi al-Qilt	7.16	6.68
al-Sultan	Wadi al-Qilt	5.58	0.29
al-Fari'a	al-Fari'a	5.31	1.9
al-Duyuk	al-Auja/Fasayil	5.04	0.25
al-Nuway'ma	al-Auja/Fasayil	2.65	0.39
Tabban	al-Fari'a	1.38	0.18
Qudayra	al-Fari'a	1.34	0.74
Sidra	al-Fari'a	1.34	2.05
Miska	al-Fari'a	1.32	0.68
Dulayb	al-Fari'a	1.27	1.89
Shibli	al-Fari'a	0.95	0.13

SOURCE: Calculated from Nuseibeh and Nasser Eddin, 1995.
NOTE:
[a]Includes the flow of al-Fawwar spring.

FIGURE 2.1 Average Annual Flow of 113 West Bank Springs, 1970–93

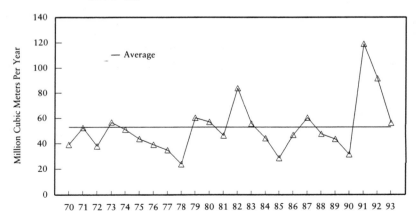

SOURCE: Calculated from Nuseibeh and Nasser Eddin, 1995
NOTE: Standard deviation = 20.6.

**FIGURE 2.2 Average Annual Flow of Three Main West Bank
Springs, 1970–93**

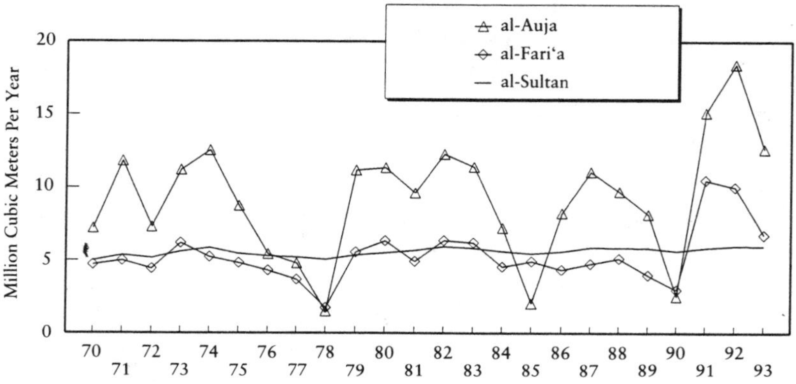

SOURCE: Calculated from Nuseibeh and Nasser Eddin, 1995
Standard deviation: al-Auja = 4; al-Fari'a = 1.85; al-Sultan = 0.29

the flow around the average of 53 mcmy. The oscillation of the
discharge is more critical from the point of view of use than its
average, notably during drought years when the soil needs more
irrigation water.

Not all springs, however, exhibited the same level of discharge
variation. The hydrological reasons differed, depending on the type
of spring and the layers from which the spring was fed. The historic
flow of three main springs, shown in figure 2.2, illustrates the
difference in interannual variation. For example, al-Sultan spring,
which was tapped by the municipality and farmland of Jericho,
seemed immune to the aberrations of rainfall, maintaining a steady
interannual discharge of about 5.6 mcmy, with a standard deviation of only 0.29 mcmy. On the other extreme, was the high variation of the al-Auja spring, which had an average flow of 9.2 mcmy
and a standard deviation of 4 mcmy. The spring all but dried up
in 1978, leading to Palestinian accusations and Israeli denials that
the wells Israel had dug in the spring's vicinity to supply Israeli
settlements were responsible, a question taken up in chapter 4 in
tandem with the treatment of the settlements' water supply. In
between lay the fluctuation of the al-Fari'a group, with its average
flow of 5.3 mcmy and standard variation of 1.85 mcmy. The fluctuation of the overall flow reflected the balance of such variations
among individual springs.

Water from springs was used for irrigation, for drinking by
livestock, and for municipal purposes. The average use was 30

mcmy, much less than the average flow of 53 mcmy, because a good portion of the winter flow, notably in peak-discharge years, like 1991, went unused, and because of losses in old aqueducts or the naturally carved channels. Proposals were made in the past for taking advantage of some of the untapped water, such as Wadi al-Qilt's, for the artificial recharge of the eastern basin.[58]

It is difficult to give a breakdown of the allocation among the three categories because the water of the same spring often is harnessed for more than one end. Without a doubt, however, agriculture received the lion's share, especially because 95 percent of spring flow was in the sparsely populated eastern basin. Overall, the Water Department estimated that 5 to 10 percent of the water of the 113 monitored springs was harnessed for irrigation and the rest for municipal purposes.[59]

The springs for the most part were common property resources and remained so under Israeli rule. Their water customarily was shared through a rotation system whereby farmers were allocated "water-time" during which they could divert the water from the feeder canals to their fields. A typical rotation worked as follows. If one dunum was allocated one hour of water-time per month (the month was lunar in some localities, such as in al-Duyuk, northwest of Jericho), it got water for 10 minutes every five days.[60] The title to a water share was tied commonly to the ownership of the land, and a title holder could not sell his water rights separately from the land. There were exceptions to this rule. In the case of al-Sultan spring, for example, the owner of water on the *falha* land, or the land that used to belong to the five clans of the town, could sell, rent, or mortgage the water share.[61] In general, the system of property rights of springs and their management need in-depth research to devise a new management system that is more conducive to spring conservation than has been the traditional system.

The rotation system was suitable for the traditional cultivation method in which plants are arranged in zigzag furrows (or *dawalib*) and irrigated by water running through these furrows. The traditional method worked according to the principle of infre-

58. Davidson and Hirzallah, 1966.
59. Nuseibeh and Nasser Eddin, 1995, p. ix.
60. Dar al-Jalil, 1981.
61. Ibid.

quent but intensive water application. The introduction of drip irrigation in the 1980s, however, required frequent, or even continuous, water application but in small doses, the opposite principle of traditional irrigation. To make water available continuously, farmers devised a technical solution. They stored their water allotments in what may be described as "earthen-pools," often lined with plastic sheets to prevent water from seeping through the soil, and used boosters to generate the pressure required for the drip pipes. They also employed the earthen-pools to mix the fresh spring water with the increasingly brackish water of the wells. The pools were used most widely in the Jordan Valley region, which claimed in the early 1990s about 85 of the 92 pools in the West Bank.[62]

Springwater was conveyed to farms via gravity canals, commonly uncovered and built of cement or gravel. The combination of such canals and the traditional furrow irrigation entailed substantial water loss to leakage and evaporation. The conveyance efficiency of the gravity canals was estimated in the Jordan Valley area in Jordan at 60 percent; the on-farm furrow irrigation efficiency was 63 percent.[63] In other words, the combined efficiency of the two systems amounted to less than 40 percent,[64] which is to say, more than 60 percent of the water was nonproductively lost. While drip irrigation itself was much more efficient than furrow irrigation, the persistence of open gravity canals meant that even with perfect on-farm efficiency, about 40 percent of the water still was lost in such canals.

A project was under way in the early 1990s to channel the water of the spring-fed Wadi al-Fari'a through pipes in order to conserve water.[65] Israel itself did not undertake water conservation projects in the West Bank and Gaza and seems to have discouraged nonofficial initiatives. For example, for several years beginning in 1978 American Near East Refugee Aid (ANERA), which has been operating in the West Bank and Gaza since 1968, tried to obtain a permit from the Israeli military to replace the old canals with pipes in the Wadi al-Fari'a area but was not granted one.[66] By allowing the project finally to proceed,[67] Israel may have begun to act on

62. Awartani, 1991a, p. 23.
63. World Bank, 1988, pp. 21–22.
64. Total efficiency = $0.6 \times 0.63 = 0.38$.
65. Center for Engineering and Analysis, 1992a.
66. Gubser, 1993; and Stork, 1983, pp. 22–23.
67. The project is no longer an ANERA project, although the organization contributes to it.

the premise that Palestinian water conservation served its own interests as well.

Other Sources

Other sources refer to (1) small-scale technologies (cisterns and pools) for collecting runoff water from rooftops, wadis, springs, and greenhouse roofs; and (2) supply from Mekorot's network, from within the West Bank and Gaza and from Israel. The potential of the first set of resources is limited, but for a place in dire need of water they may be worth looking into. Mekorot's network supplied about one-quarter of the water, and its role was planned to expand under the Taba Agreement.

Cisterns

Cisterns are an ancient method of water storage;[68] they were used inside castles and during long sieges. Some of those built in geographic Palestine during the Roman and Byzantine periods, although nonfunctional today, are scattered across the country. Cisterns traditionally were cut by hoes and axes, which were replaced in recent times by mechanical methods. In rocky terrain cisterns commonly are shaped like pears, narrow at the top and wide at the base, with whitewashed interiors. Where the ground is not firm, they are cylindrical and lined with special bricks or with reinforced concrete. Cisterns are used for storing water from rooftops, springs, or other sources, particularly in dry years. The domestic cisterns gather the water from the roofs through gutters, while those outside residential areas are located in sink like spots. People used to (and some still do) lift the water by a *dalwu* (a rubber bucket), which was replaced first by the hand pump and eventually by the mechanical pump. In houses, the water is pumped to a tank on the rooftop for storage and subsequent use. The water from the cisterns is used domestically as well as given to animals to drink.

The number of cisterns in the West Bank has been estimated at 50,000, with an average capacity of 100–150 m³. The water volume supplied by the cisterns perhaps ranged between 2 and 5

---

68. The discussion of the cisterns is based primarily on *Shu'un Tanmawiyya*, 1988, pp. 26–27.

mcmy.[69] The introduction of piped water seemed to lessen the interest in cisterns, especially in the urban areas, owing to the need for maintenance and cumbersome cleaning. However, Israel's limitations on water supply, as well as rising awareness among Palestinians of the need to conserve and develop all possible water sources, appear to have revived interest in cisterns.

In Gaza, cisterns are virtually nonexistent, perhaps because it rains less there than in the West Bank. However, it may be worthwhile to tap them as a source of extra water. A roof area of 50 sq m with 80 percent runoff efficiency could yield 8 m^3 in the south and 16 m^3 in the north.[70] For an average household of 6 people, this could provide 3 to 6 percent of present annual consumption, a small, though not a trivial, proportion for an arid area.[71] The willingness of people in both the West Bank and Gaza to build such cisterns will depend on their cost relative to that of purchased water and on whether they are offered a new type of cistern that is easier to maintain and clean than the traditional one.

Pools

In addition to collecting water in cisterns, people traditionally gathered it in pools, such as the Silwan (near Jerusalem) and Solomon pools. Today, these pools are in a dilapidated state. The largest and most celebrated of the pools are the three Solomon pools, southwest of Bethlehem, about 13 km from Jerusalem. It is unclear why they were given that name or by whom. A medieval Arab traveler mentioned them as the Pools of al-Marji' (or Return) which, according to tradition, is the place where the brothers of Joseph are thought to have returned after dropping him in the well. The third pool is reported to have been built by the Mamluk Sultan Khushqadam in 1461.[72] They are carved mainly in rock and extend east-west, nearly 50 m apart with a combined length of 0.5 km. The first pool (from the west) is higher than the second, and the second is higher than the third. Their combined storage capacity

69. Awartani, 1991a, p. 6.
70. Bruins and Tuinhof, 1991, p. 14. The implied assumption is that average rainfall is 200 mm in the south and 400 mm in north.
71. Assuming an average annual per capita consumption of 30 m^3.
72. *Encyclopaedia Palaestina*, 1984, vol. 1, pp. 379–80; and Sanad, 1992.

has been put at 340,000 m³. They collected the runoff water from the adjacent mountains and water from Wadi al-Arrub and the Artas spring.[73] During the Ottoman period, water from the pools was conveyed to Jerusalem through aqueducts and a pipeline of closely fitted stone. The pools were renovated in the 1920s by the British Mandate authorities, who also installed a pumping station to increase the efficacy of sending the water to the city. The supply from the pools continued to East Jerusalem while the West Bank was part of Jordan, but ceased after Israeli's seizure of the city in 1967.[74] Today, a visitor to the Solomon pools notices the plastic cans and bottles and other litter dumped into the pools, the algae-green water, and the idle, rusty old pumps. Yet, even under these nonhygienic conditions, young men from the neighboring communities swim in them for lack of alternative recreation.

Greenhouse Runoff

The greenhouses used in the West Bank and Gaza are half-cylindrical structures supported by metal pipe frames and roofed with special plastic that harnesses the greenhouse effect. Rainfall over the houses can be collected in tanks or small pools via gutters along the sides near the bottom of the house. Collection efficiency even could be higher than from the rooftops of houses, owing to the smoothness and curvature of the roofs. Experiments were set up in Gaza in the early 1990s in which water was gathered in covered tanks for subsequent use in agriculture. For a greenhouse enclosing an area of one dunum, the collected runoff can amount to 80 m³ for each 100 mm of rainfall. Accordingly, runoff gathered from a greenhouse can be as high as 320 m³ in the semi-coastal region of the West Bank and as low as 160 m³ in the south of Gaza.[75] Thus, for a vegetable greenhouse with drip irrigation, for example, such quantities could supply between 16 and 32 percent of annual water requirements, not insignificant proportions.[76] In terms of total supply, collection of runoff from greenhouses would remain minuscule

73. Ibid.
74. Al-Dabbagh, 1976, vol. 10, part 2, p. 340; Dumper, 1993, p. 79; and Sanad, 1992.
75. Bruins and Tuinhof, 1991.
76. Water requirements for a dunum of cucumbers cultivated under a greenhouse with drip irrigation are estimated at 1,000 cmy.

but, because yields of greenhouse agriculture are remarkably higher than those of open cultivation, the potential contribution of such water to agricultural output would be more than negligible.

The Mekorot Connection

Soon after Israel seized the West Bank and Gaza, Mekorot began building a water distribution network to deliver water to the settlements and military installations. In the 1970s and 1980s, many Palestinian towns and villages also were linked to the network, as it became the only source of water available to them. Furthermore, the company started to "transfer" water in the network from the West Bank and Gaza to Israel and vice versa, as indicated in the briefing of the Israeli Ministry of Foreign Affairs.[77] The briefing argued that Israel was utilizing the water efficiently by moving it from where it was available to where it was needed and that the exchange balance for the two years it cited, 1978–80, favored the Palestinians.[78] Whether Mekorot continued to pump water from the West Bank to Israel was unclear; some Palestinian sources claimed it did, while others discounted the claim. If it did, the amounts transferred are unknown. However, the company did divert water from Palestinian wells to the Israeli settlements.[79] Mekorot also continued to bring in water from Israel to the West Bank, 2.1 mcm in 1987 and 5.3 mcm in 1989.[80] How much of this amount went to the Israeli settlements and how much to the Palestinians was not disclosed by the company.

Overall, by 1995 Mekorot was supplying to the West Bank about 25 mcmy, or more than one-half of municipal water use, and to Gaza, 5 mcmy or about 15 percent of municipal use.[81] Mekorot's role as a supplier was furthered in the Taba accord, which committed Israel to extend 14.5 mcmy of additional water,

77. Israel, Ministry of Foreign Affairs, 1982a.
78. According to ibid., in 1978–79 the transfers from the West Bank to Israel (mainly from the Herodion well to Jerusalem) were slightly more than 1 mcm but slightly more than 2 mcm in the opposite direction; in 1979–80 the corresponding quantities were nearly 0.55 mcm and 2.7 mcm.
79. According to Awartani, 1991a, p. 19, the amount may be in the neighborhood of 2 mcmy.
80. Ibid., p, 20, citing Tahal.
81. *Jerusalem Post* (international edition), 6 January 1996.

10 mcmy for Gaza and 4.5 mcmy for the West Bank (Annex III, Article 40, schedule 10).

MUNICIPAL WATER

Traditionally, domestic water mainly was self-provided. Households that did not own cisterns or were insufficiently supplied from them fetched water from springs and wells. The task of bringing in water often was assigned to the female household members who carried it in clay jars on their heads or were aided by animals. Other households, particularly those that were "better off," and shops purchased their water from vendors, commonly males, who also either carried the water themselves in buckets balanced over the shoulders or used beasts of burden.

The provision of piped water commenced during the British Mandate. For example, Jerusalem's external water supply, which had been limited to the aqueducts from the Solomon pools, was diversified in 1936 to include water from Ra's al-'Ayn springs which drained the western basin of the mountain aquifer. Concomitantly, a partial pipe network was laid for supplying water to some households and shops.[82] Towns other than Jerusalem—Nablus in the 1930s and Hebron in the 1940s—also began to receive piped water.[83]

The network continued to spread, albeit slowly, during the period when the West Bank was part of Jordan and Gaza was under Egyptian administration. It covered most of the towns and, according to Israel's State Comptroller, 50 villages in the West Bank.[84] In the aftermath of the 1948 war, East Jerusalem had to compensate for the lost water from Ra's al-'Ayn, which was located in Israeli-held territory. At first the population resorted to traditional sources, such as cisterns and the springs of Silwan and Sur Bahir. Then the municipality, lacking finances, granted a concession to private companies to lay down pipes and sell water to customers. By 1967, about 40 percent of the city was provided with running water.[85] Similar steps also were taken by the municipalities of the twin towns of Ramallah and al-Bira, north of Jeru-

82. Dumper, 1993, pp. 79–80.
83. Haddad and Abu Ghusha, 1992.
84. Israel State Comptroller Report, 1990.
85. Dumper, 1993, p. 80.

salem, to meet water demand brought about by the influx of refugees. The two municipalities, in cooperation with the municipal council of Jerusalem, brought water from the Fara springs, northeast of Jerusalem. Subsequently, with loan money from the American International Development Agency (IDA), the forerunner of USAID, to develop municipal water in the country, the government began in 1963 to tap the wells of Samiya springs in 1966. In all, about 20 percent of the pipe networks in Ramallah in the early 1990s had been installed before 1967.

Incomplete Coverage

The extension of the network continued under Israel. According to its official estimates, 79 percent of the households in the West Bank had access to running water in 1991, and 20 percent had cisterns.[86] Because the households that were not covered by the piped water system most likely were lower income ones—which tended to be larger-sized households—the actual proportion of the total population lacking running water exceeded one-fifth. The households that did not receive piped water relied on traditional methods. To illustrate, a survey of primary health care in rural areas of three West Bank districts found that, in communities with no running water in the Tulkarm district, rainfed cisterns were the only source of water for 42 communities, spring-fed cisterns for 11, nonpiped springwater for four communities, and water carried by animals from neighboring areas for one community.[87]

In Gaza, Israeli sources reported wider network coverage. Approximately 95 percent of the households were said to have received running water, and 4 percent had courtyard taps.[88] However, a United Nations report indicated that 39 percent of the population of the camps did not receive water in their homes and that 11 percent of the houses in Gaza city itself did not get piped water.[89] The Israeli figures were probably "theoretical," assuming that connections actually delivered water. For example, a municipal employee in Gaza city was quoted as saying that "the city's piping system is outdated and partially damaged. Water pumped

86. BUNT 1994, p. 3.5.
87. Barghouthi and Daibes, 1991, report 2, p. 11.
88. BUNT, 1994, p. 3.5.
89. United Nations, 1992.

through the system never reaches neighborhoods in the southeast section of the city."[90] Thus, the fact that such neighborhoods were hooked to the pipe network did not ensure water supply.

The provision of running water in the West Bank, besides being incomplete, was distributed unevenly among regions. The lack was felt most widely in the northern districts and small-sized, usually rural, communities. To illustrate, 85 percent of the population in the Ramallah district had access to piped water in 1989, compared with 58 percent in the Tulkarm district and 45 percent in the Jinin district. Within the Tulkarm district itself, 21 percent of the population in communities with less than 500 people were supplied with piped water, 38 percent in those with 1,000 to 5,000 people, and 100 percent in those with more than 10,000 people. In the Jinin area the percentages were different; the lowest ratio of homes supplied with piped water, 42 percent, was found in communities of more than 500 persons, while the highest ratio, 80 percent, was found in communities of 5,000 to 9,999 population.[91]

In the countryside, a preliminary survey found that 179 (or 51 percent) out of 351 villages with a population of more than 100 lacked a piped water network. Moreover, only in a few villages was the entire population served by the network. Overall, only an estimated 38 percent of the rural population in these villages had running water.[92] Considering the bias against smaller communities and the 50 small villages (each with a population of under 100) left out of the survey, the proportion of the total rural population that lacked running water likely reached 40 percent.

Within the refugee camps, which number 20 in the West Bank and eight in Gaza, water distribution was chiefly the responsibility of UNRWA. The agency did not own wells in the West Bank and obtained water from the municipalities and Mekorot. However, UNRWA owned nine of the 49 municipal wells in Gaza. When it first began its services after the 1948 war, UNRWA built communal water fountains (or standposts) in one or more sites in each camp, depending on the camp's size, that brought water from towers supplied by tank trucks. Women then fetched the water from these fountains, commonly in buckets and jars carried on their heads.

90. Bellisari, 1993, p. 20.
91. Barghouthi and Daibes, 1991, reports 1, p. 8; 2, p. 11; and 3, p. 17.
92. Haddad and Abu Ghusha, 1992.

The camps of the West Bank commonly are perched on the outskirts of towns, a Palestinian version of the shantytown phenomenon, and their water services gradually were linked with those of the towns, enabling the agency to build distribution networks there. In Gaza, the camps also obtained water from the towns and private owners and, in some cases, from Mekorot.

The Formal Suppliers

The institutions involved in the delivery of piped municipal water are the Water Department, Mekorot, municipalities, village councils, water boards in villages lacking village councils, and UNRWA (for the refugee camps). As stated earlier, the municipalities and village councils owned most of the wells in both the West Bank and Gaza. The Water Department in the West Bank owned less than ten wells, UNRWA owned even fewer, and private owners only had a negligible number. The predominance of well ownership by the municipalities overstated the role played by them in the supply of domestic water, or, to put it differently, understated Israeli control over the process, particularly in the West Bank. First, through the Civil Administration, Israel held the legislative and executive reins, including budgetary allocations, that impinged on the water sector. The municipalities could propose projects and draw plans within their boundaries, but they needed to secure the approval of the Civil Administration. When the municipalities could obtain financial assistance from other sources, such as nongovernmental aid organizations operating in the West Bank and Gaza, or from abroad, the financial constraints occasionally were relaxed. However, the process of obtaining Israeli approval was arbitrary and, as a result, the ability of the municipalities to secure such assistance was erratic. The functions of the municipalities, therefore, often were confined to maintenance and bill collection.

Second, the municipalities and other Palestinian organs supplied only one-half of the 25.8 mcm of the piped domestic water used in the West Bank in 1991. The other half was supplied by Israeli organizations (Mekorot and the municipality of Jerusalem) or the Israeli-controlled Civil Administration.[93]

93. Ibid., table 8.

Third, the substantial supply by Mekorot in the West Bank mirrored the extensive penetration of its network there, albeit mainly in connection with the Israeli settlements. Thus, only the Tulkarm district did not receive water from the Mekorot network.[94] Even in Gaza, the company supplied water to the middle section, and five of the eight refugee camps received a portion of their water from it.[95] Mekorot built mainlines from which it supplied the networks inside the villages and towns, which were Palestinian public property. The role of Mekorot as a water supplier did not diminish under the Taba Agreement; on the contrary, it was planned to increase in absolute terms as mentioned earlier.

The control of the spigot by Israel put a significant part of the Palestinian communities in a vulnerable position. Palestinians whose water was under Israeli control experienced supply cutoffs or substantial curtailments before Israeli settlements in the same area during periods of water shortages. Equally important, the spatial spread of the water network further reinforced Israeli hold over West Bank territory. By transforming the institutional and legal control over the water sector into a substantial physical reality, Israel added one more hurdle in the way of resolving the water conflict.

The Running Water Runs Poorly

Official Israeli sources often have presented the expansion of the network of domestic water consumption during the occupation as evidence that Israel improved the water situation of the Palestinians in the West Bank.[96] Although the per capita domestic use grew, as is indicated in the next chapter, the extent of improvement should be assessed in light of (among other things) the quality of the coverage and the sources of finance for the extension of the network.

To begin with, the aging networks within the towns have not been modernized under Israeli rule and their water losses were

94. Ibid., tables 2.4 and 2.5.
95. Bruins and Tuinhof, 1991, p. 20, cites these camps as al-Shati', al-Burayj, al-Nusayrat, al-Maghazi, and Rafah.
96. Israel, Ministry of Foreign Affairs, 1982a; Israel, State Comptroller, 1990; and Tahal, 1990.

substantial, ranging from 25–60 percent.[97] The losses included leakage and unaccounted for water owing to technical problems related to metering and to "free riding."[98] Leakage is substantial, but the free rider syndrome grew during the intifada because of the breakdown of public order and deterioration of economic conditions. For example, total losses in the network of Jerusalem Water Undertaking, which runs probably the most efficient town network, were estimated at more than 26 percent of the water at the source: 13 percent (or one-half) of the water leaked, 11 percent was metered inaccurately, and 2 percent was abstracted by free riders.[99] In the town of Jinin, the losses were more than 45 percent, which municipal officials attributed first to free riders and second to leakage.[100] Gaza may have fared even worse, with losses reaching 50–60 percent of the supply.[101]

In contrast, losses in the networks of villages were smaller, 9–18 percent, because they were newer.[102] This indicates that had the town networks been modernized, substantial amounts of water and money would have been saved, particularly since the water supplied to the towns represented about three-quarters of the total supply of piped water.[103]

The poor state of the municipal networks was a symptom of the generally inadequate investment in infrastructure. Investment by the public sector in the social and economic infrastructure was exceptionally low. It was estimated at less than 3.5 percent of the gross domestic product (GDP), compared, for example, with more than 9 percent in Jordan and 13 percent in Egypt.[104] The low level of investment did not reflect the revenues that accrued to Israel and the Civil Administration, directly and indirectly, from the West Bank and Gaza.[105] The World Bank euphemistically dubbed the

97. European Community, 1993, p. 7, section 2.2; Haddad and Abu Ghusha, 1992; and al-Khatib and Assaf, 1992. The same situation also applied to the refugee camps because they were connected to the piped water networks of the towns.

98. Free riding was accomplished by such means as the installment of pumps before meters, tampering with the meters themselves, or nonpayment.

99. Jerusalem Water Undertaking, 1991, p. 32.

100. *Al-Nahar*, 7 July 1991.

101. European Community, 1993, p. 7, citing Israel Bureau of Statistics.

102. Haddad and Abu Ghusha, 1992.

103. Ibid.

104. World Bank, 1993a, vol. 2, p. 35.

105. The revenues included direct taxes, indirect value added taxes, fines of all kinds, deductions from Palestinians employed in Israel, etc.

difference between the revenues from the West Bank and Gaza "fiscal compression."[106] The size of the "fiscal compression" was not exactly known; the World Bank itself conservatively estimated that the indirect taxes alone that were not returned to the Palestinians in 1991 to be 8 percent of the GDP.[107] Yet, Israel's State Comptroller claimed that Tahal had planned in 1970 to connect all West Bank villages to piped water and bring up the total domestic supply network to 38 mcmy, but it did not do so owing to the shortage of funds.[108]

Moreover, the municipalities could not obtain loans to cover developmental budgets, owing to the lack of credit institutions in the West Bank. Borrowing abroad also was not possible because of the overall circumstances of the occupation. The municipalities thus spent whatever fees they collected on maintenance and services that did not generate revenues.

The minimal improvements made and the wells drilled by the municipalities depended chiefly on funds from foreign donors—such as ANERA, Save the Children, and the UNDP—and from outside Palestinian and Arab sources. Thus, when the municipality of Hebron was pondering the modernization of its network and building new water towers, it applied to the UNDP for help.[109] To build one of its wells, the Jerusalem Water Undertaking utilized funds from the short-lived Jordanian-Palestinian Joint Committee, Jordan, and Save the Children Fund. In order to finance Well No. 4 at the Samiya springs, the company received promises of financial contributions from five external sources, Arab and international.[110] The municipality of Bethlehem started in 1990 a wastewater collection and disposal project, with outlays of $12 million contributed by Italy and Germany.[111] The external sources were volatile, subject to Israeli approval and the political winds in the Arab region. Also, securing funds from numerous sources was time consuming because contacts between the West Bank and Gaza, on the one hand, and the outside world, on the other, were cumbersome, particularly if they involved travel. In sum, whatever money was

106. World Bank, 1993a, vol. 2, pp. 12–33; see also Benvenisti, 1984, p. 10.
107. World Bank, 1993a, vol. 2, p. 33.
108. Israel State Comptroller, 1990.
109. *Al-Nahar*, 7 October 1990.
110. Jerusalem Water Undertaking, 1991, pp. 15–16.
111. Nader al-Khatib, telephone interview, September 1993.

obtained to finance building and improving the infrastructure came not from the Civil Administration, needed much effort to be secured, and was insufficient. As a result, the distribution network remained in a state of disrepair.

Furthermore, the quality of the delivery left much to be desired. The water supply to households was irregular and interruptions were frequent. For example, when a water shortage occurred, Mekorot cut off water delivery to the Arab towns and villages, not to the Israeli settlements.[112] For example, in 1984 the village of al-Rujayb reportedly paid JD1,000 (or about $3,000) and the subscribers JD35 each in order to get hooked up with Mekorot's mainline.[113] In May 1989, however, water ceased to reach the houses built on higher elevations; then the cutoff expanded to other areas until by December the entire village was without piped water. In another illustration, a water council was formed in the camp of al-Burayj in Gaza, and part of the water supply that had been supplied by UNRWA was transferred to Mekorot.[114] The camp was located on a hilltop and the water supply began to be interrupted in the summer months, until, by 1988, the camp was getting only one-half of the former volume. Mekorot said that one of the five wells supplying the area went out of commission, but the wells were located in an enclosed military area and the claim could not be verified independently. When the owner of a nearby well offered to supply the camp with water for five hours a day, Mekorot threatened to take over the well. The camp's residents resorted to a variety of means: tank trucks, bathing in the sea, or doing their laundry and washing at relatives' houses in other camps. This camp, together with the other two camps in the central region, felt water shortages the most. The two other camps, al-Nusayrat and al-Maghazi, were supplied by UNWRA. This agency was able to supply only one-half of the amount of water it was supposed to supply because of disputes with Israel's Civil Administration.[115] The disputes most likely centered around the authority to control the water supply.

112. *Al-Nahar*, 7 October 1990, citing an official of the Jerusalem Water Undertaking; the villages mentioned were Iswa, Yatta, Halhul, al-Dahiriya, and al-Sammu'. See also al-Khatib and Assaf, 1992.
113. *Al-Nahar*, 6 January 1990.
114. *Al-Tali'a*, August 1990.
115. Bruins and Tuinhof, 1991, p. 20.

Irregularity of water supply was the norm, not the exception. By official Israeli acknowledgment, in the northern districts of the West Bank the towns that were linked to the pipe network received their water intermittently, and not every day of the week.[116] Hebron and Gaza also were on a rotation system, with neighborhoods getting water two days a week.[117] In summary, citing the irregularity of the supply as an example of the overall infrastructural deficiency in the West Bank and Gaza, the World Bank stated:

> The water departments and regional water undertakings have serious problems in maintaining their systems, reducing leakages, maintaining adequate pressure and in supplying the available water to consumers. Several water departments can only supply water in rotation in certain urban areas, sometimes only for a few hours once or twice a week. This endangers the quality of the water as contaminated water can infiltrate into supply pipes when water pressure drops drastically. . . .The situation in the rural areas is even more unsatisfactory.[118]

CREEPING CONTAMINATION?

Water quantity and quality are indivisible. The increase of pumping can speed up the diffusion of contamination plumes into an aquifer, while overpumping can cause saline water from the sea or from adjacent rock formations to intrude into it. Contamination of a river or an aquifer also reduces the quantity available for a certain usage. If contamination becomes pervasive, the water source may be damaged and its repair, if at all possible, is both lengthy and costly.

Numerous contaminants can find their way into the water system, whether surface or underground, during transportation or use. They may be biological (such as bacteria, viruses, parasites), organic chemicals (e.g., benzene and vinyl chloride), or nonorganic chemicals, whether toxic (e.g., lead and mercury) or nontoxic (nitrates and salt).[119] In the United States, for example, more than 80

116. Israel, State Comptroller, 1990.
117. Bruins and Tuinhof, 1991, p. 20; and *al-Nahar*, 7 October 1990.
118. World Bank, 1993a, vol. 5, pp. 52–53.
119. The Conservation Foundation, 1987, pp. 65–86.

chemical and microbiological contaminants are regulated under the Safe Drinking Water Act.[120]

Contamination may be caused by nature itself (earthquakes, volcanos) or human activity. In the present context, the main threat to the water sources are the waste-generating human activities of production and consumption. The human sources of pollution include municipal waste, industrial waste, storage (underground gasoline, for example), abandoned wells, urban storm runoff, landfills, agricultural inputs, and livestock.[121]

Water contamination is of particular concern owing to its potentially adverse impact on human health. The relationship between health, on the one hand, and water contamination, on the other, is "complex and controversial."[122] For one thing, water-related diseases can be communicated by several mechanisms. For example, they may be water-borne, when the pathogen lives in water that is then drunk (e.g., cholera), or water-based, when the pathogen spends a part of its life cycle in an intermediate aquatic host or hosts (e.g., bilharzia).[123] Second, some diseases, such as cholera, can be transmitted via media other than water, such as food exposed to fecal contamination.[124] Third, nonhygienic habits, crowdedness, and other factors can contribute to the disease incidence, making it difficult to identify precisely the role of water contamination. At any rate, the extent of the health impact of water contamination in the West Bank and Gaza is unknown. Controlled case studies, cumulative anecdotal evidence, and observations of physicians and other health practitioners suggest that it could be substantial, particularly in Gaza.[125] For a more specific discussion, the interested reader may wish to consult the sources cited by Anna Bellisari.[126]

Saline contamination also can be injurious to agriculture. Chlorides may reduce crop yields, depending on the crop's salt tolerance, and high sodium adsorption ratio (SAR), or roughly a high tendency for sodium ions to stick to the soil, may damage the

120. Fetter, 1988, p. 374.
121. The Conservation Foundation, 1987, pp. 105–67.
122. Giacaman, 1988; and Smith, 1990, p. 97.
123. Feachem, 1977.
124. Ibid.; and Smith 1990, p. 102.
125. Bellisari, 1993.
126. See ibid.

clay texture of the soil.[127] The injurious impact of high salinity has been evident most clearly in Gaza in the much reduced yields of citruses (see the next chapter). A preliminary analysis of water samples indicated that most of the water in Gaza has a high salinity and high sodium content and can be used only for salt-tolerant crops, provided there is appropriate drainage.[128] More field research, however, is needed on this topic to understand the exact relationship among water quality, soil, and plants in the specific agro-ecological conditions of the West Bank and Gaza.

The record of water quality in the West Bank and Gaza is seriously incomplete, owing to the insufficiency of testing facilities and skilled technicians. It is neither systematic nor continuous and covers only a few of the potential contaminants. Nonetheless, available information demonstrates that the water quality in Gaza has deteriorated seriously. The picture appears to be brighter in the West Bank; nevertheless, contamination of groundwater can be a slow process due to the slow movement of the groundwater itself; thus, some of the presently reassuring results about West Bank water could prove to be misleading, and it may be only a matter of time before the damage discloses itself.

Salinity

Water is classified on a freshness-salinity continuum according to its content of chloride concentration or total dissolved solids (TDS), each of which is measured in mg/l or its equivalent parts per million (ppm). Water is "fresh" when it contains less than 200–300 mg/l chloride or less than 1,000 mg/l TDS; "brackish" between 300 and 1,000 mg/l chloride or 1,000 to 10,000 mg/l TDS; and saline above these levels.[129] These are not hard and fast boundaries. The World Health Organization (WHO), for example, classifies water as fresh when its chloride content is no greater than 250 mg/l. In Israel, Tahal identifies the boundary between fresh and brackish water as 400 mg/l chloride.[130]

127. SAR = $Na^+/[(Ca^{+2} + Mg^{+2})/2]^{1/2}$. Na = sodium, Ca = calcium, and Mg = magnesium.
128. Zarour et al., 1993, pp. 215–26.
129. Fetter. 1988, p. 368.
130. Tahal, 1990, p. 2.1.

Salinity of the Mountain Aquifer

Overall, the mountain aquifer *naturally* may contain 40 mcmy of water in the western basin (that emerges at the al-Timsah [Tanninim] springs) with chloride concentration exceeding 400 mg/l; 20 mcmy of water in the northern basin and 60 mcmy in the eastern also have chloride concentrations over 400 mg/l. Thus, the western basin, the most plentiful of the three basins, includes relatively the least amount of brackish water; the opposite is true of the eastern basin.

More potentially serious salinity problems than those occurring naturally have been in the making in some parts of the mountain aquifer because of Israel's overexploitation. This practice led to the accumulation of water deficits and decline in the water tables in the various aquifers to the point where "red lines" have been crossed.[131] The decline of the water table in turn led to the leakage of brine from adjacent rock formations, causing salinity to rise. An example of such a sequence happened in the western basin in the 1950s and early 1960s as Israel overpumped the aquifer to expand the irrigated area, increasing irrigation water supply from 413 mcmy in the crop year 1950–51 to 1,047 mcmy a decade later.[132] Overpumping recurred during the drought period, 1985–90, causing an accumulated water deficit in the western basin of 1,100 mcm with respect to the red line. The deficit translated into a drop of the water table to 10 m below sea level, the designated red line of that basin.[133] Overpumping led to increased salinity, to which Israel responded by shifting the location of the wells. However, while this move lowered salinity in the short run, it led to a buildup of salts in the aquifer, and salinity may have become, in the words of Tahal, "a time bomb."[134] Similar developments also occurred in the northern basin.

131. "Red lines" signify water table thresholds that experts believe must be maintained for the aquifer not to be exposed to damage, with the provision of a reserve for years of low rainfall or periods of drought.

132. Israel, Central Bureau of Statistics, *Statistical Abstract*, various issues.

133. The deficit is defined with regard to the red line as = storage in comparison to the red line (S) + required red line operational reserve (R). For the coastal aquifer, S = −600 and R = 500; for the western aquifer, S = −30 and R = 300. In the 1985–90 period, overpumping may have averaged 34 mcmy from the coastal aquifer and 49 mcmy from the western. See further chapter 1 of this book; *Israel Environmental Bulletin*, 1991; Nativ and Issar, 1987, p. 129; and Tahal, 1990, p. 2.6.

134. Tahal, 1990, pp. 6.1–6.2.

TABLE 2.6 Chloride Concentration in Selected West Bank Wells, 1970, 1985, and 1989

Basin/area	1970 (mg/l)	1985 (mg/l)	1989 (mg/l)	1989/70 (%)
Eastern				
Marj Na'ja	600	700	800	133
Jiftlik	1,040	1,180	1,130	109
Jiftlik	740	1,290	1,280	173
al-Auja	150	264	690	460
Jericho	210	294	344	164
Jericho	190		576	303
Jericho	240	850	1,330	554
A.D.S.	660	1,080	1,164	176
A.D.S.	370	1,400	1,726	466
Northeastern				
Dayr Ghazala	155	225	270	174
Jinin (town)	100	102	104	104
Western				
Tulkarm (town)	190	155	168	88

SOURCE: Based on Awartani, 1991a, table 14, citing Hydrological Service, Israel.
A.D.S. = Arab Development Society.

Overpumping in Israel, according to Palestinian specialists (who have not offered technical details, however), may have caused the drawdowns that also were observed in both basins in the West Bank. The annual drawdown rate between 1969 and 1991 in the wells around the town of Jinin (northern basin) was estimated at about 50 cm, and about half this amount in the wells around Tulkarm and Qalqilya (western basin).[135] Although salinity has not reached critical proportions in either area, the tendency has been for it to rise steadily in some well groups (table 2.6).

Steady increases in drawdowns and salinity also were believed to have occurred in the eastern basin, more specifically in the upper aquifer that supplied Palestinian wells. In the Jericho and Jiftlik areas, the drawdown rate during the 1969–91 period was esti-mated at 7–75 cm per year or a total of about 16 m, and in Bardala

135. These are computed from Awartani, 1991a, p. 28, according to whom the total drawdown over that period was 10, 6, and 5 m in the Jinin, Qalqilya, and Tulkarm areas, respectively. Awartani based his figures on interviews with water specialists and farmers.

more than 50 cm per year or a total of 12 m.[136] At the same time, salinity levels reached alarming proportions in some wells, especially those belonging to the Arab Development Society (table 2.6). It may be that salinity could be reduced by moving the location of the wells; nonetheless, the fact that it could be that high was a cause for concern.

As for springs, the majority of them in the three basins had a chloride content of less than 100 mg/l chloride, and the principal springs, cited earlier, less than 60 mg/l, an excellent level. There were, however, several naturally saline spring groups, namely Hamam al-Malih, Ghazal, and al-Fashkha on the Dead Sea shore. In particular, the al-Fashkha group, which has the highest spring discharge in the West Bank, had chloride concentration of more than 2,000 mg/l[137] and is unfit for either agriculture or human consumption unless desalinated. Consequently, although only a few of the springs were saline, the proportion of saline springwater by volume was quite high.

Salinity of the Coastal Aquifer

The coastal aquifer's natural outlet is the Mediterranean Sea; the interface between the waters of the two poses an ever present salinity threat to the aquifer. Seawater, which is heavier than freshwater, intrudes into the aquifer at rates that are a function of the aquifer's water level at its interface with the sea: the lower the level, the greater the intrusion. The water level, in turn, depends on the balance between replenishment and pumping. The Israeli water authorities consider 1–2 km of inland seawater intrusion as acceptable.[138]

In Israel, the water levels declined sharply in the 1950s and 1960s due to overexploitation, as happened in the mountain aquifer. The water was raised to acceptable levels in the 1970s but fell once more because of overexploitation during the drought of the 1980s. The abundant rainfall in 1991–92 seems to have restored the water table to the levels of the 1970s.[139]

136. Ibid.
137. ASIR, 1986, pp. 35–36.
138. BUNT, 1994, pp. 2.9–2.10
139. Ibid.

The lowering of the water table allowed seawater intrusion and increased the salinity of the water extracted from the wells; artificial recharge was necessary to ameliorate the problem. Furthermore, overexploitation was more intensive in some areas of the aquifer than in others. This overexploitation, coupled with the uneven hydrogeology of the aquifer and its low transmissivity, led to the formation of water depressions below sea level in several parts of the aquifer.[140]

Salinity was much more acute in the aquifer's segment in Gaza than in Israel. With the exception of the fair to excellent quality water (5–200 mg/l chloride) in the upper layers of the Pleistocene aquifer in the far north and south of the Strip, where the two largest patches of sand dunes are located, the picture was generally grim. In most of the central area, where the population is concentrated, salinity exceeded 500 mg/l chloride, deteriorating in the east to 1,000–2,000 mg/l chloride.[141] In 1991, 11 of the 17 wells supplying water to Gaza city contained chloride exceeding that of the WHO's guidelines (250 mg/l), as much as 6–8 times in three of the wells. In fact, two of these wells were abandoned because of salinity. In Dayr al-Balah, three municipal wells were shut down and replaced by two new wells with chloride content between 250 and 400 mg/l.[142]

The water of the deeper Cenomanian aquifer was the most saline, with chloride content ranging from 10,000 to 20,000 mg/l (similar to seawater) to 60,000 mg/l, hardly usable for drinking or agriculture. On the whole, it has been estimated that 60 percent of Gaza's well water contained 600 mg/l chloride by the early 1990s and that its overall average chloride concentration was 380 mg/l, or 50 percent greater than the WHO guidelines.[143]

The trend has been for the salinity problem in Gaza to worsen. For example, the salinity of the well at the Khan Yunis camp increased by an annual average of 20 mg/l chloride over the decade between 1979–80 and 1989–90, and average salinity at Rafah

140. Ibid.
141. Bruins and Tuinhof, 1991, p. 10; European Community, 1993, p. 3; and Schwarz, 1982, p. 98.
142. The jettisoned wells supplying Gaza were Shaykh Radwan No. 2 and No. 6. According to Ephraim and Siniora, 1992, their salinity reached 1,500 and 2,300 mg/l chloride, respectively. The salinity of Dayr al-Balah wells had ranged between 1,200 and 1,400 mg/l chloride. See European Community, 1993, p. 4.
143. Ibid., p. 3.

increased by about 40 mg/l.[144] In all, Gaza's water has been gaining about 15–20 mg/l chloride or more annually.[145] The high salinity was caused by the water flowing from the east; possible leakage of deeper, more saline water; and intrusion of the Mediterranean Sea. The water from the east has a salinity of 600–2,000 mg/l chloride.[146]

The intrusion of seawater resulted from the lowering of the water table which, in turn, was engendered by persistent over-pumping. The drawdown was estimated at 5–25 cm between 1977 and 1982.[147] In areas south of Gaza City, Dayr al-Balah, and Khan Yunis, the water table may have dropped below sea level. In the east, it was only several meters higher. As a consequence, one estimate has put the advance of seawater at 200 m annually.[148] Even if overpumping ceased immediately, the salts would take a long time to dissipate. It is believed that pumping would have to be cut down to 55 mcmy for 10 years,[149] from the present 88–104 mcmy. The explosion of well drilling in the first days of self-government only can aggravate the situation.

Israeli sources often blamed overpumping on the Egyptian administration.[150] The Egyptian management of Gaza's water was undoubtedly responsible initially; but, as we have seen, by 1958 only 416 wells had been dug in Gaza, and overpumping would not have commenced until just a few years prior to the Israeli occupation. During 27 years of Israeli management, overpumping did not abate.

Other Contaminants

In addition to chlorides, the most widespread contaminants are those deriving from pesticides and human and animal waste. The extent of contamination by pesticides, which are borne by the return irrigation water, is unknown for either the West Bank or

144. According to Bruins and Tuinhof, 1991, p. 10, the well water of Khan Yunis camp contained between 225 and 475 mg/l chloride and that of Rafah from 800 to 1,200 mg/l chloride.
145. European Community, 1993, p. 4.
146. Schwarz, 1982, p. 98.
147. Ibid., p. 99.
148. Abu Mayla, 1990, p. 39.
149. BUNT, 1994, p. 2.13.
150. See, for example, Shuval, 1992, p. 7.

Gaza.[151] Palestinian farmers are heavy users of pesticides. In Israel, pesticide application is one of the most intensive in the world, and contamination by those chemicals may be heavy.[152] One can assume that this also is the case in the land cultivated by settlers in the West Bank and Gaza. Palestinian farmers or farm workers who apply them often do not know how to handle them. The instructions on the containers are in Hebrew, so even if the workers applying them are literate in Arabic they still do not understand them.[153] Aside from their immediate hazard to those handling them and the "residues" they leave in crops,[154] pesticides eventually find their way into the water system, contaminating surface and groundwater. Yet, standards for permissible levels of pesticides are lacking in Israel and, certainly, in the West Bank and Gaza.[155]

Pesticide pollution of aquifers is cumulative and extremely difficult, if not impossible, to reverse. If what has been said about the severity of pesticide pollution in Israel is correct,[156] the problem is likely to prove critical in the Palestinian territories, particularly in Gaza where the irrigated area constitutes 25–30 percent of the total land area, compared with less than 2 percent in the West Bank.

Fecal contamination from humans and animals is another problem. Its sources are manure or inappropriately disposed of human and animal excrement carried by the return irrigation and municipal water. Tests on the 113 monitored West Bank springs found that they contained nitrate concentrations (a marker of fecal coliform) ranging from 1 mg/l to more than 150 mg/l, or about four times the maximum permissible limit set by European Union (EU) standards. Only a few of the springs, however, had concentration levels above the EU standards.[157] A random-sample survey,

151. In Israel, the details of pesticide pollution are not well-known, at least publicly. According to Lonergan and Brooks, 1994, p. 63, the results of testing are "not always made available to the public."

152. Lonergan and Brooks, 1994, pp. 109–11.

153. Sansur, 1992; also cited in *Tanmiya*, 1992.

154. In tests conducted by the Center for Environmental and Occupational Health Sciences at Birzeit University in mid–1985, it was found that 38 percent of the vegetables tested contained pesticide residues above acceptable limits and that farmers' blood was heavily exposed to organophosphates, a common group of pesticides easily absorbed through the skin; see *Tanmiya*, 1991, p. 3.

155. Lonergan and Brooks, 1994, p. 109.

156. Ibid., p. 62.

157. Nuseibeh and Nasser Eddin, 1995.

conducted jointly by the Birzeit University Community Health Unit and the Union of Palestinian Medical Relief Committees in several communities in the West Bank, covered a variety of water sources and revealed the presence of fecal coliform (fc) concentration levels that researchers believed to pose a health hazard.[158] Although the samples of piped water contained nearly no fecal coliform, samples of water from irrigation canals, rainfed cisterns, and springs contained 100 fc/milliliter (ml) or more.[159] Water from irrigation canals and rainfed cisterns had the highest incidence, with more than three-quarters of the samples having such high levels.

Although the survey could not be considered exhaustive and was not followed up to discover trends, it was indicative. Its findings were borne out by other research. For example, one study found that the water in one-third of the 300-odd rainfed cisterns in the town of al-Bira, north of Jerusalem, had more than 100 fc/ml but the concentration was about one-half of that value when the cisterns were located more than 50 m away from septic tanks.[160] An investigation of piped water in the Bethlehem area confirmed that it was free of this type of pollution,[161] underscoring the difference that the extension of piped water and revamping the network can make in the quality of drinking water.

In Gaza, nitrate concentration was found to be high, averaging 45 mg/l, close to the maximum permissible limit of the EU standards. In the densely populated areas, especially in the refugee camps, where nearly two-thirds of Gaza's population dwell, the concentration reached 90 mg/l and in some instances 159 mg/l.[162] It has been conjectured that 30–60 mg/l nitrates are a base-level

158. The survey considered water from irrigation canals in eight Jordan Valley villages; from rainfed cisterns in seven villages in the Hebron district and one village in the Ramallah district; from nine springs in the Ramallah district; and from the piped water network; see Birzeit Community Health Unit, 1987, p. 19. The results of the research also are summarized in al-Hamidi, 1990.

159. There is no guideline as to the threshold of fecal coliform concentration beyond which the contaminant poses a definite health risk. The researchers took 100 fc/100 mm as a cutoff point.

160. Al-Hamidi, 1990, pp. 22–23.

161. Abd Rabbu, 1990, p. 58.

162. Bruins and Tuinhof, 1991, p. 13; and European Community, 1993, p. 4. The low figure is from the European Community, citing Israeli official documents, and the higher one from independent tests done as part of Bruins and Tuinhof's research.

contamination from agriculture; the higher levels derive from domestic wastewater.[163]

Lack of Sewage Systems

Human fecal contamination in Gaza and the West Bank largely stems from the lack of sewage systems. In the West Bank, there is no sewage collection network in the villages and refugee camps (the camps are discussed later in conjunction with Gaza's sewage system); in the towns where it exists the coverage is partial.[164] Thus, about 15 and 25 percent of the households were not served by a sewage network in the Jerusalem and Nablus districts, respectively; 25 percent in the twin towns of al-Bira and Ramallah; 35 percent in Hebron; and 100 percent in Jericho.[165] In the areas not served by the network, the "gray" water was disposed of randomly in the open in the rural areas and in open channels in the refugee camps. The wastewater leached into the ground from latrines, septic tanks or open sewers. In 1981, at least 21 percent of rural household in the West Bank and 15 percent of all the household reportedly lacked latrines of any kind.[166] Overall, as of 1995 probably only 20 percent of the West Bank population was served by sewage systems.

Moreover, only a few families throughout the West Bank had automatic flush toilets; most were either of the direct drop or pour flush types. The Community Health Unit at Birzeit University postulated that the provision of automatic flushes could substantially lower environmental contamination and associated intestinal infections. In the villages with piped water, the soakage pits frequently got clogged and overflowed; emptying them was expensive as it has to be done by vacuum trucks.[167]

Where sewage systems exist, treatment plants often do not exist, or, if they are present, do not function effectively.[168] The

163. Bruins and Tuinhof, 1991, p. 13.

164. The only exception among villages is Bir Nabala, Jerusalem district, where partial coverage exists; see Center for Engineering and Analysis, 1992, p. 81.

165. Ibid., pp. 81–82.

166. Birzeit University Community Health Unit, 1987, p. 22, citing figures from Israel, Bureau of Statistics.

167. Ibid.

168. Sbeih, 1996, pp. 171–72.

dearth of treatment plants in the West Bank means that the waste-water ultimately flows into the open and leaks to the aquifer system. The towns thus merely transfer their problem as negative externalities to other communities. For example, one study found that the water of al-Fariʻa springs, which provided water for a number of villages such as Jiftlik, were highly polluted as a result of the seepage of wastewater from Nablus sewage in the highlands.[169] In general, a large proportion of the wastewater flows from Jerusalem and other cities in the highlands to the Jordan Valley, turning it into sink. Considering the karstic nature of the mountain aquifer, the likelihood of groundwater contamination, especially of the upper layers of the aquifer, is very high. Therefore, it is probably a matter of time before the accumulated contamination reaches hazardous proportions in that region, which had about 30 percent of the agricultural wells and some of the freshest springwater in the West Bank. An additional, immediate hazard of untreated wastewater is that farmers, such as in the Nablus and Bethlehem areas, use it to irrigate crops, exacerbating the potential for water-related diseases.

The Israeli settlements contribute to water contamination as well. Their septic tanks regularly leak into the aquifer system; the hasty construction of the settlements without adequate sewage systems was feared, by the Israeli ministries of agriculture and energy, to pose a threat to the waters even inside Israel. Many of the Jewish settlements also are located on hilltops and ridges and let their untreated wastewater flow in the direction of Palestinian farms and villages, which they overlook.[170]

The sanitation problem was more grave in Gaza. Although all the towns were linked to a sewage network and the number of households without latrines was negligible, only 40 percent of the houses in the municipalities actually were connected to the network.[171] The refugee camps and villages were not connected to the sewage network. UNRWA initially built public latrines in the belief that the refugee camps were going to be temporary. From the early 1960s, however, UNRWA started to encourage private latrines, which gradually became common.[172] The latrines proved to be a

169. Hulayli, 1987.
170. Bellisari, 1993, pp. 11–12, citing Fletcher.
171. Ibid., p. 9.
172. Ibid., citing an UNRWA report; and Krafft, 1985.

"first rate health hazard" because they filled up quickly and over-flowed, contaminating streets and neighborhood property.[173] In all likelihood, they were also responsible for the high rate of nitrates in the groundwater in the camp area.[174]

One of the striking sights alongside the roads in the camps is the narrow, open ditches that convey the gray wastewater. These ditches in and of themselves are a health hazard. They also deliver the wastewater to open ponds at the lower ends of the camps, where water stagnates, acquiring repugnant odors and inviting microbes.

The lack of sewage systems, water contamination, and associated health problems existed before the Israeli occupation. However, since 1967 the growth of population and the increase in domestic water consumption have exacerbated the situation. Building a working sewage system could have circumvented such an outcome.

The reasons for the neglect of the sewage system were not very different from those that led to the deterioration of the infrastructure in general, as discussed earlier. The few sewage projects that have been implemented or planned resulted from external assistance. A number of projects to link the camps of Jabalia and al-Shati' in Gaza with the town's sewage system were underway in the early 1990s, financed by UNRWA and the UNDP.[175] Other plans, however, faced obstacles. In Nablus, a scheme for a wastewater treatment plant has not seen the light owing to the shortage of funds and landownership disputes.[176] A partially-implemented regional wastewater treatment scheme in the Khan Yunis area of southern Gaza was halted after it was learned that the treated water was going to go to Israel.

While the immediate adverse effects are felt primarily by the Palestinians, Israel itself could be affected in the long run because the West Bank is the chief replenishment area of the northern and western basins of the mountain aquifer. Even from Gaza the potential for negative environmental impact on Israel is not a remote possibility, as happened in the early 1990s when out of desperation the wastewater of Dayr al-Balah was diverted into the Mediterra-

173. Krafft, 1985.
174. Bruins and Tuinhof, 1991, p. 21.
175. Ibid.
176. Center for Engineering and Analysis, 1992, p. 82.

nean. In addition to worsening Gaza's already polluted seafront, the contaminants could be washed onto the Israeli shore by the sea current. On one hand, the more the water resources in the West Bank and Gaza are contaminated, the more the Palestinians will have to seek cleaner sources—which only can sharpen the water conflict. On the other hand, wastewater treatment, would make available for reuse one-third to one-half of the domestic water for irrigation.

WATER SUPPLY AFTER THE DECLARATION OF PRINCIPLES

One of the premises of peace making between the Israelis and Palestinians has been that peace would improve the living conditions of the latter. In turn, such improvement would help cement the peace. To bring about these results, at least during the transitional phase of Palestinian autonomy, Israel relaxed its grip, granting the Palestinians self-government in civil affairs and permitting economic and technical assistance from the international community. However, the overall economic conditions have worsened. The reasons for this state of affairs, which cannot be investigated here, derive from the actions of the three main "actors"—Israel, the PA, and the international aid donors—as well as the relations among them.

A primary factor that has undermined the chances for bettering the economic conditions has been the security-related, recurrent closures by Israel of its borders with the West Bank and Gaza. The closures denied entry into Israel to tens of thousands of Palestinian workers whose remittances from Israel had become a main pillar of the Palestinian economy. It hampered the movement of imported goods and equipment to the Palestinian territories as well as of Palestinian exports to Israel and elsewhere. Apart from Israel's actions, the economic management of the PA has been largely chaotic, bureaucratic, and marred by nepotism because of lack of experience and innate deficiencies. Also, the conspicuous shortage of local expertise and the weak institutional structures inherited from Israeli rule contributed to the less than stellar performance of the PA.

The third "actor," the international aid donors, which include the EU, Japan, the United States, the United Nations, and the

World Bank, at first were slow to recognize the complexity of the situation they were facing as well as the need to stabilize a fluid situation. As a result, they have not been quick in dispersing the funds they had pledged.[177] For example, of $1.562 billion pledged for 1994 and 1995, only $794 million, or about one-half, were disbursed.[178] In addition to slow disbursement, the donors' effort was met with obstacles too intricate to be discussed here.[179] As a consequence of these cumulative problems, the premise of economic prosperity thus far has remained just that, a premise.

Provisions of the Accords

In the water sector tangible improvements have yet to materialize. The Cairo and Taba accords contained provisions for increasing the water supply, protecting the environment, and giving the Palestinians a voice in the management of the water sector. Presently, reference will be made to the first two provisions; the third will be addressed in the next chapter. The water increase, according to the Taba Agreement, was to be 70–80 mcmy, including an immediate 28.6 mcmy for household use, 10 mcmy of which was to be reserved for Gaza and 18.6 for the West Bank (Annex III, Article 40.6). Gaza's 10 mcmy and 4.5 mcmy of the West Bank's increase were to come from Israel's network. However, Israel was to bear the capital costs of only 9.5 mcmy, 5 mcmy of which was for Gaza. For the remaining 19.1 mcmy, the costs were to be borne by the PA. Although economically beneficial, the water supply by Israel deepens the linkage of the Palestinian water system with Israel's, especially since Mekorot already provided about one-fourth of the municipal water in the West Bank. Regarding the overall additional 70–80 mcmy, the bulk of this volume was to come from the eastern aquifer, where the main portion of the water not yet exploited was brackish. Harnessing such water requires relatively large initial outlays and can pose an environmental hazard because of potential brine leakage into the source aquifer, as is discussed in chapter 5 in conjunction with alternative water resources.

177. The pledges amounted to about $2.4 billion for the years 1994–98, mainly for infrastructural projects, including water; see Brynen, 1996, p. 79.
178. *Journal of Palestine Studies*, 1996, table p. 142.
179. An analysis of these questions up to the end of 1995 is available in Brynen, 1996.

Projects for the extraction and distribution of the above mentioned quantities as well as the licensing and drilling of new wells had to be approved by the Joint Water Committee (JWC), which was created by the agreement for the approval of the "geo-hydrological and technical details and specifications" (Annex III, Article 40, Schedule 8.7). The JWC was to consist of an equal number of members from each side, and its decisions were to be taken by consensus (Annex III, Article 40.12.). There was no recourse for mediation or arbitration for resolving disputes. Such an arrangement effectively granted Israel veto power over decision making because it was the Palestinians who needed the new wells; the settlements' water supply was to stay at the preagreement levels. It thus left the improvement and expansion of the Palestinian water sector in the West Bank to Israeli goodwill.

In the sphere of water protection, the Taba accord included only general "principles," such as preventing any harm to the water resources including those used by the other side and the coordination of the operation, development, and maintenance of sewage systems. The principles were quite general; to be effective they would have had to be more specific. For example, in the clause on wastewater the two sides agreed to "Treating and reusing or properly disposing of all domestic urban industrial and agricultural sewage" (Annex III, Article 40.3.f). What the provision obviously omitted were treatment standards. The omission might have been a useful loophole for the Palestinians, who still lacked the resources for meeting more stringent requirements, but Israel could have accepted voluntarily to treat the wastewater of the settlements to more specific standards, perhaps with an understanding that in time the Palestinians would follow suit. As it stood, the principle was an improvement in standards but fell short of an effective commitment to water protection.

International Aid

Increasing water supply and water protection required investments in the requisite infrastructure, wells, pipe networks, sewage systems, and treatment plants. This is where the role of the donors came in. The donors, at least theoretically, defined a set of strategic objectives that would be pursued by each donor. These objectives included (1) new water sources, (2) water conveyance system, (3)

TABLE 2.7 Sample of Projects in the West Bank and Gaza Aided by International Donors[a]

Donor	Project description	End Date	Funding (US$ million) Committed[b]	Paid
Canada	Gaza water and sewage	12/1996	3.35	
European Union	Sanitation drainage Rafah (Gaza)	1997	19.50	1.30
Finland	Sewage system masterplan Ramallah (W.B.)	11/1996	0.35	
France	Assistance to Palestinian Water Authority	1/1996	2.40	.60
	Water and sewage masterplan	1996	0.60	
Germany	Drilling wells, planning institutional development Ramallah (W.B.)	12/1996	5.09	2.00
Italy	Domestic water supply, Jericho (W.B.)	12/1997	3.00	
Japan	Internal sewers, storm drainage, and road work Beach Camp (Gaza)		1.70	1.70
	Water supply phase II, Khan Yunis (Gaza)	6/1997	1.95	1.95
Netherlands	Hydraulics course development Birzeit University (W.B.)		3.00	
Norway	Establish and develop Palestinian Water Authority	1998		
Sweden	Storm water drainage Jabalia Camp (Gaza)			10.00
USA	Upgrading storm water and sewage, phases I-IV Shaykh Radwan (Gaza)	1999	40.00	12.00
	Village water supply Jinin (W.B.)	1998	5.60	

SOURCE: Local Aid Coordination Committee (LACC) for Development Assistance in the West Bank and Gaza, 1996.
NOTE:
[a]Data as of July, 1996.
[b]"Committed" is amount donor has agreed to provide; "paid" is actual sum disbursed.

wastewater collection, (4) demand side management, and (5) improved municipal capacity for collecting and generating revenues. The United States, for example, was to undertake projects related to all those objectives and the World Bank to (2) and (3).

A long list of donors and projects planned, initiated, and completed was published by the Local Aid Coordination Committee for the United Nations and the World Bank, the two bodies that emerged as the main coordinators of the donors' assistance program.[180] It indirectly confirms the critical water and sewage problems plaguing the West Bank and Gaza. The projects, a "random" sample of which is shown in table 2.7, ranged from the very small, like a training course in groundwater modeling by the Netherlands (cost, $384,000), to enhancing the water supply in the Hebron-Bethlehem area by the United States (estimated cost, $14.4 million). They were inclusive, with the attendant risk of being spread too thin. Their clear focus was on the municipalities, which handled household water supply. It was difficult from the outline to determine how far the projects would overlap and whether the available local "human resources" would be sufficient to meet the demands of this sudden influx of interest. The costs obviously reflected (among other things) the high overhead that would be paid to the nonlocal staff and price of materials supplied from the donor countries, which often had clauses in their foreign aid statutes giving preference, if not mandating, the use of their own nationals and materials.

The projects that could make a palpable local difference, notably of augmenting water supply and extending sewage systems and treatment plants, needed time for completion. When the list of projects was published in July 1996, none of the main water supply enhancement works had begun. It is, therefore, too early to assess the outcome of the donors' efforts. On the face of it, if most of the schemes were implemented they would have a positive impact, notably in the area of sewage collection. However, whether Gaza and the West Bank will end up with a few showcase projects or an enduring betterment of their water systems remains to be seen. On the supply side, the additional water provided in the Taba Agreement, even if it all materialized, would still lag behind the estimated Palestinian demand, as indicated in chapter 3.

180. Local Aid Coordination Committee (LACC) for Development Assistance in the West Bank and Gaza Strip, 1996.

3

Water Economics in the West Bank and Gaza

Little has been done by way of systematic analysis of the economics of water in the West Bank and Gaza, in contrast to Israel where the water sector has been the subject of numerous analyses. The present chapter aims to broach the topic by examining current and projected water use patterns; extending the conventional water balance to include rainfed agriculture and traded foodstuffs; estimating the marginal value product of water (MVPW) in the agricultural sector; and exploring the potential of water pricing and markets for efficient and equitable water use.

In the municipal sector, I investigate the constraints on water demand, suggest that there is a latent demand that has gone unsatisfied, and examine the Israeli argument that the low demand is engendered by low income and the Palestinian argument that blames supply restrictions. Although the level of water use is generally substandard, it is more so in some localities than in others owing to the uneven demand among them. The unevenness of demand and its possible causes are examined through the disaggregation of the overall water use patterns, by district and by type of locality—town, village, and refugee camp. The general picture of municipal water demand is summed up through the demand schedule, with a focus on past pricing policy and suggestions for the future.

To analyze water demand in agriculture, I propose that the standard water balance, which includes only the irrigated sector, be extended to include the rainfed sector and the water used in the trade of foodstuffs and agricultural crops in general. The water consumed by rainfed agriculture is estimated in terms of "irrigation water equivalent" (IWE) of the amount of rainfall on the rainfed areas. Only the West Bank is considered because the rainfed area there is relatively large and comprises 95 percent of the cultivated area, whereas the rainfed land in Gaza is of minor significance. The water effectively traded through foodstuffs is defined as the water used for growing those imported and exported commodities. It is termed here "requisite" water.

A central topic in the economics of water in agriculture is the determination of the MVPWs. These are estimated for both the irrigated and rainfed sectors and, to be viewed in perspective, they are compared with their counterparts in Israel and Jordan. In addition, I examine the potential role of water pricing and markets in achieving water efficiency, conservation, and equity among users. The opportunities for, and impediments against, establishing well-functioning water markets in the West Bank and Gaza also are outlined, drawing primarily on the experience with water marketing in the United States.

Planning for the water sector and dividing the water resources of geographic Palestine between the Israelis and Palestinians require that there be at least a general idea about future, long-term demand. Both Israelis and Palestinians have made demand projections, and selected projections from both sides are evaluated critically.

MUNICIPAL DEMAND

Municipal water in the West Bank and Gaza subsumes all water which is consumed by households, commercial establishments, and industrial plants (the latter largely in the category of family workshops) that are located in the cities and receive water from the municipalities. The chief municipal water users, however, are households, and the term "municipal" almost always can be replaced by "household." Some industries such as stone cutting and washing and food processing obtain their water independently from the municipal supply. However, such water use in the late 1980s and early 1990s comprised only a fraction of the total water consumed by municipalities (estimated at 7–8 mcmy, of which 5 mcmy is for the West Bank and 2–3 mcmy is for Gaza).[1] Water

1. Awartani, 1991b.

allocation for industry is vital from a long-term planning point of view as it can be expected to grow to a point where it could make significant claims on the water resources. The interest here, however, is in municipal water.

Estimation of end users', or final, water demand faces two sources of uncertainty in addition to those cited in the previous chapter with respect to water supply. The f st has to do with the amount of water losses in the process of distribution, which makes it difficult to know the quantities of final demand. The statistics in the literature often refer to this as "pre-losses;" the pre-losses exaggerate the amounts delivered to households.

The second source of uncertainty pertains to the size of the Palestinian population living in the West Bank and Gaza; an accurate enumeration is needed for calculating per capita water use. However, only a single population census was taken in the two regions, in September 1967. By comparison, two full censuses have been taken in Israel itself, in 1972 and 1983.[2] The West Bank and Gaza census was conducted under curfew by Arabic-speaking Israeli personnel. Although the curfew might have ensured that everyone was at home at the time of the count, the military atmosphere surrounding the census and the fact that it was carried out by Israelis rather than Palestinians raised doubts about the reliability of the respondents' answers.[3] The official population statistics that have appeared since then are updates, accounting for birth and death rates and net migration. They usually do not include East Jerusalem, which Israel formally annexed in 1967; its population since has been subsumed under Israel's. Furthermore, the various Israeli agencies offered differing population estimates.[4]

The official estimates were examined critically by the West Bank Data Base Project (WBDP) led by Meron Benvenisti; it was concluded that the Central Bureau of Statistics undercounted the West Bank's population by 24 percent.[5] In its 1993 major report on the West Bank and Gaza, the World Bank also agreed with that

2. Benvenisti and Khayat, 1988, p. 27.
3. World Bank, 1993a, vol. 6, pp. 5–7.
4. For example, the following figures for West Bank population were given in 1980: 704,000 by the Central Bureau of Statistics; 871,000 by the Ministry of Interior; and 750,000 by the military government in the West Bank. See Benvenisti and Khayat, 1988, p. 27; these figures also are cited in World Bank, 1993a, vol. 6, pp. 5–7.
5. M. Benvenisti, 1984.

conclusion, although it arrived at a lower figure for the underestimation. It estimated the Palestinian population in 1992 at 1.2 million in the West Bank and 800,000 in Gaza, or an aggregate of 2 million, in contrast to the 1.68 million figure given by Israel's Central Bureau of Statistics.[6] With respect to the higher World Bank figures, it was unclear whether the 1.2 million total for the West Bank included the Palestinian population of East Jerusalem.

The WBDP's 1987 estimate was adopted as a benchmark for the analysis of demographic trends in the survey by Marianne Heiberg et al. That study contains the most rigorous demographic and socioeconomic analysis of the West Bank and Gaza to date.[7] The survey used various scenarios of population growth rates to project the population from 1987 onward. Ultimately, however, only an unbiased census can put the uncertainty about the size of the West Bank and Gaza population to rest. In this text I employ the WBDP's 1987 estimate as a baseline and then project the population for subsequent years. I assume an exponential growth with a rate equal to the average of the rates reported by Israel's Central Bureau of Statistics between the years 1987 and 1993.[8] Thus, the 1987 population of the West Bank is assumed to be 1.2 million, with an annual growth rate of 3.7 percent. The corresponding figures for Gaza are 633,000 with a 4.6 percent annual growth rate. The growth rates may strike the reader as being too high, but they are sensitive to migration, which was characterized by a net inflow in the early 1990s, during and after the crisis in Kuwait.[9] Accordingly, the population for the early 1990s is as follows:

Year	West Bank	Gaza	Total
1990	1,344,227	726,669	2,070,896
1991	1,394,894	760,876	2,155,770
1992	1,447,472	796,693	2,244,165
1993	1,502,031	834,198	2,336,229
1994	1,558,647	873,467	2,432,114

6. World Bank, 1993a, vol. 6, pp. 5–7.
7. Heiberg et al., 1993.
8. Ibid.; Abdeen and Abu-Libdeh, 1993, table 25; and Israel, Central Bureau of Statistics, 1994, p. 786.
9. Israel, Central Bureau of Statistics, 1994, p. 786.

TABLE 3.1 Structure and Evolution of Palestinian Water Use in the West Bank

Population & water use	Year			
	1967	1985	1990	1994
Population (millions)	0.6	0.81	1.34	1.56
M & I				
Total water use	6	20	47	50
Total per capita (m³)	10	25	35	32
Irrigation				
Total water use	75	90	80	70[a]
Total per capita (m³)	125	111	59	45
M & I and irrigation				
Total water use	81	110	127	120[b]
Total per capita (m³)	135	136	94	77

SOURCES: Benvenisti, 1984; BUNT, 1994; Heiberg et al., 1993; Kahan, 1987; Tahal, 1990; and World Bank, 1993a, vol. 5.
M & I = municipal and industrial.
NOTES:
[a]For 1992.
[b]This is close to the average use of 118 mcmy according to the Taba Agreement (Annex III, Article 40, Schedule 10).

Latent Municipal Demand

The evolution of water use in the West Bank and Gaza is exhibited in tables 3.1. through 3.4 and summed up graphically in figure 3.1. The tables illustrate the structure, temporal trends, and sectoral and spatial distribution of water use. The data of municipal and industrial use in tables 3.1 and 3.2 represent "pre-losses."

FIGURE 3.1 Per Capita Water Use in the West Bank and Gaza

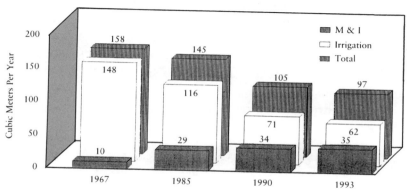

TABLE 3.2 Structure and Evolution of Palestinian Water Use in Gaza

Population & water use	*1967*	*1985*	*1990*	*1993*
Population (millions)	0.48	0.53	0.73	0.83
M & I				
Total water use	5	19	24	32
Total per capita (m³)	10	36	33	39
Irrigation				
Total water use	85	66	68	75
Total per capita (m³)	177	125	93	90
M & I and Irrigation				
Total water use	90	85	92	107
Total per capita (m³)	187	161	126	129

(column group header: Year, spanning 1967–1993)

SOURCES: Same as for table 3. 1; and Shawwa, 1993a, 1993b.
M & I = municipal and industrial.

The average per capita municipal use (including the small amount of industrial use) in the West Bank and Gaza in 1993, according to figure 3.1, averaged 35 m³, the same as was reported by Tahal.[10] Consumption more than tripled between 1967 and the end of the 1980s but has stagnated since. Whether and to what extent it might increase as a result of the Taba Agreement's provisions for additional municipal water—28.6 mcmy—will depend on the speed of making it available to the consumers. If the pace is slow, the augmentation of supply may be offset by population growth.

Whatever the case may be in the future, analysts generally agree that the current municipal water use in the West Bank and Gaza is substandard, several times lower than in Israel.[11] However, they differ as to the reasons for the modest use. The Israeli standard explanation has been to attribute it to the low income in the Palestinian territories.[12] The Palestinians, on the other hand, have adduced it to the restrictions on access to the water resources in the West Bank and to the inadequacy of the water in Gaza's aquifer. The controversy warrants further scrutiny.

10. BUNT, 1994, pp. 3.5–3.6.
11. See, for example, World Bank, 1993a, vol. 5, p. 52.
12. Boneh and Baida, 1977–78; and Israel Ministry of Foreign Affairs, 1982a.

Basic economics tells us that there is a relationship between the levels of income and demand of a particular good. Put simply, a change in income, while everything else stays constant, causes a shift in the demand curve. If income rises, the demand curve shifts upward, that is, demand increases, and the opposite happens when income drops. The extent of the shift depends on the income elasticity of demand, or the ratio of the percentage change in quantity demanded to the percentage of change in income. Formally, the income elasticity of demand, e, can be expressed this way:

$$e = [(Q_2 - Q_1)/Q_1/[(I_2 - I_1)/I_1$$

In the above equation, Q stands for the quantity demanded and I for income. If income, say, tangibly falls but demand does not drop or drops by a small amount, demand is said to be inelastic or to have a low elasticity. In other words, the demand is rigid, not responsive to the change in income.

A tally of income elasticities of demand for water from around the world show that they vary widely among countries, regions within the same countries, types of municipal use, and methods of estimation (whether based on time-series or comparative data, for example).[13] For instance, the income elasticity of demand for municipal water in Puerto Rico was 0.15 (in 1975), but in the state of Georgia (the United States) it was 0.36–0.83 (in 1968). In northern Illinois, time-series data yielded an income elasticity of demand of 0.20–0.26, whereas cross-sectional data yielded an income elasticity of demand of 0.48–1.03.

Furthermore, global studies have indicated that, in addition to being a function of income, water use is influenced by a number of other factors, including availability of water, price, metering, climate, and technology.[14] One way to illustrate these findings is by taking a comparative look at the demand for water in various countries. For example, whereas Malaysia and Mexico had comparable per capita incomes, their annual per capita municipal water demands were 175 m³ and 70 m³, respectively.[15] Malaysia is a tropical, water-abundant country whereas half of Mexico is arid and semiarid, a difference that undoubtedly affects the level of

13. United Nations, 1980b, p. 89.
14. Ibid., p. 83.
15. World Bank, 1993a, vol. 5, p. 52.

TABLE 3.3 Household Water Use/capita versus GNP/capita in
Selected Arab Countries, 1990

Country	Use (cmy)	GNP/capita[1] ($)
Egypt	75	610
Jordan	50	1,690
Oman	58	6,120
Saudi Arabia	128	7,820
Syria	61	1,160
U.A.E.	295	19,860
Yemen	11	528
W.B. and Gaza	30	1,715

SOURCES: Based on Al Alawi and Abdulrazzak, 1994; PRIDE, 1992; Wakil, 1993; World Bank, 1993a, vol. 2; and World Resources, 1992–93.
U.A.E. = United Arab Emirates
NOTE:
[1]The GNP/capita for Egypt, Oman, Saudi Arabia, West Bank and Gaza, and Yemen are for 1991.

water use. It may be said that the substantial difference in the two countries' water demand also derives from cultural factors.

In order to eliminate, or at least substantially reduce, the effect of the cultural factor, I compare municipal water demand and per capita GNP in several Arab countries (see table 3.3). The table indicates that the two variables are broadly related, with higher income countries having greater per capita water use. It does not, however, enable us to derive or deduce specific water use levels from income levels. Nor does the proportional relationship between income and water use always hold. In Egypt, for example, water use exceeded that in Oman by about 30 percent; yet Omani personal income was nearly tenfold that of Egypt. The reason for such discrepancy between income and water demand is not hard to fathom. Egypt enjoyed a total water supply of more than 1,000 m³ per person, one of the highest in the Middle East, thanks to the Nile, and many times Oman's natural supply. Oman would have to harness alternative water resources to raise the level of demand to that of Egypt.

The Palestinian territories had a higher per capita income than Egypt, Jordan, and Syria, yet had lower level of municipal water use than all of them. Even within these territories themselves, demand is not always proportional to income, as is detailed below. Last, a comparison by the World Bank of water use in the West Bank and Gaza with other developing countries with similar income levels also concluded that the Palestinian territories ranked low in municipal water use.[16]

The unavoidable conclusion is that Israel's attribution of low water use level to low income in the West Bank and Gaza does not stand. Although there is a difference in income between the Israelis and Palestinians, other conditions that affect their demand—such as availability of water, pricing, and coverage of the water and sewage networks—were superior in Israel. Clearly a latent demand in the West Bank and Gaza has gone unsatisfied because of constraints other than income. This latent demand perhaps best can be estimated by a comparative approach. The most pertinent comparison is between the West Bank and Jordan because both had a similar level of municipal water use, 10 m³ per person per year, on the eve of Israel's 1967 seizure of the West Bank.

If the West Bank had remained part of Jordan, it would be reasonable to assume that its water use would have increased at a rate at least equal to that of Jordan. I stress "at least" because there was latent demand in Jordan itself, as evident from the rationing of water supply even in the capital city, Amman, during the summer. A study has estimated that Jordan's latent municipal water demand in 1990 was 47 mcmy, or 12 m³ per capita.[17] If this was added to the 50 m³ per capita of manifest demand, the "actual" demand would be 62 m³.[18] Thus, had the West Bank not fallen under Israeli occupation, and if the estimates of Jordan's use were accurate, its annual per capita municipal water use also would have been about 62 m³. If it is assumed that Gaza's latent demand was equal to that of the West Bank, the aggregate latent demand of both regions in 1990 would be 57 mcmy. In other words, the Palestinian municipal demand in that year should have been 128 mcmy instead of the manifest 71 mcmy. Furthermore, by the time of the Taba Agreement it should have been about double the manifest demand.

Still, it does not necessarily mean that demand in the West Bank would double instantly if restrictions were lifted. For that to happen, piped water would have to be extended to virtually all the villages, and the coverage of the sewage system would have to be

16. Ibid.
17. Project in Development and the Environment, 1992, p. 8.
18. The figure of 50 m³ is from al-Fataftah and Abu Taleb, 1992, p. 160.

TABLE 3.4 Household Water Charges in Amman, Jordan, 1990

Block (m³)	1–20	21–40	41–100	>100
Rate ($/m³)	0.18	0.30	0.60	0.75

SOURCE: Jordan, Ministry of Water and Irrigation, Archives, 1992.

substantially more extensive than it is at present. Moreover, the price would have to change. Municipal water was substantially cheaper in Jordan than in the West Bank. By far, the highest water charges were in Amman. The prices were progressive, in the form of block rates, with the upper blocks subsidizing the lower, as indicated in table 3.4. The meters were read once every three months, and the blocks applied for that period. Based on table 3.4, I have estimated the average price in 1990 to have been around $0.30/m³.[19] Even such an upperbound rate was less than one-third of the average price in the West Bank, as is indicated below. How each of the factors—extension of piped water and sewage system and pricing—would affect demand can be determined only through in-depth research.

High Prices and Unequal Demand

The foregoing discussion focused on the overall, average demand. However, both price and quantity demanded are uneven among districts and types of locality—urban, rural, and refugee camp. This unevenness is illustrated in tables 3.5 and 3.6.

The demand schedule for 1993 was a step function reflecting, on the one hand, the uniformity of the price in the same district and, on the other hand, its variation among districts (see figure 3.2). One was to the left of the precipitous drop of price and applied to most of the West Bank districts, whereas the second, to the right of it, applied to Gaza and the Jericho and Tulkarm districts. About half of the water was sold at more than $1/m³ and one half at $0.40/m³ or less. In Gaza, the average was $0.40/m³, and in the West Bank $1/m³, virtually identical with the price in Israel where the average personal income was many times that of the West Bank. Overall, the average price in the Palestinian territories was about

19. This is calculated on the basis of a household size of 5.5 persons and an average annual demand of 50 m³ per capita. The average household thus consumes about 70 m³ every three months, the collection period.

TABLE 3.5 Municipal Water Supply by District in the West Bank and Gaza

District	% with no piped water[a]	Price ($/m³) 1990	Price ($/m³) 1994	Annual per-capita supply (m³) 1990	Annual per-capita supply (m³) 1994
West Bank					
Bethlehem	1	1.2	1.2	23	24
E. Jerusalem	0	1.2	1.2	44	45
Hebron	18	1.2	1.2	19	21
Jericho	11	0.2	0.3	87	94
Jinin	53	1	1	21	29
Nablus	44	1.4	1.2	38	49
Ramallah	14	1.2	1.2	32	35
Tulkarm	39	0.3	0.4	34	43
Total	25	1.0	1.0	31	36
Gaza		0.2[b]	0.4	29	32[c]

SOURCES: ARIJ-HIID, 1994; Barghouti et al., 1993; BUNT, 1994, pp. 3.5–6; and El-Jaafari, personal correspondence, January 1996.
NOTES:
[a]Percentage of households; figures for 1990.
[b]This is an average. Prices vary by locality, ranging from $0.15 to $0.45 on the basis of a monthly household withdrawal of 30 cm. (European Community, 1993, p. 8).
[c]For 1993.

TABLE 3.6 Per Capita Household Water Use by Type of Locality, West Bank, 1991

Use	Camp	Rural	Urban
Pre-losses			
Annual (m³)	16	16	36
Daily			
(liter)	43	43	99
(gallon)	11	11	26
Post-losses[a]			
Annual (m³)	10	14	24
Daily			
(liter)	28	38	64
(gallon)	7	10	17

SOURCE: Calculated from Haddad and Abu Ghusha, 1992.
NOTE:
[a]Technical losses in towns and camps = 35 percent; in villages, 10 percent.

FIGURE 3.2 Municipal Water Demand Function in the West Bank
and Gaza, 1994

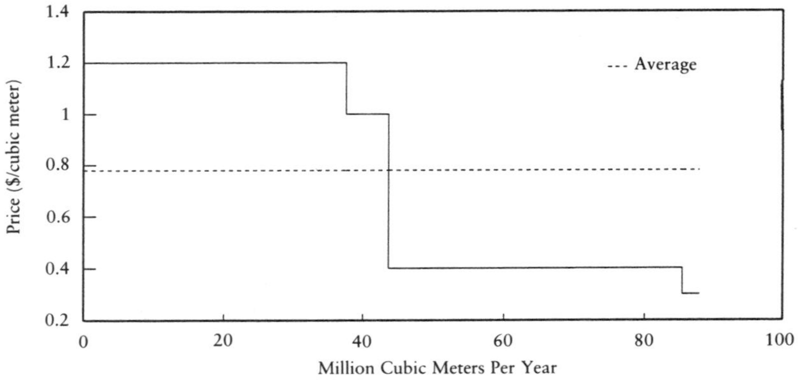

$0.80, represented by the straight line in the figure. The area under
the demand schedule, $70 million, represented what the consumers
paid and as such could be seen as a measurement of the economic
value of municipal water in the West Bank and Gaza.

The high price in most of the West Bank districts was a function of supply costs, which in turn depended on hydrogeological
factors, Israeli policies regarding water, and the general atmosphere
of the occupation. A proper accounting of supply costs would cover
both fixed and variable costs, including those of interest on capital,
extraction, and transportation. These obviously vary from one locality to another, depending on the type of water source, depth of
water table, elevation of the locality, and the locality's distance
from the water source. Reliable itemized data on supply costs in
the West Bank are lacking; what is available are some extraction
costs estimates that, nonetheless, should be indicative of the range
of supply costs. For example, in Jericho, municipal water comes
mainly from springs, which, of course, means it has no extraction
costs. Gaza's wells are shallow, and the extraction costs have been
estimated at $0.1–0.15/m^3 in the early 1990s.

In the Tulkarm district the water comes from wells shallower
than in other West Bank districts because it is located in the semicoastal zone; the extraction costs from these wells were put at
$0.16/m^3.[20] In contrast, in districts like Ramallah, the wells sup-

20. Awartani, 1991a, p. 51; and Shawwa, 1993b. It is unclear what
classes of costs are included in these figures.

plying municipal water are deep and the costs of extracting and lifting the water are greater. For deep wells, there is only one account by the Jerusalem Water Undertaking of energy expenditures for pumping the water and lifting it to the tower of Ramallah's twin town, al-Bira. This source puts the energy costs at $0.34/m^3 in 1990.[21]

The higher prices to the Palestinian municipalities, and hence to the consumers, also have had to do with Israeli price structures and policy. Drilling a deep well in the West Bank, for example, required perhaps four times the outlays of its counterpart in Jordan because the Palestinians had to use Israeli contractors, equipment, technicians, and even guards to ensure the security of the operation.[22] Moreover, when the water was supplied by Mekorot, as was about one-quarter of municipal water in the West Bank, the costs went up considerably. For instance, Jerusalem Water Undertaking calculated that the cost of water produced from its own wells was more than 50 percent cheaper than the water it purchased from Mekorot.[23] Mekorot charged that water utility and the rest of the municipalities (through the Water Department) more than $0.60/m^3. At the same time, it sold the water to the Israeli Jerusalem municipality for only $0.26/m^3.[24] The discriminatory price markups were in line with the general Israeli water pricing policy, which applied dual standards, one for its own citizens and settlers and another for the Palestinian population, as is discussed in the next chapter. In addition, the charges to households included increments by the municipalities themselves for covering their own expenditures. The accumulated costs and mark-ups added up to $1.2/m^3 charged to the consumers in most of the West Bank.

The quantities demanded in each district were also uneven. The following patterns were observed in water use data for 1990 and 1994. Jericho was by far the lead consumer, whereas Hebron consumed the least amount. In the middle range of use were most of the other districts. East Jerusalem's water demand was clearly higher than average, and that of Jinin lower than average. Incidentally, including East Jerusalem in West Bank water statistics tends to raise the overall average of water use.

21. Jerusalem Water Undertaking, 1991, p. 54.
22. Abd al-Karim As'ad, Interview, March 1992.
23. Jerusalem Water Undertaking, 1991.
24. As'ad, Interview, March 1992; in local currencies, JWU's rate was NIS1.80 and Jerusalem municipality's NIS0.77 ($1 = NIS3).

Jericho's demand estimates are sensitive to slight changes in the amount of total use and population size because its population is small, only around 15,000. Nonetheless, this district would be expected to have higher use relative to other areas. In it flow the most abundant springs; the price of water is the lowest, only 20 percent of the West Bank average; and the climate is warm in winter and very hot in the summer (when temperature can reach 45 degrees Celsius). Not an insignificant fraction—perhaps as much as one-half—of the household water in Jericho goes to home gardens, which are more prevalent and intensive than in other areas, owing to the traditional availability and low cost of water.

The low demand in Hebron must be attributed to the terribly inadequate supply in this town, as noted in the previous chapter, for it was much lower than other districts with comparable price levels. Jinin's lower use was most likely a result of the large proportion of the population—47 percent—without running water. One would have expected both Bethlehem and Ramallah to have greater demand than is indicated in the table because these two districts, together with East Jerusalem, enjoy a more privileged access to economic resources (as measured by a higher score on a specially designed wealth index for the West Bank and Gaza) than the northern and southern districts.[25] However, actual demand was only slightly above the average in Ramallah and below average in Bethlehem.

In Gaza, the average demand was close to that in the West Bank, even though Gaza's access to economic resources was less than in the West Bank. If such access were the only factor determining water demand, Gaza's demand would be lower than that of the West Bank. That demand in the two regions was nearly equal must be attributed to the fact that, in spite of all the problems that plagued the coastal aquifer in Gaza, curbs on water withdrawal there were less enforced because no water flowed from its aquifer to Israel.

The inequality of water consumption in the West Bank and Gaza was also present along the urban-rural-refugee camp divides, with the pre-losses in the urban localities being more than double those in the villages and refugee camps. The reasons were not hard to find. The population that did not receive piped water was overwhelmingly rural, and the villages and camps scored much lower

25. Heiberg et al., 1993, pp. 157–61.

on the above-cited wealth index than did the urban areas.[26] Furthermore, the living space in the camps often was limited and houses had small yards with little space to spare for home gardens. In Gaza, the rural-urban division was hard to delineate due to its small area and high degree of urbanization.

To recapitulate, municipalities in most West Bank districts paid a higher price for water than did those in Israel, where the personal income of households was many times that of the West Bank.[27] The high price was partly a reflection of the high cost of drilling wells, especially in hilly terrain where water was found in deep strata, and partly of the extra costs stemming from Israeli occupation, such as higher drilling costs and markups by Mekorot. The per capita demand in the West Bank and Gaza depended on the availability of water, price, and access to economic resources. It was unequal, notably among urban areas, villages, and refugee camps.

IRRIGATION WATER

The analysis of water demand in agriculture is essential because it is the principal water-consuming, commodity-producing sector in the West Bank and Gaza. Agriculture in all its branches contributed nearly one-third of the GDP, a high proportion compared with developing countries having a comparable income level, such as Jordan where the share of agriculture was around 7 percent. As table 3.7 shows, agriculture's contribution first gradually declined, as happened elsewhere in the world in the process of modernization, then began to increase in the mid-1980s. This "revival" is hard to explain in light of the many restrictions to which the sector was subject and the weaknesses of institutions serving it. Probably the "revival" was the outcome of a combination of factors: the boycott of Israeli produce in the early years of the intifada; an increase in illicit exports to Israel; the availability of additional labor due to restrictions on Palestinian workers entering Israel during the intifada; and loss of jobs by Palestinians in Kuwait in the aftermath of the 1990–91 Gulf crisis.[28]

26. Ibid.
27. The comparison is based on prices for the Israeli households cited in Tahal, 1990, pp. 9.1–9.3.
28. Society for Austro-Arab Relations, 1992; and World Bank, 1993a, vol. 4, p. 2.

TABLE 3.7 Agriculture's Share of GDP at Factor Costs in the West
Bank and Gaza, 1970–90

(1986 prices)

Year	Share (%)
1970–71	36
1975–76	33
1980–81	29
1985–86	26
1987–88	31
1990–91	34

SOURCE: Calculated from World Bank, 1993a, vol. 4.

Overview of Agriculture in the West Bank and Gaza

The focus in this book is on plant agriculture, although animal husbandry also is vital for the economy, diet, and water demand. The output of the livestock branch in monetary terms ranged between about one-quarter and one-half of the total value of agricultural production in the West Bank and Gaza during the 1980s.[29] In the West Bank and Gaza, animal production was historically extensive (grazing), with feed provided naturally from pastures. Access of Palestinian herders to pastures has been considerably blocked since 1967 because of land acquisition by Israel. The processes and legal instruments through which Israel acquired Palestinian land in the West Bank and Gaza are complicated and go beyond the scope of the present text.[30] It is sufficient to point out that Israel acquired land by (1) declaring it a closed military area, (2) requisitioning it for purported military needs, (3) reclassifying it "state" land, (4) declaring it "abandoned," or (5) confiscating it for public purposes.

As part of the process of land control, and soon after its seizure of the West Bank, Israel declared the eastern slopes in the Ramallah and Bethlehem districts—one of the chief pasture areas in the West Bank—closed military areas. Likewise, the Palestinians were blocked from entry into the pasture land in the Tubas area, in the northeast of the West Bank. As a consequence, large tracts

29. Society for Austro-Arab Relations, 1992; and World Bank, 1993a, vol. 4, p. 42.
30. For a full treatment of the issue see Benvenisti, 1984; and Shehadeh, 1985.

of the slopes became inaccessible and remain so. The exact amount of pasture land that has been taken away from Palestinian herders is unknown, but it is believed to be substantial.[31] The reduction of the grazing area led to overgrazing in the remaining pasture lands, further reducing that space. To make up for the losses and meet rising demand for meat and dairy products, Palestinian livestock producers resorted to intensive feeding, importing fodder from Israel and elsewhere. From the perspective of water use, this was tantamount to forcing Palestinians to import water and forego the use of the rainwater that fell over the pastures. The water quantities thus denied and their value are extremely difficult to estimate from the existing information; these issues require further research.

Plant agriculture in the West Bank and Gaza can be divided into two sectors, the irrigated and rainfed (see map 3.1). In the West Bank, rainfed crops occupy nearly 95 percent of the cultivated land of 2 million dunums, including some 0.3 million dunums of fallow land. This is more than 20 times the irrigated area of 100,000 dunums (figure 3.3). In Gaza, the rainfed area is about 80,000 dunums, small in comparison with the West Bank. However, the irrigated land in Gaza exceeds 100,000 dunums, an area that is comparable with the irrigated land of the West Bank (figure 3.4). The rainfed sector is characterized by the scant use of modern inputs and low yields due chiefly to unreliable rainfall and fragmentation of land holdings. In the late 1980s and early 1990s, its share averaged nearly 60 percent of the total output (by weight) of West Bank agriculture and 40 percent of the total crop value in the West Bank and Gaza.[32]

The two sectors also are distinguished by the type of crops cultivated. In the rainfed areas, the main crops are fruit trees, notably olives, followed by stone fruits (almonds, apricots, plums, etc.), grapes and, decreasingly, figs. Field crops—wheat, barley, sorghum, and chickpeas—are the second major class of crops, while vegetables take up minor acreage. In the irrigated sector, the dominant crops are vegetables followed by fruit trees, mainly citrus and bananas. Geographically, the rainfed agriculture of the West Bank is practiced mainly to the west of the eastern slopes, in all

31. ARIJ, 1994; Kahan, 1987; Society for Austro-Arab Relations, 1992; and World Bank, 1993a, vol. 4.

32. The 60 percent figure is for the years 1989–90; it is my estimate based on statistics in Center for Rural Research, 1989 and 1990. The 40 percent is taken from World Bank, 1993a, p. 5.

MAP 3.1 District Boundaries of the West Bank

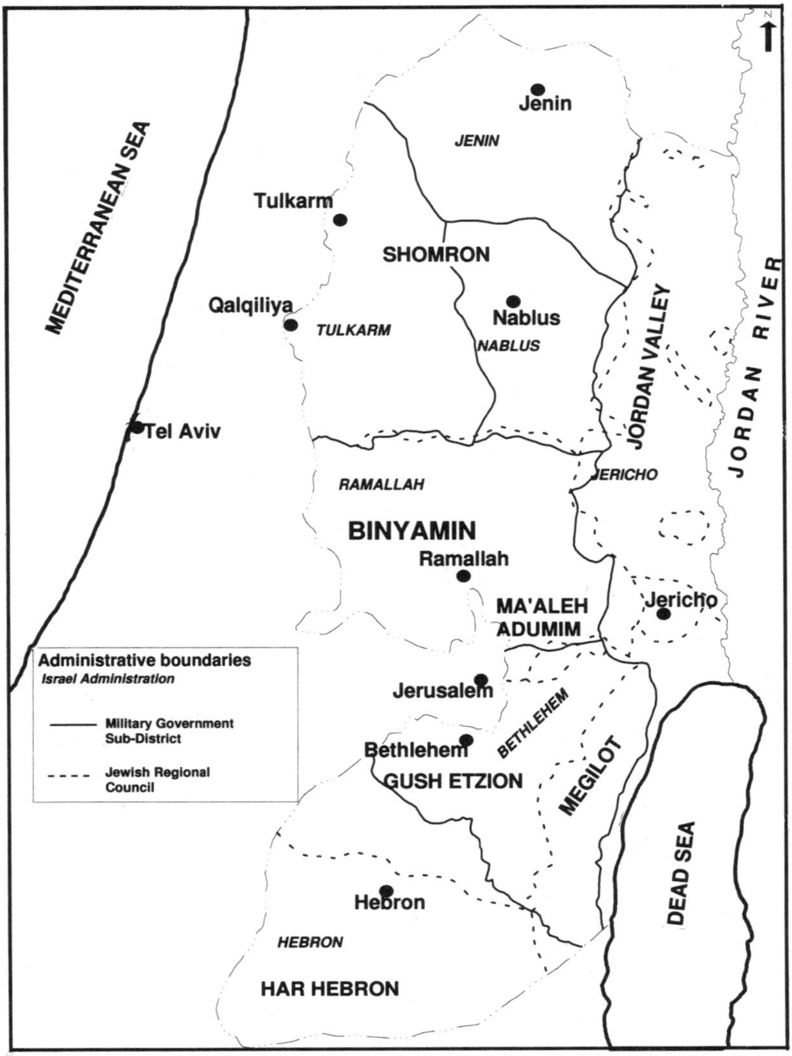

districts except Jericho; irrigated agriculture is concentrated in the three northern districts, Tulkarm, Jinin, and Nablus, as well as in the Jericho district (see figure 3.5). In Gaza, the rainfed land is concentrated in the north.

The foregoing geographical distribution is conditioned by the rainfall and topographic patterns, hydrology, and lack of irrigable land reclamation. The hills and semicoastal areas receive sufficient rain to sustain soil moisture levels during the summer that are

FIGURE 3.3 Irrigated and Rainfed Area in the West Bank

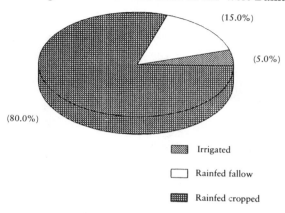

(15.0%)

(5.0%)

(80.0%)

Irrigated

Rainfed fallow

Rainfed cropped

Area in 1,000 dunums (Average 1973–91):
Irrigated 95; Rainfed cropped 1,670; Rainfed fallow 320

adequate for the types of rainfed crops cited above. The central hills also are rugged and not very well suited for irrigated agriculture. This is not the case in Tulkarm and Jinin, where the land is not as rugged and groundwater is available at easy to reach depths. In the Jordan Valley, there is a high soil-moisture deficit due to meager rainfall and high evaporation. However, the flat terrain, warm winters, and groundwater render the valley a unique region for irrigated agriculture, in particular making possible the production of fruits and vegetables in the middle of winter, and thus lending the valley a seasonal comparative advantage. Gaza also is endowed with natural conditions that provide a hospitable habitat

FIGURE 3.4 Irrigated and Rainfed Area in Gaza

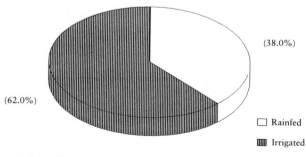

(38.0%)

(62.0%)

Rainfed

Irrigated

Areas in 1,000 dunums:
Irrigated = 115; Rainfed = 70

FIGURE 3.5 Irrigated Area by District in the West Bank

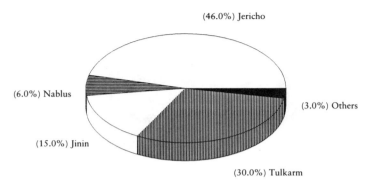

(46.0%) Jericho

(6.0%) Nablus

(3.0%) Others

(15.0%) Jinin

(30.0%) Tulkarm

for irrigated agriculture, namely sandy soil, flat terrain, warm climate, and water that can be extracted at shallow depths. In the northern part, rainfall levels of 400 mm allow for the practice of rainfed agriculture, whereas in the south the meager rainfall does not and crops must be irrigated. Because of the distinct character of rainfed and irrigated agriculture, their water-related features are examined separately.

Irrigation Quantities and Irrigated Areas

West Bank irrigated agriculture has missed out on what might be termed "the hydraulic revolution" that many Middle Eastern countries have undergone since World War II in the form of major irrigation works that, for better or worse, enabled them to enlarge considerably the irrigated land. This revolution is exemplified by projects such as the Aswan High Dam in Egypt, the al-Thawra (or Tabqa) Dam on the Euphrates in Syria, the Ataturk Dam in Turkey, and, on a smaller scale, the Water Carrier in Israel and the King Abdallah Canal in Jordan. The West Bank had no such projects and its irrigation system has remained decentralized, consisting of springs and individually owned wells. Its fall under Israeli rule led to the stagnation of the irrigation water supply at 1967 levels, a development which has proved to be an "effective constraint" on the expansion of irrigated land.[33] Likewise, the irrigation system in Gaza has remained decentralized, made up of hundreds of individ-

33. See, for example, Kahan, 1987, p. 114.

ually owned wells, and the irrigated area is constrained by the limited availability of land and water.

The volume of irrigation water fluctuated in the West Bank, staying in the range of 70–90 mcmy. It declined over time in Gaza, falling from 85 mcmy in 1967 to 75 mcmy in 1993, as indicated above in tables 3.1 and 3.2. In all, the agricultural sector's share of total water use in the Palestinian territories fell from about 85 percent in 1967 to 60–70 percent in the early 1990s, while the share of municipal use increased.

Water demand in agriculture was affected by (among other things) the size of the irrigated area, cropping patterns, and agricultural technology. The irrigated area in the West Bank declined initially after the occupation, reaching a nadir of 57,000 dunums in 1968, from 100,000 dunums in 1966. The decline was a result of Israel expropriating farmland in the Jordan Valley for inclusion in closed military areas and the destruction of water pumps along the Jordan River. During the 1970s, the irrigated area gradually was restored to its pre-occupation levels, vacillating around 85,000 to 100,000 dunums.[34] The expansion came about as a result of the reopening of Arab export markets, though these were volatile and hard to reach owing to the high transportation costs, fees charged by Israel, red tape in Jordan, and instability of inter-Arab politics. The introduction of the water-saving technology of drip irrigation also aided the expansion process. Gaza's irrigated area also grew steadily, although the trend is likely to be reversed. Farmers there extended their irrigated land to 90,000 dunums in 1968, from 75,000 dunums in 1966. They were able to do so because there was no immediate land takeover by Israel and because their citrus output found a ready outlet in Eastern Europe. The expansion continued, and by 1985 about 120 ,000 dunums were irrigated, or about one-third of Gaza's total area. The agricultural land, however, has come under pressures from population growth, intensive urbanization, and deteriorating water quality. Such pressures only can mount in the future, perhaps ultimately leading to a reduction of the cropland. In fact, there are indications that this already may be happening; by 1992 the irrigated area contracted to 110,000 dunums.[35]

34. Awartani and Juda, 1991, p. 5.
35. Shawwa, 1993b.

FIGURE 3.6 Irrigated Cropping Pattern in the West Bank

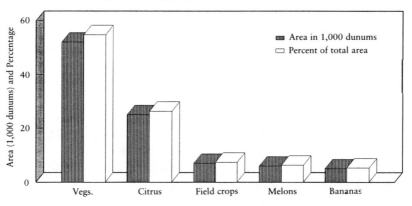

Bananas include other fruit
Vegetables include potatoes

Cropping Patterns

The major irrigated crop types in the West Bank are vegetables, with 50–60 percent of the irrigated area, and fruits, notably citruses in the Tulkarm district and bananas in the Jordan Valley (figure 3.6). Fruits and vegetables also predominate in Gaza, with citruses planted on more than one-half of the area in the late 1980s and early 1990s (figure 3.7). In the two Palestinian regions as a whole, vegetables are grown on 55 percent of the irrigated land and fruits on 45 percent. Among vegetables, tomatoes are the top

FIGURE 3.7 Irrigated Cropping Pattern in Gaza

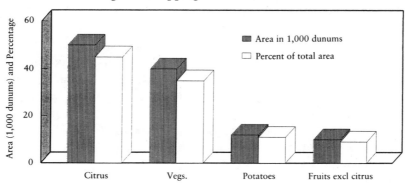

Total Irrigated Area = 112 thousand dunums

crop, followed by (not necessarily in descending order) eggplants, cucumbers, zucchini squash, and potatoes. The vegetables' acreage in both Gaza and the West Bank has expanded steadily since the early 1970s, whereas the citrus area in Gaza has shrunk.

The preceding describes the overall pattern; the fortunes of individual crops within each category are influenced by a variety of factors that ultimately translate into prices of produce. These factors include the state of export markets, regulations and costs imposed by Israel on exports, Israel's own exports to the Palestinian territories, and, in Gaza in particular, the increasing salinity of water. To illustrate, Gaza's citrus area had doubled to 70,000 dunums by 1980 from what it had been in 1968 due to the expanding export market in Eastern Europe, which actually had begun opening up before the occupation as a by-product of the burgeoning trade relations between Egypt and the eastern bloc. By 1993, however, the citrus area had been cut back to 55,000 dunums. The decline is adduced to several factors: Israeli curbs on Palestinian exports, including excessive marketing fees, to ward off competition with its own citrus exports; the loss of the principal export market in the former Yugoslavia; the increasing salinity of the water; and the spread of plant disease.[36]

Technological Change

Palestinian farmers traditionally have used straight or zig-zagged furrows (*dawalib*) for irrigating vegetables and basins for trees. These methods were suitable for the production factors existing up to the 1970s and may have had advantages in terms of washing the salts. Their water use efficiency, however, was low, as indicated in the previous chapter under the discussion of springs. The traditional methods have given way since the late 1970s to drip (or trickle) and sprinkler irrigation. In drip irrigation water is transported through pressurized hoses, with evenly spaced micro-holes from which water trickles directly around the plants' roots. This technology greatly enhances delivery efficiency (due to the virtual elimination of evaporation and seepage losses) and application efficiency (due to the slow and direct trickle of water to the plants'

36. Policy Research Incorporated, 1992, p. 13.

TABLE 3.8 Vegetable Area under Drip Irrigation in the West Bank and Gaza, 1988–90

(Area in 1,000 dunums)

Technology	West Bank	Gaza	Total
Drip and mulch	25.3	12.1	37.4
Drip and high tunnel	2.6	0.1	2.7
Drip and low tunnel	10.8	11.2	22.0
Drip and greenhouse	2.0	2.6	4.6
Total	40.7	26.0	66.7

SOURCES: Based on Awartani and Juda, 1991; Center for Rural Studies, 1989 and 1990; and Gaza Water Unit, 1990 (unpublished).

roots).[37] Apart from enhancing delivery and application efficiency and for a variety of agronomical reasons, drip irrigation significantly raises crop yields (i.e., output per unit of land area), thereby proportionally increasing water utilization efficiency (i.e., output per unit of water).[38] The impact of drip irrigation on yields is even more dramatic when it is combined with plastic tunnels or greenhouses. To illustrate, a dunum of cucumbers yields less than 1 ton under traditional furrow cultivation, 4 tons under drip irrigation without covers, and 10–15 tons under a combination of drip irrigation and greenhouse.[39]

These technologies have been diffused widely in the West Bank and Gaza owing to their water-saving and yield-augmenting characteristics, which, in the end, mean higher profitability, everything else being equal. In the late 1960s and early 1970s, Israel itself (for a host of reasons that cannot be taken up here) also encouraged their proliferation.[40] The extent of the adoption of these modern technologies in the two Palestinian regions is illustrated in table 3.8.

One of the interesting features of technological adoption has been the concentration of greenhouses in the Tulkarm district. Of the 1,960 dunums under greenhouse cultivation in 1990, a total of 1,845 dunums—93 percent—were in that district.[41] The cause of

37. See previous chapter for efficiency numbers.
38. See, for example, Elmusa, 1994a.
39. See ibid. for a detailed discussion of these technologies and their impact on agriculture.
40. Kahan, 1987, pp. 15–18.
41. Center for Rural Research, 1990, p. 17.

this remarkable spatial distribution of technological adoption is unclear. It could have been a consequence of access by the Tulkarm district's farmers to the "invisible" produce markets in Israel, owing to the proximity of the borders. However, Jinin also is close to the Israeli border and yet had only 60 dunums covered with greenhouses. Another, more plausible explanation is that farmers in the Tulkarm area may have had greater access to water than did farmers elsewhere. For example, while the irrigated area of Jinin was less than one-half that of Tulkarm, the former pumped an average 15–20 percent less from wells than the latter's.[42] The greenhouses require larger amounts of water per unit area than open-field cultivation because of double or even multiple cropping and high plant density, or number of plants per unit area. The water restrictions thus not only may have inhibited horizontal expansion of irrigated agriculture but also may have compromised certain types of agricultural intensification.[43] Nonetheless, the widespread adoption of the preceding modern technologies is what enabled Palestinian agriculture to survive under the severe constraints on water supply.

The technological change, however, was truncated and farmers have not been able to reap the full benefits of their investments. Their access to information on crop management and material use was handicapped by the cuts in the public extension personnel, transportation facilities, and office equipment, developments that are discussed in the next chapter.[44] Also, the Palestinian farmers have been restricted to Israeli input markets, the products of which may not necessarily be optimal for the physical conditions and factors of production in the West Bank and Gaza. These are not the only reasons for the inability of Palestinians to take advantage of technological change, but the purpose is not to investigate those reasons. The point I wish to make is that the limitations on technological change led to lower yields and crop quality than probably could have been achieved.

42. Data from the Water Department, ARIJ database (photocopy).
43. Whether the spread of greenhouses is desirable is another question. I have serious reservations about their spread under the present practices and management capabilities of farmers because they use heavy amounts of pesticides, including some of the most hazardous such as methanol bromide; these pesticides are harmful to workers who apply them with little protection, to consumers of the produce, and to the water resources. See further Elmusa, 1994a.
44. See also World Bank, 1993a, vol. 4.

Economics of Irrigation Water

The investigation of the economics of irrigation water in the West Bank and Gaza covers here the latent water demand, MVPW, utilization efficiency, implications of the existing pricing system on interregional equity and trade competitiveness, suggestions for an alternative pricing system, and potential for water markets. To place the findings and their ramifications in perspective, I will compare them with the corresponding parameters in Jordan and Israel. The assessment is confined to conventional inputs and outputs and does not include environmental and aesthetic considerations. These considerations are vital and must be incorporated in policy formulations, but information for their assessment currently is lacking.

Latent Water Demand in the West Bank's Irrigated Agriculture

The latent demand of irrigation water here refers to the demand that would have been manifest had the irrigated area been permitted to expand. The discussion is confined to the West Bank, where the potential for bringing more land under irrigation exists; in Gaza, the irrigated area would not have expanded more than it did under any political regime owing to its small area and rapid population growth. It has been estimated that there are 172,000 dunums—nearly double the currently irrigated area—of class-1 land in the West Bank. There is scant information on the attributes of this land, such as proximity to water. However, it is described as being readily irrigable without topographical or salinity constraints (table 3.9). This land is located mostly in the districts of Jinin and Tulkarm and the Jordan Valley. In the first two districts, as is pointed out in the next chapter, Israel left very little water for Palestinian irrigation. In the Jordan Valley, the Israeli settlers tapped 40 mcmy to irrigate land, with application rates nearly double those of the Palestinians.[45] The implication here is that had water been available, Palestinian farmers conceivably could have employed it to irrigate at least part of the 172,000 dunums.

45. Kahan, 1987, p. 113. Kahan reports that the water use was 712 cm/dunum in the Palestinian villages and 1,342 cm/dunum in the Israeli settlements.

TABLE 3.9 Soil Classes 1 and 2 by District in the West Bank
(Area in 1,000 dunums)

District	Class 1[a] Area	Class 1[a] Percent	Class 2[b] Area	Class 2[b] Percent	Total Area	Total Percent
Jericho	28.9	16.7	35.9	8.1	64.8	10.5
Nablus	14.0	8.1	57.8	13.1	71.9	11.7
Jinin	108.7	63.0	130.9	29.6	239.6	39.0
Tulkarm	11.9	6.9	42.9	9.7	54.7	8.9
E. Jerusalem[c]	9.1	5.3	174.8	39.5	183.9	29.9
Total	172.6	100	442.3	100	614.9	100
Percent of total		28.1		71.9		

SOURCE: West Bank Agriculture Department (unpublished report).
NOTES:
[a]Irrigable without physical constraints.
[b]Irrigable with salinity and slope constraints.
[c]Includes also Ramallah, Bethlehem, and Hebron.

In addition to class-1 land, there are also large tracts of class-2 land, the reclamation of which must contend with problems arising from salinity and topography. Little information is available about the potential of this land for reclamation, and not much can be added here. It is worth pointing out, however, that drip irrigation can enable farmers to surmount slope and even salinity problems in some areas. In Jordan, large areas of land in the highlands have been brought under irrigation as a result of drip irrigation and greenhouses.

Estimating the latent demand can be done, as was done for municipal water, by reference to Jordan and Israel (see table 3.10). It should be noted that the irrigated area in Israel declined after 1990, and the irrigated sector is slated to become the "shock absorber" of water deficits in drought years, as discussed in the next chapter, but this does not affect the inferences drawn here.

For the West Bank to have had per capita irrigated land equal to Jordan's in 1990, it would have had to bring under irrigation about 140,000 dunums, or 80 percent, of class-1 land and to tap nearly 125 mcmy of additional water. This might have been possible, given Jordan's own record and the West Bank's climatic conditions. In the Jordan Valley alone, Jordan brought more than 80,000 dunums under irrigation between 1968 and 1986, and the irrigated area in the country increased by more than 70 percent

TABLE 3.10 Water Use and Irrigated Area in Israel, Jordan, and the West Bank, 1990

	W. Bank	Israel	Jordan	Israel/ W Bank[a]	Jordan/ W. Bank[a]
Population (millions)	1.35	4.8	3.8	3.6	2.8
Irrigated area					
Total (1,000 dunums)	90	2,057	643	23	7
Per capita (dunum)	0.07	0.43	0.17	6	3
Water use					
Total (mcmy)	80	1,157	652	15	8
Per capita (cmy)	59	241	172	4	3

SOURCES: Previous tables; Israel Central Bureau of Statistics, *Statistical Abstract*, 1991; Project in Development and the Environment, 1992.
NOTE:
[a]Ratios other than that for populations are rounded up.

between 1973 and 1988. In the West Bank itself, the majority of class-1 land is in the semicoastal and Jordan Valley regions, where water could be tapped for irrigation if Israel were to release it. The utilization of relatively large areas would have required great amounts of labor, of course. Such labor could have been provided by the Palestinian labor force which commuted to work in Israel and/or labor from Arab countries, as happened in Jordan where the majority of farm workers on irrigated land are Egyptians.[46]

To match Israel, however, the West Bank would have had to reclaim greater land area and employ more labor than it would have needed to be on par with Jordan. All class-1 land would have had to be reclaimed, in addition to 317,000 dunums, or 70 percent, of class-2 land. To assess the possibilities of the expansion of class-2 land requires more information than is available about that land, as well as projections of the conditions that would have prevailed in the West Bank itself without the Israeli occupation. All that can be said at present, therefore, is that at a minimum the West Bank would have been able to develop all its class-1 land. Such an area would have required more than 150 mcmy of water in 1990, which may be viewed as the *minimum* latent demand of irrigation water in that year.[47]

46. Elmusa, 1994a.
47. The 152 mcmy figure is prorated according to the 1990 use: $172 \times \dfrac{80}{90} = 152$ mcmy.

Marginal Value Product of Water

Estimating the MVPW in agriculture can aid in decisions regarding the water allocation priorities among sectors, economic worthiness of investments in water projects (such as in wastewater treatment for use in agriculture), water-pricing policy, and optimum cropping patterns. The technicalities of such estimation are complicated by the lack of, or serious imperfections in, water markets; MVPW variability among crops, seasons, and over time; and mixing of water with other inputs (land, labor, materials) for agricultural production. Moreover, the results can diverge according to the method and assumptions used. For example, three attempts at measuring the value of water in Egyptian agriculture yielded widely different answers.[48] The most commonly used valuation procedure, which also will be employed here, is the method of "residual imputation."

In the residual method, the MVPW is calculated from the remainder of the gross value of output minus the costs of all inputs other than water. Formally, MVPW = (Gross value of agricultural output − fixed and variable costs excluding water's)/quantity of applied water. In other words, the residual indicates the maximum break-even point for water expenditures, or the price of one unit of water at which the farmer's net revenue diminishes to zero. For this to be valid, two conditions must hold. First, the prices of all the other resources are equal to their marginal value products. Second, the total value of the output can be divided into shares, each resource is paid according to its marginal productivity, and the total value product is completely exhausted.[49] The residual method is likely to underestimate the MVPW in the West Bank and Gaza because the two assumptions seldom hold. Input markets are imperfect and the timing and amounts of applications of the inputs are not necessarily those required for optimal yields due to the truncation of technological development. Besides not accurately reflecting the economic value of water, the residual method is time consuming: It requires gathering detailed farm budgets for each crop that include the amounts and prices of each, and crop yields and prices. Reliable farm budget data are not easy to come by in the West Bank and Gaza, and existing data are fragmented. None-

---

48. Bowen and Young, 1985; Kutcher, 1980; and Whittington and Haynes, 1980.
49. Young and Gray, 1985, pp. 1820–21.

theless, preliminary estimates are offered here from the available information for selected vegetable crops in the Jordan Valley, bananas in the West Bank, and citruses in the West Bank and Gaza. The budgets and attendant MVPWs are exhibited in tables 3.11 and 3.12.

Before delineating the MVPW for individual crops, clarifications regarding the unit water costs, which generally do not depend on the crops grown, are in order. The extraction costs of irrigation water varied according to the source, springs or wells, as indicated in the discussion of municipal water. To recapitulate, they averaged $0.17/m³ for well water and zero for springwater in the West Bank and $0.15/m³ in Gaza. Not all farmers owned wells, and those who purchased their water from wells owned by others were charged an extra $0.01–$0.02 cents/m³. How much water derived from owned wells and how much from sales is unknown, however. Anyway, the difference in the costs is minor, and I assume here that farmers paid $0.17/m³ for water from irrigation wells.

To the above costs must be added the expenditures of the earthen pools used for storing water (see chapter 3). These costs varied with the area being served by the pools and the pools' life span. Overall, I estimate that the pools added nearly $0.08/m³.[50] Thus, when farmers used pools they paid $0.08/m³ for springwater and $0.25/m³ for well water. The water quantities channeled through pools were unknown. It is reasonable, however, to impute the pool costs of $0.08/m³ to all the water as opportunity costs, on the premise that those farmers who did not own pools forewent the benefits they afforded. Accordingly, the demand schedule of irrigation water in the West Bank and Gaza in 1990 looked as follows:

	Spring water		Well water	
	Quantity (mcmy)	Price ($/m³)	Quantity (mcmy)	Price ($/m³)
West Bank	43	0.08	37	0.25
Gaza			68	0.15

50. This figure is based on the following data and assumptions: The number of pools in the Jordan Valley in 1990 was 177 serving 24,655 dunums, or about 140 dunums each; and the average cost of construction was $27,000. Assuming the average life span of the pool to be 20 years, the average annual depreciation would be $1,350. Assuming also that each dunum gets roughly 1,000 m³, the average cost would be = ($1,350)/140 × 1,000 = $0.08/m³. The data on costs and area served are from Abd al-Razzaq and Abu Salih, 1991.

TABLE 3.11 Efficiency and Marginal Value Product of Water (MVPW) for Selected Vegetable Crops in the Jericho District, 1992

Measure	Tomatoes mulch	Cucumbers mulch	Eggplants mulch	Zucchini tunnel	Melons tunnel
Yield (ton/dunum)	3	1.5	5	2.2	3
Water (m³/dunum)	700	450	900	400	600
Price ($/ton)	368	338	250	324	353
Costs ($/dunum)					
Production					
Machinery	34	29	34	7	29
Materials	284	162	294	162	241
Rent[a]	30	30	30	30	30
Labor[b]	251	126	226	206	75
Total	599	348	584	405	376
Marketing	166	59	176	82	140
Total (P + M)	765	406	761	487	515
Gross value ($/dunum)	1,103	507	1,250	712	1,059
Net returns ($/dunum)	338	101	489	224	544
Water output (ton/1,000 m³)	4	3	6	6	5
Water output ($/m³)	1.58	1.13	1.39	1.78	1.76
MVPW ($/m³)	0.48	0.22	0.54	0.56	0.91
Water costs/gross value of output[c]					
Spring water	0.05	0.07	0.06	0.04	0.05
Well water	0.16	0.22	0.18	0.14	0.14

SOURCES: Calculated mainly from data provided by Adil Brayghith, Jericho's Agricultural Station, 1993, ARIJ database.
NOTES:
[a]Land rent is estimated from the preliminary results of a survey of irrigated agriculture in the West Bank conducted by ARIJ, 1993–94.
[b]Labor costs are estimated on the basis of hired labor.
[c]Water costs are based on spring water price of $.08/m³ and well water price of $0.25/m³.

TABLE 3.12 Marginal Value Product and Efficiency of Water for
Citrus and Banana Production in the West Bank and
Gaza, 1992

| | West Bank | | Gaza |
Measure	Citrus	Bananas[a]	Citrus
Yield (ton/dunum)	3	3.5	2.3
Price ($/ton)	258	467	128
Water (m³/dunum)	700	2,500	480[b]
Total costs($/dunum)[c]	410	491	250
Gross value ($/dunum)	773	1,633	295
Water output (ton/1,000 m³)	4.3	1.4	4.8
Water output ($/m³)	1.10	0.65	0.6
Water cost/gross value	0.2	0.3	0.3
MVPW ($/m³)	0.52	0.46	0.1

SOURCES: Calculated from Abu Arafeh et al., 1992; Israel *Statistical Abstract*, 1993; Jericho
Agricultural Station, 1994, "Costs and Returns of Banana Production in the Jordan Valley" (photocopy).
NOTES:
[a]The results represent the average of the 4 years from planting to the time when the trees cease
bearing fruit.
[b]Water use in Gaza's citrus is less than the West Bank's because about 30,000 dunums of the
nearly 58,000 dunums get an average of 225 m³y/dunum.
[c]Water costs are not included. Marketing costs are included for citrus by adjusting the marketing
costs in table 3.11 in proportion to the citrus yields. Bananas have no marketing costs; they get
picked up by merchants at the orchard.

Thus, the average price for irrigation water in the West Bank and
Gaza in that year was nearly $0.16/m³.

The MVPW first will be estimated for vegetable crops. It can
be expected that the MVPW would vary by crop and region, for
these two parameters impinge on the input mix, costs of inputs,
water requirements, yields, and price of produce. No detailed data
are available that would permit the carrying out of dependable
interregional comparisons for vegetable crops. What data are available are limited farm budgets for a number of crops in the Jericho
district. The reliability of the figures themselves is hard to judge,
but they compare reasonably well with other fragments of evidence.[51] These budgets may not diverge appreciably from those of
other districts. The costs of material inputs other than water are
nearly similar throughout the West Bank. The Jordan Valley, however, enjoys a seasonal comparative advantage, and its crops may

51. See, for example, Awartani and Juda, 1991; and Society for Austro-
Arab Relations, 1992.

fetch higher prices during the winter months. In the end, the divergence in costs and benefits is minor because of the uniformity of the economic context in which production and marketing take place. Finally, the budgets give only "point" yields, whereas the yields vary with the quantities of water (and other inputs). Ideally, the water-yield response, or the elasticity of yield relative to water application, should be accounted for, but it is disregarded here for lack of data.

The differences in costs among crops derived largely from differences in labor expenditures and material inputs. The first type of expenditure was contingent on yields, and both types on plant growth period. For example, the growing season of zucchini, beginning with the preparation of the soil through the sowing of seeds and the final harvesting, was four months, half that of eggplants, and its yields were lower. Consequently, the costs of labor and material for zucchini were less than those of eggplants. The marketing costs, which went chiefly to transportation, were also a function of yields. Land rent is assumed to be equal for all crops.

The table indicates that the MVPWs for all crops were several times the price of springwater ($0.08/m³), the main source of irrigation water in the Jordan Valley. Also, with the exception of that of cucumbers, the MVPWs were greater than the price of well water ($0.25/m³). These estimates do not address the MVPW's sensitivity to changes in the cost-benefit schedule. Yet, the MVPW is particularly sensitive to the price of produce as well as to yields. For example, a reduction of the price of tomatoes by 30 percent would bring the MVPW down to nil. The variation of the MVPW with yields is illustrated best by greenhouse cucumbers, which yield more than a dozen tons per dunum and so would be expected to have a much higher MVPW than the $0.23/m³ for those grown in open fields with their inferior yields, in spite of the former's much higher production and marketing costs.

The MVPW for fruits in the West Bank compared well with those of vegetables. The MVPW for citrus was comparable to the MVPW for bananas and to vegetables under open field cultivation. It was more than double the price of water. This conclusion is significant because the two types of crops, especially bananas, are profligate water users, in the sense that they need greater quantities of water than other crops for the same amount of tonnage produced, and their cultivation under conditions of extreme water scarcity often has been cited as exemplifying economically insensible use of water. The MVPW figures suggest that the criticism may not be completely justified. Besides, the banana area was in fact small, less than 5 percent of the irrigated land in the West Bank, and the West Bank and Gaza were net importers of this fruit.

The overall inference then is that water use for the cultivation of most horticultural products in the West Bank was *not* economically unsound practice. The same also can be said regarding vegetables in Gaza because their cost-benefit schedule was similar to that in the West Bank. There was, however, a striking difference between the MVPW for citrus in the two regions, with Gaza's being quite low. It should be noted that in the table Gaza's MVPW is an aggregate and does not indicate the variations in technology as well as types of citrus crops. The low MVPW partly resulted from the inclusion of 15,000 dunums, out of 55,000 dunums, that were fairly neglected. The more important cause of the low MVPW, however, was the price. The price of Gaza's citruses has been consistently lower than those of the West Bank because they were of lower quality and geared for processing rather than final demand. The marketing problems mentioned earlier also affected the prices adversely. Thus, it can be said that water use in Gaza for at least some of the citrus production was not economically justifiable.

The preceding results of the MVPW are sketched in figure 3.8. On the left end of the curve lie the highest values of the MVPW, for crops grown under greenhouses and high tunnels; on the right end are the lowest MVPW values, for a portion of Gaza's citruses and crops cultivated by traditional methods and for other non-profitable establishments. The right end in particular requires closer investigation than is possible here to determine the width of the interval (that is, the quantities of water) with MVPW lower than the price of well water in the West Bank and Gaza. In the middle of the curve lay the bulk of West Bank bananas and citrus and West Bank and Gaza vegetables cultivated under drip irrigation and mulch or low tunnels.

The MVPW for all crops could have been greater than the preceding estimates had the prices of vegetables and citruses kept pace with the those of inputs. The price index of purchased inputs, which were imported largely from Israel, has risen consistently since the mid-1980s. For example, the price of pesticides nearly doubled between 1986 and 1992 (see figure 3.9). At the same time, the vegetables' price index fluctuated widely, and in 1992 it exceeded the 1986 index by only 25 percent; the citrus' price index

FIGURE 3.8 Marginal Value Product of Irrigation Water in the West Bank and Gaza

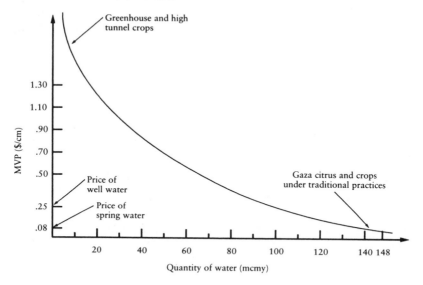

FIGURE 3.9 Input and Crop Price Indices in the West Bank and Gaza

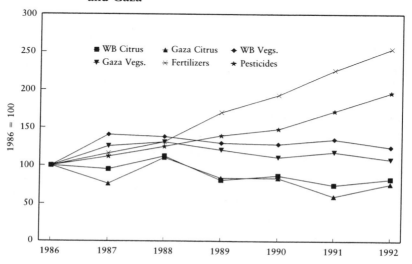

fell by 20–25 percent in the same period. The gap between the rate of increase of input and output prices meant that the financial returns were lower than they would have been had the two indices risen parallel to each other; consequently, the MVPW in both the West Bank and Gaza did not attain its potential.

Comparing Israeli and Palestinian MVPWs

The MVPWs in the West Bank and Gaza can be brought into sharp relief by comparing them with those in Israel and Jordan, although the comparison may not be totally meaningful because the costs of inputs and prices of produce in the three entities are often dissimilar. First, with respect to Jordan, there are no readily available estimates of the MVPW for the overall irrigated sector. However, I have computed the MVPW for several vegetable and fruit crops grown in the northern segment of the Jordan Valley on the basis of 1991 farm budgets from the valley.[52] The MVPW in that segment should be the highest in the valley because the yields are higher there than in the middle and south and because the temperature is lower, rendering the water requirements lower.[53] They were on the whole comparable with the values obtained in the West Bank. The reason for the parity was that labor costs in Jordan were much lower than in the West Bank and Gaza and the agricultural inputs were largely exempt from tariffs.[54] Other areas on Jordan's side of the valley, however, yielded lower MVPWs than on the West Bank.

One Israeli study using the residual method to determine the MVPW in 1991 for a wide array of crops concluded that they ranged between $0.30 and $1.50 for most fruits and vegetables.[55] However, its results "embody the returns to land" because agricultural land in Israel is leased from the state and is not subject to market valuation. The premise of embodying the returns to land in the returns to water was that the land had no alternative use, which, according to the study, might be true in some cases, but

52. Ghezawi and Khasawneh, 1993.
53. The MVPWs ($/m³) were 0.16, 0.35, 0.81, 0.83, and 0.63 for melons, eggplants, zucchini, citrus, and bananas, respectively.
54. In the early 1990s, the daily wage on the Jordanian side of the valley was $2–3, but it was about $10 in the West Bank.
55. Fishelson, 1993.

often was not. Further, the results did not account for marketing costs. The study hence must have overestimated the MVPW, although it is difficult to determine by how much.

If marketing and land rent were excluded from the list of costs of Palestinian vegetable crops, their MVPWs would go up by 30 to 90 percent. Thus, the MVPW for vegetables and fruits in the West Bank and Gaza (except for Gaza's citruses) and those of Israel would be comparable. Israel, however, irrigated large areas of field crops, including wheat and cotton. The MVPW for such crops, as calculated by the Israeli study, was much lower than the average cost of water production in Israel ($0.33/m^3 in 1990).[56]

A list of crops and corresponding MVPWs longer than the one in the above study was presented in the joint Ben-Gurion University and Tahal (BUNT) report to the World Bank.[57] The MVPWs were for 1990 with projections for 1997. The report, however, did not state the assumptions—especially whether it imputed opportunity cost to land and included marketing expenditures—which makes its findings difficult to use as a reference for comparison. Nonetheless, the results are worth stating because they agreed with the conclusions of the previous study. They indicated a convergence between the MVPWs for Israeli and Palestinian horticultural crops. Furthermore, they showed that in 1990 about one-half of the irrigation water that was considered in the study (1,064 mcmy) went to crops with MVPWs of less than $0.40, which is close to the threshold of the average production cost of water but less than the MVPWs for the horticultural crops in the West Bank and Gaza (with the exception of some Gaza citrus, of course).[58] Field crops in particular had a low average MVPW of $0.15.[59] If land and marketing costs were not included in these estimates, including them would increase the proportion of crops with MVPWs of less than $0.40 to more than one-half and decrease the MVPW for field crops to even lower than $0.15. That such crops were grown was due to the generous, politically informed subsidies of water by the state, a topic that is examined in the next chapter.

In brief, irrigated horticultural crops in the West Bank and Gaza had MVPWs comparable to those in Israel and in Jordan.

56. Tahal, 1990, p. 9.1.
57. BUNT, 1994.
58. Ibid., pp. V.1–6.
59. Ibid., p. 7.6.

Moreover, they were superior to the MVPWs of the crops that consumed approximately half of the irrigation water in Israel, and more so to those of field crops, which used 320 mcmy or about one-fourth of that water. It is therefore fair to conclude that transferring much of the water that was earmarked for field crops in Israel to the agriculture of the West Bank and Gaza, where the returns to water were higher, would have been the economic thing to do.

Water Pricing, Equity, and Competitiveness

The inequality of irrigation water prices in the West Bank and Gaza is a source of inequality among farmers, differentially affecting their profitability and attendant ability to compete. Because the Palestinian farmers also sell their produce in the Israeli and Jordanian markets, the price of water in these two states is relevant to Palestinian agricultural competitiveness and will continue to be in the future. An indicator of the impact of water price on profitability can be obtained from the ratio of the cost of water to the gross value of the produce or to total input costs. For the vegetables discussed earlier, the ratios of water costs to gross values ranged between 5 and 8 percent for springwater and between 14 and 25 percent for well water, or nearly three times as much.

To illustrate the ramifications for this difference, use of well (instead of spring) water would have reduced the net revenues of a dunum of tomatoes from $283 to $164, or by more than 40 percent, assuming the other input-output elements constant. This is an appreciable impact on income, and a clear source of intra- and interregional inequality among farmers. The springs, however, are concentrated in the Jordan Valley, privileging it over the other areas. Gaza's water costs fell between the two extremes of West Bank wells and springs, and their impact also should lie somewhere in the middle.

With respect to competition with Jordanian and Israeli horticultural crops, the situation becomes more complicated because a host of factors other than water price affect competitiveness. These factors encompass the costs of other inputs, especially labor, crop yields and quality, currency rates, and marketing capabilities and institutions. Insofar as water is concerned, agricultural competitiveness is a function of water's price and its productivity. The price of water in the West Bank and Gaza has been examined already.

In Jordan, as in the West Bank, water prices depend on the source of supply. For example, in the Jordan Valley farmers received water from the King Abdallah Canal at a subsidized price of about $.09/m³, which was even less than just the operation and maintenance costs of about $0.14/m³. In the highlands, however, water cost farmers about $0.25/m³.[60] In Israel, the price of irrigation water sold by Mekorot in 1993, which amounted to 740 mcmy, averaged about $0.14/m³.[61] Thus, in absolute terms, the price of irrigation water in Israel, the West Bank, and Jordan converged, and water prices could not have affected competitiveness in any significant way.

The same cannot be said about water productivity. Water productivity depends on a host of factors, most notably technology. It varies proportionally with yields, but it does not follow automatically that higher yielding crops also have higher water productivity because crop-water requirements are dissimilar. For example, banana and citrus yields are 3.5 tons/dunum and 3 tons/dunum, respectively, whereas the water productivity of citrus is more than twice that of bananas (table 3.12). Technological improvement also can make an immense impact on water productivity through yield augmentation or water conservation, as indicated in the discussion of drip irrigation and greenhouses.

Overall, water productivity in the irrigated sector of the West Bank and Gaza during the late 1980s and early 1990s was in the vicinity of 3 tons/1,000 m³ for vegetables, 4-5 tons/1,000 m³ for citrus, and 1.5 tons/1,000 m³ for bananas. In Israel, I estimate that water productivity for vegetables and citrus were more than 5 tons/1,000 m³ and 6.5 tons/1,000 m³, respectively. In Jordan, there were no readily available water productivity figures for the whole country, but for the Jordan Valley region the productivities in 1991 averaged 4.5 tons/1,000 m³ for vegetables, 0.86 ton/1,000 m³ for bananas, and 1.6 tons/1,000 m³ for citrus.[62] Consequently, water

60. Based on Ghezawi and Khasawneh, 1993, p. 59; and World Bank, 1993a, vol. 4, p. 66.

61. My calculation from BUNT, 1994, pp. 4.16–4.17. The 740 mcm do not cover all the irrigation water because Mekorot supplies only part of the water, about 60 percent of the total.

62. The author's calculations, based on Ghezawi and Khasawneh, 1993, p. 41.

productivity gives Israel a competitive edge over Jordan and the West Bank and Gaza.

All production factors considered, however, the produce of the West Bank and Gaza was competitive with that of both Israel and Jordan. This conclusion was confirmed by an econometric study, which found that under free trading conditions the flow of Palestinian agricultural produce would increase both to Israel and Jordan.[63] The full potential of that competitiveness, however, has not been realized because Israel erected numerous trade barriers against Palestinian agricultural exports, both to its own markets and to Jordanian and other markets. At the same time, Israeli produce has flowed freely to the West Bank and Gaza. The barriers, which were intended for the protection of Israeli producers, included such measures as permit requirements, types of trucks in which produce can be shipped, and delays at the crossing points.[64] Furthermore, Israel insisted in the Taba Agreement on fixing quotas for West Bank and Gaza agricultural exports to its market. The quotas covered poultry, eggs, potatoes, tomatoes, and melons.[65] By including the protectionist quotas, Israel only confirmed the competitive edge held by at least some branches of Palestinian agriculture.

Toward an Alternative Water Pricing System

A water pricing system explicitly or implicitly serves socioeconomic objectives, such as equity, efficiency, profit maximization, and cost recovery. Different objectives call for different pricing systems. For example, if the objective of the supplier were to maximize profits, he would sell the water at a price where marginal revenue equals marginal costs; but if his purpose were to recover costs, the price would equal the average cost of water production.

The objectives of the pricing system that prevailed under Israeli occupation in the West Bank and Gaza already have been mentioned. In the municipal sector, prices have been designed primarily for covering the supply costs of Mekorot and then for the municipalities and village councils, without regard to equity. In

63. El-Jaafari, 1995.
64. See, for example, Kahan, 1987, pp. 71–79; and World Bank, 1993a, vol. 4, pp. 12–14.
65. Elmusa and El-Jaafari, 1995, p. 195.

agriculture, prices were kept at the level of private production costs without extra tariffs or subsidies; the overriding objective of putting a ceiling on pumping was implemented administratively, not through pricing. Palestinian water managers hence may want to devise more nuanced water pricing policies that serve wider social, economic, and ecological objectives.

The objectives deemed salient in contemporary water management discourse are efficiency, equity, and sustainability, or, roughly speaking, maintaining the water supply for future generations. In the West Bank, an additional objective might be agricultural expansion. These objectives may complement, contradict, or have neutral effects on each other. Striking a balance among them, although fraught with difficulties, is usually necessary. I will address some of the implications of these objectives for pricing; my purpose is not so much to offer exact figures, for this is premature under the present uncertainties, but to highlight some of the issues that have to be considered when devising a new pricing system.

Let us begin with efficiency. Here, "efficiency" is defined in an economic, not a physical, sense as the obtaining of higher economic value for a unit of water. It can be achieved via allocations among and within sectors. Because the economic value of water in the West Bank and Gaza is higher in the municipal sector than in agriculture, raising the water price in agriculture, through such measures as levying taxes on private wells or communal springs, in theory might shift water from it to the municipal sector. However, given the extremely limited water supply and irrigated area in the West Bank, reallocation may not be desirable. In contrast, in Gaza, so much water goes to citrus cultivation with its low MVPW, reallocation may not be entirely out of the question. Raising water prices, however, is not an easy political undertaking, especially in the agricultural sector; in many countries, even removing subsidies has proved to be hard.

Reallocation among the municipal and agricultural sectors also can be done through the market by allowing well owners to sell their water, as is done at present. Diversion of large amounts of water from agriculture to the municipal sector through the market, however, is difficult because of the decentralized system of wells and their lack of connections with the municipal distribution networks. Thus, the question of whether water efficiency could be improved through a more centralized system that would facilitate the mobility of water among sectors would have to be investigated, although it is doubtful that altering the present system is worthwhile as long as the supply itself is not increased.

Allocation between agriculture and industry, where the economic value of water is generally much higher than in agriculture, raises similar questions. In addition, industry, like agriculture, is a "productive" economic sector, and its development cannot be impeded for lack of water. Without additional water, the only choice may be a "triage" entailing a loss of irrigated areas commensurate with industrial needs.

A second objective that a new pricing system can serve is equity. In the municipal sector, the flat rates in the West Bank, as elsewhere, discriminate against lower income households, in the sense that such households would have to spend proportionally more of their total budget on water consumption than those with higher incomes. Further, the rates are high relative to the average income in the West Bank—as was apparent from a comparison with Jordan's prices—and are *too* high for the lower income households. These two drawbacks, notably the second, can be overcome by the adoption of a progressive, linear or block, rate. The price and quantity of the first block would be designed so that low-income households' water consumption would be commensurate with basic needs. One problem with the block rate is that the charges for the first block may have to be lower than the cost of supplying the water, and the other succeeding blocks would have to ensure that such costs (both capital and operation and maintenance) are repaid, in effect subsidizing the first block. Determining the exact block intervals and rates calls for more specific research on consumer behavior, especially the income elasticity of demand.

In the irrigated sector, equity dictates closing the gap between the price of springwater and well water and the technologies farmers use. That might be done either by subsidizing the farmers who obtain their water from the wells or by introducing a tariff structure for the use of springwater. The first option is not desirable as it may remove some of the incentives for the efficient use of water and may not be possible in any case, considering the tremendous financial needs for reconstruction. The second option has more merit since it would make funds available for the maintenance of the springs and at the same time provide a disincentive against inefficient use. It may not be easy to implement, however. The owners of water rights in these springs, quite a few of whom are also large landowners, notably in the Jordan Valley, can be expected to oppose it.

The price of irrigation water also can be more equitable if it were set to accommodate the different farming technologies because the ratio of water costs to the total varies with the technology. To accomplish such an objective, the price of water for crops grown under greenhouses would have to be greater than for those grown in open field cultivation. It is worth noting, in fact, that private landowners charge tenants using greenhouses about double the rent they charge tenants using open field cultivation (although not for the purpose of effecting equity).[66]

With regard to agricultural growth, or at least stability, a water pricing policy cannot be formulated fully without knowledge of the trading regimes that will emerge between the Palestinians and other trading partners in the region. At present, the main trading partner of the West Bank and Gaza is Israel, where water is subsidized, and the conditions of trade favor Israel.[67] If a free trade regime were to prevail between Israel and the Palestinians and between the Palestinians and the rest of the world, then agricultural production in the West Bank and Gaza would be competitive. This would not be the case if irrigation water prices are subsidized in Israel and other countries whose crops, whether in the export or domestic market, compete with those grown by Palestinian farmers. Irrigation water prices may be negotiated with future competitors to ensure fairness; otherwise, commensurate trade barriers would have to be erected against the produce of countries that subsidize irrigation water.

Finally, pricing could serve as an important tool for ensuring the sustainability, or the continuity of both the quantity and quality, of the natural water supply for future generations. Because water sources are common, in the sense that one party's use affects that of the others, a main thrust of a sustainability price will have to be the internalization of the externalities, that is, making the

66. Preliminary results from a survey conducted in 1994 by ARIJ for its project, "The Potential for Sustainable and Equitable Development of Irrigated Agriculture in the West Bank." The reasons behind this practice are unclear; it may be because land for greenhouses is rented on a long-term basis—10 years or more—that the higher rent implicitly adjusts for inflation; or because greenhouse cultivation is more chemical-dependent than open field cultivation, it is perceived to be more exhaustive of the land. The practice also suggests that the land market is a sellers' market.

67. Elmusa and El-Jaafari, 1995.

users, or those whose activities may affect the water sources in any way, pay for them. Thus, in the municipal sector, for example, progressive rates are necessary to pay for the treatment of waste-water, which, if left untreated, would contaminate, if not altogether damage, the water supply. In agriculture, taxes need to be levied in such a manner as to make it prohibitively costly for well owners to pump beyond hydrologically sound limits. Such taxes can be used, too, to discourage pollution from the return irrigation water, especially from greenhouse farming that depends on heavy use of chemical inputs.

Thus, while it is easy to recognize unsound pricing systems, it is much more complicated to devise (and even more difficult to implement) more appropriate ones. Sound water pricing policies demand overcoming domestic political obstacles, negotiating with trade partners, and having available technical information and ca-pabilities. Nonetheless, giving appropriate price signals to water users can be a powerful tool for achieving societal objectives and sustainability of the water supply.

Water Markets

Water markets are uncommon in the world today, but they have been advocated in recent years as a way of infusing price signals into water use activities with the ultimate purpose of promoting efficiency. According to neoclassical economic theory, a perfect market with many buyers and sellers, provides, under certain con-ditions, the mechanism for achieving that purpose.[68] It ensures that the price at which suppliers are willing to sell their commodity and the price at which buyers are willing to buy reach equilibrium at the point of efficient allocation.[69]

Yet, although promoting efficiency is a desirable goal, the creation of perfect, or at least well-functioning, water markets is replete with obstacles. It requires the presence of numerous con-

68. The term "many" does not have a precise definition in economics except to mean that the number is such that one or a few sellers cannot on their own affect the equilibrium price.

69. This also happens to be the price at which some people can be better off without others being worse-off, or the Pareto optimal price. For discussion of the many issues involved in water markets see, for example, Brajer et al., 1989; Chan, 1989; Colby, 1987; Dudley, 1992; Howe et al., 1986; Israel and Lund, 1995; and World Bank, 1993b, pp. 81–92.

ditions, such as the mobility of water itself, smooth flow of information, availability of well-defined property rights, and many buyers and sellers.[70] Furthermore, water-related goods often are characterized by low subtractability and excludability, which make them suited for being public or common rather than private goods.[71] "Subtractability" means that the nondamaging use of the good or resource by one person does not subtract from, or diminish, the benefit of the resource to the next person. For example, watermelons are highly subtractable goods, whereas navigation in an ocean or a street sewer line has low subtractability. Increasing the use of a resource without the diminishment of its value to other consumers increases society's economic welfare—which may not be realized if the resource is privately owned.

Excludability is defined as the ability of the supplier to exclude the consumer from having access to the resource. Low excludability implies that the supplier cannot prevent, or can prevent only at a high price, the access of consumers to the resource if they do not meet his conditions. For example, it would be costly for a private owner to monitor a gravity canal or a piped water distribution system to exclude users. The high transaction costs, in fact, discourage private investment in such resources. However, certain water-related goods, such as bottled water or water provided by tank trucks, can have both high subtractability and excludability and hence qualify for being private goods. Often, however, either or both the subtractability and excludability of water-related goods are low. If, despite all the odds, real water markets were established, society still would have to tackle their failure to consider critical concerns, notably equity, negative externalities, and the welfare of future generations.[72]

Real water markets are absent in both the West Bank and Gaza, even though water is bought by households from the municipalities and by farmers from well owners. The foregoing premises will be used as a framework to outline the opportunities for, and some of the chief impediments against, the creation of such water

70. Brajer et al., 1989.
71. The discussion of subtractability and excludability is based on World Bank, 1993b, pp. 81–92.
72. I borrow heavily in the following discussion from the excellent syntheses by Brajer et al., 1989, and Howe et al., 1986. The two articles make similar points about the failures of, and conditions for, a well-functioning market.

markets in the West Bank and Gaza. The discussion will be buttressed by highlighting the relevance of several conclusions regarding water markets in the United States, where considerable debate over garnering them as a reallocation tool has taken place.

Prerequisites of Well-Functioning Markets

Well-functioning water markets require, first of all, that water be mobile so that it can be bought and sold, and there can be many buyers and sellers. Water mobility, in turn, depends on such factors as the availability of sound physical infrastructure and laws and low transaction costs. The physical infrastructure that mobility requires, especially an extensive pipe network hooked to the scattered wells, is limited in the West Bank and Gaza. It probably would be costly to build on a large scale in the West Bank, with its mountainous, highly uneven topography. The topography also would make the transportation of water an energy-intensive, expensive operation. In Gaza, however, the limited area, proximity of farmland and population centers, and flatness of the terrain all would simplify the extension of such infrastructure. Obviously, not all the water would have to be mobile, for there are more or less constant demands, notably for municipal use; but sufficient amounts of water would be necessary to make the costs of furnishing the infrastructure worthwhile.

Mobility also is linked to transaction costs deriving from items such as middlemen's fees, litigation, and staff payments. These costs can be high. For instance, the transaction costs of a water bank set up by the state of California in 1991 to manage drought conditions made up about 30 percent of the price at which the state sold the water.[73] Thus, for water to be mobile either the transaction costs have to be minimized or the users must be willing to pay the mark-up charges. In drought years, in particular, it may not be too difficult to find such buyers, even in a developing society such as the West Bank and Gaza.

Finally, mobility requires that water laws clearly define property rights and allow water transfer among basins, regions, uses,

73. According to Israel and Lund, 1995, p. 10, the state bought the water at a uniform price of $125 per acre-foot (1 acre-foot = 1234 m³) and sold it at $175 per acre-foot, with the $50 difference being, I assume, the transactions costs.

and individual users. Efficiency-conducive property rights for a well-functioning market have several characteristics: they are fixed by legal ownership rights, in the sense of the right to use, subject to various restrictions; they are specified, for example, as quantities of water; they are transferrable; and they are enforceable, in the sense they cannot be taken away without the consent of the owner.[74] It is difficult to anticipate the water legislation in the West Bank and Gaza in the postoccupation period; however, if water markets were to be garnered as a water management tool, the laws would have to facilitate water transfers among regions, sectors, and users.

Further, well-functioning markets rely on the smooth flow of information to connect potential buyers and sellers. The information furnishes such items as the names and locations of water sellers, quantity and quality of the water, duration of the sale, and price. It could be channeled through media that normally transmit other types of information, including word of mouth, advertisement in the newspapers, agencies set up for the purpose, agricultural extension services, and clearing houses. The flow of information is likely to be easier in the small Gaza Strip than in the West Bank. In both places, however, the communications infrastructure essential for the flow of information, such as telephones, is not well-developed, particularly in the countryside. Further, the high levels of illiteracy greatly reduce the "efficiency" of the flow of information through advertisement. Physical mobility of individuals also is more constrained than, say, in the United States. Thus, overcoming these obstacles and creating the conditions for a smooth flow of information is a long-term proposition tied to economic and social development in general.

As an aid to water mobility and marketing in general, Norman Dudley has proposed the technolegal concept of "capacity sharing," which has been used in Australian water management.[75] Simply put, capacity sharing allocates to stakeholders percentage shares of the capacity, inflows, and outflows of a central reservoir, as if each holder had his own separate reservoir. The concept thus presupposes a centralized water system in which water rights are defined in volumetric terms as stored amounts (as is the case in Australia) rather than priority use (as is the case in the United

74. See, for example, Brajer et al., 1989, pp. 495–96.
75. Dudley, 1992.

States). For trade to be effected, whether in the short-term or long-term, the stakeholders are informed by the central management about the statistically determined probabilities of supply (which is variable, seasonally and interannually). They then can compare this information against the probabilities of their own demand in order to decide whether they want to buy or sell and how much.

In a sense, a rudimentary form of capacity sharing that can be developed further exists with respect to the West Bank's communal springs, where the "water hours" owned can be thought of as being the equivalent of storage-and-flow shares and where owners of these "water hours" can sell part or all of their time to others.[76] Implementation of capacity sharing in the rest of the system, however, would be difficult, unless the water networks in Gaza and the West Bank each become more integrated. Capacity sharing would be particularly worth considering if an irrigation canal (West Ghor Canal) with centralized storage and distribution were to be built along the Jordan River. Even then, the concept would have to be modified because the other prerequisites for its functioning—such as operations research to determine probabilities, a long-term planning mindset on the part of stakeholders and other users, and smooth communication channels—all are hard to come by in a developing country context. In addition, more flexible forms that allow, for instance, "changing one's mind"—like the ability of customers to return goods to the store within a certain period of time in the United States—would need to be developed.

Addressing Market Failures

Market failures regarding equity, externalities, and welfare of future generations can be attenuated by several instruments, including legislation, pricing, and technology. With respect to equity, for example, allocation of resources strictly through the market rests on the initial distribution of society's income, or more generally on assets that are often unequal. The unequal distribution of income affords those with higher incomes greater ability, hence willingness, to pay for and acquire resources. In other words, the market fails to distribute resources equitably. This type of failure can be corrected somewhat in the household sector of the West Bank and

76. See chapter 2.

Gaza, as suggested above, by block pricing. The situation is different in agriculture. In this sector, water rights are conflated with land rights, and it is not economical for small landowners to drill wells. So they must purchase the water from the larger landowners at a higher price than the large owners sell it to themselves. It is a difficult kind of inequality to redress and could become more acute if large landowners were able to sell their water to the municipalities or industry instead of the small farmers. Subsidies to the small farmers could offset the mark up above large farmers' prices, but they effectively would end up as payments to large farmers. Agricultural cooperatives may be able to play a role here either by pooling the resources or by improving the bargaining position of their members by purchasing water in "bulk."

Another type of potential inequality in the access to irrigation water could stem from the differential use of farming technologies. For example, farmers with greenhouses have a greater ability to pay than those with open field cultivation because the proportion of water to total costs is lower in the former than in the latter. Taxation of water to greenhouses, as was proposed above, could close the purchasing power gap between the two groups of farmers.

Markets also produce negative externalities that affect a third party—whether an individual, a group, or nature—that may not be involved in the transactions. For example, the decision of a landowner to sell his well water to a municipality may lead to the unemployment of farm workers or sharecroppers. It may have further ramifications for society at large, such as abetting the immigration to the towns of rural inhabitants, who would abandon the rural infrastructures and at the same time burden that of the urban areas. Such externalities, among other reasons, have prompted some economists to question whether the market, while it may be an efficient mechanism, is, in fact, an efficient allocation institution.[77] Yet another common type of negative externality is the impact of return water, either its loss from a locality or its addition somewhere else where it may not be desirable because it usually is contaminated. Legislation for the protection and compensation of potentially or actually injured third parties obviously would be necessary.

The third category of market failure is the market's lack of incorporation of the welfare of future generations because it tends

77. See, for example, Chan, 1989.

to favor short-term profits. Left to its own, market-based allocation could result in the depletion (through overpumping) or pollution of the aquifers. In a sense, this is a kind of negative externality whose objects are not present to defend their interests. It is hence harder to tackle, and its prevention needs strong public and expert attitudes toward water, and nature in general, that favors sustainability. The hope also is that the water of the aquifers would be divided equitably between the Israelis and Palestinians so as to reduce the incentive for their depletion. In brief, to ensure equity among potential users and sustainability of the water resources, water markets would have to be closely regulated and established in tandem with integrated resource management. The result is not likely to resemble what the word "market" normally evokes.

Lessons from the United States: Markets or Just Economic Incentives?

The discourse on water marketing has burgeoned since the 1980s, most notably in the United States, thanks to the "promarket atmosphere" that began to prevail after the assumption of power by the political conservatives (represented by Ronald Reagan and his supporters).[78] More specifically, the discourse was triggered by a watershed 1982 decision by the U.S. Supreme Court, which held that groundwater was an article "in commerce," effectively making it tradable across state lines like any other commodity.[79] Four major types of conclusions from this discourse illuminate further some of the themes examined above and present new ones. The conclusions are based mainly on empirical studies of water marketing in the arid and semiarid areas of Arizona, California, Colorado, and New Mexico.

A first conclusion comes from a study of water markets in northern Colorado, which found that, to be acceptable and reliable, water markets should satisfy a number of conditions.[80] Several of these conditions already have been mentioned as prerequisites for well-functioning markets. Two additional conditions, however,

78. Dudley, 1992, reviews the literature of water marketing and the management of common property resources.
79. The decision was handed in *Sporhase v. Nebraska ex rel. Douglas*, 458 U.S. 941, 1982.
80. Howe et al., 1986, p. 440.

are worth pointing out: guaranteed tenure security for established users and predictable outcome (because changing to a new system of water allocation brings with it uncertainties and makes water suppliers and users reluctant to change from the more predictable ways). These two conditions, in fact, detract from the competitiveness of the market.

A second conclusion concerns the entity that ought to manage the water markets. At least two studies found that state-run, integrated water marketing or banking holds several advantages. Based on their analysis of the 1991 California water bank, Israel and Lund infer that the bank was able to reduce substantially transaction costs, provide initial capital, and coordinate with other water-transfer operations.[81] Likewise, Hrezo and Hrezo have argued that the state, as opposed to municipal or federal government, can accommodate various competing interests and pursue state wide policies; provide a basin wide view necessary for treating the water resources as a hydrological unit; and integrate water policy goals with other societal objectives, such as land management and economic development.[82] This obviously may be a peculiarly American phenomenon owing to the federal system and the size of the states, all but two of which dwarf the combined size of the West Bank and Gaza. The point, however, is to find the appropriate unit of management that can shoulder functions similar to those that a state in the United States carries out.

Third, well-functioning water markets rarely are found, perhaps because of the stringent prerequisites of their establishment. What actually seems to have happened historically in the United States was in some cases a transition from private to communal property rights. Such markets as may have arisen involved minor exchanges among users or were subject to strong state intervention. They have been described as being publicly managed property systems with economic incentives, rather than markets.[83] For example, the 1991 California water bank that was run by the state sold the water it bought according to a hierarchy of priorities (needs) rather than the value of bids.[84] Whatever name one gives for such arrangements may be immaterial; the crucial thing is to understand their complexity and not reduce them to slogans.

81. Israel and Lund, 1995, pp. 19–20.
82. Cited in Brajer et al., 1989, p. 505.
83. Dellapenna, 1994, p. 158.
84. Israel and Lund, 1995, p. 10.

Finally, quantifying the costs and benefits from water transfer, whether through markets or otherwise, is not easy, nor is determining the extent of public policy regulations.[85] (It is useful in this context to recall the problems of estimating the economic value of water.) After all is said and done, it may be that the best to be hoped for from water marketing is the realization of second-or nth-best efficiency levels. The transfer of water through the California water bank may have put water into higher value uses than would have been possible without the bank, but this result is a far cry from the efficiency that a well-functioning market theoretically could achieve. Accordingly, the desirability of establishing water markets in the West Bank and Gaza would have to be assessed in light of the costs of creating them versus the efficiencies that could be practically harnessed, not the theoretical efficiency of a perfect market.

WATER AND RAINFED AGRICULTURE IN THE WEST BANK

Rainfed agriculture in the West Bank has been a low-input and low-yield enterprise due to the lack of investment in modern inputs, a situation that derives from the uncertainty of rainfall and attendant risks, fragmentation of landholdings, migration of labor into Israel, and insecurity of property rights as a result of the ever-present threat of land confiscation by Israel. Furthermore, the neglect of the sector, in a kind of vicious circle, has led to increasing soil erosion and desertification that, if left unchecked, could be detrimental to agriculture.

Still, in spite of its low yields, rainfed agriculture remains at the core of Palestinian crop production in the West Bank owing to the extensive area it covers. Its eminence becomes even more apparent if one takes account of its role in the preservation of the soil, fine climate, respectable levels of rainfall, and the aesthetic value of the landscape. Moreover, the maintenance of favorable soil and climatic conditions translates into minimization of runoff and evaporation, or the maximization of water available for aquifer recharge. The use and economic value of water in the rainfed sector, therefore, warrant closer inspection.

85. According to Bonnie Colby Saliba, based on the analysis of water markets in northern Colorado; cited in Dudley, 1992, p. 761.

TABLE 3.13 Crop Yields of Irrigated and Rainfed Agriculture
(In kg/dunum)

Crop	Irrigated		Rainfed	
	Yield	Region	Yield	Region
Olives	500	Jericho district	100	W. Bank
Wheat	400	Jordan[a]	200	W. Bank
Grapes	1,700	Jericho	550	W. Bank
Watermelon	3,000	Jinin	1,100	Jinin district
Vegetables	2,800	W. Bank	700	W. Bank

SOURCES: ARIJ, 1994; Center for Rural Studies, 1989 and 1990; El-Hurani and Duwayri, 1986; and World Bank, 1993a, vol. 4.
NOTE:
[a]In the Jordan Valley.

Irrigation Water Equivalent (IWE)

The water utilized by crops in rainfed areas, or the agronomically *effective* water, is equal to rainfall less runoff and aquifer replenishment. Yet, to consider the total volume of this effective water as part of a region's water use would exaggerate greatly its value as a productive asset, as is demonstrated by a comparison of the yields of the rainfed and irrigated lands (table 3.13). A more realistic gauge of the utility of rainfall would have to take into consideration the water productivity of the rainfed land compared with that of the irrigated land. From such a comparison one can measure what may be termed the IWE that is tapped in the rainfed areas, or the quantity of irrigation water that gives the same amount of crop output as does effective rainfall. Formally, the IWE can be defined as follows: IWE = (output of rainfed land/output of irrigated land) × water used in the irrigated land. If the interest is in monetary comparison, the output quantities can be replaced by their monetary values.

A main problem with the IWE is that the land and water productivity of irrigated agriculture is not constant and changes with technology. Thus, the IWE must be thought of in terms of a specific technological state prevailing in the domain under study; should the technology and yields change in either of the two sectors, the IWE would have to be altered accordingly. A second problem is that the crops of the two sectors and the regions in which they are grown may not be identical, which presents difficult estimation problems, as clarified below. Still, identifying the IWE is superior either to overlooking the water consumed by the rainfed sector or to exaggerating its productive contribution. The IWE can be thought of as a lower bound of water use: The difference between it and the actual amount of effective rainfall is a measure of the water that is lost unproductively, or, put positively, an indicator of the potential of water gains from improvements in the rainfed sector.

The average rainfall and corresponding crop-type distribution in the rainfed areas are shown in table 3.14. These are approximate figures obtained by superimposing the district map and rainfall contour (isohytes) map and visually estimating the rainfall level. They do not account for variations in the cultivated areas or rainfall from year to year; the latter, of course, is considerable. Furthermore, they are the total, not effective, rainfall. The effective rainfall in the West Bank may amount to two-thirds of the total, as indicated in the chapter 1 discussion of evapotranspiration. Accordingly, the effective rainfall over the rainfed areas would be 670 mcmy.

I estimate that the West Bank's crop output in the late 1980s and early 1990s averaged about 270,000 tons in the rainfed areas and 220,000 tons in the irrigated.[86] The irrigation water volume during that period was about 80 mcmy. The IWE thus would be 98 mcmy, or about 15 percent of the effective rainfall. However, the two areas did not have identical crops and so in a sense this is like comparing apples and oranges, thereby underestimating the IWE. The reason is that the rainfed areas had crops with exceptionally low yields, such as stone fruits, which were planted on nearly 220,000 dunums, whereas the irrigated areas were planted mainly with vegetables and citrus. For example, the yield of almonds, which alone occupied 95,000 dunums, was less than 50 kg/dunum, or 0.1 ton/1,000 m^3 of water. The same was true of olives, which were cultivated on a much larger scale. These and other low-yielding crops, like wheat, tended to depress the overall output of the rainfed land. However, if the rainfed lands were planted only in fresh vegetables, their production would be close to 1.2 million tons, with an attendant IWE of 300 mcmy. The actual IWE for the rainfed areas, therefore, should be somewhat greater than 15 percent of the effective rainfall.

86. Calculated from various tables in ARIJ, 1994; Center for Rural Research, various years; and Society for Austro-Arab Relations, 1992.

TABLE 3.14 Crop Area and Rainfall in Rainfed Agriculture of the West Bank, by District
(Crop area in 1,000 dunums)

Crop	Jericho	Jinin/ Tulkarm	Nablus	Hebron	Ramallah/ E. Jerusalem/ Bethlehem	Total
Field crops[a]	5.1	217.0	98.7	186.7	77.3	585
Vegetables		59.1	3.6	13.1	9.8	86
Melons		2.6[b]	0.1	0.1		3
Fruits	0.1	455.0	193.5	150.9	225.0	1,025
Olives		368	162	48	163	741
Total area	5.2	733.7	295.9	350.8	312.1	1,699
Annual rainfall (100 millimeters)	2–3	5–6	5–6	5–6	5–6	5.48[c]
Rainfall volume over crop area (mcmy)[d]	1–2	369–440	148–178	175–210	156–187	849–1,017

SOURCES: Based on Benvenisti and Khayat, 1988; Center for Rural Studies, 1990; and Society for Austro-Arab Relations, 1992.
NOTES:
[a]Field crops include cereals (wheat, barley, sorghum, and dura), legumes (chickpeas, broad beans, lentils) tobacco, sesame, and vetch.
[b]Jinin only.
[c]Average.
[d]Rainfall volume over crop area = rainfall in millimeters × crop area.

MAP 3.2 Cultivated Areas in the West Bank (Irrigated and Non-irrigated)

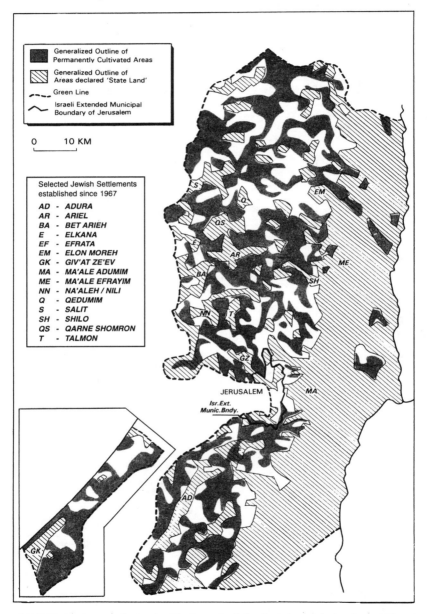

SOURCE: Jan de Jongard printed in The Center for Policy Analysis on Palestine, *Beyond Rhetoric* (1996), p. 11.

The MVPW for Rainfed Crops

The MVPWs for wheat and several types of rainfed fruit trees are illustrated in table 3.15. They are calculated from farm budgets collected in a field survey and represent averages for the West Bank.[87] The data for olives are the mean of two years, incorporating the peak and trough yields of olives.

If the figures are accurate, olives, nontrellised grapes, almonds, and wheat had low MVPWs. These crops were grown on more than two-thirds of the rainfed land, with olives alone claiming close to one-half.[88] The only crop planted over a significant area that had a high MVPW was the plum. It should be noted, however, that these values are "point" estimates, and, like those of irrigated crops, are sensitive to prices and yields, as is apparent from the gap between the MVPW for the different types of grapes.

The low MVPW for olives in particular deserves attention because of its spatial preponderance. The area planted in olive trees was estimated at 670,000 dunums in 1978–80, and increased to 800,000 dunums by 1990–92, or by 20 percent.[89] The common explanation for this expansion is that olive trees were planted by land owners as a defensive measure against the takeover of land by Israel. In the 1980s, the right-wing Likud government designated large tracts of land, amounting perhaps to 40 percent of the total area of the West Bank, as state land in order to speed up land acquisition. It did so under the guise of applying the previously existing Ottoman and British land codes, which, it alleged, permitted the government to declare as state land any property that had not been "used" for a number of years.[90] The Palestinian landowners believed the olive trees would demonstrate that their land was not idle and thus could not be declared state land. Assessing the effectiveness of planting olive trees to prevent land takeover goes beyond the scope of the present study. The concern here is with the ramifications of planting olive rather than other trees for the economics of water use. From the point of view of water scarcity, the choice of olive trees was inferior because of their low MVPW.

87. ARIJ, 1994.
88. The total rainfed area planted in trellised grapes was unknown.
89. World Bank, 1993a, vol. 4, p. 69.
90. See Benvenisti, 1984; and R. Shehadeh, 1985.

TABLE 3.15 Marginal Value Product of Water (MVPW) for Rainfed Crops in the West Bank

Crop	Area (1,000)	Yield (kg/d)	Price ($/t)	Value ($/d)	Costs ($/d)	MVPW[a] ($/m³)
Olives (oil)[b]	742	24	3,100	75	50	0.10
Stone fruits	114					
Almonds	78	45	1,000	45	20	0.05
Apricots	5	530	1,000	530	60	0.94
Peaches	1	450	340	153	60	0.19
Plums	30	390	740	289	60	0.46
Grapes	81					
Ground		500	240	120	149	0.06
Head		600	340	204	58	0.09
Trellised		1,500	340	510	201	0.62
Wheat	209					
Grain		200	240	91	55	0.07
Straw		250	172	48		
				43		

SOURCE: Calculated from ARIJ, 1994.
d = dunum, t = ton.
NOTES:
[a]Based on average annual rainfall of 500 millimeters (or 500 m³/dunum).
[b]Average for two years; approximately five tons of olives make one ton of oil.

WATER REQUIREMENTS FOR FOOD CONSUMPTION

In the last two decades, Arab countries in general have experienced what has been dubbed "the food gap," or the excess of consumption over production, evident from the steady growth of food imports. It commonly has been recognized that a fundamental, although by no means the only, factor in the making of this gap is the water constraint. J. A. Allan, for example, defines the water deficit in terms of the food gap.[91] In a similar vein, the fear of a water "crisis" has prompted concern that the use of water to irrigate export crops in the region may not be the best or most efficient way of utilizing this resource.

Detailed water-food budgets, however, seldom have been drawn for the countries of the region. Such budgets would show the amount of water needed to satisfy the food demand and how much of that water was imported and/or exported indirectly through foodstuffs. The reasons for the lack only can be surmised and may be adduced to the relatively recent emergence of water scarcity as a critical issue, as well as to the uncertainties in making the estimates.

Determining a country's water requirements for meeting the food demand can be done first by establishing the total water demand coefficient, or the water required to meet one person's food consumption. The aggregate requirements are equal to this coefficient multiplied by population size. The total demand coefficient is the sum of individual coefficients, each being a function of two variables: the amount a person consumes of, and the water it takes to produce, the individual commodity. In turn, the first variable depends on culture and income; and the second on climate, production technology and management, and whether the constituent crop is irrigated or rainfed. The total demand coefficient, being the aggregate of individual coefficients, is also a function of the ingredients of the diet. The demand coefficient is a convenient planning unit to work with as it permits relatively easy calculations of water demand "scenarios" for a variety of projected diets and population sizes.

The second aspect of the water-food budget, the water in food trade, is the water that enters into the production of the traded food commodity, not just the water embodied in the commodity

91. Allan, 1994.

itself, and will be called here *requisite* water, or what has been called independently by Allan "virtual" water.[92] For example, a ton of sugar embodies very little water, but it may take 1,250–2,000 m³ of irrigation water to produce the sugarcane from which one ton of sugar is extracted.[93] Requisite water refers to that irrigation water. On a country level, it can be determined from the balance of the water required for the production of its food imports and exports, just like other traded commodities.

A plausible estimate of the water demand coefficient requires the overcoming of intractable informational and technical difficulties, a sample of which will be delineated shortly. Before attempting such an undertaking for the West Bank and Gaza, it is useful as a basis of comparison to cite several coefficients that have appeared in recent literature. In its demand projections for the West Bank and Gaza in the year 2000, the 1994 BUNT report to the World Bank uses a partial irrigation coefficient of 90 m³ for fruits and vegetables and 25 percent of the dairy consumption.[94] On a global scale, Sandra Postel postulates a preliminary coefficient of 400 m³ for the entire diet.[95] Allan offers a ballpark coefficient of 1,000 m³ for semiarid areas, and qualifies it as being "very" approximate and "very" conservative, or an underestimate.[96] A third coefficient of 1,570 m³ reportedly has been suggested by the United Nations Food Organization (FAO).[97] This coefficient is said to be sufficient for the provision of 2,700 daily calories per person, 2,400 of which are plant based and 400 animal based. FAO views these levels as constituting a good nutritional standard.[98] Clearly, there is no standard figure to go by, and determining a specific coefficient for the West Bank and Gaza (and for Israel in the next chapter) is warranted.

92. J.A. Allan has brought to my attention that he had used the term *virtual* instead of *requisite* water to refer to the same phenomenon. The term virtual is certainly appealing, and in one sense the water in food trade is virtual in that one does not actually see water in the imported sugar or flour. However, when a country exports crops, the water is not virtual. Also, the word virtual now is used ubiquitously (virtual education, virtual money, etc.).
93. This is based on estimates of crop water requirements, land yields of sugarcane, and an extraction ratio of 10–12 percent made by Doorenbos et al., 1986.
94. BUNT, 1994, p. 7.14.
95. Postel, 1996.
96. Allan, 1994, pp. 32–33.
97. Falkenmark, 1996, p. 2.
98. Ibid., citing FAO.

I will explain the procedure for estimating such a coefficient (table 3.16) and then cross-check it against the foregoing values. The per capita food consumption figures in the table are averages for the West Bank and Gaza; the latter are somewhat lower than the former for the majority of food items owing to Gaza's lower personal income. They are not derived from household surveys, but from the net of aggregate production, exports, imports, and carryover averaged for population size. As such they include post-harvest losses. They also agree with similar statistics for the mid-1980s.[99] The water efficiency (or the utilization efficiency of the evapotranspired water for the harvested crop) is based on data from a FAO study of twenty-six vital irrigated crops.[100] It should be stressed that these data are not the amounts of water that farmers apply; they are smaller by the amounts of return water and evaporation losses through conveyance. Using water productivity is more useful for comparison than the quantities supplied by farmers because it eliminates the question of conveyance losses, but it does not tell accurately how much irrigation water must be supplied to produce the given crop under the irrigation methods that exist in a particular region.

FAO's data, moreover, are based on adequate water application and high levels of inputs and crop and water management. FAO quotes ranges, a kind of lower and upper bounds, rather than single point values of water efficiencies. The ranges also are used here because of the uncertainty regarding the farming conditions under which FAO's data were obtained in comparison with those prevailing in the West Bank and Gaza. Still, the rainfed areas in the Palestinian territories, with their low inputs and often inadequate water supply—which translate into extremely low yields—can be expected to have values that are even much greater than the upper bound. The efficiencies in table 3.16, therefore, pertain only to the irrigated, not rainfed, sector. At any rate, the question of how well they apply to the West Bank and Gaza may be largely "academic" because, as the food self-sufficiency ratios in the table demonstrate, both territories import significant proportions of their basic food staples and animal feed.

Clarifications regarding specific food items must be made as well. To begin with, missing from FAO's list are numerous fruit

99. Kahan, 1987, p. 157, citing the *Statistical Abstract of Israel*.
100. Doorenbos et al., 1986.

TABLE 3.16 Water Demand Coefficient for Food in the West Bank and Gaza, 1992

Item	Food		Water	
	Consumption (kg/capita)	S.S.R. (%)	Requirement (m³/100 kg)	Demand coefficient (m³/capita)
Wheat	120[a]	9	115–144[a]	138–173
Rice	15[a]	0	108–170[a]	16–26
Sugar	35	0	125–200	44–70
Potatoes	25	112	14–22	4–6
Dry pulses	7	9	167–330	12–23
Seeds (e.g., sesame)	2	10	200–500	4–10
Fresh vegetables	150	122	20–22	30–33
Melons	40	26	13–20	5–8
Bananas	26	13	25–40	7–26
Citrus	43	182	20–50	9–22
Grapes	25	101	25–50	6–13
Other fruits	47	50	40–50	19–24
Olives	7	100	50–67	4–5
Vegetable oil	15	59	500–800	75–120
Miscellaneous[b]				15–20

Red meat[c]				
Meat	10	76	875–1,750[c]	88–175
Feed		20		
Poultry				
Meat	22	87	188–375	41–83
Feed		5		
Fish[d]	2	22	75–150	2–3
Milk[e]	120		69–138	83–166
Feed		20		
Eggs[f]	5	195	300–600	15–30
Feed		5		
Total		716		614–1,017
Average				815

SOURCES: Calculated from Appendix 3.1 and previous tables; Doorenbos et al., 1986; El-Jaafari and Shaaban, 1995; and U.S. Department of Agriculture, 1981 and 1991.
Daily calorie intake per person: 2,700, of which 2,400 are plant based and 300 animal based.
S.S.R. = Self-sufficiency ratio
NOTES:
[a] After adjusting for moisture content.
[b] Includes such items as tea and coffee.
[c] Beef, sheep, and goats. The water requirements, however, are for beef.
[d] Assuming fish from fish ponds.
[e] This is the fluid milk equivalent of both fluid milk and dairy products consumption.
[f] Egg consumption usually is given in number of eggs, rather than in weight; 15 eggs are assumed to weigh 1 kg.

and vegetable crops that are subsumed in the table under the categories fresh vegetables and "other" fruits. I based the water efficiencies of these two classes of crops on approximations from the West Bank's and Gaza's irrigated sectors. Second, the water efficiency for vegetable (or more accurately plant) oils are derived on the following bases. The per capita consumption is assumed to have consisted of one-half olive oil and one-half other vegetable oils. This is a plausible assumption because the Palestinian territories produced 60 percent of their vegetable oil demand, and essentially all the oil they produced was olive oil. In addition to the quantities of oil, I assigned conversion factors from crops to oils, that is, how much crop it takes for the extraction of one unit of oil. The conversion factor, by weight, from olives to oil in the West Bank is 5 to 1. The other oils were imported, and tracking their types and quantities is impractical for our purposes. Their conversion factors vary; for example, the conversion factor for cottonseed oil is 5.9, for soybean 5.5, and for linseed 2.8.[101] I used an average of 5.5, which may be an overestimate. It is essential, however, to get more precise figures because of the apparently high water requirements for oil.

A third clarification pertains to the category "miscellaneous," which in the table covers items not incorporated under other categories, such as tea, coffee, and nuts, as well as flowers—a "not by bread alone" item. The corresponding water demand coefficient of 15 to 20 is arbitrary. Fourth, not included in the table are tobacco and alcohol. Although the latter may be "negative" foods, they still need water for their production. Smoking is widespread in the West Bank and Gaza and its exclusion lowers the water demand coefficient; the same is not true for alcohol, however.

Finally, the determination of the water demand coefficients for meat and dairy is particularly daunting, in part because it involves an intermediate step, namely the conversion of feed to meat and dairy. Establishing the feed-to-meat conversion factors (CFs) is replete with methodological and information-gathering difficulties. Animals consume a wide array of feed grains and grasses with dissimilar nutritional values, and tracking the proportions can be a statistical headache. Even the same type of meal may not carry identical nutritional value. For instance, grass fertilized with nitro-

---

101. These figures are taken from the United States Department of Agriculture, 1981.

gen contains more protein than unfertilized grass. Animals, moreover, are fed crop residues (e.g., straw or cottonseed meal) that often are equal to or exceed the edible food components. Including the water used in the making of such residues is tantamount to double counting because the source crops would have been produced anyway for human consumption. A further problem in estimating feed-to-meat and dairy CFs is that feeding practices vary among countries and regions within countries and for different animals. For example, about 80 percent of cattle feed in the United States comes from forage and 20 percent from the intensive feeding of concentrates (feed grains, protein feeds, and by-product feeds). In the Far East, however, animal feeding (except in China and Indonesia) is a backyard operation with crop residues and supplemental meal.[102] In the West Bank and Gaza, feeding is mainly intensive.

There are no data from the West Bank and Gaza that allow one to deduce relationships between feed and meat. However, one can employ approximations from the United Stated Department of Agriculture that are aggregated as corn-feed equivalent, presumably arrived at after grappling with the foregoing uncertainties and other factors. The technology of animal husbandry and types of breeds obviously are not the same in the West Bank and Gaza and the United States; thus, the CFs cannot be expected to be similar. Nonetheless, in the absence of data for the West Bank and Gaza, the U.S. numbers should be adequate for our purposes. These numbers are cited for beef, poultry, and fish (catfish) and for dairy products in table 3.17. Fish is included in the table, although it is consumed in minor amounts in Gaza, and even less in the landlocked West Bank. The fish is mainly from the Mediterranean Sea, as there are no fish ponds in either area. Israel, on the other hand, produces fish in fish ponds, for which it used about 100 mcmy in 1990. Some of this fish finds its way to markets in the West Bank and Gaza.

Table 3.17 shows how many kilograms (kg) of corn it takes for 1 kg of animal weight gain, and how many kg of live animal to produce 1 kg of retail meat. The latter values are presented here for information only; I will use CFs from corn to live animal weight only, on the assumption that most of the live animal is consumed. The assumption should not be wide off the mark for Palestinian

102. *World Resources Report*, 1988–89, p. 78.

TABLE 3.17 Conversion Factors from Water to Meat and Dairy

Meat and dairy	Kg corn per kg of animal	Kg live animal per kg retail	Kg corn per kg of retail
Beef	14[a]	2.4[b]	33.6
Poultry	3[c]	1.8[b]	5.4
Catfish	1.1	1.2	1.4
Milk	1.1[d]		1.1
Eggs	4.8[e]		4.8

SOURCE: United States Department of Agriculture, 1981, table 77, p. 57.
NOTES:
[a]A lower figure of 11 has been suggested by Gustafson et al., 1978, pp. 22–25.
[b]These are "rules of thumb" suggested to me by Lawrence A. Duewer, USDA, Economic Research Service, in a fax on 8 November 1996.
[c]The ratios for broilers are 2.6 and turkeys 4.1. In the Palestinian territories the poultry are for the most part chickens; the "3" accounts for the turkey fraction.
[d]Per kg of milk.
[e]Per kg of eggs.

society, especially if we also account for the fact that animals produce large quantities of manure that augment crop yields, ultimately raising crop-water productivity.

The second CF that should be established is from water to corn. The water efficiency for harvested corn, as for the other crops, is in table 3.16 and has been taken from the FAO study. This efficiency ranges between 0.8–1.6 kg/m^3, or the equivalent of 625–1,250 m^3/100 kg. Using this efficiency and the corn-to-meat figures from table 3.17, the CFs from water to meat and dairy look like this:

Meat and dairy	Water/meat and dairy (m^3/kg)
Beef	875 – 1,750
Poultry	188 – 375
Catfish	75 – 150
Milk	625 – 1,250
Eggs	300 – 600

In table 3.17 red meat includes both beef and sheep, although the water requirements are those of beef, which are somewhat lower than those for sheep. Furthermore, the figure for milk consumption refers to fluid milk equivalent. It is conjectural because the disaggregated data for dairy consumption are sketchy and the aggregated data usually are given as "milk and dairy." However, 1 kg of any dairy product is constituted of more than 1 kg of milk; for some types of cheese, for example, the ratio (by weight) of milk to cheese may be 10 to 1. The 120 kg are based on an average consumption of 70 kg of "meat and dairy." They are derived by comparison with data for Israel, where an individual's yearly consumption of milk and dairy averaged 100 kg derived from 200 kg of milk (Israel's diet is outlined in the next chapter). The 120 kg thus are 60 percent of Israel's per capita consumption; they also are about 15 percent larger than the corresponding ratios of red meat or poultry consumption. Although an accurate tally may show a different level of demand, it would not be so substantially different as to compromise the accuracy of the total water demand coefficient. Considering all of the foregoing uncertainties, in addition to those commonly faced in the preparation of baseline data, the current estimates only can be viewed as provisional.

A Staggering Water Deficit

The average diet in the West Bank and Gaza illustrated in table 3.16 may yield approximately 2,700 daily calories per person, of which 2,400 calories are plant based and 300 are animal based, similar to FAO's "guidelines" of 2,700 calories.[103] It ought to be kept in mind that the 2,700 calories were the average for the West Bank and Gaza: the daily calorie intake in the West Bank was about 2,900 and in Gaza 2,500.[104] Further, they are greater than the amount an average person actually consumes because they include postharvest losses. The 1992 calorie intake in the West Bank, as Kahan indicates, represents an improvement over the 2,430 reported for 1964.[105] The improvement is due to the rise of personal income owing mainly to the wages of Palestinian workers

103. This is my estimate obtained by comparing Israeli and Palestinian diets. The calorie make-up of the Israeli diet by food category is given in the "Food Balance Sheet" in the 1993 *Israel Statistical Abstract*. I proportioned the Palestinians' calories according to their consumption (by weight) of various foods relative to Israelis'. The figure of 2,700 calories is corroborated in World Bank, 1993a, vol. 4, p. 3, as well as in Kahan, 1987, p. 156, citing the *Israel Statistical Abstract*. Kahan reported the average West Bank diet in 1985 as yielding 2,857 daily calories per capita and containing more meat and dairy than the combined West Bank and Gaza diet in 1992.

104. World Bank, 1993a, vol. 4, p. 3.

105. Kahan, 1987, p. 156.

in Israel and remittances from Palestinians working in the oil-producing Arab states. The dietary improvement is also in line with the progress of dietary standards in adjacent Arab countries, such as Jordan, following the rise of oil prices in 1973.[106]

According to my calculations, the 1992 diet of the West Bank and Gaza corresponded to a water demand coefficient of between 614 and 1,017 m³, or an average of 815 m³. (It ought to be reiterated that this water demand coefficient is less than what farmers would use because it does not include water losses during conveyance.) How does this coefficient compare with the other coefficients cited earlier? The partial irrigation coefficient by BUNT, 90 m³ for fruits and vegetables and 25 percent of dairy products, is close to the lower range (96 m³) of the coefficient for the corresponding items in table 3.16, but is appreciably lower than the average, 131 m³. BUNT does not state how it arrived at its figure, especially the dairy coefficient. It does not specify the amount of milk or whether the irrigation water for fodder production is only supplementary and whether the fodder produced would be the sole source of nutrition for the animals (i.e., no foraging). Thus, whether the convergence between my lower bound coefficient and BUNT's figure is coincidental remains unclear. At any rate, the partial coefficient does not suffice as a basis for cross-checking the overall coefficient.

The average overall coefficient, 815 m³, lies midway between Postel's 400 m³ and the FAO's 1,570 m³, and it is close to Allan's 1,000 m³. Postel assumes that the average worldwide grain consumption is 300 kg per person, that the nongrain portion of the diet needs about one-third as much water to produce as the grain-based components, and that the water input is 1,000 m³ per ton of grain. It may be that her assumption of 1,000 m³ is somewhat low and does not account for rainfall over the rangelands that are a key source of animal feed. Nonetheless, her water demand coefficient of 400 m³ and my lower bound coefficient, 617 m³, may not be too far apart, considering that Postel's figure is global while mine is region specific. Allan does not back up his number with any data, and neither does the source consulted regarding the FAO coefficient; thus, I have no grounds for judging the present results vis-à-vis theirs. Consequently, the conclusion that must be drawn is that further investigation is needed for a definitive answer re-

106. Elmusa, 1994a, p. xix.

TABLE 3.18 Water Shares of Foodstuffs in the West Bank and Gaza, 1992

(Percent)

Food Category	Demand Coefficient	Water Deficit
Meat and dairy	42	49
Basic staples	28	33
Fruits and vegetables	12	0
Vegetable oil	12	14
Other	6	4

SOURCE: Calculated from Table 3.16.

garding the reliability of the water demand coefficient estimated here for the West Bank and Gaza.

Nonetheless, it still is a useful exercise to analyze the ramifications of the water demand coefficient for Palestinian food self-sufficiency. Its value will be assumed as the average of the range, 815 m³. Of the total, 42 percent was required for meat and dairy; 28 percent for the basic staples of wheat, rice, and sugar; 12 percent for vegetable oils; and 12 percent for the whole gamut of fruits and vegetables (table 3.18). Irrigation water in the Palestinian territories was earmarked for the last category of food crops; rainwater produced some of the wheat, vegetable oil, and animal feed; and the imported requisite water was responsible for providing the rest of the diet.

The imported water can be estimated in the following manner. The irrigation water, including the 100 mcmy IWE from the rainfed land, was in the vicinity of 250 mcmy, or 110 m³ per person. Subtracting this from the average coefficient yields a food-related water deficit of 705 m³ per person, or 5.7 times the irrigation supply. In aggregate terms, the water deficit for the Palestinian population in 1992 (2.24 million) thus was 1,577 mcmy. This is a staggering deficit and would be even higher if irrigation conveyance losses were accounted for. It is larger than the water that was allocated under the Johnston Plan for the five riparians of the Jordan River basin, 1,287 mcmy, and it is in the vicinity of Israel's total water use.

The deficit equaled the difference between the imported and exported requisite water. The exported requisite water, I estimate, was about 100 mcmy, of which one-half derived from the export of eggs (i.e., re-export of chicken feed); more than one-fourth of citrus; and the rest of fresh vegetables, olive oil, and potatoes. Thus, if the re-export of the requisite water for eggs, 50 mcmy, is disregarded, the requisite water imported to meet the domestic food demand would be 1,630 mcmy.

The major sources of the deficit were the basic staples—rice, sugar, and wheat—and meat and dairy. The three staples contributed one-third of the deficit. Rice and sugar need (in addition to large volumes of water) specific climate and soils not present in the West Bank and Gaza; thus, their portion of the deficit would have been inevitable. Wheat, which alone was a source of more than one-fifth of the deficit, was grown in the West Bank. However, the area sown in wheat has declined by more than 65 percent since the beginning of the Israeli occupation as a result of the land confiscation by, and the opening up of labor markets in, Israel;[107] relatively inexpensive grain imports as world commodity prices declined in the 1980s;[108] and lack of technological development that could have raised and stabilized wheat yields. In other words, the entire wheat deficit was avoidable had a more favorable political climate prevailed.

Still, the largest portion of the deficit, close to one-half, was engendered by meat and dairy. That was not just because some of these commodities themselves were imported but (and primarily) because the bulk of the intermediate input, animal feed, was imported. The meat and dairy contribution to the deficit underscores the negative impact on the water deficit of Israel's closure of large tracts of the West Bank's traditional pastures to Palestinian herders.

The demand for foodstuffs, and with it the demand for the import of requisite water, only can increase with the growth of income and population. Income growth not only raises the quantitative demand for foodstuffs but also is conducive to shifts in the dietary pattern toward greater meat and dairy demand. Such demands can be satisfied partially by increasing the area of irrigated agriculture, which calls for more water. It goes without saying that technological improvement and enhancing management skills also would boost greatly the yields of crops, particularly when it comes

107. According to ARIJ, 1994a, p. 41, the wheat area dropped by 300,000 dunums between 1967 and 1992, from 460,000 dunums to 160,000 dunums.
108. *World Resources Report*, 1992–93, p. 97.

to wheat, olives, and the vegetation of pastures. Enhancing the yields of these crops in the West Bank would be the equivalent of gaining water and ameliorating dependence on food imports. Investments in technologies and institutions that augment the yields of such crops thus may be worthy of comparison against investments for increasing irrigation water supply.

All the foregoing measures, however, would not be sufficient to balance the domestic output of the basic staples, meat, and dairy against demand. Dramatic increases in wheat yields are difficult to achieve, and rice and sugar are not likely to be produced in the West Bank and Gaza. Furthermore, although improvement of the productivity of the grazing areas can be beneficial, it cannot possibly keep up with population growth because of the high water requirements for the production of these food commodities. The realistic, albeit unhappy, conclusion is that the West Bank and Gaza because of limited water resources are destined to rely on substantial food imports.

Standard and Extended Water Budget

Having determined water supply and demand in the various sectors, one may construct an extended water budget or balance for the West Bank and Gaza. The standard budget covers municipal, industrial, and irrigation water, as indicated in table 3.19. As already demonstrated, however, rainfall was tapped directly in rainfed agriculture, and water was exported and imported indirectly through foodstuffs. There was also latent municipal water demand. An extended budget that factors in these sources of supply and demand offers a more accurate profile of the water situation than does the standard budget.

The standard budget drastically underestimates both water supply and demand, and it shows demand as being in equilibrium with *domestic* supply, with each being around 237 mcmy. According to the extended balance, however, water demand, excluding that which goes to export crops, is 2,000 mcmy, or more than eight times the water demand in the standard budget. Furthermore, *domestic* supply and demand are not in equilibrium; in the extended budget, demand surpassed supply by 1,663 mcmy, an amount that represents the total water deficit.

TABLE 3.19 Standard and Extended Water Balance in the West Bank and Gaza, 1992

Standard		Extended	
Item	*(mcmy)*	*Item*	*(mcmy)*
Demand		Demand	
M & I	87	M & I	
Irrigation	150	Manifest	87
Total demand		Latent	87
	237	Food consumption	1,826
Supply	237	Total demand	2,000
Balance	0	Domestic supply	
		M & I	87
		IWE	100
		Irrigation	200
		Total domestic supply	337
		Balance	−1,663

SOURCE: Previous tables and text.
M & I = municipal and industrial; IWE = irrigation water equivalent.

FORECASTING DEMAND

The demand for water can be expected to increase in the future and with it the deficit, unless supply is increased proportionally. Forecasting demand and its sectoral allocations is fraught with uncertainties. Several simplified projections based largely on judgment and prescription rather than rigorous analysis have been made for the West Bank and Gaza; not much would be gained by adding to them another projection of this type. What is required now is more rigorous analysis based on accurate baseline information. In the meantime, I will use some of the projections as a vehicle for clarifying a few of the strategic water demand and supply issues. In order to do that, it is necessary first to recall the main sources of uncertainty that would be encountered in making water demand projections for the West Bank and Gaza.

Future demand will be shaped by population and economic growth rates, the extent of horizontal agricultural expansion, and water policies, such as those related to pricing and conservation. Anticipating these factors in the abnormal conditions of the West Bank and Gaza can be even more uncertain than in more stable societies. For example, the future population of the West Bank and

Gaza will depend, like in any other society, on future birth and mortality rates. This alone is difficult to project. To it must be added two other sources of uncertainty. First, the baseline estimate, that is, current population, is controversial; only an accurate population census could rectify this problem. Second, the number of Palestinians who might return to the West Bank and Gaza is unknown. This likely will be the outcome of an agreement with Israel and the willingness and ability of those permitted to return. Future economic growth rates are linked to the overall political situation, the level of investment, economic policies, and type of government institutions. All of these variables are hard to foretell before a political settlement is sealed and the shape of future governance has become reasonably clear.

Further, the target dates of projection are important. The short-term (e.g., to the year 2000) is easier to predict than the medium- or long-term (e.g., to the year 2040). The interest here, however, primarily is in the less certain long-term. Postulating long-term demand is necessary for planning purposes and for establishing a needs basis for reallocating water rights in the common Israeli-Palestinian water resources, as is demonstrated in the next chapter.

Finally, the method of estimating future demand, whether normative or extrapolative, can affect the forecasts significantly. The normative method specifies targets that the analyst or planner deems desirable and anchors the overall demand estimates in them. The extrapolative method relies on past trends to project those of the future. The two methods overlap, and in each of them assumptions must be made about population and other variables, but they still are distinct methods. In the present context, the extrapolative method, starting from the present inequalities between Israelis and Palestinians can prejudice the projection of future demand in favor of the former. To be sure, the normative method can have the same effect, but the forecaster would have to be explicit about assuming unequal per capita targets for the two parties.

The projections examined below of future Palestinian water demand in the West Bank and Gaza are primarily of the normative type and apply for the medium and long terms. They come from two sources, the 1994 report by BUNT and the study that ARIJ undertook in cooperation with the Harvard Institute for International Development (HIID). Their results are cited in table 3.20 and illustrated in figure 3.10. The two forecasts were made after

TABLE 3.20 Projections of Water Demand for the West Bank and Gaza in 2010, 2020, and 2040

Item	BUNT	ARIJ-HIID Low	ARIJ-HIID High
Year 2010			
Population (millions)	3.2	4.2	5.7
Irrigated area (1,000 dunums)		393	479
Per capita demand (m³)			
Household	70	100	125
Irrigation	104		
Aggregate demand (mcmy)			
Household	222	425	576
Industrial		24	59
Irrigation	330[a]	273	334
Total aggregate demand	552	722	969
Year 2020			
Population (millions)	4.3	4.9	8.6
Irrigated area		504	681
Per capita demand (m³)			
Household	80	125	125
Irrigation	101		
Aggregate demand (mcmy)			
Household	342	619	1,082
Industrial		30	122
Irrigation	431[a]	352	479
Total aggregate demand	773	1,001	1,683
Year 2040			
Population (millions)	6.4		
Irrigated area			
Per capita demand (m³)			
Household	100		
Irrigation	93		
Aggregate demand (mcmy)			
Household	635		
Industrial			
Irrigation	594[a]		
Total demand	1,229		

SOURCES: ARIJ-HIID, 1994; BUNT, 1994.
NOTE:
[a]BUNT, p. 3.15, states that the availability of arable land would limit irrigation to 300 mcmy.

FIGURE 3.10 Water Demand Forecasts for the West Bank and Gaza

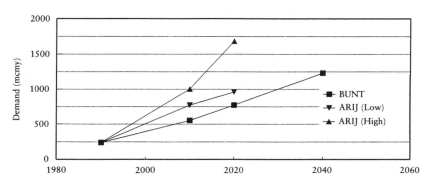

the Oslo accords and implicitly assumed favorable conditions— which so far have proved elusive—for economic development and implementation of water-related projects; thus, they ought to be viewed within this context. BUNT projects demand until the year 2040, whereas the ARIJ-HIID projections go only to 2020. Nonetheless, much insight may be gained about the future water profile by comparing and contrasting the two studies.

I will address their projections of municipal and irrigation demand only. Industrial demand is not forecast by BUNT, unless the study subsumed it under municipal demand. The ARIJ-HIID projection includes a fair amount of guesswork owing to the lack of reliable baseline data and the difficulty of envisioning the types of industries that would be established and their water demand.

A key feature of water demand in both forecasts is the change of sectoral allocation in favor of the municipal sector, which is consistent with the historical trend. The two forecasts, however, tangibly differ on the volume of this demand. The reason for the difference is the wide divergence in their estimates of the municipal demand coefficients (per capita annual demand) and population size. Neither forecast provides sufficient supporting details about how their figures were calculated. BUNT's coefficient of 70 m^3 by 2010 is double the 1990 figure of 35 m^3, representing approximately a 3.5 percent annual growth. ARIJ-HIID's coefficient of 100 m^3 translates into a 5.3 percent annual growth rate. It is equal to that of Israel in 1990. BUNT's growth rate would be reasonable under normal conditions, but because the existing demand has been kept low artificially by (among other things) restrictions on supply, rates closer to the ARIJ-HIID projections in the first period (ending in 2010) are more plausible. In any event, although the two forecasts differ on the pace of growth of the demand coefficient, they concur that eventually it will grow significantly, tripling or quadrupling to reach 100–125 m³.

Equally significant for future municipal demand is the size of the population. Here, as well, there is a marked disagreement between the two forecasts. The uncertainty regarding population size has been addressed earlier in this chapter. Suffice it to say that BUNT uses the low figures of Israel's Central Bureau of Statistics and does not factor in any returning refugees. ARIJ-HIID extrapolates the population size from the Heiberg et al. survey (cited earlier), which uses a variety of scenarios for birth and mortality rates and other parameters affecting population growth. The difference of the population size between the two forecasts compounds the gap in their projection of total municipal demand that derives from their varying estimates of the demand coefficient. It is not surprising then to find that even the low demand scenario of ARIJ-HIID for 2020 is close to BUNT's projection for 2040. Both sources, however, indicate that the municipal sector becomes eventually the leading one in terms of demand for water.

Apropos irrigation demand, the two forecasts take different routes. BUNT calculates it on the basis of the water demand coefficient, cited earlier, that would be adequate for self-sufficiency in fresh fruits and vegetables and 25 percent self-sufficiency in dairy products. It also assumes an increase in irrigation water productivity of about 20 percent over the present levels. The coefficient it posits even for the year 2000, 90 m³, exceeds the Palestinian per capita irrigation water use in the early 1990s, incidentally underscoring the meagerness of past supply. Furthermore, BUNT suggests that irrigation water demand would have a ceiling of 300 mcmy, owing to the limited availability of irrigable land. Nonetheless, BUNT projects demand apart from the land constraint because one of its purposes is to compare water demand versus supply in Israel, the West Bank, and Gaza as one agrohydrological unit without regard as to which side would produce the agricultural crops, a point to be elaborated further in the next chapter under the discussion of Israel's water demand. ARIJ-HIID, in contrast, computes irrigation demand from suppositions about the expansion of the irrigated area. It does not include changes in water productivity. In its high-demand scenario it postulates reclamation of class-2 land.

In spite of the different methods of projection, BUNT's estimates fall between the low and high scenarios of ARIJ-HIID. This is a coincidence and not because of any convergence in outlook. The demand coefficient that BUNT assumes and the population size that it projects make its forecast close to those needed to irrigate the available irrigable land according to ARIJ-HIID. Had the population size, demand coefficients, or irrigable land area been different, the projections of the two studies would not have converged.

Overall, the projections point to a demand in 2020 and 2040 ranging between more than three to seven times the use in the early 1990s, according to the standard water budget. Had ARIJ-HIID carried its calculations into the year 2040, it would have indicated a ratio five times higher than that of BUNT. Still, it is sobering to look at BUNT's smaller demand of 1,230 mcmy by 2040 against the potential supply from natural water resources. Suppose, for argument's sake, that the Palestinians obtained in a final settlement the equivalent of the water of the mountain and Gaza aquifers and their quota under the Johnston Plan from the Jordan basin. Together, these sources would total about 800 mcmy, an amount that would fall short of the projected demand of 1,230 mcmy. Furthermore, most of that quantity would be earmarked for municipal use, leaving irrigation as a "residual" sector in the sense that its demand would be satisfied after municipal demand, which presumably would have priority, and industrial demand, which can outbid agriculture because the returns to water in industry exceed those in agriculture. In such a case, the only way to satisfy the requirements of agricultural expansion would be from recycling municipal water and raising the technical efficiency of irrigation.

A central consideration of recycling would be that its benefits be on a par with its costs. The costs of recycling to agriculture may be deemed as those incurred in the extra treatment beyond the standard processes that are called for to make wastewater conform to public health and environmental standards, as well as transportation. The operating costs of treating wastewater to make it fit for irrigation have been estimated at $0.10/m^3 in 1993 prices and technology.[109] These are rough figures subject to variation according to population density, size of treatment plants, and crops (water for industrial crops requires less treatment than water for fresh

109. Assaf et al., 1993, p. 62.

fruits and vegetables). Still, the $0.10/m³ is encouraging because it is well below the MVPW for many of the horticultural crops in the West Bank and Gaza and the cost of water from the wells. That is not the whole story, however. The construction of a sewage system and treatment plants may require as much as $300 per person, which means major initial capital outlays. In the West Bank and Gaza, where other infrastructural facilities present stiff competition for scarce capital, securing the necessary outlays may not be so easy.

ARIJ-HIID's projections pose an even a greater challenge than those of BUNT. They intimate that the Palestinians would have to secure water from alternative resources (e.g., desalination), a difficult proposition at best. Otherwise, they would have to lower demand, which they can do either through checking the birth rate or pervasive conservation measures. Furthermore, lack of water (not to mention other factors) ultimately may block the reclamation of at least a portion of class-2 land included in the ARIJ-HIID forecast.

The significance of the projected population growth and agricultural expansion can be appreciated still further in the light of the water requirements for food production. The water demand for food production, conservatively assuming a diet similar to that in 1992, would be 5,525 mcmy. Consequently, if one takes BUNT's figures for 2040, the irrigation deficit would be around 5,000 mcmy. This figure amplifies the conclusion drawn above that meeting food demand is only possible through the importation of large quantities of foodstuffs. The ability of the Palestinians to secure the necessary imports would hinge on the pace of their economic development and the availability of food on the world market, each of which is a major topic.

4

The Matrix of the Israeli-Palestinian Water Conflict

The Israeli-Palestinian water conflict is nearly as old as the political conflict between the two sides. Its history and that of the wider Arab-Israeli water conflict, particularly over the waters of the Jordan basin, have been chronicled and analyzed in numerous publications, and little would be gained by going through the exercise one more time.[1] The focus of this chapter is the conflict's "content," that is the issues that drive it. The goal is to clarify these issues in order to prepare the ground for exploring, in the next chapter, how they might be resolved equitably and cooperatively.

The issues can be divided into six categories: (1) the land-water nexus or control of hydrospace; (2) the maldistribution of water rights in the common resources and attendant water use gap between the two sides; (3) the encroachment by Israeli settlers on Palestinian water resources; (4) Israel's control of water institutions, information, and legal mechanisms; (5) out-of-basin water transfer; and (6) future management of the common resources. The first issue refers to the interlocking of the historical control over land, recent claims by Israeli policy makers and strategists about the need to retain land in the West Bank for securing Israel's water supply, and ramifications for Palestinian water supply of Israel's potential retention

1. See, for example, Inbar, 1984; Kahhaleh, 1981; Lowi, 1993; Naff and Matson, 1984; Saliba, 1968; and Wolf, 1992.

TABLE 4.1 The Matrix of the Israeli-Palestinian Water Conflict

Issue	Transboundary	Occupation related
Equitable utilization	X	
Joint management	X	
Out-of-basin transfer	X	
Land-water nexus		X
Israeli settlements' water		X
Israel's institutional and legal control		X

of land for reasons other than water. The second issue deals with the unequal distribution of water rights between the Israelis and Palestinians in favor of Israel and the attendant wide gap in water use between them.

The third issue concerns the appropriation of water from the West Bank and Gaza for the benefit of the Jewish settlers in these territories. The fourth issue, institutional and legal control, arises out of Israel's takeover of the management of water production. The fifth issue, out-of-basin water transfer, concerns Israel's transfer, beginning in 1964, of water from the Jordan basin to the coastal plain and the Negev Desert. The sixth issue has to do with the opportunities for, and constraints against, multilateral (Arab-Israeli) management of the Jordan basin and bilateral (Israeli-Palestinian) management of the common groundwater.

It is obvious from the brief statement of these issues that some of them—the maldistribution of water rights, joint management, and out-of-basin transfers—are present in transboundary water conflicts elsewhere. Others, however, such as the institutional control and land-water nexus, are perhaps unique to the Israeli-Palestinian case. It is hence possible by characterizing the issues as "general" (transboundary) and "unique" (occupation related) to construct a matrix of the Israeli-Palestinian water conflict as shown in table 4.1. The superimposition of the second category of issues, which derive from the peculiarity of the Israeli-Palestinian conflict, on the first helps explain the seeming intractability of the water feud.

In terms of presentation, all the issues are discussed in this chapter, with the exception of out-of-basin transfer (issue 5) and joint management (issue 6). Not much can be said analytically about the former issue, which is discussed within the context of equitable utilization in chapter 5. Joint management (issue 6) is a future, not a past, issue and occupies a good part of the next chapter. The management of the Palestinian water sector has passed into the hands of the PA as a result of the Taba Agreement; consequently, the institutional and legal control by Israel (issue 4) may be only of historical significance and not highly germane to the final status talks. Israel, however, still wields considerable legal and other powers regarding water in the West Bank, such as the power to license and inspect Palestinian wells. More important, it is not possible to understand Israeli water policy or the water maldistribution and gap (issue 1) without examining the question of Israel's institutional control. Furthermore, the adverse impact of such control will remain a legacy for the Palestinians to grapple with for a long time to come.

In addition to the issues themselves, the perception of water by, or its position "in the cognitive map"[2] of, the antagonists has been cited by analysts as a possible factor affecting the amenability of the conflict for resolution. It has been argued that water has an ideological dimension in Israel by virtue of its association with agriculture, which itself was perceived ideologically by early Zionists. According to this argument, the ideological dimension has come to the fore in key moments of the conflict and could do so again. I posit that, whatever the case may have been in the past, the material foundations of the ideological perception of water in Israel have all but disappeared, and a water-specific ideology will play little role in water decisions. In contrast to Israeli perceptions, few people have paid attention to how Palestinians perceive water. The Palestinian perception of water has been evolutionary in nature, linked to economic and political developments. Under Israeli occupation, it has acquired a moral hue in light of what the Palestinians view as unjust Israeli policies. Such a perception is not ideological and can be attenuated to by removing the causes.

THE LAND-WATER NEXUS

Whatever the locus of the Arab-Israeli dispute was yesterday or is today—immigration, Jerusalem, settlements, history, or meta-

2. This term is used in Naff and Matson, 1984, pp. 186–88.

physics—control over land always has been at the core of arguments and actions. Water also has been a primary object of contention. One does not need to subscribe to the "hydraulic imperative," or the notion that the desire to seize the water resources propelled Israel's territorial expansion, to see that, in fact, at more than one phase of the protracted conflict, the competition for the two resources was intertwined and control of one resource abetted the control of the other. This "land-water nexus" will be illustrated by historical examples. The key concerns here, however, are Israeli claims that West Bank territory is needed to safeguard the water supply within its pre-1967 boundaries, the technical validity of such claims, and the water-related consequences for the Palestinians of potential Israeli retention, for whatever reason, of West Bank land.

Historically, leaders and planners of organized Zionism perceived water as an indispensable economic resource necessary to control for large-scale irrigation—a prerequisite for absorbing large numbers of immigrants and for laying the foundation of an economically viable Jewish entity in Palestine. Moreover, because Palestine lacked coal and other fossil fuels, water was seen as a means of generating hydroelectricity for powering industry.[3]

The first source of water to enter the equation of the Arab-Israeli conflict was the Jordan basin because it was visible; the groundwater potential initially was not understood well. The idea of diverting water from the upper Jordan basin into the Negev Desert had been broached in the late nineteenth century in a report published by Zionist sympathizers in the London-based Palestine Exploration Fund.[4] As long as the Jordan basin was part of the Ottoman empire, however, there was no transboundary water dispute. The conflict developed after the region fell under British and French tutelage following their victory over Turkey in World War I. During the negotiations between the two European powers for carving up the territory of the "Fertile Crescent" between them, Zionist leaders lobbied both powers, notably at the 1919 Paris Peace Conference, to secure what they viewed as desirable or viable boundaries for what was to become Mandate Palestine. In fact, Britain had promised in the 1917 Balfour Declaration to help set

---

3. See, for example, Frischwasser-Ra'anan, 1955, pp. 86–88.
4. See Kahhaleh, 1981, p. 9.

up a "Jewish homeland" in Palestine.[5] The boundaries of the Mandate were justified on several grounds, among them the inclusion of ample water resources. The rationale for the boundary proposals was introduced thus:

> The boundaries are sketched [in an attached sheet] with the general economic needs and historic traditions of the country in mind. . . . The economic life of Palestine, like that of every other semi-arid country, depends on the available water supply. It is, therefore, of vital importance not only to secure all water resources already feeding the country, but also to be able to conserve and control them at their sources . . . it is highly desirable, in the interest of economic administration, that the geographical area of Palestine should be as large as possible.[6]

The proposals then enumerated the water sources sought: Mount Hermon (which the report dubbed "the Father of Waters"), most of the Jordan River system, and that part of the Litani River after it bends westward toward the Mediterranean. The proposed boundary was to extend east of the Jordan River parallel to the Hijaz railway and down to the Gulf of Aqaba on the Red Sea. Aqaba, the Zionist statement recalled, was also "the terminus of an important trade route of Palestine from the days of Solomon onward."[7]

Other plans were submitted and demands were made by Zionist leaders, but it was, of course, Britain and France that disposed of the territories in protracted negotiations.[8] Water resources mattered and were bargained for;[9] and when the boundaries of the British Mandate of Palestine eventually were demarcated in 1923, they included key components of the above water sources, such as the Hula and Tiberias lakes and the entire, above ground course of the Dan River.[10] At the same time, however, they excluded the Litani River and vital segments of the Banyas, al-Hasibani, and Yarmuk rivers. After half a century and several major wars,

5. Balfour was the British Foreign Secretary at the time.
6. Toye, 1989, vol. 2, p. 217.
7. Ibid., p. 218.
8. How much weight they accorded to pressures from the Arabs and Zionists is controversial and beyond the scope of the present text.
9. Garfinkle, 1994, pp. 109–34.
10. Ibid; and Toye, 1989, vol. 3.

however, the Zionist movement and Israel have been able to extend control over the entirety of the water resources of geographic Palestine and the headwaters of the Jordan River. The combined control over the water resources and the territories that contain them was chronicled in chapter 2. Presently, the concern is with the extent to which the control of one resource was, or could be in the future, motivated by, contingent upon, and aided by the control of the other.

The Role of Water in Israeli Territorial Acquisition

Israel's historical preoccupation with water resources and expanded control over them in 1967 led some analysts—one might call them "water imperativists"—to postulate a water or "hydraulic" imperative behind Israel's wars.[11] Certainly, the notion of "water wars"—not just between the Arabs and Israel but in the Middle East as a whole—has been popularized in the media. It is also true that armed confrontations in the 1950s and in 1964 between Syria and Israel were related to water, and Israel's diversion of the Jordan prompted a special Arab summit in 1964.

Nonetheless, the fact that Israel has benefitted enormously from the water it seized in 1967 does not necessarily make the "water imperative" in this instance plausible. The outcome of the June 1967 war was by no means as certain at the time as it appears in retrospect, just as the fact that Israel benefitted tremendously from cheap Palestinian labor does not suggest that it would have fought a war for it. Further, by 1967 the share of agriculture, the chief water-using sector, in the Israeli GDP was less than 10 percent. Research on the events that culminated in the 1967 war also reveals that water was not a strong factor (if a factor at all) in the eruption of the war.[12]

Nevertheless, the special geographical character of the water resources in question must have encouraged Zionist and Israeli attempts to secure physical control over them. That is because a takeover of relatively minor land areas, notably in the upper part of the Jordan basin between Lake Tiberias and Mount Hermon,

11. See, for example, Cooley, 1984; Nijim, 1990; and Stauffer, 1984. For a discussion of the question, see also Lowi, 1993; Naff and Matson, 1984; and Wolf, 1992.
12. See Lowi, 1993, pp. 115–44; and Wolf, 1992, pp. 118–31.

ensures command over significant quantities of the basin's waters. A similar situation also prevails regarding the West Bank aquifer system, especially its northern and western basins. Thus, it was sufficient for Zionist planners to roll the pencil on the map one centimeter or two to the right and upward to bring the headwaters within the territory they wanted. Likewise, Israel's armored tanks did not need to roll more than a few kilometers to the east and the north to bring the headwaters under Israeli dominion. By contrast, Egypt, for instance, would not be able by comparable actions along the Nile to enhance its access to water, because that river's headwaters are located thousands of kilometers away in the Ethiopian highlands; thus, a land-water nexus like Israel achieved would not be easy to establish for the Nile.

Of course, one never may know exactly what informed the territorial aims—and actions to achieve these aims—of organized Zionism, and later of Israel. These aims, which one scholar called "elusive and ambiguous,"[13] were justified on different grounds at different times, sometimes by the same leaders.[14] In the 1919 proposals by the Zionist Organization, the suggested borders were justified according to several criteria—economic (water, agricultural land in the Jordan Valley, and the Hijaz railway), strategic (the railway control of Aqaba on the Red Sea as an opening to Asia and Africa), and historical (from Dan to Beersheba). If one can tailor a "designer state" from scratch, why not draw optimum borders that will secure all the perceived needs, including water, especially when all it takes is a stroke of the pen?

Zionism's territorial aims, however, always were tempered by pragmatic considerations. For example, the Zionists found it politic to accede to Britain's decision to separate Transjordan from Palestine, with the Jordan River forming the border between the two. Further, Jewish settlements in Palestine before 1948 were confined largely to the plains (coastal, Marj ibn 'Amir, and al-Hula) and the Baysan Valley, areas with irrigable land and sufficient irrigation water. It is striking how the location even of the settlements established before 1930 already had defined in an embryonic form the eastern borders of the Israeli state (see map 4.1). Furthermore, Jewish immigrants did not settle in the Jordan Valley below the Baysan district or in the mountainous terrain of Palestine, i.e., in

13. Taylor, 1971.
14. Ibid.; and Kimmerling, 1983b.

MAP 4.1 Jewish Colonies in Palestine, ca. 1930

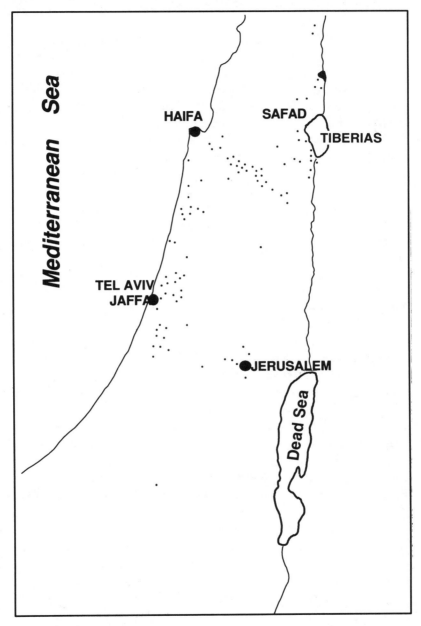

SOURCE: Walid Khalidi, ed. *From Haven To Conquest: Readings in Zionism and the Palestine Problem Until 1948.* (1971), p. 315.

the area that became known as the West Bank in 1950. Their avoidance of these areas probably was due to the harshness of climate in the lower part of the Jordan Valley and the low economic value of agriculture owing to the lack of irrigation water and security assets (transportation in particular) in the mountain areas. This pattern of Jewish (non)settlement attests not only to the importance of water resources in the making of Israel but also to the pragmatism with which the land question was approached.

Pragmatic considerations also may have contributed to the Zionist leaders' acceptance of the exclusion of these areas from the Jewish state proposed by the United Nations' partition plan of 1947; they always could go beyond the more circumscribed boundaries when the opportunity arose. This is as much suggested, for example, by Baruch Kimmerling in a commentary on a statement by David Ben-Gurion, Israel's first prime minister, advocating acceptance of the UN plan against those who saw it as impairing the "the country's wholeness."[15] The thrust of Ben-Gurion's statement was that in biblical times, the borders of Palestine under Jewish control expanded and contracted. Kimmerling sees in this argument both a nod to the existing balance of power at the time and a "hint of other borders in the future."[16] Indeed, since then Israel's boundaries have expanded and contracted continuously, sometimes in modest increments and at other times in leaps and bounds.

It was not until the peace treaty with Egypt in 1979 that Israel agreed to define some of its borders. It did so again in the peace treaty with Jordan in 1994; in both treaties the borders were delimited according to those specified for Mandate Palestine. If treaties are to be concluded with Syria and Lebanon, Israel again will be summoned to mark its borders.

In the case of the occupied Palestinian territories, however, Israel's aims have remained "elusive and ambiguous." In the decades following 1967, numerous statements and "plans" by Israeli officials and top strategists have been issued identifying the areas slated for annexation or effective control by Israel. Some of them advocate total annexation and others partial. Total annexation often has been associated with the Likud and other right-wing political parties, whereas the partial annexation of the remaining 23 percent of Palestine—often presented as "ter-

15. Kimmerling, 1983b, pp. 61–62.
16. Ibid.

ritorial compromise"—is associated mainly with Labor. Those advocating total annexation generally do so on historic-religious grounds, although water and security reasons also are used. However, the partial annexationists, like the early Zionists, justify their calls for land retention on broad strategic considerations including security, economics, and water.[17] The hydrologic arguments of both schools are considered below.

The Water Argument of the Total and Partial Annexationists

The water arguments of those advocating the total annexation of the West Bank were enunciated most clearly in two advertisements placed in the *Jerusalem Post* in the summer of 1990 by the Ministry of Agriculture, the agency responsible for water affairs in Israel.[18] This was during the tenure of Raphael Eitan as minister of agriculture, a post he reassumed when Benjamin Netanyahu's Likud-led government came to power in 1996. The advertisements cited two reasons for retaining the West Bank: uncontrolled extraction of water by Palestinians would seriously damage Israel's capacity to pump water from its side; and the high risk of water pollution, especially owing to the lack of a sewage system in the West Bank.

The Likud Party and Eitan's Tsomet Party, both advocate the retention of the West Bank (or "Judea and Samaria" in their lexicon) for historic-ideological reasons and consider it part of "the land of Israel" (*Eretz Yisrael*). They view the Palestinians living in it as residents with no rights to land or water. It is therefore likely that water, as a pretext for annexation, must have come as an afterthought, a seemingly technical justification for a stance already taken. It also could have been a scare tactic to frighten the Israeli public about the consequences of returning territory to the Palestinians because the advertisements came in the summer of 1990 at the end of a long drought, when fear of water shortage was very much present.

Likud's political use of the water argument for the purpose of territorial expansion, moreover, had been given "scientific" justification by Israeli experts, some of whom were mentioned in the

17. See, among others, Cohen, 1986; and Schiff, 1989. See also Benvenisti and Khayat, 1988, for a series of maps of some of the annexation plans, including a 1976 plan by the Labor Party and a 1981 plan by Ariel Sharon.
18. The *Jerusalem Post*, 10 and 17 August 1990.

second advertisement. In the same vein, Joshua Schwarz concluded in a paper given at the American Enterprise Institute, a conservative Washington think-tank, that:

> Cutting Judea and Samaria off from the rest of the country may result in the mismanagement of groundwater resources. Increasing groundwater pumpage will draw the water below the red line and cause irreversible salination of the aquifers in the plains adjoining Judea and Samaria.[19]

Schwarz himself believes that the West Bank and Gaza are part of Israel, and the annexationist conclusion of his paper seems preordained, arrived at before an examination of the hydrology. His introductory sentences read:

> Judea and Samaria and the Gaza Strip . . . were separated politically and economically from Israel in the period of 1948–1967 . . . [Or they] are climatically and hydrologically interconnected with the other regions of Israel.[20]

One notes Schwarz's assumption that groundwater sources would be mismanaged if they came under Palestinian control. Ironically, the overexploitation and pollution of water resources in Israel and the West Bank and Gaza occurred under Israeli management and were occasioned by policies Israel pursued, not by the lack of technical expertise. Certainly, the Palestinians would have to build their water management expertise after years of obstruction by none other than Israel itself and devise a legal code conducive to water conservation. However, they would have an incentive to care for the groundwater resources and might not need to overpump if they were to receive their fair share from these resources. Schwarz's solution to the water problem in the West Bank and Gaza is to rely on water imports or desalination.[21]

On technical grounds the annexationists are erroneous. Only those areas that constitute the headwaters of the western and northern basins in the West Bank are hydrologically connected in a significant way to the Israeli system. Annexation of all the West Bank therefore makes no hydrological sense.

19. Schwarz, 1982, p. 100.
20. Ibid., p. 81.
21. Ibid., p. 100.

MAP 4.2 Aquifer Areas Mentioned for Israeli Annexation

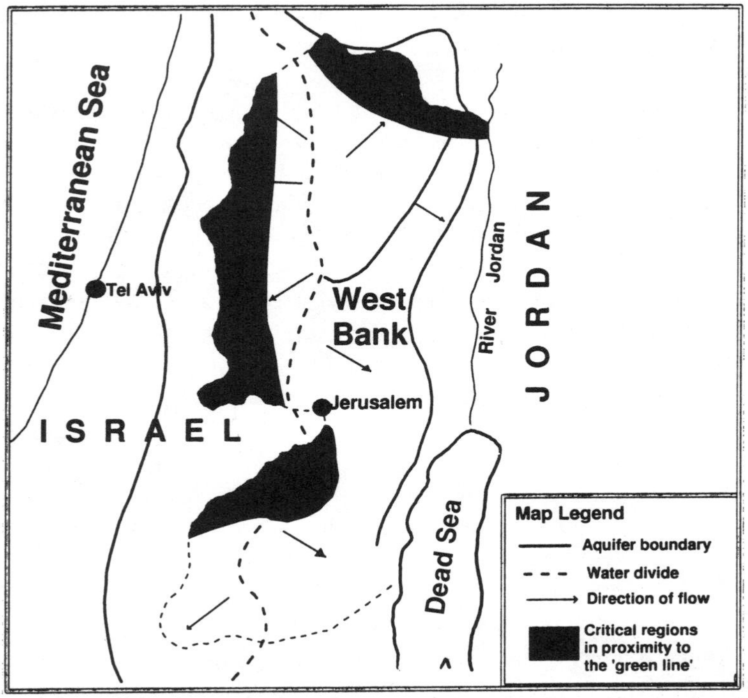

SOURCE: Adapted from David Newman, "Boundaries in Flux," *Boundary and Territorial Briefing*, University of Durham, 1995.

Indeed, those advocating partial annexation for water-related reasons "limit" themselves to the retention of a 2- to 6-km-wide strip of the West Bank along the western and northern borders with Israel, an area which they believe contains critical hydrological zones (see map 4.2).[22] The size of such a strip varies with the expert, and may be adjusted because of factors other than water, such as the need to exclude Palestinian population centers within the strip from falling inside Israel. Yet, even advocacy of this more modest annexation seems to contradict the technical explanations of some Israeli specialists that depict the West Bank as only a recharge area of the western basin and Israel as the storage area, or the area from which substantial amounts of water can be tapped. On the basis of this explanation, Haim Gvirtzman, for example,

22. See Cohen, 1986; Movement for Preservation of Israel's Water, 1994; Schiff, 1989; and Wolf, 1992 (Wolf is not necessarily an advocate of land retention but is cited here for his discussion of the question).

claims a large share of natural water rights for Israel from the western aquifers, a point elaborated in the next chapter.

Other analysts have pointed out that the costs of significant water abstraction from the West Bank would be quite high because the mountainous terrain renders the water table deeper and harder to reach. The costs could go higher with increased pumping by Israel from its side of the border, as such increase would lower the water table in the West Bank. These analysts, moreover, assert that the complex drilling technology required for reaching the water table is not available to the Palestinians. They view the high costs and lack of technology as a possible impetus for the Palestinians to agree to obtain water at cheaper rates from inside Israel, where pumping costs are lower, a topic that will be revisited in the next chapter.[23]

Water Ramifications of Land Loss for the Palestinians

Whether or not Israel uses water as an argument for the retention of West Bank territory, such retention will have marked implications for Palestinian access to water. How much of the West Bank Israel will demand is not yet known. The DOP signed by Israel and the PLO did not clarify the size of the area of the settlements in Gaza or the West Bank; protracted negotiations and two subsequent accords—Cairo and Taba—were required to define them. As for the final borders between Israel and the West Bank, they are expected to be the subject of final negotiations between Israel and the PLO, which were inaugurated on 5 May 1996 and are supposed to conclude by mid-1999.

Despite current uncertainties, it is worth noting that one of the latest annexation plans, titled "Enclaves for Peace," was presented to the Israeli cabinet on 24 October 1993, after the DOP was signed.[24] The territory it marked for annexation is an expanded version of the 1970 Allon Plan, the best known of such plans and named for Yigal Allon, then deputy prime minister and a Labor Party leader. The new plan takes into account the spread of the settlements since 1970 and the expansion of Jerusalem. It does not allow for a Jericho corridor (which was present in the Allon Plan),

23. Fisher et al., 1994.
24. A map of the plan is in Gilbert, 1993.

and it splits the West Bank into three enclaves—northern, central, and southern—rather than the two enclaves of the Allon Plan. More specifically, the various annexation plans[25] often mark three areas for annexation or for effective control by Israel: Jerusalem, the Jordan Valley, and the northwestern quadrant of the Dead Sea. None of these areas has come under the jurisdiction of the PA in the last interim agreement (Taba) on the West Bank and Gaza.

In the Israeli definition, "metropolitan Jerusalem" has come to mean about 10 percent of the West Bank territory. If Israel retains this area, Palestinian water claims (based on natural rights) could be affected, because the recharge area under Palestinian sovereignty would shrink. Annexation of the Jordan Valley would vitiate the status of the West Bank as a riparian of the Jordan basin and deny it water rights in that basin. The Jordan Valley is potentially one of the main areas of agricultural expansion and perhaps of resettlement of Palestinian returnees. If Israel were to annex it and to deny Palestinians access to the water of the Jordan River, this potential of the valley would be undermined. Further, the territory marked for annexation in the Jerusalem and Jordan Valley areas commonly includes the eastern slopes that control the headwaters of the eastern aquifer where Israel has drilled many wells to supply the settlements. Equally important is the spatial fragmentation of the West Bank into "peace enclaves" which, if it comes to pass, would make the transfer of water from one "enclave" to another subject to Israeli will and place the water conduits under Israeli control. Finally, retention of the northwestern quadrant of the Dead Sea could compromise any Palestinian claims to partake of the benefits from potential projects linking the Red or Mediterranean seas to the Dead Sea for hydropower generation. In short, the land-water nexus entailed and could entail for the Palestinians a double loss of land and water.

Maldistribution of Water Resources and Water Gap

The maldistribution of water rights has been viewed by the Palestinians as the core of the water conflict with Israel. It precipitated the other issues as well, especially the takeover of the management of the water sector in the West Bank, which Israel pursued as a

25. See also f. 101.

TABLE 4.2 Indicative Israeli and Palestinian Withdrawals from the Water Resources in Geographic Palestine

Source	Available (mcmy)	Percentage of withdrawals	
		Palestinians	Israelis
Renewable aquifers			
Mountain			
Eastern	100	57	43
Northeastern	140	29	71
Western	360	6	94
Coastal	340	25	75
Galilee			
Eastern	45	0	100
Western	155	0	100
Carmel	70	0	100
'Araba (Arava)	25	0	100
Surface water			
Jordan River basin	615[a]	0	114[b]
Floodwater	90	0	45
Nonrenewable aquifer			
Negev Desert	70 billion m^3		

SOURCES: BUNT, 1994; Taba Agreement (Annex III, Article 4, Schedule 10); and tables 1.1 and 3.2.
NOTES:
[a]This is the combined share of the West Bank and Israel under the Johnston Plan.
[b]Israel diverts about 700 mcmy from the Jordan basin.

way of maintaining its water privileges and of legitimatizing land retention to protect the water supply. The maldistribution is evident in the diversity of the water sources to which the two sides have access and the water quantities they extract. It has resulted in a striking water use gap between them in both the municipal and irrigation sectors.

The maldistribution of water rights is clearly illustrated by the statistics in table 4.2 and their aggregates in figure 4.1. The figures show that Israel and Jewish settlers in the West Bank and Gaza extract water from all the water resources of geographic Palestine. Israel draws and distributes the water through an extensive, integrated network of water conduits, centered on its Water Carrier, which affords it flexibility in managing the water resources, notably in times of drought and in mixing water of different qualities. In contrast, the Palestinians are limited to the

FIGURE 4.1 Israeli and Palestinian Water Extraction by Source

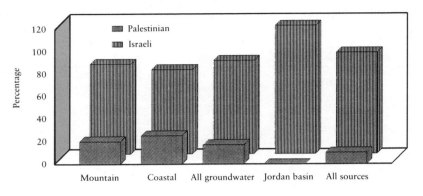

SOURCE: Table 4.1

mountain aquifer and the portion of the coastal aquifer underlying Gaza, and their water distribution system is highly decentralized. These conditions rigidify the management system and render the supply more vulnerable than in Israel.

Overall, Israel takes more than 83 percent of the groundwater of geographic Palestine,[26] and it alone impounds surface water, notably from the Jordan basin. From the mountain aquifer, Israel takes 483 mcmy (including 40 mcmy for the settlers in the Jordan Valley), compared with 118 mcmy for the Palestinians, or four times as much. It also pumps more than 280 mcmy from the coastal aquifer, or three-quarters of the water that the two sides extract from it.

The preceding are averages; in actuality Israel may take more or less than the above proportions as dictated by rainfall conditions. That is because Palestinian allocations are nearly stable, notably from the western and northeastern basins of the mountain aquifer, while Israel, mainly in response to rainfall levels, varies its annual extraction. In the dry years Israel usually extracts more water than in the wet years to meet irrigation requirements. The variations of the water output (pumping and spring flow) of the western basin of the mountain aquifer, which are essentially the result of Israel's, not the Palestinian's, shifting use are illustrated in the following figures.[27]

26. It is hard to be precise here because of overpumping.
27. Figures are from Netanyahu et al., 1994, p. 175.

Crop year	Pumpage (mcmy)
1987/88	377
1988/89	379
1989/90	419
1990/91	356
1991/92	255
1992/93	392

The figures indicate that during 1989–90, the peak of a drought cycle, extraction from that basin exceeded its safe yield by about 60 mcmy. The Palestinian water share in that year was about 20 mcmy, or less than 5 percent. The situation was different in 1991–92, a crop year of plentiful rainfall, and the Palestinian share was somewhat larger and Israel's smaller than they were in 1989–90.

As for surface water, Israel impounds water from the western wadis that commence in the West Bank's watershed, whereas the Palestinians get virtually nothing from those wadis. In addition, Israel by 1993 was thought to have had impounded an average of 1 mcmy from Wadi Gaza (Bessor) and was planning a total of 9 mcmy.[28] Palestinian specialists have contended that Israel takes away even larger quantities. However, they probably would be unable to specify those quantities accurately, because only the tail end of the wadi traverses Gaza. Overall, Israel impounds about 40 mcmy, or 45 percent, of the potentially extractable runoff in geographic Palestine; the Palestinians impound negligible amounts.

Israel also draws large quantities from the Jordan basin, whereas the Palestinians are denied access to it. To put the situation in the basin in perspective, reference should be made to the water quotas allotted by the Johnston Plan and to the water agreement between Israel and Jordan included in their peace treaty of 26 October 1994. The total amount of water allotted by the plan to all the riparians was 1,287 mcmy, according to their respective irrigation requirements in the basin. The share of each riparian and the source of diversion are listed in table 4.3. The quotas are straightforward; the West Bank, then part of Jordan, was accorded a share subsumed under that of Jordan; water for it was slated for diversion through a gravity channel, the West Ghor Canal, across

28. Schwarz, 1993.

TABLE 4.3 Actual Use Versus Quotas under the Johnston Plan in the Jordan River Basin

Country	Johnston Plan quota (mcmy)	Percent of total	Actual use (mcmy)	Percent of total
Lebanon[a]	35	3	20	<2
Syria[b]	132	10	200	17
Israel[c]	400	31	690	60
Jordan[d]	720	56		
East Bank[e]	505	39	250	22
West Bank[f]	215	17	0	0
Total	1,287	100	1,160	100[g]

SOURCES: Based mainly on American Friends of the Middle East, 1964; BUNT, 1994, pp. 2.6–2.7; Naff and Matson, 1984, pp. 41–42; and Naff, 1991c.

NOTES:

[a]Both quotas and use from the al-Hasibani.

[b]Quotas: 90 from the Yarmuk, 22 from the Jordan, and 20 from the Banyas; actual use: all from the Yarmuk.

[c]Quotas: 375 from the Jordan, 25 from the Yarmuk; actual use: 550 from the Jordan and 70–100 from the Yarmuk.

[d]Quotas: 100 from the Jordan, 377 from the Yarmuk, and 243 from the western and eastern side wadis.

[e]Quotas: 297 from the Jordan and the Yarmuk and 206 from the side wadis; actual use: 130 from the Yarmuk and 120 from the side wadis.

[f]Quotas: 180 from the Jordan and the Yarmuk and 35 from the side wadis.

[g]Percentages do not add up due to rounding.

the western Jordan Valley (see map 4.3). It is possible to estimate what the West Bank's separate quota ought to be under the Johnston Plan. In fact, a 1992 PLO report put the West Bank's share at 290 mcmy (220 from the Jordan River and 70 from the Yarmuk River).[29] Another report by a group of Palestinian water specialists, some of whom are or were members of the official negotiating team, estimated the West Bank quota at 100 mcmy, adding, without further elaboration, that "a rational allocation" would accord the Palestinians "at least 200" mcmy.[30] However, neither of these reports explained how their figures were derived.

I submit that the West Bank's share can be calculated as a percentage of Jordan's quota and be in proportion to the irrigable area on the eastern and western banks of the Jordan Valley, as estimated by the Chicago-based engineering firm, Baker-Harza. The rationale behind this proposition is that Jordan's share was allocated according to the water required for the irrigable area on

29. PLO, 1992.
30. Water Resources Action Program Task Force, 1994, p. 7.

MAP 4.3 The Johnston Plan

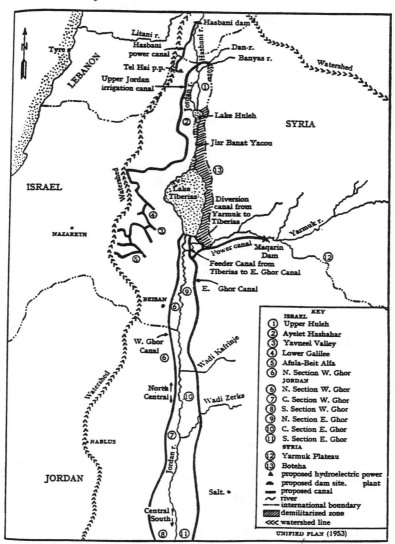

SOURCE: Saliba, *The Jordan River Dispute* (Dordrecht, The Netherlands: Kluwer Academic Publishers, 1968), p. 91.

both sides of the river. The West Bank share is illustrated in the following table.[31]

31. Table is derived from American Friends of the Middle East, 1964, p. 79.

	Total (dunums)	West Bank (dunums)	East Bank (dunums)	WB/total (%)
Irrigable area	519,846	155,762	364,084	30

In accordance with the above table, the West Bank's share would be about 215 mcmy: 180 from the river itself (including the Yarmuk) and 35 from the side wadis. The remaining 505 mcmy of Jordan's share of the water under the Johnston Plan is for the East Bank. Israel extracts water from the basin at Hula plain, from Lake Tiberias and from the Yarmuk River. It is thought to have adhered to its quota under the Johnston Plan until 1967, when it expanded its zone of control in the basin and began unilaterally to exceed the quota. Tahal put the distribution of Israeli extraction of about 700 mcmy as follows:[32]

Source	mcmy	
Lake Tiberias	380	
Hula Plain	150	
Direct	80	
Yarmuk River	70	
Lower Jordan	10	(for the settlements, not mentioned by Tahal)

Israel thus diverts about 54 percent of the total allocated flow under the Johnston Plan, compared with its quota of 31 percent that mainly was a nonguaranteed residual.[33] Israel's 1994 water agreement with Jordan required it to reduce its intake immediately from the Yarmuk and the lower Jordan rivers by about 45 mcmy. However, the agreement envisioned joint projects to impound floodwater from the two rivers that, if implemented, probably would make up for, if not exceed, this quantity.[34]

The Arab riparians were slow in the early years to capture their water quotas under the plan, mainly because of the lack of financial resources and, especially in the case of Syria, the continued tensions along its borders with Israel. With the aid of the United

32. BUNT, 1994, pp. 2.6–2.7.
33. Of the 400 mcmy, 375 mcmy were a residual and 25 mcmy from the Yarmuk River were a priority.
34. For analyses of the agreement, see Elmusa, 1995b; and Hof, 1995.

States, Jordan was able to tap only a portion of its allocations, beginning in the early 1960s. It did that by diverting Yarmuk River water (110–130 mcmy) into the East Ghor (King Abdallah) Canal, which conveys water through the Jordan Valley south to the vicinity of the Dead Sea. It also impounded an estimated 130 mcmy behind small dams on the side wadis, bringing its diversion to 250 mcmy, or about one-half of its share.[35] Jordan also made several attempts to augment its water production by building jointly with Syria the Maqarin Dam on the Yarmuk River. The two countries agreed to the project in 1953, and it was an element in the Johnston Plan as well. When Jordan first tried to erect the dam in the 1980s on its own, Syria objected. Then the two sides reached an agreement in 1987 to build an alternative dam, which they dubbed al-Wihda (or Unity), close to the original site. At that point, Israel vetoed the project. Jordan and Syria continued to mention it even after Jordan's water agreement with Israel, but the dam has yet to be built. The water agreement that Jordan signed with Israel (if all the quantities it earmarked for Jordan as estimated by its own experts materialized) could bring that country's water withdrawal from the basin close to its quota under the Johnston Plan.[36] (The allocations of Israel and Jordan under their water agreement are summarized in table 4.4.)

Jordan failed to construct the West Ghor Canal in the West Bank before 1967, and building it under Israeli rule has not been possible. After Israel seized the territory in 1967, it declared the land strip alongside the river a closed military area and barred Palestinians from entering it. The closure deprived Palestinian farmers not only of the benefits of the canal but also of the modest amount of water they used to pump directly from the river to irrigate fields on the riverbank before the June 1967 war.

Syria did not initially undertake projects to divert water from the basin. When it lost its access to the upper Jordan River in 1967, it concentrated on the Yarmuk River. It built a series of small dams on the numerous streams that fed the river from within its borders. These dams reportedly have enabled Syria to impound in the vicinity of 200 mcmy. This is a greater quantity than Syria's quota under the Johnston Plan, but it does not match Israel's excess.

---

35. That is, of the share of what was the East Bank of Jordan at the time of the plan.

36. The foregoing account is based on Elmusa, 1995b; and Hof, 1995.

TABLE 4.4 Water Quotas of Israel and Jordan Under the 1994 Water Agreement

(In mcmy)

Source	Amount	Priority	Season	Effective date and notes
Jordan				
Yarmuk River				
King Abdallah Canal				Existing (no mention
(KAC)	130[a]			in treaty)
Stream	8[a]	Residue	Sum.	Immediate
Stream	17[a]	Residue	Win.	Immediate
Flood	50[a]			Future (into KAC)
Total	205[a]			
Lower Jordan River				Existing (no mention
Side wadis	130[a]			in treaty)
Stream (exchange)	20[b]		Sum.	Immediate
Flood	20		Win.	Future
Additional	40[a]	Residue		Future (storage and
Total	40 + 40[a]			rehabilitation)
Saline springs	10		Sum.	"non-immediate[c]"
To-be-identified	50			
Total	245[a] + 100			
Israel				
Yarmuk River				
Stream	12		Sum.	Immediate
Stream	13		Win.	Immediate
Stream (exchange)	20[b]		Win.	Immediate
Flood	(?)			
Total	45 + (?)			

Table continues on next page

Lebanon, too, did not divert its share from the basin before 1967 and was unable to do so afterward, because of internal disorder and Israel's occupation of the headwaters. Tahal, however, states that the Lebanese villagers directly divert 20 mcmy, presumably from al-Hasibani River and its tributaries.

To summarize, Israel translated its successive hydrostrategic gains into significant increases in water exploitation, to the point that it now takes 85–90 percent of the groundwater of Mandate Palestine and perhaps 54 percent more than its quota under the Johnston Plan from the Jordan basin. At the same time, it meticulously curtailed Palestinian access to the mountain aquifer and the

TABLE 4.4 Water Quotas of Israel and Jordan Under the 1994 Water Agreement *(Continued)*

(In mcmy)

Source	Amount	Priority Season	Effective date and notes
Lower Jordan River			Existing (to be as-
Stream			sessed jointly)
Flood	(?)		Future
Additional	3		
Total	3 + (?)		
Saline springs	10		Future
Total	58 + (?)		
Israeli use in Wadi			
'Araba[d]			Existing (to be as-
Groundwater	8[a]		sessed jointly)
Groundwater	≤10		Future (jointly)

SOURCES: "Treaty Between the State of Israel and the Hashemite Kingdom of Jordan," annexes I-II, *Journal of Palestine Studies*, vol. 23 (winter, 1995), pp. 133–39; and *Jordan Times*, 20 October 1994.

Sum. = Summer (15 May–15 Oct.); Win = Winter (16 Oct.–14 May).

NOTES:

[a]These figures are not specified in the water annex II; they are estimates by Munthir Haddadin. All, except those for use in the Wadi 'Araba area south of the Dead Sea, appeared in the above cited *Jordan Times*. Use in Wadi 'Araba was to be assessed jointly by 1 December 1994; based on the information that Jordan received from Israel, Haddadin made the preliminary estimate of 8 mcmy (correspondence, 26 January 1995); he also confirmed the accuracy of the estimates in the *Jordan Times*.

[b]Jordan "concedes" 20 mcmy of winter water from the Yarmuk to Israel, while Israel "concedes" 20 mcmy of summer water to Jordan from the lower Jordan River at Deganya, south of Lake Tiberias (Annex II, Articles I.1.b and I.2.a).

[c]The saline springs are earmarked for desalination within four years. Meanwhile, Jordan is to draw the 10 mcmy from Lake Tiberias.

[d]An area south of the Dead Sea that Israel occupied between 1968 and 1970; it reverted to Jordan's sovereignty under the treaty. Israel would continue to pump water from the area as shown in the table.

Jordan River through direct, unilateral management of the Palestinian water sector. Consequently, the Palestinians today tap a minor portion of the groundwater and no water at all from the Jordan River.

Israel's Water Use

The water budget of Israel will be drawn in a manner similar to that of the West Bank and Gaza, by identifying the demand of the standard sectors—municipal, industrial, and irrigation—and then adding to them the water of the rainfed agriculture as well as the

FIGURE 4.2 Israel's Water Use, 1950–93

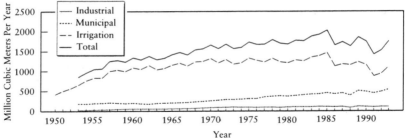

SOURCE: Statistical Abstract of Israel, various years

requisite water in food trade.[37] In addition to past water budgets, I will examine the long-term demand projections that were made by BUNT's 1994 report to the World Bank.[38]

Israel's municipal, industrial, and irrigation water use between 1950 and 1993 is exhibited in figure 4.2. The trend has been for use to grow over time, with interannual, rainfall-related fluctuations. The sources of growth varied; in some periods, such as from 1948 to the early 1960s, the chief source was groundwater (which also was overexploited, as pointed out in chapter 2) and to a much lesser extent the water yielded by the drainage of the Hula lake and marshlands that was completed by 1958. Subsequently, surface water from Lake Hula and the Yarmuk River distributed through the National Water Carrier significantly boosted the water supply. The Jordan basin also contributed to the increase after 1967, as a result of Israel's acquisition of additional hydrospace. By the early 1970s, Israel reached its hydrologic limit by exploiting all the natural freshwater resources it could muster, with the exception of the Negev's fossil aquifer. Subsequent increases had come either from overexploitation as happened in 1985, the peak year of water use (2,050 mcmy), or from alternative resources, such as treated wastewater. Since the mid-1980s, recycled water increasingly has begun to constitute an important fraction of the water budget: 80 mcmy in 1985 and 200 mcmy, or nearly 10 percent of the total, in 1992.

After peaking in the second half of the 1980s, Israel's water use conspicuously dipped in 1991 and 1992 owing to heavy rainfall

37. The main sources of data for this section are BUNT, 1994; and Israel, Central Bureau of Statistics, various years.
38. BUNT, 1994.

and attendant reduction of irrigation demand. It picked up again in response to higher irrigation demand, which in 1993 stood at 1,112 mcmy due to the drop in rainfall. Such fluctuations are likely to persist in the future.

Agriculture historically claimed, and still does, the bulk of the water, although the trend in recent years has been for the irrigation curve to stabilize and for the municipal one to move upward in response to population growth. The cropped area in Israel has exceeded 3.5 million dunums since the mid-1950s. It bifurcates into rainfed and irrigated branches, as in the West Bank and Gaza. The irrigated acreage, however, consistently expanded until in the early 1990s it comprised 55 percent of the total, up from 25 percent in 1955. The acreage of the two branches has alternated by 5–10 percent; in years of good rainfall the rainfed area expanded and the irrigated area contracted, while the opposite occurred when rainfall was poor.

The enlargement of the irrigated land was motivated by the desire for food self-sufficiency, a cornerstone of the ideology of Labor Zionism, to be outlined in the final section of this chapter. It was driven by the enhancement of irrigation water supply and aided by a steady improvement of irrigation efficiency that was considerably sped up by the diffusion of drip irrigation in the 1980s. The volume of irrigation water between 1955 and 1993 grew from 830 to 1,112 mcmy, or by one-third, whereas the irrigated area nearly doubled, from 966,000 dunums to 1.86 million dunums. The application rate per dunum thus dropped from 860 to 600 m³ over the same period.

Municipal and industrial demand, on the other hand, expanded from 220 mcmy (including perhaps 20 mcmy for industry) in 1955 to 642 mcmy (including 106 mcmy for industrial use) in 1993. Thus, municipal and industrial demand comprised 21 percent of the 1955 aggregate water demand and 36 percent of the 1993 total. Put differently, agriculture's share of water use fell from 81 to 64 percent. The trend for the relative expansion of municipal and industrial demand and the relative contraction of irrigation demand can be expected to continue in the future, as will be explained in the subsequent discussion of demand forecasts.

Whereas the tendency has been for aggregate use to rise, the per capita use has fallen because supply has not kept up with population growth. The per capita consumption fell from 587 to 340 m³ for all sectors and from 464 to 216 m³ for irrigation.

FIGURE 4.3 Average Cropping Pattern in Israel, 1990–91

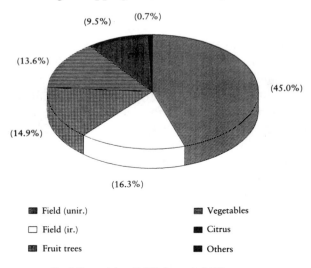

(9.5%) (0.7%)

(13.6%)

(45.0%)

(14.9%)

(16.3%)

- ▨ Field (unir.)
- □ Field (ir.)
- ▦ Fruit trees
- ▤ Vegetables
- ■ Citrus
- ■ Others

Total Cropped Area (1,000 dunums): 3,539
Field unir. 1,591; Field ir. 576; Fruit trees 529; Vegs. 482; Citrus 332; Other

Municipal per capita use, however, went up, from 80 m³ in 1960 to more than 100 m³ in 1993.[39] Industrial per capita demand was only 20 m³ in 1993. The obvious inference here is that the leveling off of the water supply has affected per capita irrigation use.

Irrigation water in Israel was centrally allocated (mainly), according to crop requirements. Israel cultivated innumerable kinds of crops, from grains, legumes, fruits, and vegetables to cotton, flowers, and fodder, thanks to the richness of agro-climatological variations and irrigation. Another water-consuming agricultural activity, fresh ponds, was allotted 100 mcmy in 1990. The average cropping pattern during the early 1990s is exhibited in figure 4.3, and the distribution of water among crop types in table 4.5. According to the table, fruit trees have been, and will continue to be in the near future, the major water-consuming crop, with about one-fifth of total irrigation going to citrus, a principal export crop. Vegetables were allocated 16 percent in 1993; however, it was planned that by 1997 citrus and vegetables would exchange places in terms of percentage of water used.

39. The reason I compared 1993 and 1960 instead of 1955 is that municipal and industrial uses were combined in the 1955 statistics.

TABLE 4.5 **Water Distribution by Agricultural Sector in Israel, 1990 and 1997**

(In mcmy)

Sector	1990	%	1997 (planned)	%	Change
Field crops	319	27	239	21	(−)
Fodder	65	5	85	8	(+)
Other	254	21	154	14	(−)
Vegetables	194	16	251	23	(+)
Tree crops	527	44	460	41	(−)
Citrus	256	22	192	17	(−)
Other fruits	271	23	268	24	(−)
Flowers	25	2	40	4	(+)
Fish ponds	86	7	76	7	(−)
Livestock	40	3	40	4	(0)
Total	1,191	100[a]	1,116	100[a]	(−)

SOURCE: Based on BUNT, 1994, p. 7.6.
NOTE:
[a]Percentages do not add up due to rounding.

Altogether, about 60 percent of the water has been going to horticulture, and plans are to maintain that proportion in the short-term. Field crops, mainly wheat and cotton, have absorbed nearly 27 percent, and fish ponds, livestock, and fodder 15 percent. The foregoing statistics suggest that the pattern of water distribution has been almost the reverse of the cropping pattern: While horticultural crops occupied 38 percent of the acreage, they absorbed 60 percent of the water. Water supply also has been scheduled to drop for all major classes of crops, except for vegetables, fodder, and flowers so as to accommodate the dictates of economics (e.g., the poor returns of field crops and satisfactory returns of flowers) and domestic food demand (e.g., the increase of demand for milk and dairy). In all, irrigation supply in 1997 was scheduled to remain at about the same level as the early 1990s.

Water use in the rainfed sector will be measured by the IWE, with all the caveats that were cited for the West Bank in the previous chapter. The rainfed area in Israel in the early 1990s averaged around 1.6 million dunums. More than 90 percent of it was planted with field crops, with wheat claiming about one-half of the acreage.

Assuming an average annual rainfall of 500 mm, the total rain-water received by the rainfed land was 800 mcmy. The effective water, or that which did not run off or percolate to the aquifers (see chapter 1), was two-thirds, or about 530 mcmy. The crop output by weight from this water, I tentatively estimate, was in the vicinity of 10 percent of the output of the irrigated sector. Thus, at a minimum, the associated IWE was about 100 mcmy, or 20 percent of the effective rainfall.

The final item in Israel's water demand is the requisite water in food trade (see table 4.6). The steps for determining it and pertinent qualifications are basically similar to those for the West Bank and Gaza, as discussed in chapter 3. The main difference between the two procedures is that in the case of Israel one can use "point" values for water efficiencies (m³/100 kg in the table) instead of the ranges used for the West Bank and Gaza. These point values are the lower bound of the range because the upper bound values are probably too high for Israel's advanced farm management and technology.

Table 4.5 shows that Israel produced a substantial portion of its food consumption, was self-sufficient in poultry and dairy products, and had a surplus of horticultural crops, notably citrus, which was exported. Nonetheless, Israel imported the bulk of the demand of dry pulses, and all its rice and sugar. It also imported one-half of its red meat consumption and a portion of its animal feed. Not knowing the exact percentage of animal feed that is imported, I have not been able to determine its corn-feed equivalent value. To reiterate the discussion in chapter 3, the corn-feed equivalent is the basis on which the water requirements for food and dairy were estimated.

The Israeli diet cited in table 4.6 provides 3,080 total daily calories, of which 2,420 were plant based and 660 animal based. The total calories are 14 percent greater than the FAO "guideline" of 2,700, and the animal based calories are more than twice as much as FAO's 300 calories, as cited in the previous chapter in conjunction with the Palestinian diet. The water coefficient of the Israeli diet is 896 m³. This is about 50 percent larger than the Palestinian coefficient, 617 m³, derived from similar water efficiencies. One reason for the discrepancy is that Israelis consume greater amounts of meat and dairy than do the Palestinians. By way of cross-checking the present estimate of the Israeli coefficient, I compare it with a partial coefficient cited by BUNT, 107 m³ for fresh

TABLE 4.6 Water Demand Coefficient for Food in Israel, 1992

Food item	Food Consumption (kg/capita)	S.S.R.* (%)	Water Requirement (m³/100 kg)	Demand coefficient (m³/capita)
Wheat	97.1ᵃ	48ᵇ	115	112
Rice	6.8	0	108	7
Sugar	40.4ᵃ	0	125	51
Potatoes	32	137	14	10
Dry pulses	5.7	38	167	16
Seeds and nuts	7.8	90	200	4
Vegetables	203	128	20	41
Melons	30	128	13	4
Citrus	43	446	20	6
Other fruits	75	145	40	30
Vegetable oil	21	96	500	105
Miscellaneousᶜ				20
Red meatᵈ	23	55	875ᶜ	201
Poultry	48	105	188	90
Fishᵉ	11	38	75	8
Milkᶠ	200	100	69	138
Eggs	18	117	300	54
Total	862			896

SOURCES: Calculated from tables 3.16 and 3.17; BUNT, 1994; and "Food Balance Sheet," in Israel, Central Bureau of Statistics, *Israel Statistical Abstract*, 1993.
Daily calorie intake per person: 3,080, of which 2,420 calories are plant based and 660 are animal based.
*S.S.R. = Self-sufficiency ratio.
NOTES:
ᵃInclude an assortment of other items; for example, sugar includes half of the jam consumption.
ᵇOnly for direct consumption; it does not cover feed grain.
ᶜIncludes tea and coffee. The 20 m³ are arbitrary.
ᵈBeef, sheep, and goats. The figures for water requirements, however, are for beef.
ᵉAssuming fish from fish ponds. The water that goes into the fish ponds, about 100 mcmy, is not included.
ᶠThis is the fluid milk equivalent of both fluid milk and dairy consumption.

fruits and vegetables and 25 percent of dairy. The corresponding quantity from table 4.6 is 116 m³, which is close to BUNT's. Nonetheless, the present estimate of the Israeli coefficient ought to be thought of as provisional and requiring further corroboration, for reasons similar to those regarding the Palestinian coefficient.

The coefficient of 896 m³ yielded for Israel in 1992 an aggregate water-for-food demand of 4,660 mcmy (Israel's 1992 population was 5.2 million). If the amount of the domestic water (both

TABLE 4.7 Water Demand Forecast for Israel According to Tahal

	Year			
Item	*2000*	*2010*	*2020*	*2040*
Population (millions)	6.5	7.7	9.2	12.8
Per capita demand (m³)				
Municipal & industrial	120	120	120	110
Irrigation	107	104	101	93
Aggregate demand (mcmy)				
Municipal & industrial	784	805	1,098	1,406
Irrigation	703	928	924	1,189
Total aggregate demand (mcmy)	1,487	1,733	2,022	2,595
Irrigation for export crops[a]	289	289	289	289

SOURCE: BUNT, 1994, pp. 7.13–17.
NOTE:
[a]The distribution of this quantity between Israelis and Palestinians is not specified.

irrigation and IWE) used for food production was about 1,200 mcmy, then the requisite water deficit was 3,430 mcmy, something that does not appear in the standard water budget.

Israel's Future Demand

The only projections that will be considered here are those made by BUNT (table 4.7). They are the most pertinent projections because Tahal is a central player in water planning in Israel. Moreover, there are no counter Palestinian projections of Israel's demand as there were Israeli forecasts of Palestinian demand, a symptom of the asymmetrical relationship between the two sides. BUNT follows the same procedure in forecasting Israeli demand as it did in its projections for the West Bank and Gaza. It assumes municipal, industrial, and irrigation demand coefficients and multiplies them by projected population size. The following assessment of the forecast centers on these two variables.

BUNT offers three population growth scenarios—low, medium, and high—but uses the medium scenario, indicated in table 4.6, as a working hypothesis. Projections of the Israeli population, unlike those of the Palestinian, do not face the problem of uncertain baseline population size. Future demographic growth, however, will be a function of whether massive new immigration or net out-migration (as occurred during some years in the 1980s before the inflow of Soviet immigrants) occurs, as well as of the natural rate of population increase. These factors depend on political and economic developments inside and outside Israel that are hard to predict.

As for the municipal and industrial demand coefficient, BUNT postulates that it would go up from 100 m^3 in 1990 to 120 m^3 by the year 2000, a 20 percent increase, then drop to 110 m^3 by the year 2040 as a result of conservation measures. These coefficients are bigger than their West Bank and Gaza counterparts. Although such difference may be valid in the short term, it is difficult to see why, by the year 2040, Palestinian demand would not catch up with Israel's 110 m^3.

BUNT prescribes an irrigation demand coefficient equal to the water needed for total self-sufficiency in fruits and vegetables and 25 percent self-sufficiency in dairy products, as it does for the West Bank and Gaza. The coefficient begins at 107 m^3 in 2000, then drops to 93 m^3 by 2040 as a consequence of enhanced irrigation water productivity. Unlike the municipal and industrial coefficient, it coincides in the long run with the Palestinians'. In addition to this coefficient, the BUNT forecast factors in water for export crops that could achieve acceptable economic returns to water, the threshold of acceptability being \$1/m^3, a figure that is in the vicinity of the estimated marginal cost of water. It fixes the volume of this water, a bit too accurately perhaps, at 289 mcmy throughout the period of the forecast. The study does not, however, specify how much of that water would be demanded by the Israelis and how much by the Palestinians, that is, how much of the export crops each side will grow. There is no indication, either in the agreements already signed or in the on going talks, that the Palestinians will be able to obtain any of that quantity in the short term. Also, BUNT does not foresee Palestinian irrigation demand as going beyond 300 mcmy because of what it views as constraints on irrigable land. Yet, even that quantity would be inadequate for self-sufficiency in fresh fruits and vegetables. It seems that BUNT tacitly assumes that the water for export crops would go to Israel.

Keeping the preceding qualifications in mind, the projected aggregate Israeli water demand profile for 2040 may be summarized thus: The municipal and industrial sectors could become the leading water demanders as a consequence of a long historical trend of population growth and industrialization. Irrigation demand,

TABLE 4.8 Comparative Israeli-Palestinian Economic Statistics, 1992

Item	Palestinian	Israeli	P/I (%)
Population (millions)	2.25[a]	5.2	48
GNP ($ millions)	3,435	63,240	5
GNP/capita ($)	1,527	12,170	13
GDP ($ millions)	2,650	64,510	4
Agriculture (%)	31[b]	3	1,000
Industry (%)	8[b]	21	38
GDP/capita ($)	1,178	12,420	10
Employment (1,000)	219	1,650	13
Agriculture (%)	33	3	1,100

SOURCES: El-Jaafari and Shaaban, 1995, table 9; Israel, Central Bureau of Statistics, *Israel Statistical Abstract*, 1993 and 1994; and World Bank, 1993a, vols. 2, 4 and 6.
NOTES:
P = Palestinian; I = Israelis.
[a]From text in chapter 3.
[b]For 1991.

however, would not be far behind or could be slightly ahead, depending on the division of the 289 mcmy for export crops between Israelis and Palestinians. To put the demand figures in perspective, I note that Israel's municipal and industrial demand alone would be nearly equal to the entire Israeli standard water budget in 1991 (1,484 mcmy) and to two-thirds of the entire natural, renewable freshwater resources of geographic Palestine of about 1,790 mcmy. The total projected demand would exceed these resources by 600 mcmy, or the equivalent of one mountain aquifer. Such demand, as postulated by BUNT, can be met only from alternative resources.

The Israeli-Palestinian Water Use Gap

Although the long-term projections show a convergence between Israeli and Palestinian demands, water consumption has been characterized by a conspicuous gap between the two sides because Israeli demand has been met and the Palestinians' suppressed. To appreciate better the significance of the gap, I have outlined some relative Israeli-Palestinian economic indicators for 1992 (tables 4.8 and 4.9). The year 1992 was selected because the economic gap, although considerable, was still smaller than in subsequent years.

TABLE 4.9 Palestinian Trade Statistics with Israel, 1992
(In $millions)

Item	Value	To/From Israel %
Total exports	290	42
Total imports	1037	91
Food exports (non-processed)	67	55
Food imports (non-processed)	197	80
Total trade deficit with Israel	−995	
Food trade deficit with Israel	−119	

SOURCE: Based on El-Jaafari and Shaaban, 1995.

After 1992, Israel resorted to prolonged closures of its borders to Palestinian workers on security grounds, a policy that led to a decline in Palestinian income. At the same time, Israeli income since the start of the peace negotiations has grown at a rapid pace.

If the figures are accurate, the Palestinian per capita GNP in 1992 amounted to $1,527, and the GDP to $1,178. The sizable difference between the two indicators largely mirrored the reliance of Palestinian labor on employment outside the West Bank and Gaza, notably in Israel. The largest sector of the Palestinian domestic economy was agriculture. In 1990–92, agriculture contributed one-third of the GDP and absorbed a similar share of employment. The industrial sector, largely in the form of household workshops and modest plants, was in its infancy.

Israel's population in 1992 was more than double that of the Palestinian territories. However, the size of its economy, as measured by GDP, was twenty-four times larger than the Palestinian economy; its GNP per capita was seven times larger. Structurally, the Israeli economy was far more sophisticated than its Palestinian counterpart, and its industry contributed about one-fifth of the GDP in the early 1990s. By comparison, agriculture played a minor role in the Israeli economy; its share was less than 3 percent of the GDP although a slightly larger percentage of total employment. Nonetheless, Israel was able to produce a larger portion of its food especially because of the greater amounts of irrigation water, as indicated earlier. Furthermore, the West Bank and Gaza since 1967 have become exceptionally dependent on Israel, notably in trade and employment. To illustrate, in 1992 the Palestinians imported from Israel 90 percent of their total commodity imports and 80 percent of their nonprocessed foods. Meanwhile, they sold to Israel more than 40 percent of their total commodity exports and 55 percent of their nonprocessed food exports. Palestinian trade thus exhibited a remarkable concentration of trade "partnership" with Israel; the same cannot be said of Israeli trade, however, because its exports to, and especially imports from, the West Bank and Gaza comprised only a fraction of its foreign trade, including of foodstuffs.

The Municipal Water Gap

In the municipal water sector, the share of the average Palestinian consumer was about one-third that of the Israeli (see table 4.10). Further disaggregation of water consumption in the Israeli munic- ipal sector, however, discloses a more fundamental distribution gap than just between Palestinians in the West Bank and Gaza and Israelis. Water allocation in Israel was ethnically based, character- ized by discrimination against Palestinian-Israelis. For example, a comparison of water allocations in 1987 for 23 Palestinian-Israeli and 14 Jewish-Israeli localities in the Northern District, where the majority of Palestinian-Israelis live, indicated that the Jewish-Israeli localities obtained significantly higher water provisions than did their Palestinian-Israeli counterparts.[40] The least per capita provi- sion for a Jewish locality, 87 m³, was greater than the largest for a Palestinian-Israeli locality, 72 m³. Overall, the average per capita allocation for the Jewish localities, 134 m³, was nearly 2.9 times greater than the average of 47 m³ for their Palestinian-Israeli coun- terparts.[41] Tahal put the 1990 countrywide average per capita de- mand in the municipal sector at 100 m³ per year, but noted that per capita demand in the Palestinian-Israeli localities, which it eu- phemistically dubbed "low income municipalities," at only 35 m³, an amount that was strikingly close to the level of Palestinian utilization in the West Bank and Gaza.[42]

40. Israel is divided into the following districts: Northern, Haifa, Cen- tral, Tel Aviv, Jerusalem, and Southern. The figures are from Falah, 1990, citing Israeli official statistics.
41. Compare with the average per capita water use of 196 m³ for all Israeli rural areas (in 1986–87), according to Tahal, 1990, p. 3.1.
42. Tahal, 1990, p. 3.1. I have argued at length in the previous chapter against imputing lower water consumption among Palestinians in the West Bank and Gaza to their lower income level. The same argument can be made about the Palestinian-Israelis.

TABLE 4.10 Summary of Israeli-Palestinian Water-Use Gap, 1993

Item	Palestinian[a]	Israeli[a]	P/I (%)
Aggregate use (mcmy)	225	1,754	12
Irrigation	145	1,112[a]	12
Municipal	70	536	13
Industrial	10	106	9
Annual per capita use (m³)			
Aggregate	97	330	29
Irrigation	62	210	29
Municipal	31	100	31
Industrial	4	20	20
Total use increase (1967–93) (mcmy)	25	345	7
Price per cubic meter			
Absolute ($/m³)			
Municipal	1	1	100
Irrigation	17	13	
Relative to GNP/capita			
Municipal			700
Irrigated agriculture			
Total area (1,000 dunums)	200	1,864	11
Area per capita (dunums)	< 0.1	0.35	< 29
Irrigated/cultivated (%)	10	55	18
Irrigated/irrigable (%)	33	> 90	< 36
Growth, 1966/67–93 (1,000 dunums)	0	276	0
Water for meat and fish (mcmy)			
Feed	0	65	0
Fish ponds	0	100	0

SOURCE: Previous tables and text.
NOTES:
P = Palestinian; I = Israeli.
[a]Palestinian population in 1993 = 2.33 million; Israeli = 5.33 million.

The duality of water allocation in Israel means that the typical Jewish per capita use is about 115 m³, or 15 percent above the average. It also suggests that the water gap between the Palestinians in the West Bank and Gaza and Israeli Jews is even wider than is suggested by comparison of allocation between Israel as a whole and the Palestinian territories. Therefore, one can speak of a "Jewish-Palestinian" water gap within geographic Palestine.

The municipal water gap was manifested further in the quality of services and prices. The Israelis did not suffer from the irregularities of water supply as did the Palestinians in the West Bank and Gaza or from salinity and contamination as did the Gazans. The coverage of the piped water network in Israel was also universal, whereas one-fourth to one-third of the West Bank population was without running water. Further, Israelis enjoyed a more egalitarian pricing system and much lower prices relative to their income than did the Palestinians in the West Bank. A typical Israeli household was charged around $1.0/m^3$.[43] Accordingly, although consumers on both sides were charged nearly the same rate, West Bank Palestinians in 1993 paid seven times more than the Israelis for a cubic meter of water relative to their GNP per capita income, and the price differential widened in subsequent years as the income of Israel relative to the West Bank rose. In fact, the price gap would be even wider if one compared the rates for the first block within which Palestinian consumption largely fell. In this block the Palestinians paid three times as much as the Israelis in absolute terms and 15 times as much in relative terms. Finally, the progressive, block-rate system in Israel had the advantage of assuring the poorer households a minimum quantity of water at a reasonable price, which the uniform rate in the West Bank did not. These were remarkable asymmetries for water sectors managed by the same body, Mekorot. Because Mekorot will go on supplying a fair portion of Palestinian municipal water in the foreseeable future and because the PA is not expected to have the financial capability to subsidize water, it is likely that the pricing gap will persist if not widen further.

The Irrigation and Food Production Gap

The Israeli-Palestinian water gap also can be observed in irrigated agriculture and food production. It can be summed up as follows. The ratio of the irrigated land per person in the West Bank and Gaza in 1993 was less than 30 percent of that in Israel; the ratio

43. The $1.0/m^3$ is based on the assumption that a typical four-person household consumed 100 m^3 of water per month. According to Tahal, 1990, p. 9.3, in 1990 households were charged monthly $.32/m^3$ for the first block of 8 m^3, $0.75/m^3$ for the second block of 8 m^3, and $1.23/m^3$ for quantities in excess of 16 m^3.

of irrigated to cultivated land was 20 percent; and the ratio of irrigated to irrigable land was 35 percent. What must be underscored in these figures is that Palestinian per capita irrigation use was only 60 percent of the irrigation demand coefficient required for self-sufficiency in horticultural crops and fodder supply for 25 percent of dairy demand. In contrast, Israeli irrigation use was more than double the demand coefficient. Moreover, between the eve of its seizure of the West Bank and Gaza in 1967 and the DOP in 1993, Israel expanded its irrigated area by about 275,000 dunums, an amount greater than the combined Palestinian irrigated land in both of the Palestinian territories. In the same period, the Palestinians' irrigated acreage stagnated. Although water-saving technologies contributed to the expansion in Israel, the additional water supply acquired as a result of the June 1967 war played a critical role in this expansion.

The greater supply of irrigation water in Israel meant that it could produce more of its food consumption than could the Palestinians, as is clear from their respective food self-sufficiency ratios in tables 3.16 and 4.6. This was true even though the 3,080 daily calories of the average Israeli diet surpassed those of the Palestinians (2,700 calories), and the animal-based calories—660 per day—were more than double the 300 animal-based calories per capita of the average Palestinian diet. The dietary gap was a reflection of the differential income of the two protagonists; nonetheless, Israel was able to devote 165 mcmy for fodder production and fish ponds, an amount of water that was larger than the total irrigation supply for the West Bank and Gaza. The difference between the ability of the two sides to produce food for local consumption was summed up in the fact that the per capita Palestinian import bill of nonprocessed food commodities in 1992 was fourfold that of the much richer Israel.

Not only did Israel produce more food for domestic consumption than did the Palestinians, it also dedicated more irrigation water for export crops. The export gap was apparent, for example, in the fact that Palestinian agricultural exports in 1992 were only 6 percent of Israel's. It is also worth recalling the relatively large agricultural trade deficit the Palestinians had with Israel itself. Finally, Israel still was planning in 1997 to earmark 336 mcmy, or 29 percent of the total irrigation volume,[44] for export

44. BUNT, 1994, pp. 7.7–7.8.

crops; no such amounts (on relative basis) were available to the Palestinians, who could not generate foreign currency from industrial exports as could Israel.

The irrigation gap was equally evident in the types of crops grown by the two sides. The Palestinians irrigated virtually no crops other than vegetables and fruits, whereas the Israelis irrigated, in addition to horticultural crops, large areas of field crops, such as cotton, that generally were acknowledged as having questionable economic value. The MVPW for the field crops in 1990 was estimated at $0.15/m^3$, less than one-half of the average water costs. Cotton, in particular, planted in the hot Negev Desert and the southern coastal plain, consumed large quantities of water, but its productivity was only one ton/1,000 m^3, less than that for bananas. Thus, growing cotton was neither economically nor ecologically sound. Nevertheless, the irrigated cotton area, even after a period of shrinkage, stood at 165,000 dunums in 1993.[45] The water earmarked for this area was more than double the volume of irrigation water in the West Bank. True, the water used for growing cotton was treated wastewater; but water, like money, is fungible. Treated wastewater could be utilized for fruit trees instead of vegetables had there been unease about its use.

That Israelis were able to irrigate relatively extensive land and field crops was due to the heavy subsidization of agriculture. Subsidies included the low prices of factors of production, especially land and water, concessional credit rates, and guaranteed minimum prices for certain crops. According to one estimate, the value of such subsidies averaged 32 percent of the value of the sector's output in the period 1984–90.[46] Price subsidies for water, as indicated in the previous chapter, were significant as well, reaching on the average more than half the production costs. Nonofficial estimates indicated even higher levels of subsidization: "The real cost of water is four to eight times (depending on the locality) more than the farmer actually pays."[47]

The high level of subsidies was the result of a combination of natural conditions and political objectives. Because most of the water was available in the north while the irrigable land was in the south, the water had to be transported long distances with com-

45. Israel, Central Bureau of Statistics, 1994.
46. Nashashibi and Kanaan, 1994, p. 11.
47. Associates for Middle East Research Water Project, 1987, p. 107.

mensurate cost increases. Furthermore, the subsidies were originally instituted to serve political more than economic objectives: to enhance population dispersion and settlement of areas where the scarcity of water might discourage potential settlers. They also have served as an aid for channeling new immigrants into farming. They were enshrined in the 1959 water law that created the Water Charges Equalization (or Adjustment) Fund, an agency tasked with reducing the difference in water prices among sectors and various parts of the country. Twenty percent of the Fund's resources came from a surtax on areas that pay less than the average price for water; 20 percent from households; and 60 percent from the government.[48]

The subsidies initially bolstered economic growth, equity, and the competitiveness of Israeli produce. They have continued, however, in spite of mounting evidence that the MVPW in crop production has been on the decline. They still may persist, at least partially, in the future owing, in part, to the "statutory policy of water subsidization for agriculture."[49] Yet, the diversion of irrigation water from Israeli to Palestinian agriculture could have benefitted Israeli consumers by relieving them from paying for the subsidies and by offering them cheaper produce, thanks to the lower costs of Palestinian labor. It may be said that the subsidies are an internal Israeli economic and political affair, the costs of which are borne by the Israelis. This may be so, but the argument overlooks the fact that, by encouraging profligate water use patterns, they aid and abet the deprivation of much-needed water to the Palestinians.

THE ENCROACHMENT OF ISRAELI SETTLEMENTS

The Israeli settlements in the West Bank originally started in the Jordan Valley during the early years of the occupation and were viewed as a means of enhancing security in an area that Israel might keep if it withdrew from the territory. Subsequently, under the Allon Plan cited earlier, and supported by various means and justified on various grounds, the settlements spread throughout the West Bank. In Gaza, there were two groups of settlements: one cluster in the northernmost segment of the strip and the second in

48. These are rounded up figures from ibid., p. 114.
49. BUNT, 1994, p. 7.2.

the south along the shore, between the sand dunes and Palestinian citrus orchards. The spatial distribution of the settlements is illustrated in map 4.4. Depending on who is doing the counting, by 1992 around 120 to 128 settlements were built in the West Bank, excluding Jerusalem, and 14 to 16 in Gaza.[50] The number of settlers was disputed as well. In 1991 they may have been close to 105,000, of whom 100,000 were in the West Bank and 5,000 in Gaza. The growth of settlements and the settler population did not abate after the signing of the interim peace accords. By 1994 there were reportedly more than 127,000 settlers in 136 settlements, 14 of which were urban and accounted for 60 percent of the settler population.[51]

The Settlements' Water Use

In order to supply water for the settlements, Israel has encroached since 1967 on the water of the eastern basin of the mountain aquifer in the West Bank and on the coastal aquifer in Gaza. The encroachment raised many questions about the legality (from the standpoint of international law) of the utilization of this water for the citizens of the occupying power. This matter has been probed by other investigators.[52] The focus here is on the extent of the settlements' water utilization and its impact on Palestinian water use and resources, as well as on the water gap between the settlers and Palestinians.

The exact amounts of water drawn by the settlers have not been made public on a regular basis. According to the fragments of disclosures by official and unofficial Israeli sources, the settlements' water withdrawal was around 50 mcmy in the West Bank and 5–10 mcmy in Gaza.[53] According to the Taba Agreement (Annex III, Article 40, Schedule 10), the settlers get water "From

50. The lower figures are official and the higher are from Peace Now (a political movement in Israel). The reasons for the difference between the two counts are discussed in Hyatt et al., 1992, p. 16.

51. Aronson, 1996.

52. See, for example, Dillman, 1989; al-Hindi, 1990; and United Nations, 1992.

53. Kahan, 1987, put the settlers' "allocations" in 1986–87 at 37.8 mcmy. The 1990 Israel State Comptroller report, however, critically pointed out that the settlers' actual withdrawal exceeded formal allocations; for example, in 1985, the allocations were 26.6 mcmy, but withdrawal reached 36.4 mcmy.

MAP 4.4 Israeli Settlements in the West Bank and Gaza

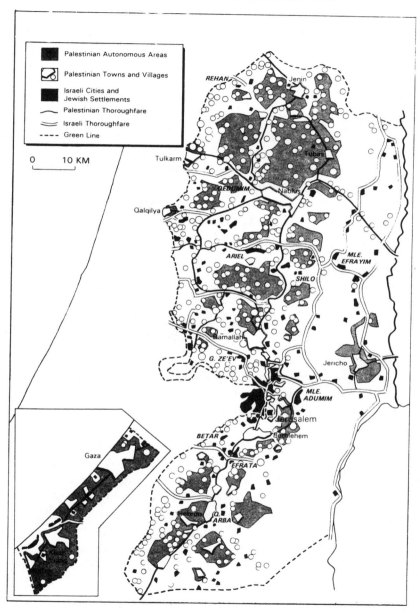

SOURCE: Reprint of the Ta'ba Interim Agreement Map.

the Eastern Aquifer: In the Jordan Valley 40 mcm to Israeli users from wells." This is all that the agreement mentions about the quantity of the settlements' use. However, Kahan's report to the West Bank Data Base Project had indicated earlier that the settlers drew an additional 10 mcmy from the Jordan River, mixing the brackish water (2,000 mg/l chloride) with fresh groundwater.[54] Most of the settlements' water was supplied by Mekorot, mainly from wells it drilled in the West Bank itself. In Gaza nearly all the water to the settlements was supplied by Mekorot from its own network and from wells inside the strip.

It is important to examine the impact of settlements' water withdrawal on Palestinian access to water and the claims made by Palestinian and outside specialists that the settlements' wells caused some springs and wells to run dry and the salinity of others to rise. The settlers' total water provisions were around 40 percent of those of the Palestinians. Owing to the relatively small number of settlers, this translated into 5–6 times the Palestinian per capita use, an even wider gap than the one between Israelis inside Israel and the Palestinians. In Gaza, not only was there a conspicuous consumption gap between the Palestinians and settlers, but the settlements themselves also happened to be located in the areas that contained some of the freshest (if not *the* freshest) water in the strip. Whether this happened by accident or design may not be known for some time; the important point is that while Gazans were pumping highly saline and contaminated water, the settlers were exacerbating the situation.

The bulk of the settlements' water was allotted for irrigation. The cropped area of the settlements was about 65,000 dunums in 1985–87 (table 4.11), apart from more than 20,000 dunums of natural pasture.[55] Subsequent official statistics suggest that it has declined to 28,000 dunums in 1992, of which about 23,000 dunums was in the Jordan Valley (table 4.12). The land in the Jordan Valley was some of the most fertile, thanks to the alluvial soils deposited by the Jordan River. It was irrigated and planted mainly with fruits and vegetables. If the official statistics about its size and about the water drawn by the settlements are accurate, the rate of water application would be remarkably high, 1,700–2,100 m³ per

54. Kahan, 1987, p. 102.
55. Ibid., p. 111.

TABLE 4.11 Irrigated Area of Jewish Settlements in the West Bank and Gaza, 1985, According to the West Bank Data Base Project
(In 1,000 dunums)

Region	Irrigated	Cultivated	Irrigated/cultivated (%)
West Bank			
Matei Binyamin (Ramallah)	5.0	5.7	88
Etzion Bloc (Bethlehem)	3.8	17.0	22
Samaria (Nablus)	0.7	0.9	78
Har Hebron (Hebron)	4.2	7.1	59
N. Dead Sea (Jordan Valley)	3.2	3.2	100
Jordan Valley	22.0	22.4	98
Total	38.9	56.3	69
Gaza	6.7	11.1	60
Grand total	45.6	67.4	68

SOURCE: Kahan, 1987, pp. 110–11.

dunum.[56] This was 3–3.5 times the overall rate inside Israel and 2.4–2.9 times the Palestinian rate in the West Bank.

In Gaza the cultivated area of the settlements increased initially, then contracted under drought conditions. The irrigated area

TABLE 4.12 Evolution of Cropped Area of Jewish Settlements in the West Bank and Gaza, 1985–92, According to Israel, Central Bureau of Statistics
(In 1,000 dunums)

Region	1985	1987	1988	1992
West Bank				
Jordan Valley	33.4	30.5	32.8	23.1
Nablus-Ramallah	6.4	8.5	7.2	0.9
Bethlehem-Hebron	4.3	7.1	2.2	1.3
Total	44.1	46.1	42.2	25.3
Gaza	21.6	19.5	14.6	2.7
Grand total	65.7	65.6	56.8	28.0

SOURCE: Israel, Central Bureau of Statistics, *Israel Statistical Abstract*, various years.

56. This is based on the 40–50 mcmy cited above.

per settler was 2 dunums, compared with 0.15 dunums per Palestinian, or a ratio of 13 to 1.[57] The disparity between the two sides was clearly more profound than in the West Bank.

As for water pricing, the settlements belonged to the Israeli system. In general, the settlements enjoyed a handsome package of subsidies for housing, education, and health that were superior to those in Israel itself. The subsidies were the main vehicle of the government and international Jewish organizations that supported the settlement project for encouraging nonideologically motivated Jews to move to the West Bank.[58] I have not been able to locate sufficient information about the rate of water subsidization for recent years, but they were at least comparable with the levels in Israel itself.[59] The difference between the costs to Mekorot and the sale price to the settlements was picked up by the Jewish Agency (the main organization in charge of agricultural settlement and absorption), substituting for the Water Charges Equalization Fund. The settlers, like other Israelis, thus enjoyed a substantial price differential relative to the Palestinians.

The future of the settlements' water supply depends on the final status of the settlements themselves, which is ultimately a political, not a hydrological, question. For instance, if the settlements were removed, the issue of supplying them with water would become automatically nonexistent, but it is not clear what would happen to the water supply infrastructure that includes the pipe networks and the wells. Would Israel just dismantle the pipes and decommission the wells or would it use them as part of an economic bargain? Would the Palestinians be interested in keeping some wells and capping others? These questions can be dealt with only after a detailed physical and economic inventory of the settlement water system is made available to the Palestinians and after a comprehensive assessment of their water and infrastructural requirements has been undertaken.

Water supply to the settlements would pose a different set of questions if the final status accord gave the settlers the option of remaining under Palestinian rule. What kind of supply regime would be set up for the settlers who stay? Recalling that the settlers'

57. These ratios are calculated on the following basis: 3,500 settlers for 7,000 dunums of irrigated area; and 730,000 Palestinians for 110,000 irrigated dunums (see chapter 3).
58. See, for example, Aronson, 1990; and Benvenisti, 1984.
59. Israel State Comptroller, 1990, citing January 1986 prices.

quotas and prices differed from those of the Palestinians, would the settlers be subject to Palestinian water laws, regulations, quotas, and prices, or would the Israeli government insist on keeping their former privileges, and who would pay for the subsidies? Answers to such questions obviously transcend considerations of water; among other things, they touch on the modalities of Palestinian sovereignty.

The Drying Up of Palestinian Springs and Wells

In order to supply the settlements, Mekorot reportedly drilled around 35 wells.[60] About 20 of these wells were in the Jordan Valley, especially on the upper eastern slopes, and some were very close to Palestinian springs and wells (see map 4.5). They drew water from the richer lower Cenomanian aquifer at depths reaching 500–600 m, as opposed to Palestinian wells that drew water from the upper Cenomanian aquifer. They thus enjoyed two advantages over Palestinian wells. First, their output capacity exceeded by more than a dozen times that of the Palestinian wells which, irrespective of the size of wells and pumps, would not have been possible had they been confined to the upper layers.[61] Second, by being drilled on the slopes, rather than in the depression itself, they avoided the saline rock layer deposits that engendered some of the salinity in the upper aquifer.

Not only were the wells of the settlements superior, they also reportedly have led to the depletion and drying up of numerous Palestinian wells and springs in the eastern basin since the mid-1970s.[62] Some of the villages that have been affected were al-Auja, north of Jericho; 'Ayn al-Bayda; and Bardala, in the northeastern corner of the West Bank. The hydrological reasons for the drying up of the springs and wells in these three villages are complex and cannot be pinned down definitively, particularly in the absence of detailed and specific spatial and temporal data about the "source" and "target" of injury. They might be linked in that the lower and upper aquifers are not totally insulated from each other, and water leaks from the lower aquifer upward through

60. This figure was provided to me by local Palestinian experts; the company has not disclosed the exact number.

61. Awartani, 1991a, p. 30.

62. Dillman, 1989; Rowley, 1990; and United Nations, 1992.

MAP 4.5 Palestinian Springs and Israeli Settlements' Wells

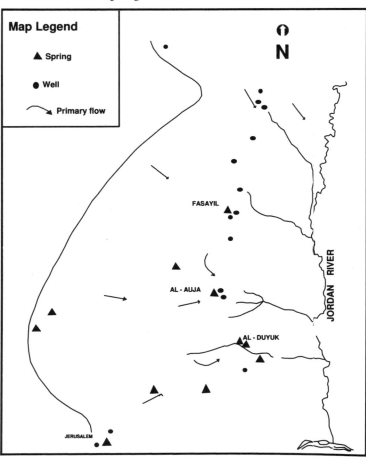

SOURCE: Adapted from Rosenthal and Kronfeld, 1982.

faults. At work also is the cone-of-depression effect that, by the act of suction, lowers the water table around the well, sometimes to considerable distances. The presence of many wells may intensify such an effect owing to the overlapping of multiple cones of depression. When this happens, springs and shallower wells could dry up.[63]

The difficulty of "proving" the cause-and-effect relationship between Israeli wells and depletion or damage to Palestinian water sources has given rise to controversy: Palestinians have charged

63. Although these are known hydrological phenomena, the first scholar to bring them to bear on the Palestinian-settler situation was Rowley, 1990.

that the settlements' wells harm their wells and springs while Israel has denied the accusations. The Israeli Ministry of Foreign Affairs, for example, asserted that "In no case has the sinking of a well for a Jewish village [settlement] been allowed adversely to affect the water supply available to the Arab inhabitants."[64] It also has been claimed that any recently observed decline in the endogenous Palestinian water sources was the result of a long-term drop in the water table due to prolonged low rainfall conditions, rather than because of the intrusion of the settlements' wells.[65] Nevertheless, Israel has acknowledged that the well it had dug near Bardala and 'Ayn al-Bayda caused wells and springs in the two villages to dry up.[66] It since has provided villagers and farmers with compensatory water from a new well it drilled in the area. Israel, however, did not offer technical information regarding what caused the damage.

In another notable case, that of the virtual drying up of al-Auja spring, Israel did not make a similar acknowledgment. This spring, with an average discharge of about 6 mcmy, was drastically depleted in 1979. The depletion occurred after Mekorot had dug three wells in its vicinity for the benefit of the adjacent settlements, Yitav and Gilgal, and following two subsequent years of low rainfall. As a consequence, 1,300 dunums of bananas and 150 dunums of citrus worth $2.7 million reportedly were lost; 2,000 dunums were taken out of vegetable cultivation; and 1,500 villagers migrated away.[67] The plight of al-Auja's farmers received international attention. Israel maintained that the spring had dried up due to the poor rainfall but then relented and licensed the drilling of two replacement wells in the village.[68]

The al-Auja spring is fed by the upper Cenomanian aquifer, which causes its discharge to fluctuate from year to year and, especially, from season to season.[69] Israel employed this property of the spring to support its claim. In fact, the spring did dry up for a period in the early 1930s, according to Palestinian experts at the Water Department in the West Bank. The findings of a subsequent uranium isotopic study on a number of wells and springs in the

64. Israel Ministry of Foreign Affairs, 1982a.
65. Rowley, 1990.
66. According to al-Maw'id, 1990, p. 137, six wells and eleven small springs were damaged.
67. Stork, 1983, p. 22; and United Nations, 1980a, p. 14.
68. Israel Ministry of Foreign Affairs, 1982a; and Stork, 1983, p. 22.
69. See, for example, Rosenthal and Kronfeld, 1982, p. 150.

West Bank further complicate the story.[70] They showed that the isotopic activity ratio of the al-Auja spring were midway between those of the lower and upper aquifers,[71] suggesting that the spring also may be fed by leakage from the lower aquifer. The possibility of lower aquifer leakage is buttressed by the Rofe and Raffety study that found many springs in the West Bank to be caused by faulting.[72] The size of the leakage in the case of al-Auja spring, however, is unknown.

Rosenthal and Kronfeld's findings are significant in that they could inform in advance those planning to drill a new well in the vicinity of a spring or an already existing well whether these sources are linked to the lower aquifer and therefore can be affected by a new well. Yet, even without this technique, it is difficult to fathom how Mekorot's engineers, who had accumulated substantial experience in drilling wells and who purposely dried up the freshwater springs that drained the mountain aquifer inside Israel, could not have anticipated that the new wells could harm those already operating close by. That Mekorot did not conduct the necessary investigations in the West Bank could not have been for lack of technical knowledge. Equally significant, the affected Palestinian communities did not have recourse to the courts to demand that advance investigations be taken to ascertain the potential impact of new wells because Israel had changed the pre-existing Jordanian law that would have permitted them to initiate legal action.

INSTITUTIONAL AND LEGAL CONTROL

The stagnation, if not deterioration, of the Palestinian water sector and the wide water gap between the Palestinians, on the one hand, and the Israelis and Israeli settlers, on the other, were made possible through Israel's takeover of the water sector's management. Israel altered the pre-existing codes and marginalized the role of the Palestinian institutions that had run the water sector before the occupation. The Israeli-enacted water laws and the framework of its management of the water sector in the West Bank and Gaza were significantly truncated, inferior versions of its own water laws

70. Ibid.
71. As measured by the 234U/238U ratio.
72. Rofe and Raffety, 1965a, pp. 85–87.

and management system. This can be demonstrated by an examination of Israel's own water laws and management framework.

An Outline of Water Law in Israel

The principal legal framework that guides water management in Israel is the water law of August 1959 and its subsequent modifications.[73] The most salient feature of the 1959 law is that it considers water sources—whether surface or underground, natural, regulated, or improved—as state property. This is affirmed by the stipulation that a land title does not confer on its holder rights to water beneath or crossing it. Further, the law defines water rights in terms of quantities without specification of the source. By rendering water state property, Israel introduced a fundamental change into Ottoman and British Mandate laws that had been in force in Palestine before the establishment of Israel in 1948.

The implementation of the 1959 law, according to the provisions of the law itself, is vested in the minister of agriculture to whom all water agencies and institutions must answer. The minister introduces water policy and is responsible before parliament (*knesset*) on behalf of the government. He is advised by a Water Board or Council consisting of 36 members, one-third from the government and two-thirds from the public; half the members are suppliers, and the other half are users. The body that drafts policy, however, is the Water Commission, headed by the water commissioner, who is responsible to the minister of agriculture. The commissioner is appointed by the government, although the Water Commission itself is, at least in theory, an autonomous body. The Water Commission includes administrative and technical divisions that enable it to implement its tasks: an allocation and licensing division; a hydrological service; and economic, judicial, agricultural, and water infrastructure planning. In the 1970s, the minister of health was accorded authority to set drinking-water standards that suppliers were required to meet and guarantee through appropriate testing.

Some insights into how the management system actually operates cam be obtained by reviewing two central domains of water

73. The description of the management of the Israeli water system is based on Associates for Middle East Research Water Project, 1987; Tahal, 1990, section 7; and Virshubski, 1961.

management: allocation of water rights and pricing. In order to lay claim to specific water quantity rights, a legal entity (individual, cooperative, municipality, etc.) must obtain a license from the water commissioner. Adherence of the user to the licensed allocation is ascertained through metering. In theory, the water commissioner has great discretionary powers in granting licenses. His powers, however, are tempered by the Water Board, two-thirds of whose members represent the public. Another constraint comes from the general guidelines that the water commissioner must take into consideration. The guidelines include conforming water policy with overall government policy, plans of the state planning agencies, the most beneficial use of water, and the economic conditions of the target community. For example, the allocation of irrigation water is based on, inter alia, the technical requirements of the crops, while the allocation of municipal water is based on what is viewed as optimum levels in the technical and social studies by a specialized department within the Water Commission. More crucially, however, the water commissioner's decisions can be challenged before water courts (tribunals). As Mordechai Virshubski noted:

> Control of the courts is the most important safeguard against the abuse of power by governmental agencies and all the decisions will have to follow a clearly stated policy.[74]

Water prices are set by the minister of agriculture, who must consider the financial condition of the consumers, as well as the costs of water supply. He receives input from the water commissioner, Mekorot, Tahal, and the ministries of Finance and the Interior (which funds municipal water activities). He also consults the Water Board, which holds public hearings on issues. Further, the water commissioner's proposed prices are subject to review and approval by the water committee in parliament, which itself receives price proposals from the Water Commission. Finally, the water charges fund, as pointed out earlier, plays a crucial role in water price determination.

To recapitulate, although the water law treats water resources as state property and gives the minister of agriculture and the water commissioner vast nominal powers, in practice the determination

74. Virshubski, 1961.

of water allocations and prices is shaped by an ensemble of factors. These factors include the strategic objectives of the state, social and economic development, and input from users, who may exert pressure to influence the policy-making process by challenging it in courts.

Overall Israeli Governance in the West Bank and Gaza

Soon after it captured the West Bank and Gaza, Israel established a Military Government under the command of the Israeli Defense Forces (IDF), which also handled civil and administrative functions. In 1981, it created the Civil Administration, separating military and civilian functions with the declared purpose of preparing the Palestinian territories for autonomy in line with the Camp David accords.[75] However, "effective authority and source of power" remained in the hands of the military governor,[76] and the main form of legislation under both regimes was military orders. Military Proclamation No. 2 (the first three military orders were called "proclamations") gave the military governor, who was appointed by the IDF chief of staff, all "powers of government, legislature, appointment and administration in relations to the region or its inhabitants;" at the same time, commanding officers were to be "responsible for security and the maintenance of order."[77]

The Military Government proceeded to consolidate its authority over the Palestinian territories by (among other things) modifying the pre-existing laws and controlling the administrative organs. The pre-existing laws in the West Bank were those enacted by the government of Jordan after the merger of the East and West Banks into the "Hashimite Kingdom of Jordan" in 1950, as well as extant segments of British Mandate and Ottoman laws in force in Palestine prior to the creation of Israel in 1948. In Gaza, which was administered by Egypt between 1948 and 1967, most of the basic legislation was Ottoman and British Mandate law; the Egyptian administration introduced legislation that was, for the most

75. The Camp David accords signed by Egypt and Israel in September 1978 and March 1979 laid the principles for peace between the two states and also included general provisions for Palestinian autonomy. According to Lesch et al., 1992, p. 22, the purpose of the change might have been to consolidate the Israeli grip on the autonomous entity.
76. Kuttab and Shehadeh, 1982, p. 14.
77. Cited in Lesch et al., 1992, p. 21.

part, regulatory, procedural, and administrative. One exception was the Constitutional Order of 1962; it emphasized Palestinian identity and proclaimed that all laws and court judgments were to be issued and implemented in the name of the "Palestinian People."[78]

The extant laws, according to Military Order No. 2, were to stay in force so long as they did "not conflict" with military orders or with "the changes arising by virtue of the occupation" of the West Bank and Gaza by the Israeli army.[79] With these sweeping powers in hand, and "whether through extensive lawmaking by the military authorities, through extraterritorial prescription of Israeli laws, or through case law of the Israeli courts, large segments of the law of the territories" became Israeli-enacted law.[80] Much has been written about whether these radical alterations of the pre-existing laws violated the international law of belligerent occupation, especially the 1907 Fourth Convention Respecting the Laws and Customs of War on Land and its annexed regulations (commonly known as the Hague Regulations). Israel never acknowledged itself as an occupying power in the Palestinian territories, but it *formally* accepted the international law of belligerent occupation as binding and repeatedly has claimed that its legal and other moves there were consistent with it.[81] Irrespective of whether such claims were valid, Israel, according to Eyal Benvenisti, employed "the fiction" of its adherence to the law of belligerent occupation to absorb the West Bank and Gaza "without having to share political or economic power with the local population, or resorting to a symbolic act of annexation."[82]

The legal position of the Palestinians that emerged under Israeli occupation differed from that of the Israeli settlers. The legal status of the settlers was made equal with the status of Israeli citizens inside Israel itself, and the settlers were granted numerous privileges above and beyond their fellow citizens, as enticement for settling in the West Bank. In other words, at operation here was

78. Kassim, 1984.
79. Cited in Kuttab and Shehadeh, 1982.
80. E. Benvenisti, 1990, preface.
81. See ibid.; and Shehadeh, 1988, p. xiii.
82. E. Benvenisti, 1990, p. 58. Whether Israel actually has absorbed the West Bank and Gaza, in the sense that the occupation has become irreversible, is arguable. This writer does not believe the occupation has become irreversible.

what Benvenisti called "legal dualism" in the West Bank and Gaza, with one system of laws applying to the Palestinians and one to the settlers.[83] It is within this broader context that the following investigation of the institutional practices of Israel vis-à-vis the Palestinian water sector ought to be viewed.

The Israeli-Enacted Water Laws

The Israeli Military Government introduced two types of legislation that affected water use in the West Bank and Gaza; one targeted the water sector itself, and the second land use. I will delineate here only the first type; the second type has been partially covered in the previous chapter, notably the military orders that designated significant portions of the Jordan Valley and the eastern slopes as closed military areas and a number of other areas as natural reserves. Moreover, a fair treatment of land use legislation is too involved and would not add significantly to the direct understanding of Israel's water policy.[84]

Israel targeted the West Bank's water resources promptly after the occupation because of the significant hydrogeological linkages they have with those in Israel; Gaza's water was targeted later, in 1972. Military Order No. 92 of 15 August 1967 "entrusted" the water officer in the West Bank "with all the powers conferred by the Water Provisions." It defined the water provisions as including all the pre-existing laws and regulations pertaining to aspects of production, distribution, consumption and sale, licensing, metering, pricing, etc. Just in case something escaped this "water-proof" definition, the order sealed it with the clause "and any other matter that has not been specifically mentioned but is dealt with in any form whatsoever as regards to water issues."

Subsequent military orders handled specific issues, such as licensing and valuation of water property rights, or amended Jordanian laws. Thus, Military Order No. 158 of 30 October 1967 amended Jordanian Law 31 of 1953 even though that law actually had been repealed in 1959.[85] The order addressed mainly the central question of licensing and stipulated that licenses be obtained

83. Ibid.
84. A chronological examination of the land-use orders is available in al-Labadi, 1990.
85. *Palestine Yearbook*, 1989, p. 351.

for any "water establishment," which it exhaustively defined as "Any construction or building intended for the production of surface water or ground water, including drilling or the diversion of water from any water source whatsoever." It also specified the procedures and penalties against violators. Most crucially, though, it empowered the water officer to deny permits "without giving reasons." Further, it affirmed that there would be "no appeal against the decision" of the water officer. The uncontestable power of the water officer not to grant licenses was complemented by the power to "cancel," "change," and "impose conditions on" permits that had been granted.

Military Order No. 457 of 15 February 1974 dealt with the valuation of natural resources, including water, and amended the relevant Jordanian Law 37 of 1966. It vested the authority to estimate the value of water or land allocations in the "competent Authority," defined as an official appointed by the commander of the IDF in the West Bank. Objections were permitted, but they were to be presented to a toothless "Objections Committee."[86]

No military orders appear to have been issued regarding prices. In the municipal sector, pricing for the final consumers, as has been detailed earlier, was in the hands of the municipalities. Mekorot, however, determined the price of the water that the municipalities purchased from the Water Department. The portion of the price charged by this company comprised the bulk of water charges and was much greater than the rates Mekorot charged Israeli municipalities. Mekorot did not intervene in the pricing of irrigation water, which stayed decentralized.

Similar military orders were also issued in Gaza, the most sweeping of all being Military Order No. 498 of 11 April 1974.[87] It went further than the military orders in the West Bank by adding pricing and combatting water contamination to the powers of the water officer. The power to set overall as well as area-specific water prices was placed in the hands of the "competent authority"—the equivalent of the water officer in the West Bank. The order did not provide that authority with guidelines for price determination. With regard to pollution, the order may be thought of as consisting

86. Ibid., pp. 357–58.
87. This order repealed the "Safeguarding of Public Water Supplies Ordinance, 1937" issued during the British Mandate and designed to protect water intended for household use, although it did not restrict irrigation water. See ibid., pp. 365–68; and al-Za'im, 1993.

of "preventive" and "corrective" provisions. The preventive provisions empowered the competent authority to regulate the use of industrial materials and agricultural inputs (notably manure), as well as to oblige local authorities to issue their own regulations and suppliers to maintain the water pipes that deliver the water. The corrective provisions required suppliers to treat polluted sources and restore them to their state before pollution but did not stipulate guidelines or standards that suppliers should meet.[88] Clearly, the military orders were far-reaching, covering every water use related activity, placing the reins of water management in the West Bank and Gaza entirely in Israeli hands.

A Comparative View of the Water Laws

The Israeli-enacted laws superseded the pre-existing Jordanian and Egyptian legislation and introduced elements of Israel's own laws. A comparison of the Israeli-enacted laws with those in Israel itself and with the pre-occupation legislation demonstrates more starkly their discriminatory nature than if they were examined in isolation. It also can reveal the role of law in water management as well as strengths and weaknesses of various legal water regimes. The centerpiece of the Israeli-enacted laws was the vestment in the person of the water officer unlimited powers over the water sector in the West Bank and Gaza. He could grant permits for any water-related project (or establishment), could deny them without having to offer an explanation, and could cancel or modify the terms of permits already granted; he could set water prices without reference to broad, socially responsive criteria and could determine the value of water establishments or damage to water interests from actions taken by him; his decisions were final and uncontestable, and he was the authority of first and last resort.

The delegation of such vast powers to the water officer was tantamount to rendering water resources state property, leaving Palestinian farmers only with a right to the use of water; even this usufruct right could be revoked without explanation. With such legal tools, Israel did not need to declare formally that the water resources of the Palestinian territories were state property, and it

88. Other relevant military orders in Gaza were No. 360 of 13 October 1970, No. 558 of 17 July 1977, and a series of announcements by the regional military commander during the 1970s; see al-Za'im, 1993.

thus could avoid formally annexing them. Rendering water effectively as state property also revised the status of groundwater resources under Jordanian Law 37, which had treated them as private property.[89]

What was left of the old regime was the microlevel arrangements, especially in agriculture. Although the Israeli water officer was in control of permits and allocations, once a farmer was granted a license, he could sell water if he so wished. Moreover, the old rotation system of property rights in springwater continued. However, the more fundamental issue here is not the formal form of property rights, private or state, but rather such issues as the law's distribution of power among the decision makers and among them and the rest of the society, the extent to which it protects the citizenry from the arbitrary exercise of power by those who wield it, and the vision and criteria it provides for decision making. Whereas in the West Bank and Gaza, the authority to make decisions was vested in one person, in Israel it was multi-centered and negotiable among the Ministry of Agriculture, the Water Commission, and the Water Board, on which suppliers and users were represented equally and on which the public held majority representation. Decisions by the minister of agriculture also were bound by the approval by the water committee in the parliament.

Nor did the military orders accord the affected Palestinians the chance to appeal the decisions of the water officer before a water court as did the law in Israel. The inability to take their case before water courts deprived the Palestinians of a pivotal instrument against the arbitrary exercise of power by the water officer. In the case of assessing the value of water rights subject to acquisition, the objections committee could hear complaints, but that committee was bound neither by rules of evidence nor by law, and its decisions were not binding. Rather, its decisions were in the nature of recommendations to the military governor, who had the final say in the matter. In sum, Israeli water legislation in the West Bank and Gaza thoroughly stifled the Palestinian voice in the decision-making process.

This situation had not been the case before Israel's capture of those territories. Jordanian Law 37 designated an "authority" to be the legal entity responsible for all natural resources, including land and water, and stipulated that it comprise seven members,

89. *Palestine Yearbook*, 1989, pp. 348–49.

headed by the prime minister. Further, it specified that land and water rights acquisition by the authority was to be subject to compensation based on an evaluation by a committee of three members, headed by a judge. Moreover, the decisions of the committee could be contested before an appellate committee headed by a judge from the court of appeal.[90]

Regulatory legislation subsequently was enacted (Law 88 in 1966) concerning the procedures for obtaining licenses for water works, determining permissible water rights and their potential impact on the rights of others, and filing objections against the applicant. These procedures also were superseded by the military orders, effectively depriving Palestinians of the legal tools to demand that Mekorot conduct studies to demonstrate that the wells it planned to drill for the settlements did not cause appreciable harm to existing water supply sources, as pointed out earlier in relation to the drying up of wells and springs in the West Bank.

Moreover, Israeli water legislation in the West Bank did not formulate criteria in which the water officer could anchor his decisions. This also contrasted with Israeli water law in which water pricing (for instance) had to take into account the financial conditions of the users and the supply costs, apart from adjustments that could be made by the water charges fund. In the absence of such guidelines, the West Bank's municipal water was priced uniformly for cities and villages. The Israeli law also sought to allocate municipal water in amounts that were considered optimum by experts. Thus, the optimum per capita consumption recommended for Israelis was 80 m^3 annually in the period immediately after the enactment of the law, subsequently increased to 100 m^3.[91] Given this experience, one legitimately can ask on what basis Israel considered an annual 35 m^3 per capita water consumption optimum for the Palestinians in the West Bank and Gaza?

On a more general plane, the water law in Israel stated that water utilization was to serve the development of the country and the interests of the inhabitants of a region and to accord with government policy. The military orders did not provide any such guidelines for Israeli water policy makers in the West Bank and Gaza. The inescapable conclusion is that Israel's overarching concern was with how water use in the occupied territories affected

90. Ibid.
91. Virshubski, 1961.

Israelis and Israeli settlers, not how it might improve the welfare of the Palestinian population.

Arrest of Institutional Development

In most sectors, including water, the Military Government essentially retained the official institutional apparatus that was in place before the occupation, keeping the majority of the Palestinian personnel in their jobs. Yet, while Palestinian employees stayed on the job, the Israeli officers controlled the hiring, firing, budgets, and policy making.[92] Palestinians attempted to offset the lack of capable, responsive public institutions by creating other forms of institutions, such as professional associations, cooperatives, and non-profit companies. Although there were some "success stories," the outcome seems to have been generally less than successful. The lack of success has been adduced in part to pressure by Israel—which viewed institution building as resistance by other means—in the form of such actions as the denial of licenses for new organizations. Israeli pressure was strongly abetted by the dependence of the institutions on outside and foreign funders with various development philosophies and motivations; by competition among political factions, regions, and families; by the absence of an overall development strategy; by the lack of modern institutional tradition; and by the widespread tendency for a single person to dominate a given institution.[93]

Although the water sector fitted within this overall picture, it would seem that the arrest of water-related institutional development was more an outcome of Israeli policies than in other sectors. The main reason for this was that water management was a function of public, rather than private, institutions. For example, while in the health sector private doctors and medical facilities could compensate for the absence of governmental health care, much less could be done by private hydrologists and engineers who had no facilities to manage, wells to drill, pipe networks to lay out, or public policies to formulate.

Before the water sector in the West Bank was seized by Israel in 1967, it was managed by the Water Department, which was

92. Lesch et al., 1992, p. 22.
93. See Nakhleh, 1994, pp. 25–63; and Roy, 1995, pp. 265–66.

under the jurisdiction of the Natural Resources Authority (NRA) centered in Amman. In order to develop the groundwater resources on a planned, scientific basis, the NRA in the early 1960s had commissioned the British firm Rofe and Raffety to undertake what has become the seminal hydrogeological study of the mountain aquifer.[94] Other investigations, including a study of groundwater in the Jericho area, were conducted with the participation of Palestinian engineers.[95] Wells were drilled by local contractors and plans were made to increase the irrigated area by 40 percent. Those were modest achievements, and much remained to be done to develop the institutional capability of water management in the West Bank when Israel's occupation beginning in 1967 aborted the process of institutional development. By the 1990s, Palestinian water management capability compared poorly with its Jordanian counterpart.

In Gaza, water management during the Egyptian administration was entrusted to the Department of Municipal and Rural Affairs, and it appears that less attention was paid to the water sector in Gaza than in the West Bank. The reasons can only be conjectured. It may be that Egypt did not take much interest in Gaza's water because the strip did not become part of Egypt as the West Bank became part of Jordan. It also may be that the modest quantities of water in the aquifer, especially in comparison with the Nile River, did not make careful management or study of the aquifer seem like an urgent matter. Further, because water abstraction in Gaza did not affect Israel, the Egyptian government perhaps did not feel compelled to look closely into the water sources as Jordan had to do in the West Bank. As a consequence, only one hydrogeological investigation was undertaken in 1965, after a sudden acceleration in well drilling in the early 1960s induced by the opening of export markets for citrus.[96]

Under Israeli rule, the Palestinian personnel in the West Bank's Water Department were left with the administrative tasks of reading meters and identifying violators. They were entrusted with basic technical assignments, such as collecting water samples for testing, measuring spring flows, and keeping rainfall records. Well-drilling, a relatively demanding hydrological task if scientifi-

94. Rofe and Raffety, 1965a; and idem., 1965b.
95. Davidson and Hirzallah, 1966.
96. Shata and Salim, 1965.

cally based, was passed into Israeli control. This not only hampered the development of Palestinian expertise, but it also raised the costs of drilling.[97] The exclusion of Palestinians from the technical sphere was reinforced by the staffing policy. Although the overall staff of the Water Department grew, the technical staff did not. In fact, the Water Department did not hire a single Palestinian hydrologist after June 1967. A similar situation prevailed with respect to Israeli management of water in Gaza, with the exception of well-digging, which, because of the shallow, sandy nature of the aquifer, the Gazans undertook without the heavy equipment required for drilling in the West Bank. Israel exempted well-drilling from scrutiny because there was no danger that the depth of the wells would affect its water supply.

The conditions of the municipalities, which administered water supply, were no brighter. The powers of the municipal councils, which had included building, sanitation, sewage, and licensing, among others, diminished under the occupation. An Israeli officer in the military government representing the Ministry of Interior approved their budgets and any changes in their bylaws and set tax rates; thus, he could influence the councils' decisions through the threat of reducing financial allocations, which were minuscule anyway.[98]

Because the bulk of water was earmarked for irrigation, agricultural research and extension could have had important implications for the water sector. However, the departments of agriculture in the West Bank and in Gaza experienced similar conditions to those of the Water Department and municipal councils. For example, officials in the agricultural station at Jericho, the center of the most important irrigated agricultural area in the West Bank, revealed that between the late 1970s and the 1990s the station's extension staff was reduced from fifteen to ten and the number of vehicles from eight to two.[99] Also, at a time when computer use has become widespread, the station did not have even a typewriter.

The only establishment to escape this fate was the Jerusalem Water Undertaking (JWU), perhaps because it supplied water to the Civil Administration headquarters and to Israeli settlements and had consented to take water from Mekorot's network, which

97. Interviews with Water Department staff, March 1992.
98. Lesch et al., 1992, p. 26.
99. Interview with Adil Brayghith and other staff, March 1992.

was part of the process of "creeping annexation" during the 1977–83 period of Likud-led government. Within the constraints of Israeli restrictions, the JWU, by all accounts, has been an efficient, reliable water manager. After the severe snowstorms in 1992, for instance, the company promptly replaced meters and restored service.

Whatever institutional capability the Palestinians developed in the West Bank and Gaza occurred in spite of the occupation and within the nongovernmental domain. The nongovernmental institutions either were foreign based or indigenous. The foreign based institutions, such as the United Nations Development Program (UNDP) and ANERA, had Palestinian staff who acquired vital experience for advancing institutional capability as they moved into other jobs with local organizations; here, however, the focus is on the indigenous institutions. Private initiative gained momentum notably during the intifada, perhaps later than it should or could have begun. The institutions that emerged after 1987 commonly were started by individuals who may be thought of as "institutional entrepreneurs." In particular, two pioneering institutions—the Palestinian Hydrology Group (PHG) and ARIJ—deserve mention. The PHG started with the idea of helping small farmers on a modest scale through investigating the conditions of the water springs, with a view to their rehabilitation. Its work expanded, and in 1993 the PHG started a hydrogeological study of a catchment area in Wadi Zimar. Intended as a pilot project, this study was the first of its kind in the West Bank. It already has resulted in a technical report on the reliability of rainfall data concerning the catchment and the northern segment of the West Bank.[100] The PHG also participated in 1993–95 in the study and execution of drilling a well (Dayr Sharaf) for Nablus municipality, with financial assistance from Germany.[101]

ARIJ is an environmental research institute that has done work on water, agriculture, and pollution. In the early 1990s, it conducted a research project on the rainfed sector and in 1994 undertook an ambitious, three-year project to study the irrigated sector in the West Bank, with the object of investigating its potential for equitable and sustainable development.[102] The study of the

100. Husary et al., 1995.
101. Aliewi et al., 1995.
102. ARIJ, 1994.

water resources, including wells and springs, as well as irrigation technology, was a central component of the study. ARIJ also has been building a computerized database on agriculture and the environment in the West Bank.

These water-related institutions in the West Bank and Gaza are new, have yet to accumulate effective experience, and need senior technical and social science staff if the quality of their efforts is not to plateau rapidly. They also need to become *institutionalized*, in the sense of not having their futures tied to the entrepreneurs who started them. Their work has been fragmented and sometimes has overlapped; to become cumulative it has to be part of a coherent macrolevel water management strategy. Moreover, they have depended on external funding for their survival. The future evolution of these institutions thus hangs in the balance. Still, whether or not they continue as institutions, the experience gained by their personnel should prove valuable to any institutions that might absorb them.

There is no substitute, however, for developing modern, effective governmental institutions and creating a water management system and legal regime based on trust and collaboration between the mangers and the managed; on incentives, not just on disincentives; and on policy, not just on policing. Such is the challenge that lies ahead for the Palestinian Water Authority, whose creation was declared officially in June 1994. The interval that has passed since its founding has been too short for a fair evaluation of its work. It also has been a time of closures and confrontation, a situation not conducive for development. Nonetheless, the preliminary picture that emerges from numerous reports is that the managerial performance of the PA in general leaves something to be desired.

During the interim phase, the Palestinian water sector in the West Bank is managed jointly with Israel under essentially Israeli regulations. The agreements stress environmental aspects and conservation, but such measures need the kind of practical steps that have not been possible in the context of the overall relationship between the two sides. Furthermore, Israel's approval is mandatory for any change in the status quo ante in the West Bank, and Israeli representatives on the joint "Supervision and Enforcement Teams" have the power to monitor and ensure Palestinian compliance, as discussed in chapter 2.

IDEOLOGICAL WATER IN ISRAEL?

Some analysts have argued that water has an ideological dimension in the Israeli "cognitive map."[103] They base their argument on the fact that water is an indispensable input in agriculture, which itself was perceived ideologically, not just instrumentally, by the once-dominant current of Labor Zionism in the Zionist movement. Itzhak Galnoor summarizes the thesis of ideological water as follows:

> From the outset water has not been conceived of in Israel as merely a means of production. It was also given a central position in Zionist ideology and the social priorities of the state . . . and leaders like Ben-Gurion, Eshkol and Sapir were personally involved in it.[104]

Although the ideological perception of water is not an issue per se, it is a factor that, if present, could complicate the resolution of the conflict by lending an emotional or irrational element to the Israeli position or could be manipulated in the service of other aims, such as was done in the aforementioned 1990 *Jerusalem Post* advertisement (see The Water Argument of the Total and Partial Annexationists in this chapter). Nevertheless, I argue that, even if water had been perceived ideologically in the past, the material foundations for such a perception have practically disappeared; where the perception persists, it is likely to be an atavistic phenomenon confined to the few who still are involved in agricultural work.

In contrast, Palestinian perceptions of water, which have been examined inadequately, may have taken an opposite trajectory. I propose that earlier Palestinian views of water were grounded culturally and instrumentally, rather than ideologically. Perhaps ironically, as the ideological outlook on water has receded in Israel, for the Palestinians the water question appears to have moved onto center stage as another symbol of their dispossession. Such symbolism is less ideologically induced than it is a cognitive mirror of the daily reality facing the Palestinians.

103. See in particular, Galnoor, 1980; Lowi, 1993, pp. 51–52; and Naff and Matson, 1984, pp. 184–88.
104. Galnoor, 1980, pp. 158–59.

Labor Zionism and Agriculture

"Labor Zionism" refers to the groups and factions within organized Zionism that were broadly socialist in orientation, despite the many differences among them on some basic issues and details.[105] Its foundation was laid during the second wave of Jewish immigration (1905–14) to Palestine, a movement that brought about 35,000 Jews from eastern Europe, particularly from Russia, in conjunction with the failure of the Russian revolution of 1905.[106] The parties associated with Labor Zionism were the pivotal factions in the establishment of the State of Israel and provided its political leaders until their hold on power was broken in 1977 by the electoral victory of the Likud bloc. Consequently, Labor Zionist social and economic philosophies predominated within the Zionist movement and in Israel itself, and they were concretized in such social institutions as the *kibbutz*, or collective agricultural settlement, and the Histadrut, the primary labor union.

A main tenet of Labor Zionism held that Jewish labor was essential for the "normalization" of Jewish society which, in the "diaspora," was engaged mainly in commerce and the professions rather than the "productive" pursuits of the peasants and working class. Further, many Labor Zionists also advocated the use of Jewish labor alone, which meant, at least theoretically, the exclusion of Palestinian workers from their enterprises. As a corollary, some also called for the purchase of only "Jewish produce," that is, produce from Jewish farms.

For Labor Zionism, agriculture, more than industry, was to serve some unique goals. Apart from its utilitarian value as a food supplier and a factor of economic development, Labor Zionists viewed agriculture as a means for the "redemption" of the land from the "desolate" state they perceived it to be in,[107] as a means to make the desert bloom, as a source of spiritual renewal for Jewish immigrants, and as a means to help them strike roots in Palestine. As Mordechai Bar-On has written:

> The early Zionist settlers primarily saw large stretches of uninhabited land, malaria-infested swamps and many ruins

105. Patai, 1971, pp. 695–97.
106. Laqueur, 1989, pp. 277–337; and Tessler, 1994, p. 61.
107. Zionists used the term "desolate" in the text they presented to the 1919 Paris Peace Conference for drawing the boundaries of Palestine; cited in Toye, 1989, vol. 2, p. 215.

everywhere, since these lands were those available to their colonizing efforts.[108]

A corollary, not necessarily logical or inevitable, was the Zionist denial of even the presence of the indigenous inhabitants, which has been summed up by the well-known phrase coined before World War I by Max Nordau, a prominent Zionist orator born in Hungary, who described Palestine as "the land without people [for] the people [the Jews] without a land."[109]

The Labor Zionist conception of the land and agriculture thus was essentially romantic, if not mystical. It was informed first by the distance from which it was viewed and the inability of Jews to cultivate land elsewhere; and second, upon arrival in Palestine, by some natural features of the narrow space in which Jews could settle. This conception also endowed the early generation of Zionist settlers—the "pioneers"—with a mythic aura that was to become one of the central founding myths of the state of Israel.

However agriculture was perceived, it needed water. By being indispensable for agriculture, water hence acquired what might be termed "ideology by association." The thesis, however, fails on its own to explain the proposals for, and/or implementation of, key water schemes, such as the draining of the Hula lake and marshlands, the diversion of the Jordan River to the Negev, and projects to link the Mediterranean and Dead seas by canals. The water-to-the-Negev scheme, as noted earlier, first was broached in the nineteenth century by Zionist sympathizers from England even before the emergence of Labor Zionism. The idea of a Med-Dead canal was mentioned in the memoirs of Zionist movement founder Herzl, who was given the idea by an engineer colleague. Moreover, the transportation of Jordan River water to the south was given credibility by the American engineers Lowdermilk and Hays, who were not known for being Labor Zionists.

Gerald Steinberg asserts that prestige and big projects in Israel have been informed by Baconian philosophy (after the thirteenth-century English philosopher Roger Bacon) in its broadest sense, which encouraged the exploitation and domination of the natural environment for the benefit of human development.[110] Obviously,

108. Bar-On, 1996, p. 15.
109. Cited in Childers, 1971, p. 168.
110. Steinberg, 1987.

this is a caricaturist view of that philosophy and of European attitudes toward nature, a topic with copious discourse.[111] Whatever European philosophical attitudes toward nature might have been in the past, during the nineteenth and early twentieth centuries Europe was in the throes of the industrial revolution, creating a new world with mammoth projects and subduing the natural environment in the process. The early leaders of the Zionist movement came out of that milieu and could imagine the aforementioned water projects in Palestine without difficulty, and then tried to seize the appropriate moment to execute them.

More than just philosophy, however, was needed. The projects were conceived because Zionists considered agriculture, which the projects were to serve, to be pivotal for the realization of national objectives. It was viewed, inter alia, as a means of economic development; as a means for progress toward food self-reliance; as a means for securing an uninterrupted Jewish presence and settlement in outlying areas; as a means toward security; as a means of laying claim to the land; and as a means of excluding the indigenous Palestinians from the land.[112] For the "Zionists/Israelis," as Lowi sums it up, "Agricultural development has remained a national goal, embodying a socially accepted value and dictated by ideology."[113]

The foregoing analysis of the perception and role of agriculture may be valid for the prestate period and the early years after its establishment. However, to suggest that it has persisted in subsequent decades, as the authors of the thesis of ideological water seem to do, is misleading. In the decades since 1948, the role of agriculture, and hence the material foundations on which the Labor Zionist ideology of agriculture rested, have diminished considerably.

The End of Ideological Water

The steady decline of agriculture's role in Israel's economy, notably its minor share of 3 percent of the GDP, and even the decline of the profitability of some branches, was discussed earlier. As oc-

---

111. For a nuanced historical view of European attitudes toward nature, see Schama, 1995; for Zionist and Israeli attitudes, see Zerubavel, 1996, pp. 60–99.
112. Lowi, 1993, pp. 50–52; and Naff and Matson, 1984, pp. 84–88.
113. Lowi, 1993, pp. 51–52.

curred historically in many societies in the process of economic development, industry and the services have replaced agriculture as the locus of economic growth in Israel. Nevertheless, food self-sufficiency or food security has remained a social and political objective in Israel, a goal that perhaps goes back to one of the central ideas of Labor Zionism, "Jewish produce." Israel produces significant amounts of food for local consumption. However, it also imports the bulk of its basic staples of rice, sugar, and wheat flour, while earmarking a significant fraction of irrigation water for export crops rather than for domestic use. It may be said that earnings from the exports of food and other agricultural commodities enable Israel to finances its imports. Financing food imports from agricultural exports is another prevalent notion of food self-sufficiency, but is it appropriate to ask the agricultural sector to pay for food imports, especially when most of the food is consumed by urban populations not engaged in agricultural production? What is essential for financing food imports is the availability of foreign exchange, which Israel can secure more readily from industrial exports and tourism than from exporting citrus, which uses scarce, subsidized water.

However that may be, the future does not look bright for food self-sufficiency. This sentiment has been expressed, for example, by Avram Katz-Oz, a former Israeli minister of agriculture and head of its water delegation at the peace talks in 1994: "Ideas on food security and self-sufficiency are of the 1950s and the 1960s, not of today."[114] More concretely, and indicative of a wide acceptance of this shift in thinking, are BUNT's long-term projections of Israeli water demand that are based on domestic self-sufficiency in fresh fruits and vegetables and 25 percent sufficiency in dairy products. This is a modest vision compared with the vision of complete food self-sufficiency from domestic production.

What about the argument that agriculture enhances Israeli military security? The subject of military security is beyond our competence, but common knowledge leads one to question this claim. It may be that, prior to the creation of the state of Israel, some frontline agricultural settlements had an important role to play in security, but it is unclear how they would do so today, considering the sophisticated and destructive potential of military

114. Cited in Katz, 1994; I thank J. A. Allan for bringing this source to my attention.

equipment and the advanced reconnaissance technology. Moreover, it seems that irrigated agriculture would not be a great security asset because it is often found in flat terrain that is hard to defend, as was amply illustrated, for example, by the experiences of the Egyptian army in the June 1967 war and the Iraqi army in 1991 during the Gulf war after their air defenses had been decommissioned. Furthermore, why should settlements and population dispersion be dependent on agriculture rather than on industry? In fact, the only Jewish agricultural settlements in the West Bank are those located in the Jordan Valley, and these have more to do with the availability of water and irrigable land in that region than with security considerations. One seldom reads about agriculture being depicted elsewhere in the world as a military asset, and no one has made a convincing case that it is in Israel either.

Further, the ideological character of agriculture may well have become history. In order for agriculture to fulfill ideological functions, such as the creation of a new Jewish man or effecting rootedness in the land, a significant number of people in the society would have to work in this sector. The urban population in Israel on the eve of its founding was already three times larger than its rural counterpart; by 1990 the former had outstripped the latter by a ratio of approximately 10 to 1.[115] In the latter year, the number of Israelis employed in agriculture was less than 63,000, or slightly more than 4 percent of the total labor force of about 1.25 million. Significantly, of those working in agriculture, about 10,000—16 percent—were, in the lexicon of the *Israel Statistical Abstract*, "non-Jewish," that is, Palestinian-Israelis. In addition, not counted in the 63,000 figure were more than 12,000 agricultural laborers who commuted daily from the West Bank and Gaza; including them in Israel's agricultural labor force raises to 30 percent the total number of Palestinians working in Israeli agriculture. Thus, only a small minority of Israeli Jews were engaged in agricultural work. In fact, in the *kibbutzim* (plural of *kibbutz*), the bulwark of Labor Zionism, manufacturing has become the dominant economic sector, contributing in the late 1980s around 60 percent of the value of their production.[116] Likewise, 50–60 percent of the members of the *moshavs*—the other type of cooperative settlements that

115. Government of Palestine, 1946, p. 157; and Israel, Central Bureau of Statistics, 1992.
116. Aharoni, 1991, p. 208.

after 1948 absorbed immigrants (who were often reluctant to join them)—did not work in agriculture.[117]

Besides the number of people engaged in agriculture, the nature of agricultural work itself also has a bearing on the attitude toward land. Agricultural tasks in Israel, from tillage and irrigation to pesticide and fertilizer application, are highly mechanized. The labor of operating machinery is quite different from the manual work of pioneer Labor Zionists, who, in spite of their tendency to exaggerate the hardships,[118] undoubtedly experienced more intimacy with the soil, flora, and fauna than do the operators of modern farm equipment.

Hence, it is hard to fathom how agriculture can be the means to rootedness in the land when the vast majority of the population in Israel is urban; when so few Jews, even in the communities that are the core of the sector, work in agriculture; when a significant proportion of the agricultural workforce is composed of Palestinians; and when the tasks themselves are mechanized. Indeed, the words of Haim Weizmann, the first Israeli president, no longer seem relevant:

> that the real soul of a people—its language, its poetry, its literature, its traditions—springs up from the intimate contact between man and soils. The towns do no more than "process" the fruits of the villages.[119]

It may be that the towns only "process" the fruits of the village, and that the *kibbutzim* exert more influence than their relative population size would warrant. Still, few would dispute that language, poetry, literature, and traditions in Israel today are produced mainly in the towns and more so in the cities, not by people engaged in agriculture.

In fact, the ideology of agriculture and of making the desert bloom, which was never without its opponents in the Zionist movement, has come under scrutiny in Israel itself. For example, a 1991

117. Ibid.
118. Much has been written about the hardships that Labor Zionist "pioneers" suffered and the great toil they exerted prior to the establishment of the state of Israel; their story has become one of the founding myths of the Israeli state. The story needs to be recast, but that would be too far a digression for this study. For a flavor of some critical views about the "pioneers" by their fellow Jewish contemporaries, see Kimmerling, 1983a, p. 4.
119. Cited in Aharoni, 1991, p. 63.

editorial in the *Jerusalem Post* dubbed that ideology "anachronistic" and "irrelevant in a modern state."[120] It also is interesting to note that, in the previously cited advertisement by the Ministry of Agriculture calling for the annexation of the West Bank purportedly to preserve "Israel's" water resources, water was used as a rational, technical reason to brush aside the ideological motivations underlying the call for annexation:

> It is important to realize that the claim to continued Israeli control over Judea and Samaria is not based on extremist fanaticism or religious mysticism but on a rational, healthy and reasonable survival extinct.[121]

Although the Ministry of Agriculture clearly was resorting to hyperbole by invoking the "survival instinct," especially in light of the diminishment of the role of agriculture in the economy, the significance of water and the impact of the "loss" of the West Bank on water supply were presented in the advertisement as "dry facts" that could be challenged objectively without reference to ideology.

Ideologies sometimes are inscribed and outlive the disappearance of the milieu in which they emerged. The demographic and economic transformation of Israel, however, would suggest that water no longer holds the ideological baggage it once carried (or is said to have carried). Where it does, it is perhaps chiefly among the older generation of Labor Zionists and the small fraction of the population working in agriculture. The critical comments of the *Jerusalem Post* and, more important, the increasing calls among Israeli professionals in the water field for according priority to the economic and environmental calculus over the political, as well as the fact that agriculture has diminished to a residual sector that bears the brunt of droughts, are strong indicators of the fading of the ideological perception of agriculture and water.

PALESTINIAN PERCEPTIONS OF WATER

The land tenure system and social stratification of the Palestinian agrarian sector have been studied adequately, but the cultural aspects have been much less probed, perhaps for the lack of recorded

120. *Jerusalem Post*, 4 January 1991.
121. Ibid., 10 August 1990.

material. Thus, constructing a credible argument on Palestinian perceptions of agriculture and water, notably before the establishment of the state of Israel, may not be possible. The remarks below are largely impressionistic, derived from general knowledge rather than in-depth research.

Broadly speaking, farming in Palestine was carried out by males and females from various social strata in the countryside: owners, sharecroppers, and agricultural laborers. Both owners and sharecroppers mobilized members of their households, and family labor was the cornerstone of agricultural work. Not all landowners worked on the land, however. There were absentee landlords, who eventually came to be associated in the minds of many Palestinians with land sales to the Jews, although they were not the only group to sell land. They resided in the towns and owned relatively large tracts of land, notably in the plains and valleys, and tended to hire sharecroppers to do the farming. There were innumerable share-cropping arrangements, centering around the division of inputs and output among landowners and sharecroppers. Labor, however, invariably was contributed by the sharecroppers and their families. In addition to owner-operation and sharecropping, there was another form of land tenure, namely the *musha'*. The land under *musha'* tenure belonged to the whole village, but individual plots were reallotted periodically among stakeholders; labor was family based. The land tenure system and the fortunes of the peasantry varied regionally, especially along the rainfed-irrigated cultivation axis, and shifted in response to macroeconomic and political changes. The *musha'* system, for instance, largely was dismantled during the British Mandate. Describing such shifts, however, is beyond the scope of this book. The present concern is with how Palestinians perceived agriculture and water.

For Palestinian peasants, as for most agriculturalists, working on the land was a way of life. The proper way to look at it is as broadly cultural, rather than ideological. The villagers used simple implements and drought animals, although machines were introduced from the 1930s onward in the irrigated areas, as Palestine increasingly was incorporated into the world market. Agricultural labor was hard and backbreaking, in spite of occasional romanticization by urban dwellers of village life and of the peasant as being the source of moral values.[122] Furthermore, although the peasants

122. For example, Miller, 1985, pp. 22–23, cites testimonies mirroring this sentiment by Jamal Bey al-Husayni and the Palestinian historian George Antonious before Britain's Palestine Royal Commission in 1937.

themselves were undoubtedly proud of being the producers of the food and much of the wealth of the country, a principal social status cleavage existed between them and city dwellers: Becoming a peasant was not something to aspire to in Palestinian society. For example, in one folk song, a girl beseeches her mother not to marry her to a ploughman or a shepherd, but to a horseman—an old romantic symbol in Arab culture—or a preacher, a secure, "white collar," employee, perhaps even living in the city.[123]

Needless to say, Palestinian peasants generally neither saw themselves nor were perceived by the rest of the society as heroic figures like the early Zionist settlers, even though the two groups performed similar types of work and the peasants supplied the bulk of the recruits in the confrontation with these settlers. Depending on their fortunes, one can expect that some peasants found satisfaction in tilling the land or accepted it as their lot in life. Others, however, probably wished to leave agriculture but could not, whereas a few did jettison it and head for the towns, either permanently or during the slack agricultural season. Certainly, peasants, unlike the early Jewish "pioneers," did not need to prove to themselves or to others that they could endure the hardships of agricultural labor or to be anxious about attachment to a land in which they were rooted economically and existentially.

During the first thirty years of the twentieth century, Palestinian laborers also worked on Jewish farms. They were either former tenants on the land before it had been purchased by the new Jewish owners or landless peasants seeking a livelihood. The Jewish enterprises hired Palestinian workers because, among other things, those who managed them did not necessarily subscribe to the ideology of Labor Zionism or they experienced a shortage of Jewish workers. In time this practice came to a halt because Palestinians began to feel that the Jewish immigrants, whom they did not believe had a right to Palestine, were intent on taking away the land and eventually the country. This feeling was dramatized by some key events, such as the protracted strife that lasted from 1929 to 1933 between the tenants of Wadi al-Hawarith, a village about 17 km northwest of Tulkarm, and the Jewish National Fund (JNF), the World Zionist Organization's body for land purchase and development at that time. The JNF sought to evict the tenants after

123. Sirhan, 1989, vol. 2, p. 390.

buying the land from an absentee owner.[124] The 1936 Palestinian "great revolt" against both British colonialism and the Zionist project for a Jewish homeland in Palestine witnessed much agitation against land sales to the Jews and put an end to Palestinian work on Jewish farms.[125] Such land-centered consciousness was not so much ideologically informed as it was anchored in the Palestinians' fear of losing the land. At any rate, one need not belabor the argument about the absence of an ideologically informed engagement in agricultural labor.

The absence of agricultural ideology, and hence an associated water ideology, however, ought not be mistaken for a lack of rich cultural associations and symbolism. Villagers always performed agriculture and water-related rituals, prayers, songs, and other expressive practices.[126] For example, where the land was communally owned, *musha'*, they named the individual plots after the physical property of the land or historical and geographical references.[127] The harvest of grapes, olives, and wheat was ritualized in some localities, with the rituals bringing the community together in work, song, and sharing.[128] Water, of course, always figured prominently in Arab symbolism and aesthetics, perhaps because of its scarcity and the preponderance of the desert in the Arab world. To illustrate, Muslims consider water as a purifying agent in performing ablutions before prayer; as a centerpiece of Paradise; and as a manifestation of God's blessing in times of plentiful rain and His curse during droughts. Aesthetically, water was a focal point in the houses and palaces of the elites who could afford the elaborate gardens. A widely quoted Arabic verse says: "Three things make life bright with their loveliness: water, greenery, and a handsome face." Home gardens in Palestine were not confined to the houses of the elite, however; they also were likely to be found in many rural and urban houses, as a source both of food and beauty.

That the Palestinians did not translate the need for water into large irrigation schemes may have been the outcome of a combination of demographic, cultural, and political factors. Water must not have seemed to them to be in short supply: Scarcity is a relative matter both in the subjective and objective senses, subject to his-

124. See, for example, Adler (Cohen), 1988.
125. Kimmerling, 1995a.
126. Sirhan, 1989, vol. 2, pp. 374–402.
127. Sirhan, 1989, vol. 2, p. 374.
128. There is a rich description of such rituals in ibid., pp. 408–13.

torical and cultural change. For example, the thirteenth-century Muslim geographer, Yaqut al-Hamawi, in his compendium, *Mu'jam al-Buldan,* described the water situation in Jerusalem thus: "Water is plentiful in Jerusalem, and it has been said, that nothing is more ample there than water and the calls for prayer; seldom is there a house that does not have one, two, or three cisterns."[129] Obviously, no one today considers a house with two cisterns as having an ample water supply. In the first half of the twentieth century, Palestine's water was sufficient when measured against the population size—as late as 1946, estimated at about 1.2 million Palestinians and 0.5 million Jews—and the state of technology.[130]

Further, the attitude of planning and social engineering in general had not yet permeated Palestinian culture, like in other pre-industrial cultures. Although the Hula marshlands were a source of malaria, drying them up artificially would not have been a pre-occupation, notwithstanding an aborted nineteenth-century effort at doing so by two entrepreneurs from today's Lebanon; they had been granted a concession by the Ottoman authorities that subsequently was abandoned, reportedly due to a lack of finance and British reluctance to assist the project.[131] The Palestinians had access to other agricultural land and, unlike Jewish immigrants, did not perceive the marshlands as mere swamps; the villagers actually harvested the marshlands' papyrus for making straw mats and their ditch reed for building houses.[132] To these factors may be added that governance after 1918 was in the hands of the British, not the Palestinians. During the intense period of strife between the Palestinians and the Zionists, the development of water resources was subject to Britain's policy in Palestine, and the thrust of that policy did not favor change in the Palestinian villages, presumably to avoid destabilization.[133] The situation of the Palestinians thus contrasted sharply with that of the Zionists, who were compelled to plan by virtue of their vision of a future state in a distant land with a large immigrant population which, it must be admitted, was the original cause of the imbalance between resources and population in geographic Palestine and the Jordan basin in general.

129. Cited in Abd al-Salam, 1990, p. 227.
130. Government of Palestine, 1946, p. 141.
131. *Encyclopedia Palaestina,* 1984, vol. 1, p. 144.
132. Khalidi, et al., eds., 1992, p. 232.
133. Miller, 1985.

Palestinian perceptions of both agriculture and water drastically shifted after 1948 as many villagers were dispossessed of their land and gathered into desolate refugee camps. The lost village acquired a romantic aura and Palestine began to be remembered as paradise on earth, although the hardships of agricultural work were not entirely forgotten. Between 1948 and 1967, Palestinians shared with neighboring Arabs their concern about Israeli plans to divert the waters of the Jordan River, viewing the diversion as a means of strengthening Israel and, obversely, of impeding their return to their homes. It was perhaps symbolically significant that the first raid in 1964 by the guerrillas of al-Fateh, which would become the main faction of the PLO, was aimed at the Israeli National Water Carrier that diverted the Jordan River's water to the Negev. To be sure, the Palestinian refugees wanted the water, but they wanted it in their own homes in Palestine. Thus, even though one of the main goals of the 1955 Johnston Plan was the resettlement through irrigation schemes of those refugees who had fled to the Jordan Valley, the refugees opposed the resettlement attempt.[134]

Israel's stringent curbs on Palestinians' access to water after its seizure of the West Bank and Gaza in 1967 made the denial of water, like land confiscation, seem like an integral part of its endeavor to dispossess them. The Palestinians deemed the curbs as impediments confining their ability to produce their food, if not to pursue economic development. Symbolically, water has become for the Palestinians another sphere of Israeli injustice toward them. This feeling has been sharpened by what they see as profligate water use in Israel and by Israeli settlers in the West Bank and Gaza (poignantly symbolized by the swimming pools in the settlements) and by the fact that the groundwater denied to them comes largely from the West Bank. Israeli water-related policies and actions thus are seen as "usurpation" of Palestinian water rights and a violation of international law and conventions and the basic precepts of justice. An excerpt from a statement presented by the Palestinian delegation to the MWGW in Vienna sums up those sentiments:

> Not only did Israel impose severe restrictions on freedom for Palestinians in the OPTs [Occupied Palestinian Territories] to drill wells and use their own water resources, it also built

134. Elmusa, 1994a, pp. 35–8.

illegal settlements that are supplied with large water quantities from resources belonging to the OPTs ... Thus the Israelis currently use about 80 percent of the OPTs water resources ... On a per capita basis, an Israeli citizen uses 3–4 times more water than a Palestinian ... In sum, the water situation in the OPTs is approaching a critical phase which is threatening daily life and hindering further economic development ... The Hague regulations of 1907 and the IVth Geneva convention of 1949 place restrictions on the powers of a belligerent occupier like Israel, and provide safeguards for the protection of the resources of the occupied territories.[135]

Still, such morally and materially grounded perceptions differ from the earlier ideological perception of water by Labor Zionism because they do not involve transcendent beliefs of redemption and rootedness. The issue can be addressed, the statement demands, as a practical matter of water rights, taking control of management and providing compensation for past wrongs.

135. MWG-W, 13 May 1992.

5

Toward Equitable Utilization and Joint Management

With the signing of the Declaration of Principles (DOP) in 1993, the Israelis and Palestinians crossed a rubicon in their all-consuming political conflict. After three subsequent agreements imparted some flesh to the skeletal DOP, and in spite of the coming to power of the Likud-led coalition in Israel, few people on either side see a practical alternative to negotiations for resolving the conflict. A negotiated settlement, however, is likely to be protracted because it has to deal with such weighty matters as borders, settlements, security, Jerusalem, refugees, and water. The resolution of these questions is meant to define the final status of the West Bank and Gaza and, implicitly, Israel. Whether the talks will be completed by mid-1999 in accordance with the dates and schedules stipulated in the DOP remains to be seen; so far the timetables fixed in the DOP and other agreements have not been adhered to, and delay has been the rule.

With regard to water, the talks are supposed to commence with an agenda, specified by the DOP and the Taba Agreement, that includes two paramount issues: the equitable allocation of water rights in the common resources and their joint management. These two issues are the focus of this chapter. The two sides also concurred in the Taba Agreement that they "recognize the necessity to develop additional water for various uses" (Article 40.2). Although enhancing the water supply is indispensable for meeting the projected demand growth, as discussed in the previous two chapters, it is not necessarily an agenda item. There are three potential sources for boosting supply: wastewater treatment, desalination of brackish and seawater, and imports from water-surplus countries like Turkey. The economics of, and constraints against, these options have been discussed in a host of publications, and the topic will be highlighted only briefly in connection with equitable utilization.[1]

The DOP identifies equitable water utilization and joint management only as principles, without defining them. Translating the principles into quantities, management tasks, and institutional mechanisms presumably will be the subject of bargaining. The purpose here is not so much to predict the outcome of such bargaining as to explore what constitutes an equitable and cooperative resolution. To this extent the present exploration does not depend on who is in power in Israel or in the PA. Nonetheless, one can delineate the salient water-related factors that could provide (dis)incentives for both parties to reach an agreement.

The nature of an equitable and cooperative settlement is examined within the framework of international water law. Despite the widely recognized weaknesses of international water law, as a framework for discussion it can serve as a vehicle for analyzing the various official and nonofficial demands and positions expressed by both parties. In particular, the doctrine of "equitable utilization" and the "factors" it enumerates as equity criteria are singled out as a basis for the allocation of water rights because they generally are accepted, even if just in theory, by the international community. Furthermore, the principles of mutuality, equality, and respect for sovereignty, which international law stresses must be observed in joint management arrangements, are discussed with reference to special tasks, verification, water protection, dispute resolution, and water trade and conveyance. The scope of such tasks and the willingness of the two sides to undertake them may be constrained by political and economic issues that must be acknowledged and dealt with. The principles of international water law seldom have been analyzed for particular situations, and the discussion below may help clarify some of the general concepts or principles embodied in the law.

1. In the Israeli-Palestinian context, summaries of the economics of wastewater treatment and desalination are available in BUNT, 1994; and Sbeih, 1996.

The narrative often will deal with the Jordan River basin separately from the other, predominantly groundwater, resources within geographic Palestine proper. The reason for the separation is that the river basin is common to three other riparians besides the Israelis and Palestinians and, insofar as the water conflict and its resolution are concerned, has had historical and legal idiosyncracies different from those of the other resources.

CONTEXT OF FINAL STATUS NEGOTIATIONS

The literature on international water conflict identifies an assortment of factors as influencing the potential for conflict and cooperation in common international water resources. The list covers the disputants' relative power resources (military, economic, and political); hydrostrategic or stream position (up, mid-, or downstream); extent of dependence on the resources in conflict; and overall relations. It also includes an external factor, namely, mediation by a third party. For example, some of these factors were employed by Frederick Frey for constructing a simple, expository model to rank the potential of conflict or cooperation in the Nile, Euphrates-Tigris, and Jordan basins.[2] They were also used by Miriam Lowi as a framework for analyzing the historical evolution of the Jordan basin conflict.[3] However, even after the identification of these factors, and for various reasons, the ability to predict conflict/cooperation remains elusive. More elusive still would be forecasting the terms of cooperation, should this be the outcome.

Although forecasting the outcome of the Israeli-Palestinian negotiations is not an objective of the present text, I will offer an outline of factors, particularly those that are water related, which could shape the terms of a water accord. Nonwater related issues, such as the overall balance of power, that might affect the whole gamut of issues are too complex to be taken up here. I begin with a recapitulation of where the two sides stand as a result of the Oslo process.

Multilateral and Bilateral Negotiations

Since the inauguration of the peace talks in 1991, the water issue has been debated bilaterally between Israel and the Palestinians

2. Frey, 1992.
3. Lowi, 1993.

and in the international MWGW.[4] Without delving into the history of these negotiations, the MWGW veered away from discussion of water rights, largely at the behest of Israel and the United States, and took up topics like databanks, enhancement of water supply, and water supply and demand projections.[5] In early 1996, Syria proposed that the matter of water rights in the Jordan basin be discussed in the MWGW. If Syria's call is heeded, it can have repercussions for the Israeli-Palestinian negotiations, as will be pointed out shortly.

For Palestinians, the MWGW afforded small sums of money (or at least pledges) for various projects and recognition in international fora.[6] For Israel, the MWGW and other multilateral fora (like the economic summits) served first and foremost as a portal for "introducing" it into Arab capitals and for establishing footholds for future normalization. One clear example is the creation of the desalination research center in Oman in 1995, with Israeli membership. Israel is keen on using desalination and selling desalination technology to the Gulf and Saudi markets, the largest such markets in the world. For both sides, the members of the MWGW have undertaken a number of studies on technical and management aspects of water, especially demand forecasting, which could serve as a common ground for negotiations.[7]

In the bilateral track, Israel under Yitzhak Shamir's Likud government held an extremist position that deemed the Palestinians mere residents of the West Bank and Gaza and rejected any discussion of water (or land) rights, but it did agree to discuss the use of these resources.[8] The Likud's position gradually was modified by the Labor government, and the scope of the talks was broadened in principle beyond water use to include water rights and joint management.

4. The MWGW is one of five groups in which forty countries participate, including European Union member states, Russia, and the United States, in addition to Middle Eastern countries.

5. Summary statements of various MWGW sessions. These statements are made by the gavel-holder and are not considered binding.

6. For example, in the Muscat, Oman, session, $10.5 million were pledged to the Palestinians for work on a data bank, irrigation projects, and a dam on Wadi Gaza to help recharge the aquifer. Israel received $7 million worth of pledges. FBIS, 28 June 1994.

7. For example, Germany is conducting a two-phase study of water supply and demand in the Middle East, the first report of which was presented to the MWGW in 1996; see CES Consulting Engineers, 1996.

8. Mansour, 1993.

The result of the negotiations has been the three water agreements included in the DOP and the Cairo and Taba accords. The following is a summary of their most salient aspects. The DOP (Article III.1) stipulated two general principles for the resolution of the conflict: equitable allocation of water rights in the common resources and the joint management of these resources. The Cairo Agreement (Annex II.31) applied only to Gaza and Jericho and essentially maintained the status quo ante, except for the transfer of water management to the PA in the territory under its control. The Taba Agreement is more elaborate than the DOP or the Cairo accord. It gave the Palestinians "Additional Water," as detailed in chapter 2, and preserved the settlements' water supply at the pre-existing levels. It also made joint Israeli-Palestinian management arrangements for the Palestinian sector only, the primary purpose of which is to check any Palestinian attempt at extracting quantities beyond those in the accord.

Overall, the agreements apply chiefly to the interim stage and only broadly to the final status phase. For this last phase, they define in broad strokes a time frame, two major agenda items, and an institutional framework for the talks. These first were spelled out in the DOP (Annex III, Article 1), which stated that a "Water Development Program" would be

> prepared by experts from both sides, which will also specify the mode of cooperation in the management of water resources in the West Bank and Gaza, and will include proposals for studies and plans on water rights of each party, as well as on the equitable utilization of joint water resources for implementation in and beyond the interim period.

Thus, the DOP unequivocally slated two items—the equitable allocation of water rights in, and joint management of, common water resources—for future negotiations. The loosely defined time horizon for implementation—"beyond the interim period"—in the DOP was fixed in the Taba Agreement to be coterminous with the final status talks: "These [water rights in the West Bank] will be negotiated in the permanent status negotiations and settled in the Permanent Status Agreement relating to the various water resources" (Annex III, Article 40. 1).

After initial objections, the Israelis agreed to include in the Taba Agreement this statement: "Israel recognizes the Palestinian water in the West Bank" (Annex III, Article II, 1). The statement helped the interim-period negotiations to move on, but legally, as Iain Scobbie argues, it may not add much because water rights in the West Bank and Gaza are vested in the Palestinians under the doctrine of permanent sovereignty.[9] Still, one cannot overemphasize that Israel's recognition of those rights was significant, considering that the Likud government under Shamir did not acknowledge that Palestinians had any water rights. Thus, with the DOP and the Taba Agreement specifying general principles, the two sides have before them the task of agreeing on which resources are common and on water-rights allocation and joint management regimes.

Water and Other Issues

By identifying water as a final status issue, the two sides apparently have elevated it to the rank of "high" as opposed to "low" politics. Still, figuring out the importance each party will assign to it relative to other issues is difficult. If the water question is to be negotiated as part of a "package deal" involving other major final status issues, the weight assigned to it could be influenced by how each side assesses its gains and losses regarding the other issues. For example, would the Israelis compromise over water if the Palestinians were forthcoming on security arrangements? If the Palestinians secured a decent deal on the settlements or Jerusalem yet water seemed like a stumbling block to an accord, would they then downplay its prominence? Although such questions may not be spelled out explicitly, they could be factored into the bargaining process implicitly.

For Israel, water is an area where it can afford to be flexible because it can deploy considerable economic and technological power to tap treated wastewater and to desalinate seawater. Also, because water has lost its ideological dimensions, it is easier for its politicians, if they so choose, to compromise. In all likelihood, Israel can be expected to attach whatever concessions it might make on water rights to securing deals for joint, water related projects for augmenting water supply and for creating (inter)dependencies to cement the peace, as well as to guarantee financial gains (from third parties) to implement such projects.

9. Scobbie, 1996, p. 105.

As for the Palestinians, an accord on water simultaneous with ones on the other final status issues could be politically easier for the leadership than a separate one, owing to the ambiguities and stakes inherent in an overall peace accord. Also, tucking water provisions somewhere in the thicket of an agreement (in the extraordinarily long text of the Taba accord, water appeared in Annex III, Article 40) and fragmenting water quantities from various sources (as was done in the Israel-Jordan agreement) would discourage close public scrutiny of the outcome. Whether these considerations would weigh heavily in decisions germane to water cannot be foretold, for the Palestinian leadership will be under pressure to consider how the lack of water might affect the new entity's quality of life and carrying capacity. In addition, the leaders are aware of the extent to which water has been an everyday, high-profile issue for many Palestinians since 1967.

Hydrologic Constraints

The contested Israeli-Palestinian water resources possess several attributes with significant ramifications for the water conflict and its resolution. For one thing, the heavy dependence of the parties on, and interconnectedness of, these resources have contributed to the conflict's intensity and to Israel's iron-clad measures to control them. Yet, those very same factors also can be a goad for the two sides to resolve the dispute if they are "to move on." Another vital feature of the common resources is that Israel contributes very little to the mountain aquifer, the centerpiece of the groundwater resources, and the Jordan River basin. That is why Israel could appropriate the bulk of these resources only through the use or threat of force and through occupation of the headwaters. However, it also is why Israel would have a significant incentive to compromise, if it decided to withdraw from the Arab territories that contain the headwaters.

Opposed to these facilitating hydrostrategic factors are complicating ones. Bargaining over water rights in common aquifers may be particularly hard. Aquifers are superior to rivers or lakes as natural storage "facilities": They lose much less water, especially to evaporation, and are not as easily pollutable. Functionally, on the other hand, they are less versatile, offering a smaller "basket" of goods that can be traded among the conflicting parties. In a river system, for example, the riparians may exchange water for other goods, such as dams or other flow-regulating structures, hydro-power, or in-stream use (recreation, fishing, culture, religion). Such tradeoffs do not obtain in groundwater, and bargaining essentially would be confined only to the water itself.

This type of bargaining difficulty, however, is different from a suggestion by an Israeli specialist that the complexity of the aquifer system—as manifested in the inability to control the flow of the aquifer, the differential pumping costs, and the lack of a complete understanding of the system—renders "a one-time division of [the aquifer's] water most likely infeasible."[10] It is true that the mountain aquifer, for example, is complex and incompletely understood, but the conclusion about the infeasibility of a one-time division needs to be looked at within a wider perspective. For one thing, the Palestinians have been allotted fixed quotas by Israel since 1967, while Israel has been free, within the hydrological constraints, to pump as much as it wanted. Nor is it clear why the differential costs of pumping should be an obstacle to a one-time division; although they may be a critical variable that may offer an incentive for water transfer and exchange between the two sides, these costs should have no bearing on the assignment of initial property rights. As for uncertainty and inability to control the flow of groundwater, Israel has a cumulative, time-series record concerning the flows of, and pumping from, the aquifers, and this can be used to map out approximate safe pumping regimes from various zones. The uncertainty can be reduced also by fixing the shares as percentages, rather than quantities, of the total amount that the two parties would agree to pump each year. Also, the two parties could agree at the outset that if the pumping schedules appear to pose a threat to certain parts of the aquifer system, they would be revised in a balanced manner. Lastly, the allocation of shares every year or two may lead to perpetual disputes and to the neglect of the main tasks of joint management, such as the protection of the aquifer against pollution.

Whereas groundwater may be hard to bargain over owing to its physical attributes, the Jordan River has its own complicating properties, notably its being common to five parties. An agreement in the Jordan basin is tied particularly to future relations between Israel and Syria. Eventually, the river would have to be managed

10. Feitelson, 1994, pp. 216–17.

as an integral unit, which entails a pact among the five riparians. The Israelis might prefer a series of bilateral pacts because these would place them at the hub of the management of the river system and because they might be concerned about being in the minority in a multilateral institution including four Arab riparians. On the other hand, regional cooperation in the river area may not be counter to Israel's self-interest and was a key theme in the diplomacy of the Labor government. Moreover, past Zionist and Israeli plans envisioned a unified basin. However, it is uncertain whether or when a multilateral accord will come about, in part because the time frame of the Israel-Syria talks and their handling of the water question are unpredictable.

Israel-Syria Talks

Three "scenarios" for the Israel-Syria talks and their ramifications for the Israeli-Palestinian track can be considered. In the first scenario, the Israel-Syria negotiations would be protracted and no accord would be forged until after the final status talks between Israel and the Palestinians. In this case, the Palestinians can be expected to demand the release by Israel of their share of the water that Israel now diverts for its own use. A trilateral management arrangement including Israel, Jordan, and the Palestinian polity may have to be devised in the interim.

In the second scenario, Israel and Syria would ratify a water agreement before Israel and the Palestinians do. If the allocations in such an agreement were different from those of the Johnston Plan, Palestinian demands in the aquifer system would be affected by how much water is left for them after Israel, Jordan, Lebanon, and Syria take their shares. Moreover, the Jordan-Israel water agreement, even in the absence of an Israel-Syria accord, has made it harder for the Palestinians to squeeze out their share in the basin from Israel. That is because, according to the agreement, Jordan and Israel would impound essentially all the untapped water from the segments of the lower Jordan and Yarmuk rivers covered by the agreement, leaving the Palestinians to demand that Israel release water it already exploits. Overall, this second scenario is perhaps the most disadvantageous to the Palestinians owing to their downstream location in the basin and a lack of means to effect a different outcome.

In the third scenario, the question of the Jordan basin's waters would be tackled in the international MWGW, as Syria proposed in early 1996.[11] If the multilateral parley adopts the proposal, the Israelis and Palestinians might elect to include all the common groundwater resources in these talks as well. Even if they do not choose this route, the course of their bilateral talks certainly would be influenced by developments in the multilateral parley. Whatever the scenario, the size of Syria's demands in the basin is critical and will be discussed subsequently. For the Palestinians in particular, their fortunes in the Jordan basin clearly depend not just on Israel's stance, but on Syria's as well, assuming Syria regains the Golan Heights.

Negotiation Methods

The method of negotiations refers to direct bilateral talks, mediation, or arbitration. Negotiations over reallocation of water shares and management have been conducted in a direct, bilateral manner. This is the same route that presumably would be taken, at least initially, in the final status forum. Whether mediation becomes necessary would depend on the progress of these talks. Mediation could be undertaken by the United States, from within the trilateral (Israeli-Palestinian-American) committee, or by a multilateral lending agency, notably the World Bank.

Both the United States and the World Bank are in a favorable position for mediation. In addition to its key role in the overall peace negotiations, the United States sits with the Israelis and Palestinians on a trilateral committee that was formed in August 1995. One of its tasks, in addition to addressing economic issues and political coordination, is water production.[12] The Taba Agreement also stipulated that the bilateral Israeli-Palestinian water committee would cooperate with the trilateral committee "on water production and development" (Article 40. 20.c). Enhancement of water supply has been central to Israeli thinking. The Palestinians have not stressed it, not because they do not need the extra water, but because Israelis view it as a substitute for the reallocation of water rights. One may expect that the American role will be largely to

11. Ibrahim Hamidi, citing the Syrian information minister, *Al Hayat*, 1 February 1996.
12. See *Journal of Palestine Studies*, 1995, p. 147.

locate technical and financial assistance for water augmentation, conservation, and quality improvement.

It is possible that the trilateral committee will be a forum for debating other topics, especially water rights or joint management, particularly if the bilateral talks get bogged down. Likewise, the World Bank is well-situated for a mediation role. It has coordinated international assistance to the PA, funded projects on its own in the West Bank and Gaza, and participates in the MWGW. The Europeans and the Japanese also could play a facilitating role. However, Israel so far has discouraged powers other than the United States from influencing the outcome of the talks.

In addition to ideas or middle-ground positions, the mediator is likely to present inducements for the parties to compromise through financial and technical assistance as, for example, the World Bank did in its well-known facilitative role in the 1950s deal between India and Pakistan over the Indus River basin. However, because the Palestinians need financial assistance for reconstruction in virtually all economic and social spheres, external funding may be less assured for water-related projects than in the case of the Indus basin. Moreover and for various reasons, not all aid pledges by international donors to the PA have been delivered. In the end, whatever mediation may offer, it cannot be expected to create a context that would change the relative abilities of the two sides to realize their demands.

Arbitration (for example, through the International Court of Justice) can be resorted to only if the two sides agree to abide by the resulting verdict. Its advantage over the other two methods is that its decisions are less susceptible to the pressure of power. This is unlikely to be acceptable to Israel, but Palestinian officials invoked it as an option in past parleys, when talks over water seemed deadlocked. Its outcome would be uncertain for Israel, and it is not risk-free for the Palestinians. The magnitude of risk for the Palestinians would hinge on what they are offered in the bilateral talks. Still, it could become the only course if bilateralism or mediation fails. It has a precedent in the case of Taba, when both Egypt and Israel accepted arbitration to settle their claims to this Red Sea resort area.

To summarize, each side will enter the negotiations with a core demand on the agenda. The symmetry of their stream positions provides incentives for an agreement. Incentives also could come from third parties acting as mediators and providing financial and technical assistance. However, there are complicating factors stemming from the heavy dependence of both sides on the same resources, the lack of functional versatility of groundwater, and the regional character of the Jordan River basin. In the end, if neither bilateralism nor mediation works, the two antagonists have the option of arbitration.

EQUITABLE WATER RIGHTS

"Water rights" may be defined as mutually recognized access by both sides to water quantities (fixed and/or percentages) under specific conditions pertaining to such things as points of extraction, seasons, and priorities.[13] They also involve mutual obligations as well as responsibilities for the resources themselves. Accordingly, the present allocations are de facto and must be signed and agreed to by the two parties to become de jure. Furthermore, Israel's acceptance in the DOP that such rights would be allocated equitably may imply also its recognition that the existing allocations are unequal (a situation amply demonstrated in the preceding chapters).

Neither the DOP nor subsequent accords spelled out criteria by which equitable utilization can be assessed. There is more than one guide for devising an agreed-upon sharing regime between Israelis and Palestinians. One such guide is international law, which will serve as the framework for this chapter; another relies on analytical methods based on optimization and cost-benefit analysis, such as Paretian environmental analysis, super fairness, and cooperative game theory. Neither international water law nor the other procedures, however, can produce a magic formula or number that would be acceptable to all the parties. At any rate, the outcome of the negotiations is more likely to be shaped by the foregoing factors rather than by rational persuasion or considerations of fairness. The adage "negotiations are non-principled solutions," coined by a former member of the United Nations' International Law Commission (ILC), may reek of cynicism, but it also contains much truth.[14] International law itself leaves much room for this to be the

13. This is a restatement of a definition of water rights in Saliba and Bush, 1987, p. 1.
14. Khassawneh, 1995, p. 26.

case, as will be discussed shortly.[15] Adjudication before the International Court of Justice can be taken up only when the parties to a conflict voluntarily agree to appear before it and abide by its rulings. Nonetheless, grounding the claims of a riparian in international law lends those claims legitimacy while at the same time it circumscribes them—two essential ingredients for the creation of a stable water-sharing regime. On the conceptual plane, it provides a context for clarifying many of the arguments on both sides as to how water should be allocated, such as the Israeli insistence on maintaining prior or existing use and telling Palestinians to import water instead of demanding reallocation or Palestinian advocacy of nature-based reallocation.

Several doctrines of international water law have been invoked over the years in water disputes among countries. These include prior use, absolute hydrologic sovereignty, absolute hydrologic integrity, avoidance of appreciable harm, and limited hydrologic sovereignty.[16] *Prior use* means that in any new division of water rights, the historic or established uses are paramount. *Absolute hydrologic sovereignty* accords the riparians absolute freedom to use international sources within their territories as they please. *Absolute hydrologic integrity* is the diametrical opposite of absolute sovereignty; it grants priority of access to the downstreamer. *Avoidance of appreciable harm* advocates that before a riparian undertakes a water project, it has to ascertain that the negative externalities, or economic and environmental costs to other riparians, are not significant. *Limited hydrologic sovereignty* is a midway doctrine between absolute sovereignty and integrity. Of the five doctrines, only "limited hydrologic sovereignty" has gained wide acceptance. It has been translated imperfectly into operational form through the principle of "equitable utilization" by incorporating the other doctrines as "factors" to be weighed in the calculation of equitable utilization and adding other factors to them as well.

All these doctrines will be discussed in the context of equitable utilization, with the exception of the absolute integrity doctrine, which has not been brought up, nor is it likely to be invoked by

15. The literature on international water law is extensive. See, for example, Barberis, 1991; Caponera, 1994; Dellapenna, 1995; Lipper, 1967; and Khassawneh, 1995.

16. The literature generally uses the term *territorial* instead of *hydrologic*. Territorial is not imprecise, but it is indirect; hydrologic is more immediately indicative of the intent of the doctrine.

either side. However, because there is a pre-existing, albeit non-ratified, treaty in the Jordan basin in the form of the Johnston Plan, I first examine its legal standing and why it still should serve as a benchmark.

Legal Standing of the Johnston Plan

In the multiriparian Jordan basin, the Palestinians and Lebanese base their water claims on the quotas of the Johnston Plan. Jordan has been consistently favorable to the plan. Israel's water supply forecasts are predicated on its current share, which exceeds its quota under the plan. Syria has not taken a public stance regarding the plan during the peace negotiations. Assuming it regains the Golan Heights, it probably would rest its demands, as upstream riparians usually do, on its sizable contribution to the system. Cognizant of its location downstream of its major water source, the Euphrates River, Syria may not carry the geography-based claim too far.[17]

The allocations of the Johnston Plan were accepted by the Arab states, which conducted the negotiations under the umbrella of the Arab League, and Israel. The plan, however, never was ratified. The reason for the nonratification was that the Arab countries, although they approved of the allocations, viewed the provisions of joint management and cooperation as being a political vehicle to draw them into recognizing Israel. In fact, eventual recognition of Israel through the plan was a goal the United States sought to accomplish, but for the Arab countries recognition was contingent upon a resolution of the Palestinian problem.[18]

Nevertheless, before 1967, Israel and Jordan adhered in their water withdrawals to the plan's quotas, and the United States conditioned its aid to the two countries for water-related projects in the basin on such adherence.[19] In fact, as late as 1964, when Israel was on the verge of inaugurating its major diversion project from Lake Tiberias, it regarded the plan as an achievement (and it was,

17. Syria shares the Euphrates with Turkey, the upstreamer, and Iraq, which is downstream from Syria.
18. See, for example, Lowi, 1993.
19. See Department of State, vol. 1, chapter 4.H.2, case no. NLJ 83-223; Eisenhower Papers, 28 March 1958, case no. 80-331; and Lowi, 1993.

considering that it gave Israel close to one-third of the water).[20] The plan thus can be thought of as having "in effect functioned as a customary legal regime for the surface waters of the [Jordan] Valley," at least for Israel and Jordan.[21]

Even after 1967, when Israel increased its water extraction from the basin, it justified its action partly by pointing to its control of the West Bank (consult the relevant sections in chapters 1 and 4 for the Johnston Plan's allocations from the Jordan basin). During the negotiations with Jordan on the Maqarin Dam, Israel demanded a share of the water of the dam on the same grounds.[22] Interestingly enough, after Jordan accused Israel of not delivering on its promises in their water agreement and discussed with Syria the revival of the Maqarin Dam, Raphael Eitan, Israel's minister of agriculture, reportedly invoked the Johnston Plan as being the basis for the distribution of the Yarmuk River water.[23] He probably was implying that Israel's share included that of the West Bank. Even though they lack legitimacy, such Israeli demands strengthen the case that the Johnston Plan has become customary law in the basin. Israel's demands equate occupation with sovereignty, as the late Palestinian geographer Bashir Nijim remarked, and they ignore the fact that the West Bank's share was slated for its Palestinian population, not for the population of the ruling power.[24]

Another important legal consideration is Israel's transfer of water outside the Jordan basin. In the course of Johnston's mission, Israel demanded to be allowed to transfer water out of the Jordan basin to the coastal plain and the Negev Desert. The Arab riparians, at least initially, opposed this transfer on the grounds that customary law did not allow such transfers until after the needs within the basin itself had been met. It has been suggested by several scholars that the Arab side probably approved Israel's demand implicitly, the approval being conditional on Israel's adherence to

20. In a press conference on 11 January 1965, for example, Israeli Prime Minister Levi Eshkol noted that "there are commitments in the world toward us in the wake of the Johnston Plan." On 17 May, he reportedly remarked that the plan was "regarded as agreed from an international point of view." Cited in Department of State, Case no. NLJ 83-223.

21. The quote is from Dellapenna, 1990, p. 27. See also ibid., p. 43; Dellapenna, 1995; and Naff and Matson, p. 169.

22. Based on discussions with an authoritative Jordanian source, 3 March 1996. See also Schmida, 1984, p. 11.

23. *Jerusalem Post* (international edition), 28 August 1996.

24. Nijim, 1990.

the quotas.[25] This seems to have been the position of the United States as well.[26] Later, Arab objections to the Israeli National Water Carrier also were based on fears—borne out by subsequent events—that Israel would exceed its quotas when the opportunity arose.

During Johnston's mission, Israel argued that the water it was going to transfer would not have been used efficiently by the Arab riparians, and therefore it was surplus water.[27] This argument confounded efficiency with equity, and it failed to identify the type of efficiency meant (i.e., whether technical or economic). Even if such an argument was acceptable in the 1950s, it is no longer acceptable in the 1990s, as was indicated earlier in the discussion of Israeli and Palestinian agriculture. If this is so, then the Palestinians are on solid grounds legally, historically, and economically for insisting that their water needs within the basin must be met before Israel's out-of-basin transfers can be authorized.

A number of analysts, such as the Israelis Elisha Kally and Arnon Soffer, contend that the plan has become dated owing to the changes that have occurred in the basin. The changes, according to them, include locations of scarcity and surpluses, the technical facilities, the political context, technology, winter and summer needs, and population growth. Neither author, however, analyzes the implications of the individual changes for the plan, except to conclude categorically that a new water-sharing regime would have to acknowledge existing uses.[28] This arbitrary conclusion does not follow logically or practically from the changes enumerated by the authors. It is self-serving because existing uses favor Israel. Further, Israel accepted in its water agreement with Jordan to reduce its post-1967 use from the Yarmuk River effectively to its allocation under the plan.[29]

It is true that conditions among the basin's riparians have changed since the time of the plan, but the shifts in the main factors that drive water demand, notably population growth and urbanization were more or less even. For example, Jordan received an influx of refugees from the West Bank as a result of the June 1967

25. American Friends of the Middle East, 1964, p. 46; Lowi, 1993, p. 98; and Saliba, 1968, p. 103.
26. Saliba, 1968, p. 106.
27. Ibid., p. 100.
28. Kally, 1993, p. 33; and Soffer, 1994, pp. 115–16.
29. Elmusa, 1995b, pp. 70.

war and from the Persian Gulf countries as a result of the 1991 Gulf war, while Israel received Soviet immigrants beginning in the late 1980s. Likewise, the Palestinian population has risen considerably by the inclusion of Gaza in addition to growth in the West Bank. Further, the natural population increase in both Jordan and the West Bank has been even greater than in Israel and also has been quite high in Syria. Only Lebanon's population did not multiply as much as the other riparians' due to the civil war-induced high emigration rates. In sum, Israel's population comprised close to 17 percent of the basin's total in 1950 and just under 19 percent in 1992.[30]

Any attempt to overhaul the plan's quotas in all likelihood would come at the expense of the Palestinians and probably the Jordanians, the two vulnerable downstreamers. Lebanon's share is small and cannot be reduced further without making it irrelevant. Furthermore, given the fragmentation of the Arab position (in contrast to their coordinated stance during the Johnston mission) and the heightened concern in the region over future water shortages, assigning new quotas for the five riparians would be a protracted process, resulting in large opportunity costs for the Palestinians and Lebanese, who do not have access to the basin.

All of this is not to suggest that the Johnston Plan is perfect or that it cannot be improved. To illustrate the kinds of improvement, the aggregate allocations could be broken down on a seasonal basis, as was done in the Israel-Jordan water agreement.[31] Another improvement would be to state the quotas as percentages, in addition to fixed quantities, to account for the variations of rainfall and the concomitant water availability in the basin. A third improvement would be to give Syria a choice between the water it impounded behind dams built on the Yarmuk's tributaries and the water that the plan assigned to it from the Banyas and the Jordan rivers. If Syria were to choose the latter, the dams still can be used to regulate the flow downstream, and the Palestinians would get part of their share from the Yarmuk. Moreover, regional cooperation, if it occurs, may permit the undertaking of projects that are

30. My estimate based on figures from the United Nations Environmental Programme, 1993, pp. 218–19. The following assumptions were made regarding the Palestinian population: Gaza was not included in the 1950 estimate; and the combined West Bank and Gaza population in 1992 was 2.4 million (see further chapter 3).

31. Elmusa, 1995b, p. 66.

more efficient than, and ecologically superior to, those proposed by the plan. Finally, any plans to harness and redivide the waters of the Jordan River basin must factor in the instream value of the river's water that derives from the waterway's unique historical, religious, and geological features. None of the preceding modifications needs to breach the plan's basic allocation regime.

The Factors of Equitable Utilization

Equitable utilization is an imperfect translation of the doctrine of limited sovereignty into a practical guideline for allocating water rights in common international resources. For utilization to be equitable, several "factors"—hydrogeological, historical, and socioeconomic—have to be weighed against each other. The first list of factors was composed in 1966 by the International Law Association (ILA), a nongovernmental body devoted to international law, and has become known as the Helsinki Rules of Equitable Utilization.[32] Since then, other legal bodies and international law authorities have issued their own lists of factors, which were often variations on the Helsinki Rules. In particular, the United Nations ILC incorporated equitable utilization rules in the draft "Rules on Non-Navigational Use of International Watercourses," which it submitted in 1991 to the 43rd Session of the General Assembly for revision and approval.[33] The doctrine of equitable utilization "enjoys wide acceptance today and is part of general international law."[34] It is worth underlining as well that the Palestinian-Israeli DOP used the term "equitable utilization" as the criterion for the allocation of water rights—the same term used in the Helsinki and the ILC Draft rules.

The factors may be aggregated as (1) the natural attributes of the water source (effectively equivalent to absolute sovereignty); (2) prior or existing use; (3) social and economic needs; (4) availability of alternative resources and their comparative costs; and (5) avoidance of appreciable harm. These are common to the Helsinki Rules, the ILC's series of reports, and the 1989 Bellagio Draft Treaty, which is a model treaty for groundwater drafted by an

32. See, for example, ILC, 1994, p. 342; Flint, 1995; Goldberg, 1992; and Hayton and Utton, 1989.
33. Flint, 1995, pp. 197–204.
34. Barberis, 1991, p. 175.

interdisciplinary team of international experts.[35] All of these factors are to be weighed, and none is paramount. According to two prominent members of the panel that drafted the treaty, Robert Hayton and Albert Utton: "This language [weighing all the different factors] has become accepted virtually universally."[36]

Before discussing the implications of each factor for the reallocation of the Israeli-Palestinian common waters, several remarks regarding them as a group are in order. The five factors are not exhaustive. Legal authorities have listed other factors, including the stage of economic development,[37] financial compensation, population,[38] and environmental sensitivity.[39] Some of these factors are incorporated into the discussion of the five factors, while others may not be essential to the case at hand. The asymmetry in the development of the Israeli and Palestinian economies will figure directly and indirectly in the examination of all five factors, with the exception of natural attributes. A one-time financial compensation is unlikely to be acceptable to either side as a price for foregoing water shares because the scarcity value of water will go up in the future; it may be accepted, however, on a limited basis and in specific localities. The population factor need not be listed separately as was done in the Helsinki Rules because it automatically is incorporated in the social and economic needs—themselves a function of population size. Environmental sensitivity should not affect the proportion of water allocated to each of the parties but would necessitate, for example, limiting the total amount set for allocation to the safe yield of an aquifer.[40] It also may require in some instances limiting the pumping of one party from a given location because of the critical nature of the source to the water system as a whole.

The factors may be faulted for being too numerous and stated in too general a fashion to be useful for negotiations. They also are

35. Garretson et al., 1967, pp. 782–91; Goldberg, 1992, p. 72; and Hayton and Utton, 1989, pp. 695–97.

36. Hayton and Utton, 1989, p. 669.

37. Third Report to the ILC, 1982, cited in ibid., p. 700.

38. Financial compensation and population are mentioned in the Helsinki Rules.

39. Mentioned in the Bellagio Draft Treaty and the ILC 1988 Report.

40. *Environmental sensitivity* is defined in the Bellagio Draft Treaty as "vulnerability or susceptibility to changes detrimentally affecting the quality of life of one or more biological or physical systems." Text in Hayton and Utton, 1989, p. 678.

not assigned weights, which renders them even more elastic than if they were stated hierarchically. As such, the factors open the door for the parties to the conflict to accent those that are advantageous to them, and the resulting apportionment may end up reflecting the relative power position of the parties rather than equity. The elasticity of the factors, together with the nonbinding character of international water law and the lack of serious enforcement mechanisms, severely limits the utility of the doctrine of equitable utilization.

Nonetheless, the multiplicity of factors ensures that they rarely are stacked against one side, and, if—by no means a small if in the Israeli-Palestinian case—approached in good faith, they would balance the interests of the various parties. To illustrate, if the natural attributes of the joint sources favor one party, prior use may serve the other. This may not be an uncommon situation because the downstream of rivers, with their alluvial soil deposits and flat terrain, were historically more suitable for irrigated agriculture than the upper reaches. The Nile, the Euphrates, and the Tigris basins are major examples. In the case of the Nile, for instance, prior use favors Egypt, which taps about two-thirds of the river's discharge, whereas the natural attributes favor Ethiopia, the principal source of the river's water. In addition, the factors take into account the water requirements and economic and technological capabilities of the disputants by specifying the social and economic needs as well as the costs of alternative resources as criteria for apportionment.

The factors, moreover, are not merely theoretical; they are based on treaties and conventions ratified by governments, custom, generally accepted principles, decisions in the judiciary, and the opinions of qualified authorities.[41] In fact, the doctrine of equitable utilization and some of the factors are found implicitly or explicitly in the few international water agreements reached in the Middle East itself. The social and economic needs factor, for example, was very much evident in the allocations in the Johnston Plan, which were based on the irrigation needs of the Jordan Valley region (broadly defined). Geography also figured in the plan regarding the source distribution of the allocations of each of the parties, as exemplified by the small quantity rendered to Israel from the Yarmuk River, which appears in its territory in its final few kilometers

41. Goldberg, 1992; and Lipper, 1967.

before joining the Jordan River. The allocation according to needs, geography, and other criteria that can be found in those treaties underscore the relevance of the factors for future negotiations over the disputed water resources.

One must assume that both Palestinians and Israelis would abide by international water law if their post-1993 accommodation is to move forward. They have agreed in the DOP that the final settlement of the political conflict will be based on the implementation of United Nations' Security Council Resolutions 242 and 338, irrespective of differences in interpretation.[42] More to the point, they accepted the principle of equitable utilization itself. Still, even if the two sides agree to consider the factors as a frame of reference, they are likely to disagree on their interpretation.

There is little by way of guidance in the literature on international water law as to how to "operationalize" the preceding factors. Hence, one task of the following discussion is to provide interpretations as to the meaning or implications of each of the factors. The interpretations also ought to be of more general applicability than just for the case at hand.[43]

Prior Use

Israel has been inclined officially to view prior use as paramount in any future negotiations on water rights and enhancement of water supplies as a way to offset Palestinian water shortfalls. To illustrate, a position paper submitted in August 1992 by the Israeli delegation to the MWGW under the title "Proposed Activities in

42. Resolution 242 was passed in the aftermath of the June 1967 war; Resolution 338, passed after the October 1973 war, urged the parties to implement Resolution 242, which essentially calls for swapping land for peace: Israel would give back the land it captured in 1967 in exchange for peace. The Arabs interpret the resolution as referring to all the land, while Israel interprets it as referring to only parts of it. The texts of the two resolutions are available in Institute for Palestine Studies, 1975.

43. The discussion of prior use, natural attributes, avoidance of appreciable harm, and the relative costs of alternative resources extends my articles on the same topic; see Elmusa, 1994b and 1995a. Moore, 1994, independently applied the factors to the division of the common Palestinian-Israeli aquifers. He included prior use, natural attributes, and population. He also offered an intuitive mathematical formula to calculate an equitable solution. For the formula to be more persuasive, however, it needs to be provided with a rationale as to why *it* was selected over another formula, or at least indicate what weight it implicitly gives to the various factors.

Desalination" stated that enhancement of water supply was "preferable" to "optimizing the distribution and usage of already existing water."[44] This is not a selectively chosen statement; the whole tenor of Israeli official discourse on regional water problems is single-mindedly focused on enhancement of water supplies, brushing aside the question of reallocation. In this vein, Meir Ben Meir, the Israeli water commissioner, was cited as having said that he dreamed of setting up desalination plants to supply an annual 800 million m³ of drinking water. Of this amount, he would earmark 200 million m₃ for Israel and 600 for the Jordanians, Palestinians, and "perhaps even the Syrians." He then added: "We have to talk about the right to water of the peoples of the region, and not about water rights, as regrettably set down in the peace agreements."[45]

Israel's advocacy of prior use seems to ignore that the doctrine has "given origin neither to rules of international customary water law, nor to general principles of law recognized by civilized nations."[46] The most that can be said for prior use is what the doctrine of equitable utilization imputes to it, namely, that it is one factor to be weighed against others.

Israel's position is tantamount to invoking an absolutism of history rather than the absolutism of geography or the absolute sovereignty doctrine, even when its history of use is of such short duration compared, say, to Egypt's use of the Nile. Nor does it take into account that much of the short history of this prior use has been imposed by force or the threat of force and in the face of repeated protests by the Palestinians and the other Arab riparians of the Jordan basin. Moreover, the Israeli position overlooks the point that if the Israelis were entitled to prior use in the mountain aquifer, the Palestinian refugees, by the same logic, would be entitled to have access to the coastal, the Galilee, and other aquifers in geographic Palestine. The refugees have been prevented from access to these sources because of their expulsion in 1948 for which Israel bears at the very least partial responsibility, as is now widely acknowledged.

Other arguments could be marshaled against Israel's prior use claim. It may be said that it was lucky for Israel that prevailing

44. Israel, MWGW, August 1992 (photocopy).
45. Globes [Internet] 5 February 1997 in World News Connection, 7 February 1997.
46. Caponera, 1994, p. 174.

social and economic conditions before 1967 did not permit Palestinians to extract larger amounts from the common aquifers. Now that Israel has exploited that very water successfully to spur its own economic development, it is time that Palestinians be given the chance to develop their own economy, a process hamstrung by lack of water, among other things. This would be in line with some of the rules of equitable utilization which specify the "stage of economic development" as one of the factors to be weighed.[47] In any case, prior use remains a de facto condition and does not acquire legitimacy or become de jure unless the co-riparian agrees to it.

Israel also had not given "prior notification," as international water law requires, to Jordan, then the co-riparian, when it began in the early 1960s to extract substantial quantities of water from the common aquifers and to modify the hydrology of the basin by extracting water from hundreds of wells and letting the spring discharge diminish.[48] In fact, I was told by Joshua Schwarz, a high-level manager at Tahal, that Israel was not obligated to notify Jordan because the water from the aquifers "had always been flowing to the springs emerging in Israel, and nobody except Israel's Water Commission has to be notified on their use."[49] This stance may be faulted on two grounds. First, Israel, by supplanting the wells with springs, altered the natural character of the aquifer.[50] Second, and more important, is that Israel unilaterally was establishing a prior use level that subsequently it would claim as its legitimate share of the common aquifers, when in fact it should have been established by mutual agreement with Jordan. Be that as it may, the Palestinians cannot be expected to accept a grossly unfair status quo.

There is, finally, a lesson to be learned from the Egyptian-Sudanese treaties for dividing the Nile's waters. In the first treaty (1929), the principle of prior use was, according to one student of the Nile basin, "resoundingly affirmed" in favor of Egypt, which

47. Third Report to the ILC, 1982, cited in Hayton and Utton, 1989, p. 700.
48. Palestinian Hydrology Group and Palestine Advocacy Group, 1992.
49. Schwarz, 1993.
50. Some of the changes, such as salinity and lowering of the water table, have been indicated in the previous chapter. Moreover, principles of hydrogeology suggest that the direction of water flow in the aquifers changed because the wells are scattered and pumping is based on different mechanical processes than those of natural spring flow.

historically had been the main Nile water user.[51] However, he continues, "With hindsight we may say that such a lopsided and geopolitically unrealistic formula was not likely to endure. It did not."[52] It had to be renegotiated at the insistence of the Sudan, which obtained more favorable terms in the 1959 treaty.

Natural Attributes and Absolute Hydrologic Sovereignty

According to the doctrine of absolute hydrologic sovereignty, or the "Harmon" doctrine, countries have absolute say in how to use a common water resource in their territory stemming from their sovereignty over the territory. The doctrine is favorable to the upstream states that normally provide the replenishment, and for them to speak of natural attributes or absolute sovereignty often amounts to the same thing. Absolute hydrologic sovereignty is essentially the declared position of the Palestinians. This is exemplified in their demand that the groundwater rights be allocated in accordance with the replenishment area of the aquifers, which is tantamount to invoking absolute sovereignty.[53] Their contention is that the West Bank should come under their sovereignty in fulfillment of UN Security Council Resolutions 242 and 338, the terms of reference for the peace negotiations. Should water rights thus be divided, the Palestinians would be entitled to 80–90 percent of the water of the northeastern and western basins of the mountain aquifer and essentially to all the water of the eastern basin.

In fact, common international mineral resources are divided in a manner akin to absolute sovereignty, and it can be maintained, as some Palestinian and other experts have done, that the approach ought to be applicable to water as well.[54] The Palestinians also can maintain that Israel itself has set a precedent by acting as an absolute hydrologic sovereign, even when it lacked absolute territorial sovereignty over substantial portions of the common water resources.

Against these legitimate arguments, one must set other considerations. The history of water allocation among individuals and countries differs from that of other natural resources. For instance,

51. Waterbury, 1979, p. 67.
52. Ibid.
53. PLO, 1992, p. 76.
54. Barberis, 1991; and Zarour and Isaac, 1994.

Egypt—the gift of the Nile—exists as a country because Egyptians for millennia harnessed the Nile's waters, even though Egypt contributes almost no water to the river. To suggest that its waters be divided now according to the natural characteristics of the Nile would seem precipitous. Elsewhere, use of this factor as the sole criterion for apportionment could be wielded by powerful upstream riparians to deny those in the downstream water they may be entitled to on other grounds.

However that may be, the doctrine has had only a fleeting, if any, legal standing as the sole factor of allocating water rights in common international resources. The doctrine derived "its strength if not genesis"[55] from a 1895 opinion by U.S. Attorney General Harmon in the dispute over the Rio Grande River between the United States, the upstreamer, and Mexico, the downstreamer. Harmon claimed that international law imposed "no liability or obligation" on the United States not to intervene in the flow of the river, and that if it chose not to intervene, it would be "from considerations of comity."[56] The opinion, although invoked occasionally by some upstream states, has not been implemented even by states that asserted water claims on its basis; it was considered "dead" a long time ago,[57] and "has produced no rules of customary international water law."[58]

Legal and general principles aside, some practical matters would have to be considered. If the Palestinians invoke the principle of absolute sovereignty, which is advantageous to them with respect to the mountain aquifer, they would have to be willing to forfeit their claims in the Jordan basin. This option still may give them more water than appealing to other factors, as shall be seen later; but it is not certain as the operations of the mountain aquifer are not fully understood. The Palestinians also have to consider the economics of water supply from the Jordan River and the mountain or other aquifers. On the other hand, it is hard to fathom how Israel would accept the principle of absolute sovereignty when it is the downstream riparian in both the mountain aquifer and the Jordan basin and contributes little to both. In short, the natural attributes or absolute sovereignty factor, for legal and practical

55. Lipper, 1967, p. 20.
56. Ibid.
57. Ibid., p. 24.
58. Caponera, 1994, p. 175; see also Lipper, 1967, pp. 20–22.

reasons, ought to be weighed as one of the factors, not the sole factor.

What are the critical natural attributes of a common water resource that should be taken into account? Palestinian experts hold that the crucial attributes are the recharge area and quantity, prompting some of them to call the waters of the joint aquifers "Palestinian waters" because they are recharged primarily from the West Bank.[59] In addition to these two attributes, Gvirtzman includes the water volume stored within the aquifer on each side of the border, a consideration that increases the quantities that Israel can claim on the basis of this factor.[60] In response to Gvirtzman, it can be said that the storage volume is germane only to nonrenewable aquifers where it is the only variable owing to the absence of recharge. It is not so obvious, however, that the storage volume is relevant when it comes to a renewable resource, whether a river or an aquifer.

The reasoning above may be deduced from the intention of the doctrine of limited sovereignty. The doctrine was meant to safeguard the downstreamer because the natural attributes of water sources commonly enable the upstreamer, if it were to exercise absolute sovereignty, to use most of the water before it reaches the downstream. Thus, along the Nile, for example, more water reaches Egypt than just Ethiopia's contribution to the river because the Nile gathers water from other sources in Sudan and elsewhere before reaching Egypt; yet, Ethiopia could harness sufficient water from the river so as to render Egypt dry. The critical attribute then is how much water Ethiopia, not Egypt, can take away. In the case of the mountain aquifer, it is technologically possible today for the Palestinians to tap "a substantial amount, if not most, of the groundwater" of the western basin in the West Bank.[61] Although they may not at present possess the technological or economic wherewithal to do that, this situation is likely to change in the future as their capabilities improve. Further, the fact that substantial amounts of water can be drawn from within the West Bank casts doubt about the validity of Gvirtzman's definition of the storage area as being solely a function of hydrogeology unrelated to drilling technology or economics.[62]

59. See, for example, al-Jarbawi and Abd al-Hadi, 1990.
60. Gvirtzman, 1994, p. 212.
61. Brawer, 1994, p. 58.
62. It is not totally obvious what hydrogeological criteria Gvirtzman

Social and Economic Needs

International water law offers little by way of guidance as to the meaning of "needs" or the time frame of their assessment. Thus, some conceptual clarifications for establishing a frame of reference for these are in order. With regard to the time frame, long-term planning is necessary because water itself is a primary substance that has no substitutes, and because needs are diachronic and rise over time due to population and income growth and urbanization. Providing water to the citizenry is often the responsibility of governments, whether central or provincial, and they have to be able to anticipate the water demand and supply. Water projects, moreover, require large initial outlays and need planned budgeting.

In the present context, Israel has been a long-term planner; its demand and supply forecasts reach as far as the year 2040. In contrast, the Palestinians have been unable to do their own planning, and, since 1967, Israel has done it on their behalf. In order to plan, they have to be able to anticipate well into the future not only their water demand, but also, and especially, supply. So, the apportionment of the common groundwater would have to be assessed on the basis of long-term demand, but with prompt implementation.

What constitutes needs? Needs are a portmanteau concept, and, to limit disagreement, they must be assessed according to the same criteria for each of the disputants. This may not be entirely fair to the party that is economically less developed, as will be pointed out subsequently. Nonetheless, it is a useful starting point. The needs are taken here to mean prescribed levels of demand, in the sense described in the forecasts of water demand for both sides in chapters 3 and 4.

To reiterate, these forecasts were made by BUNT for both Israel and the Palestinians and by ARIJ for the Palestinians. They both specify water demand coefficients (or per capita water requirements) for the municipal sector and multiply that by the projected population size. The postulated demand coefficients for both Israelis and Palestinians converge in the long run; the projections of the Palestinian population size, however, do not. For irrigation, the forecasts employ different approaches. BUNT posits a water

used to claim that the storage area lies only in Israel; for example, he excluded the semicoastal Qalqilya and Tulkarm region in the West Bank from his definition of the storage area.

demand coefficient sufficient for meeting a person's consumption of fresh fruits and vegetables and 25 percent of the dairy and then aggregates it according to population. It also adds 289 mcmy for export crops without specifying how they would be allocated between the two sides. ARIJ, however, calculates Palestinian irrigation demand on the basis of the irrigable area. In spite of the different starting points, their demand projections for Palestinian irrigation needs are not far apart. The Palestinian forecast, however, extends only to the year 2020, whereas the Israeli counterpart extends to the year 2040.

The foregoing projections, with minor amendments, will be used to illustrate how equitable utilization can be rendered on the basis of social and economic needs (table 5.1 and figure 5.1). The amendments apply to the Palestinian population and the water demand coefficients for both sides. I use a Palestinian population size between that of the ARIJ and BUNT projections; the assumptions are explained in the footnotes of the table. The water demand coefficients are assumed to be equal for both sides, 220 m³/capita: 120 for municipal and industrial use and 100 for irrigation. The municipal and industrial demand is accorded priority in allocation, with irrigation picking up the surplus water. The 100 m³/capita municipal water is the same as the present level of Israeli consumption, and the 100 m³/capita for irrigation would be approximately sufficient for total self-sufficiency in fresh horticultural crops and 25 percent self-sufficiency in dairy products. The only exception is the Palestinian demand coefficient of municipal and industrial water, which is assumed as 100 m³/capita instead of 120 m³ in the year 2010.

It has been pointed out often that equitable utilization does not mean equal use. Such an interpretation tacitly refers to overall quantities, in the sense that equity does not mean that a resource common to two riparians ought to be divided into two equal portions, and one common to three into three equal portions, and so on. It is fair, however, to suggest that the individual or per capita shares be equal. This even may be fairer to the Israelis than the Palestinians because the former's personal income is much higher (see chapter 4) and they can afford to import more food than the latter.

If it is accepted that allocation of water rights would be made according to equal per capita shares, the total quota of each side would be proportional to the population size. Accordingly, if the

TABLE 5.1 Israeli and Palestinian Water Demand and Natural
Supply

(In mcmy)

Item	Year 2010	2020	2040
Palestinian			
Population (millions)	4.2[a]	5.4[b]	7.5[c]
Demand			
M & I	420	594	825
Irrigation	420	540	750
Total	840	1,134	1,575
Israeli			
Population (millions)	7.7	9.2	12.8
Demand			
M & I	924	1,012	1,408
Irrigation	770	920	1,280
Total	1,694	1,932	2,688
Israel and Palestinian			
M & I demand	1,344	1,606	2,233
Total Demand	2,534	3,066	4,263
Supply[d]	1,790	1,790	1,790
Balance:			
Supply—M & I demand	446	184	−443
Supply—total demand	−744	−1,276	−2,473

SOURCES: Tables 3.18 and 4.6; and BUNT, 1994.
NOTES:
[a]This represents an annual growth rate of 3.7 percent between 1990 and 2010. See Abdeen and Abu-Libdeh, 1993.
[b]This represents an annual growth rate of 2.5 percent.
[c]Same growth rate as Israel's.
[d]Includes 170 mcmy of brackish water which Israel can use for agriculture and industry.

year 2040, for example, is taken as a target date, the Israeli quota would be 1,129 mcmy and the Palestinian 661 mcmy. Consequently, the Palestinian share would increase by about 435 mcmy over the 1993 level, or nearly triple, while the Israeli share would be reduced by the same amount.

Figure 5.1 clearly illustrates that there would be a huge gap between the projected demand and supply from the natural resources of geographic Palestine. Those would provide only 88 m^3 per capita, or 40 percent of the postulated total demand coefficient

FIGURE 5.1 Future Water Supply and Demand in Geographic Palestine

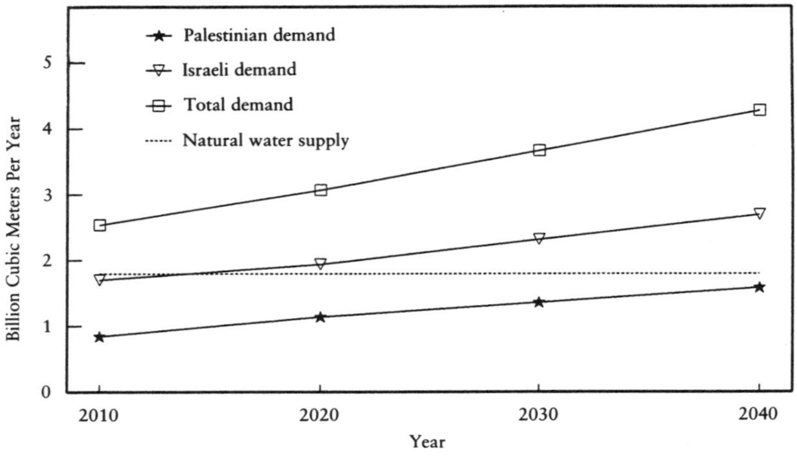

SOURCES: Tables 3.18 and 4.6; and BUNT, 1994

of 220 m³ per capita, and even less than the municipal and industrial demand coefficient.

Comparative Costs of Alternative Resources

Alternative water resources refer specifically to potential sources—such as desalination of brackish groundwater, seawater, and imported water. Those sources, by increasing the size of the "bucket," could facilitate an equitable sharing agreement. However, they cannot be viewed as an alternative to equitable utilization, as the Israeli government seems to think.

How the alternative water resources influence the equation of equitable utilization depends on (1) their physical availability and (2) the comparative costs of harnessing them. Naturally, the relative availability of alternative resources must be assessed at the start since for a riparian without alternative sources comparative costs are an academic question. The comparative costs are a yardstick of the parties' ability to harness alternative resources when they exist. The party that is more able to do that would be entitled to a smaller share of the common sources (just within the confines of this factor).

The Israelis and Palestinians theoretically have three ways of obtaining alternative water: importation, wastewater treatment, and desalination. Regarding importation, numerous schemes have been suggested for transporting water via pipelines or canals from the "water-rich" countries in the Middle East to the poorly endowed. Those schemes include water conduits from the Seyhan and Ceyhan rivers that empty into the Mediterranean in Turkey, the Euphrates in Syria, the Nile in Egypt, and the Litani in Lebanon to Jordan, Israel, the West Bank, and Gaza, as well as to the Gulf countries and Saudi Arabia. Others have centered around transporting water by sea in specially designed, large-volume bags (so-called Medusa bags) that are still under development.[63]

The interregional schemes require a separate treatment. All that can be said here is that, in principle, there is nothing wrong with these ideas; long-distance transportation of water is a basic feature of modern water-supply systems in most countries. However, the proposed conduits are interstate schemes, and some of them would extend over much longer distances than those of intrastate and/or would supply water to countries that are not riparians of the basin from which water originates. Building them entails overcoming numerous political, legal, environmental, and economic obstacles in order for the schemes to be realized. Further, for the importing countries not to be vulnerable to interruption of water supply (witness the interstate oil pipelines that have been made temporarily or permanently inoperative by war and politics in the region), they would have to have sufficient primary sources and use water from these conduits as a supplement or as a reserve. Thus, it would seem that interstate water transfer remains a potential, long-run option to be taken up after a discernible stabilization of regional politics and after local natural and alternative resources have been exhausted.[64] At any rate, it is more viable for the Israelis than for the Palestinians because Israel could project its military power far afield to protect the water conduits, whereas the Palestinians lack such an option.

The second option, desalination, can be used to extract freshwater from either brackish or saline water. In the West Bank, it may be possible for the Palestinians to tap brackish water from the eastern basin of the mountain aquifer. The quantity of such water

63. See, for example, Duna, 1988; Haddadin, 1992; and Kally and Fishelson, 1993.
64. I expressed this view in Elmusa, 1994b; BUNT, 1994, seems to share the opinion that importation from regional sources at present is not in the cards.

is limited to 22–42 mcmy, assuming also that the environmental problem of disposing the brine, which could contaminate the surroundings or the source aquifers, can be overcome. In Israel, the volume of renewable brackish water that can be exploited is unclear but may be as much as 140 mcmy with "an additional potential theoretically estimated at 240–290 mcmy."[65] It also is not obvious whether these figures, given by BUNT, include the West Bank. More significantly, however, is the fossil aquifer in the Negev, which conceivably could meet the water needs of that agricultural region for a century. It even could be used to irrigate crops in the central coastal area.[66] This source seldom is mentioned in Israeli discourse on water, whether official or not, save by the scientists and economists who advocate mining it.

Other than brackish groundwater, there is seawater. Israel possesses a broad seafront extending in the north from the border with Lebanon to Gaza in the south, and this gives it flexibility in plant location. The West Bank, in contrast, is landlocked, while Gaza has only a modest seafront that may be able to support one major desalination plant, especially when considering the competing demands for developing recreational, fishing, and harbor facilities (which the PA wants to build to lessen dependence on Israeli ports).

Wastewater treatment, the third option, has become an environmental and health necessity, even where it is not needed for reuse. In the West Bank and Gaza, the nontreated sewage water—whether it percolates to the aquifers; is left to run in open channels in the villages, refugee camps, and even some of the towns; or is used by farmers—has become a health hazard, as discussed in chapter 2. In addition to attenuating the risks to health, treated water can be a boon for agriculture, both as water and as source of fertilizers.

Israel is better served with sewage systems than the Palestinian territories. Although it treats 200 mcmy, two-thirds of the municipal and industrial water still goes untreated. The Palestinians have started wastewater treatment on a small scale using mainly external assistance. The available amounts for both sides depend on how much water is consumed and the proportion of that water that can

65. BUNT, 1994, p. 6.11
66. Huerta, 1991; Issar and Nativ, 1988; Nativ and Issar, 1987; p. 128; Pearce, 1991, citing Issar; and Tsur et al., 1989.

be treated. The main sources of wastewater for treatment are the municipal and industrial sectors. The effluent available for treatment from these two sectors commonly ranges from 40–60 percent of water use. The volume of water (per capita) that can be treated from the two sectors by Israel and the Palestinians is proportional to the rate of their respective consumption (per capita), which is three to one.

The second factor that touches on the capability of both sides to harness alternative resources is the relative economic costs. Here we have to consider the initial capital investments and the capability of consumers to pay. The costs vary by the water's salinity content and type of desalination technology. According to 1995 World Bank estimates, desalination costs $0.45–0.70/m³ for brackish water and $1.0–1.5/m³ for seawater.[67] The initial investment in a desalination plant was estimated in Israel at about $2.5/m³, at an interest rate of 7.5 percent.[68] The costs do not cover the connection either to the feedwater source or to the consumer supply system and brine water disposal. It is probably reasonable to assume that initial investments in all parts of the system would be $4.0–5.0/m³, or $150 million for a plant with 30-mcmy capacity module.

Wastewater treatment may cost $0.4–0.6/m³, or less than the costs of desalinating brackish and, especially, seawater.[69] Wastewater treatment also helps solve an environmental problem, whereas the brine from desalination could be a pollution hazard, notably to the source aquifers in the case of inland brackish water, something to be factored in when comparing costs. Initial investment in sewage systems and treatment in the West Bank and Gaza has been put at an average of $200 per capita for collection and $60 per capita for treatment.[70] At these rates, the initial investment in collection and use facilities for the urban and refugee populations, not including the villages, would amount to $600 million by the year 2000. In Israel, the initial outlays have been calculated as being $0.7–1.3/m³ for the treatment plants and $0.2–0.7/m³ for the conveyance infrastructure.

Based on the foregoing description and the consumer water prices cited previously for Israel and the Palestinian territories

67. The World Bank, 1995, p. 20.
68. BUNT, 1994, pp. 6.21–6.23.
69. World Bank, 1995, p. 26.
70. Estimates cited in Sbeih, 1996, p. 173.

(chapters 3 and 4), the following can be inferred regarding their capability to tap alternative resources. In the West Bank, desalinated brackish water might be affordable for municipal use, and even for agriculture in the Jordan Valley. However, it has the drawback of being a potential environmental hazard and is limited in quantity. Desalinated seawater is a remote possibility for the West Bank because it does not have a seafront. Theoretically, it could import desalinated water from Israel, but that would add considerably to the costs. In addition, the costs of vulnerability of the supply would have to be incorporated into the calculation of costs and benefits. Furthermore, considering that treated wastewater is cheaper than desalinated water, even the brackish type, and that capital is extremely scarce, investment requirements in wastewater collection and treatment preclude desalination in the foreseeable future. However, there is a "Catch-22" situation: In order to reclaim wastewater in quantities commensurate with demand growth, the West Bank would have to secure supply increases first. Gaza's long-term options will be discussed in detail in the section on joint management; for the time being, however, it can be said that the collection of sewage water and treatment of both this kind of water and of that from the polluted aquifer are the only viable options.

As for Israel, desalinated brackish water is economical for municipal use as well as for irrigation, except for field crops, even if the sector were to be charged the full costs. Charging full costs, however, is not a mandatory course because the water has to be treated anyway and agricultural land even can be thought of as a sink for that water. The drawbacks of desalinating brackish water are similar to those in the West Bank. Desalinated seawater is affordable for domestic use and may be economical for some specialty crops. Moreover, Israel's broad seafront and enormous economic resources enable it to invest in desalination. In fact, in 1995 former Israeli Water Commissioner Gideon Tzur announced plans to build a desalination capacity of around 400 mcmy by the year 2020, and 900 mcmy by 2040. According to him, the desalination would commence with 100–120 mcmy.[71] It is unclear, however, whether the "dream" of the new water commissioner, Meir Ben Meir, to desalinate 800 mcmy refers to the same plan. At any rate, Israeli officials and government publications have been in the fore-

71. FBIS, 4 April 1995.

front of desalination advocacy. Furthermore, with respect to waste-water recycling, Israel already has made great strides and treats about one-eighth of its water budget. It uses this water to irrigate cotton, as mentioned in chapter 4.

In summary, Israel is much better positioned to exploit alternative resources on a significant scale than are the Palestinians. According to the foregoing reasoning, and from the standpoint of comparative ability to harness alternative resources, the Palestinians in the West Bank and Gaza would be entitled to a larger portion of the common waters than the Israelis.

Avoidance of Appreciable Harm

"Appreciable harm" refers to costs that can be measured objectively as a result of denial of water rights. For there to appreciable harm, "There must be," according to the 1988 report of the ILC, "a real impairment of use, i.e., a detrimental impact of some consequence upon, for example, public health, industry, property, agriculture or the environment."[72]

Two aspects of the appreciable harm principle need to be clarified. The first is the traditional contradiction in international law between appreciable harm and equitable utilization. Opinion has varied as to whether priority ought to be accorded to equitable utilization or to appreciable harm. Until recently, the latter was given the upper hand, perhaps because it was easier to ascertain than the former, despite the ambiguity of the threshold of "appreciable."[73] Although the World Bank, for example, "does not take a position adverse" to the principle of equitable utilization, it has had the avoidance of appreciable harm "firmly embodied" in its Operational Directives.[74] The priority of avoiding appreciable harm has been criticized, inter alia, on grounds that it is a static principle favoring the early developers of common international water resources.[75] In response to criticism and through the pressure of states that were, or potentially will be, adversely affected by the principle of appreciable harm, the ILC's rules appear to have swung in favor of equitable utilization. In the articles it adopted at its 43rd

72. Cited in Goldberg, 1992, p. 72.
73. Khassawneh, 1995, p. 23.
74. Goldberg, 1992, p. 73.
75. Khassawneh, 1995, p. 24.

session in 1991, the ILC accorded the "obligation" not to cause appreciable harm primacy over the "obligation" of equitable utilization.[76] In its 46th session, however, the primacy of no appreciable harm was watered down, if one can put it this way. Instead of an "obligation" not to inflict appreciable harm, the ILC replaced "obligation" with the "exercise" [of] "due diligence."[77] Where the two principles of equitable utilization and appreciable harm come into conflict, it made the former the guiding criteria: "Generally, in such instances [when the two principles are in conflict], the principle of equitable and reasonable utilization remains the guiding criterion in balancing the interests at stake."[78]

Nevertheless, it would seem that including social and economic needs (and obviously environmental concerns) as criteria of equitable utilization renders the opposition between the two principles superfluous. For what else would be harmed appreciably if not social and economic needs? Is there any other way of determining whether appreciable harm would be, or has been, inflicted on a riparian by another state's actions except by assessing the impact of the actions on such needs? Avoidance of appreciable harm and the satisfaction of social and economic needs indeed are the same side of the same coin despite the negative phrasing of the one and the positive rendering of the other.

A second, and related feature, of appreciable harm is that it commonly has been assumed to be "damage" caused by upstream riparians. The World Bank, for example, does not usually require the approval of an upstreamer for implementing water-related projects in a downstreamer's territory. The assumption is plausible when it comes to pollution, for pollution in the downstream does not harm the upstream. However, water allocations—to the extent that they do not have an adverse environmental impact—take into account only hydrology, not power and other factors that influence allocations.[79] Even if an upstreamer's dam can withhold water from the downstreamer, the latter might be able to deny the former water by political and other means, thus effectively reversing their stream positions. Appreciable harm, therefore, should be regarded from the point of view of the denial of water, whether by dams, power, or other means.

76. Ibid.
77. ILC, 1994, p. 343.
78. Ibid.
79. See also the discussion in Flint, 1995, p. 198.

When reallocation is demanded by the party that feels aggrieved, the party causing the infringement is likely to contend that it would be appreciably harmed by any reallocation. In such a case, both claims must be examined and ways must be found to balance the relative harm incurred by each of the co-riparians. For example, Palestinians undoubtedly have sustained appreciable harm, and the case for reallocation has been partly made on this ground. The impact of reallocation on Israel depends on how much water it would have to give up, or rather, give back to the Palestinians.

The Israeli sector most likely to be affected directly by reallocation is agriculture. Because the sector's share of GDP and employment is quite small, appreciable harm is not likely to result from reducing the water allocation to this sector. However, employment and economic indicators by themselves cannot serve as reliable predictors, and a more detailed impact analysis would be required before any reallocation plan is devised. At least one such study has relevance for any reallocation proposals. An input/output impact analysis by Gideon Fishelson found that cutting irrigation water usage in Israel by one-half would reduce the GDP by 2 percent.[80] Fishelson's estimate was for 1982/83, a time when agriculture contributed 6 percent of the GDP. In the late 1990s, the impact is likely to be even smaller because agriculture's share of the GDP has diminished. Furthermore, future projections of demand and Israel's capabilities to harness alternative resources would guarantee that it would not sustain appreciable harm in the future. Maintaining the present allocations, however, would have detrimental consequences on the Palestinian economy and quality of life.

Lastly, this is not a zero-sum game, and Israel would be able to capture significant benefits from regional cooperation in the wake of a peaceful settlement. Although the benefits would transcend the water sector, Israel could profit even in this sector, as well as in water related technology trade. Israel's possession of desalination technology undoubtedly would make it keen to exploit the regional desalination market, the largest in the world due to the paucity of water and the abundance of energy resources. A second area from which Israel could benefit is hydroelectric power generation. The reference here is to the megaprojects, such as the Med-Dead and Red-Dead canals. These projects require large cap-

80. Fishelson, 1994.

ital outlays, and no multilateral aid agency, such as the World Bank, would be in a position to assist without the approval of the Arab parties that share the Dead Sea.

How To Assess Equitable Utilization

Examination of the factors unambiguously suggests that were water rights to be designated according to the doctrine of equitable utilization, the Palestinians would be entitled to a much larger share of the water than they have had. Moreover, in the absence of a large increase in their share, their ability to satisfy their water-related social and economic needs would be impaired. As an exercise, I will consider each factor, with a summary of the arguments and a rough quantification of the implications for equitable utilization.

To begin with, it was suggested that the traditional opposition between the principles of appreciable harm and equitable utilization may not be as pertinent as it appears. In fact, one may go further and say that the avoidance of appreciable harm is essentially a duplication of the social and economic needs principle and need not be considered as a separate factor.

Second, Israeli claims to prior use are highly problematic, considering the circumstances under which such use was secured: lack of notification before 1967 and forcible curbs on Palestinian extraction from the mountain aquifer after 1967; out-of-basin transfer and force in the Jordan basin; alteration of the natural ecology without consulting, and even against the wishes of, other riparians (such as the draining of Lake Hula and the supplanting of natural springs in the mountain aquifer with wells); and over-extraction from several aquifers. Depending how far in time "prior" is taken, moreover, the Palestinians can lay claim to prior use in the resources of geographic Palestine to which they were denied access after 1948. Finally, even if for argument's sake prior use were to be considered for Israel, it would have to be the quantity used on the eve of the 1967 war, which was about 1,000–1,100 mcmy.

Third, geography favors the Palestinians in the mountain aquifer and Israel in the rest of the aquifers. Both Israel and the Palestinians, however, are at a great disadvantage under this factor in the Jordan basin, where Syria, Lebanon, and Jordan contribute

TABLE 5.2 Division of Water Rights between Israel and Palestinians According to Needs and Capabilities in 2040

(In mcmy)

	Palestinians	Israelis
1. Division according to needs	661	1,129
2. Capabilities		
Waste water	331	565
Desalination	140	900
Desalination recycle	70	450
Total	540	1,915
3. Grand total from 1 and 2	1,202	3,044
Per capita (m³/year)	160	238
4. Division according to needs *and* capabilities	895	895

SOURCE: Calculated by author based on previous tables and text.

most of the water. The share of geographic Palestine, according to its contribution to the drainage area and flow of the Jordan River system, would be only around 100 mcmy. This would reduce the total supply to about 1,250 mcmy, instead of 1,790 mcmy (table 5.1). Of the 1,250 mcmy, the Palestinian and Israeli shares would be nearly equal, 625 mcmy each.

Fourth, consideration of the social and economic needs, defined essentially as basic needs for a modern mode of living, indicated that they cannot be met by the available natural freshwater resources. By the year 2040, the municipal and industrial needs no longer can be met from these resources, and harnessing alternative resources will be indispensable for their satisfaction. The capabilities of the two sides for tapping such resources, however, are unequal. If the water resources are divided without the inclusion of the capability to harness alternative resources, the Palestinians would fare worse than the Israelis, as illustrated in table 5.2. Israel's supply from all the resources would be 238 m³ per capita, larger than the postulated needs of 220 m³ per capita, whereas the Palestinians' supply would be only 160 m³ per capita. If the capabilities are included, the 1,790 mcmy would have to be divided into two approximately equal portions, or 895 mcmy each. Obviously, the foregoing figures are illustrative, and the two sides would have to agree on the population figures, demand coefficients, and resource availability.

It may be that, in the final analysis, focusing on needs and capabilities would be the best course of action. The water can be seen as a means, a utility, and thus subject to rational calculation rather than legal arguments that easily could turn Talmudic. Viewing water as a utility forces the two sides to look to the future, instead of the past. It is worth repeating here that the allocations of the Jordan basin water under the Johnston Plan were devised in accordance with irrigation needs, which at the time were the priority needs in the region. Finally, as Jerome Lipper observed many years ago: "It is precisely because the water is often inadequate to satisfy the just needs of all [riparians] that rules [for equitable utilization] are required."[81]

According to the preceding statistics, an equitable utilization of the 1,790 mcmy would give the Palestinians 650–800 mcmy, or the equivalent of their share under the Johnston Plan plus from two-thirds to nearly 100 percent of the mountain aquifer. This is 425–575 mcmy more than they used in 1993. Israel's allocations would be 990–1,140 mcmy, or 415–565 mcmy less than its share in 1993.[82] Israel could make up for this quantity from alternative resources.

JOINT MANAGEMENT: TASKS AND CONSTRAINTS

International water law has advocated consistently the joint management of common water resources and their treatment as unitary basins or watersheds. For example, the 1991 Draft Articles of the ILC submitted to the UN General Assembly stated that riparians of a watercourse "shall, at the request of any of them, enter into consultations concerning the management of an international watercourse, which may include the establishment of a joint management mechanism."[83] The objectives of joint management include sustainability, optimal use, protection, and control of the water resources. They are to be undertaken on the basis of the riparians' sovereign equality, territorial integrity, and mutual benefit.[84]

81. Lipper, 1967, p. 44.
82. Israel's use in 1993 was 1,754 mcmy, 200 mcmy of which were treated wastewater.
83. Article 26.1, cited in Dellapenna, 1995, p. 95.
84. Article 8, cited in ibid.

At present, only the water resources under Palestinian jurisdiction are managed jointly, a remarkably asymmetrical arrangement and unlike anything intimated by international water law. A
final status accord would have to rectify this situation and devise
a joint management regime that is responsive to hydrologic boundaries rather than political expediency. Such an accord also must
specify the tasks to be shouldered cooperatively, as well as a commensurate joint management body.

Broadly speaking, the level of cooperation between Palestinians and Israelis and the associated institutional arrangements they
opt to make can be expected to vary according to the type and
intensity of the tasks or functions that are assigned for joint management to serve.[85] At the same time, selection of the tasks necessitates weighing what may be ideal from a technical or engineering
perspective against the political, economic, and other constraints.
Such constraints against joint management are more profound in
the case of the common groundwater than of the surface waters.
For the latter, the Israel-Jordan agreement may provide a broad
model of principles. However, as has been pointed out by an Israeli-
Palestinian workshop on the joint management of the common
aquifers, there is a dearth of experience, especially successful experience, with joint management of shared aquifers, and no tailor-
made models exist for them to emulate.[86] The two parties hence
must strive to develop their own mode of management.

Nonetheless, the Bellagio Draft Treaty, mentioned earlier,
may have some relevance to the Israeli-Palestinian case. The treaty
was based on the U.S.-Mexican experience in their semiarid border
zones and was meant to serve as a model for other groundwater
basins.[87] It covers a wide range of tasks—including protection
against pollution, database collection, and declaration of
drought—that a joint water institution might undertake. It also
contains sections on reconciling differences and resolving disputes,
which often have been missing from water treaties.[88]

The Bellagio Draft Treaty is mainly about the procedures to
be followed by, and the authority accorded to, the joint management body. Although the rationale for these procedures is not

85. S.D. Sylvan, cited in Feitelson, 1994.
86. Feitelson and Haddad, 1994, vol. 1.
87. Hayton and Utton, 1989.
88. Bingham et al., 1994, p. 142.

furnished in the text, the basic premise is that despite a possible commonality of interests, there also will be divergences stemming, for instance, from the different stages of economic development. The treaty also deals sensitively with sovereignty-related matters. These premises are particularly germane in the Israeli-Palestinian case. Although not all the tasks it enumerates need to be adopted in a joint Palestinian-Israeli management project, it is a document well worth careful reading by the Palestinians, especially for its rigorous details, precise language, and the gamut of issues it raises. Still, although the Bellagio Draft Treaty may offer some clues, the two parties would have to design their own mode of management.

The type of joint institution would be too speculative in the absence of an agreement on the tasks that it would be set up to perform. The above-cited joint Israeli-Palestinian workshop explored types and possible evolutionary trajectories of collaborative "management structures."[89] It did not, however, broach the ramifications of the tasks. Those ramifications and how they can be accommodated within the economic and political constraints are discussed in the remainder of this chapter.

The management tasks, broadly speaking, are alike for the groundwater and the Jordan basin, although their details and implications, notably for sovereignty, are different. Yet, because the Jordan basin is common to five riparians, the bilateral arrangements would have to give way to multilateral institutions that manage the basin as an integrated unit. Integrated management of a river system is advocated by the ecologically conscious modern management discourse, originally was envisaged by the Johnston Plan, and even was proposed by Israel itself during the course of the Johnston mission.[90]

Several tasks will be tackled: protection of the water quality and quantity, verification and notification, and transboundary water marketing and conveyance. There are others that are equally salient, such as drought management and establishment of a common database, but I will not take these up as my purpose is to illustrate the potential areas of, and constraints on, cooperation, not to prepare a blueprint for joint management.

89. Feitelson and Haddad, 1995, vol. 3.
90. Elmusa, 1995b, p. 72.

Protection of Water Quantity and Quality

That the common water sources need protection, both preventive and corrective, cannot be overstressed.[91] Palestinians, whose dependence on them is almost entire, would have to undertake such protection even more vigorously than the Israelis, whose ambitious desalination program could compensate for the potential contamination of household water resources. In fact, the Israelis appear to have made the pessimistic assessment that groundwater, the main source of household water, indeed will become polluted. This was acknowledged in the statement by former Israeli Water Commissioner Gideon Tzur when he announced the outlines of the desalination program cited earlier; he said that he was "afraid that the quality of fresh water will continue deteriorating."[92] The pressure on the water resources and attendant danger of their contamination only can mount with population growth and relentless urbanization and industrialization on both sides of the border. The rampant contamination of Gaza's aquifer which has rendered it nearly moribund is an object lesson.

The ubiquitousness of contamination sources and the multiplicity of contaminants (see chapter 2) render the protection of water, particularly groundwater, from pollution economically costly, institutionally demanding (laws and enforcement), and fraught with technical uncertainties. Joint management would compound these problems by adding external political constraints. These hurdles perhaps go a long way in explaining the dearth of successful protection experiences of transboundary resources, notably groundwater.

Protection of Surface Water

Middle Eastern states do not have a distinguished record when it comes to the protection of water resources. Regarding transboundary resources, the only water accords that have included water-protection clauses are the Israel-Jordan water and environment agreements and the 1994 nonbinding Bahrain Environmental Code

91. The Bellagio Draft Treaty broadens the notion of protection to include the "underground environment"; see Hayton and Utton, 1989, p. 677.
92. FBIS, April 4, 1995.

of Conduct issued by the Multilateral Working Group on the Environment.[93] In the Israel-Jordan agreements, which are pertinent here, the two sides have identified numerous areas of cooperation in ecological protection; more specific clauses for water protection are spelled out in the water agreement. The two notable provisions for the protection of the water of the Jordan and Yarmuk rivers are, first, the prohibition against dumping municipal and industrial wastewater into the two rivers before they are treated to a degree that make them suitable for agriculture, and, second, desalination of the saline springs that Israel diverted into the Jordan River in 1964 (Annex II, Articles III.3 and 5).[94] Insofar as the Jordan basin is concerned, these provision could be viewed as a model for a provisional tripartite arrangement (Israel, Jordan, and the Palestinians) or a multilateral one inclusive of all the riparians.

Protection of Groundwater

Groundwater protection entails more far-reaching measures and a higher level of cooperation between Israelis and Palestinians than does protection of the Jordan basin surface water. There are three reasons why this is so. First, the groundwater has to meet stringent drinking and other household-use standards, whereas the basin's surface water needs only to meet less stringent irrigation standards. Second, the aquifers extend under an extensive area and thus are more vulnerable to point-source contamination than is the river system. Third, rehabilitation of damaged aquifers is generally more costly and time-consuming than that of rivers.

The measures needed to achieve quality standards include regulations regarding extraction, sources of contamination, and land use. The subsequent discussion of standards and measures borrows liberally from a succinct U.S. review of the topic that was prepared by the National Policy Forum.[95] Although that study does not address transboundary problems, it contains a rich variety of relevant examples.

93. Scobbie, 1996, pp. 107–108, provides a brief analysis of the legal standing of the Bahrain Code.
94. The first measure becomes effective three years after signing, and the second four years after signing.
95. The Conservation Foundation, 1987; the National Policy Forum included members of major environmental institutions, universities, and corporations, in addition to two state governors, farmers, and others.

Protection of water quantity requires the regulation of extraction through an array of instruments: legal (e.g., licensing, ceilings on pumping); economic (e.g., pricing); and technical (e.g., metering). Each party would deploy whichever instruments it deems effective within its own borders. Israel's principal regulatory tools are licensing, metering, and quotas. The Palestinians, however, may be reluctant to regulate pumping by legal means because restrictions on pumping have become associated with the heavy hand of the occupation. Employing legal instruments, however, is inescapable.

For the protection of water quality, standards, or limits on types and quantities of permissible contaminants, must be agreed upon. The standards can apply to the water itself (ambient standards) or to the sources of contamination (source standards). In reality, the ambient standards are unlikely to be realized without source standards, and a joint management accord may combine both. In the case of ambient standards, which in most locations should conform to household water standards, the permissible levels of contaminants would have to be apportioned between the Israelis and Palestinians because contamination is cumulative. The bone of contention in this situation is the distribution of the "contamination quotas" between the two sides. One way to do this would be to base them on relative economic capabilities and derived benefits.

Many of the protection activities, such as the treatment of wastewater or construction of technically sophisticated storage facilities for gasoline, entail economic costs that the Palestinians are less capable of shouldering than are the Israelis. The differences in the "stage of economic development" hence dictate either financial compensation by Israel or greater contamination quotas for the Palestinians. Otherwise, the "moral hazard" for the Palestinians of not adhering meticulously to the quotas would be high. Even if contamination quotas were approved, pinpointing the source of violation in an aquifer, unlike in a river where the water is enclosed in a well-defined course, is hard, especially if it is a nonpoint source. Further understanding of the hydrogeological properties of the aquifer would not eliminate uncertainty, but undoubtedly it would be helpful.

Source standards are too cumbersome to set jointly because the sources of contamination are numerous, change over time, and cover a large, hydrologically nonhomogeneous area. All that may be practical to spell out in an accord are general provisions, such as banning the dumping of wastewater before removing particular toxic materials and, as was done in the Israel-Jordan water agreement, treating wastewater to qualitatively stated standards. It may be possible, too, to agree to prohibit altogether the disposal of certain toxic or hazardous wastes onto designated areas of the aquifers.

The policy measures for controlling the sources of contamination do not readily lend themselves to management by a joint institution. Such measures can be complex and ubiquitous. They may be regulatory, designed for a particular source, or empower appropriate levels of government (e.g., municipal, ministerial) to review discharge plans. This point can be illustrated by some examples from the regulatory measures.[96]

The regulatory measures may apply to the performance, technical aspects, or best management criteria of the source. Performance regulations may specify the level of treatment of wastewater before disposal or how much a particular source, such as septic tanks, can discharge. Further, they may ban outright the disposal of certain pesticides or hazardous industrial wastes that can leach into the groundwater, or require an enterprise to clean up its waste site before it can sell the property. Technical regulations also may set construction standards, such as type and thickness of liners for landfill sites or storage tanks. Best management regulations specify provisions as to how a source or a facility ought to be managed, operated, or maintained. For instance, in agriculture such regulations may ask farmers to observe those techniques that are most effective in the control of runoff water and pesticides.

Apart from contamination sources, regulatory measures may target land use itself and be incorporated into zoning laws. They may prohibit the establishment of industries in certain locations, or declare limited areas around municipal water wells as "protected," and curtail potentially polluting activities in their vicinity. In the West Bank, one particular type of land use may have to be targeted for regulation, namely, quarrying. Besides the aesthetically disagreeable sites it leaves behind and the air pollution it inflicts on adjacent communities and agricultural fields, quarrying removes impermeable rock layers that may be critical for impeding contaminants. Regulations often need to be bolstered by financial incen-

96. These are from the Conservation Foundation, 1987, pp. 171–91.

tives to encourage such preventive actions as the building of a particular type of septic tank or gasoline storage facility and to promote agricultural conversion from the profligate use of pesticides to a less chemically reliant, integrated pest management system.

What emerges from the foregoing illustrations is that protection measures may touch on virtually every activity in the aquifer area. Their implementation calls for the enactment of laws and the creation of an extensive institutional network that can act on the macro and micro levels. They entail immediate economic costs to society, resulting from the increased production costs of goods and services, financial incentives, or transactions costs (e.g., from litigation). Hence, it is difficult to see how they can be entrusted to a joint management institution rather than to each party's relevant agencies. The joint institution, however, should not be excluded from making recommendations. In particular, it should be able to recommend declaring limited areas as "conservation" zones, of both water quantity and quality as, for example, was stipulated in the Bellagio Draft Treaty.[97] Special measures would be applied in such an area and the joint institution may be given additional authorities, subject to the approval of the governments.

Verification, Notification, and Dispute Resolution

The three categories of action—verification, notification, and dispute resolution—are indispensable for the implementation and survival of a water agreement. They pertain primarily to the water shares that each party is allocated, water quality, and construction of new water-related facilities insofar as they may affect the existing properties of the hydrological system.

Each side would need verification and notification with respect to activities upstream of the source in which it is located in the downstream. With respect to the Jordan River, provisions of verification and notification can be similar to those in the Israel-Jordan water agreement. The provisions specify that verification of water flows and quality would be carried out by the use "of jointly established stations to be operated under the guidance" of the joint water committee (Annex II, Article III.2). In addition, they demand

97. Hayton and Utton, 1989, pp. 692–93.

that notification be given "six months ahead of time" regarding "any intended projects which are likely to change the flow of either of the above [the Jordan or Yarmuk] rivers along their common boundary, or the quality of such flow." The last provision is predicated on the understanding that artificial changes in the course of the two rivers only can be made by mutual consent (Annex II, Article V.1 and 2).

The procedures of verifying adherence to water quotas are more demanding in groundwater than in rivers. Gauging the flow of a river is not a technically demanding task and can be made at a relatively small number of fixed stations along its course. Consequently, it does not visibly encroach on sovereignty. Withdrawal from the aquifers, on the other hand, takes place from hundreds of wells scattered across the aquifer's area. Each party, of course, can monitor pumping through meters on its side of the border. But how would the other party be informed? The Bellagio Draft Treaty suggests that the joint institution be the medium and that governments notify it rather than each other.[98] Relations between the United States and Mexico, however, are different from those between Israel and the Palestinians. Furthermore, the common transboundary groundwater sources of the two North American states, unlike those of geographic Palestine, have limited regional, rather than national, scope. Thus, notification alone may not do. This leaves only two options: one is *in situ* verification and the other is technical. The first option involves the inspection of the wells of one party by the other, as is done in the mountain aquifer where Israeli and Palestinian personnel inspect Palestinian wells, a procedure stipulated by the Taba Agreement. *In situ* verification obviously is a political question, and it can bear heavily on Palestinian sovereignty. To minimize encroachment on sovereignty, perhaps some statistical random sampling procedure that requires the checking of only a limited number of wells could be worked out. There is also a technical solution that can substitute for *in situ* verification: Electronic devices can be installed on the pumps to keep track of the wells' activities, and the logs can be transmitted either electronically or manually to the joint institution for inspection. If Israel insisted on *in situ* verification, it would have to reciprocate by accepting similar Palestinian activity on its territory.

98. Ibid., p. 687.

Verification of groundwater quality applies, in principle, to both water quality in the wells and springs (ambient verification) and the sources of contamination (source verification). Because of the ubiquity of the attendant measures, however, verification can seriously compromise sovereignty. In the Bellagio Draft Treaty, only notification is stipulated.[99] According to the treaty, the governments would "promptly" notify the joint management institution of any actual or planned contamination sources that might result in significant leaching into the groundwater. The joint institution would review the situation and decide whether it should declare the areas that might be affected "conservation areas," as indicated earlier. These procedures also could be adopted (or adapted) by the Palestinians and Israelis.

A third activity that needs verification is drilling new wells on both sides of the border, because wells influence not only the quantity of the flow but also its direction. This may not be a formidable task and can be facilitated greatly by remote sensing and aerial photography. The need for ground truthing would be minimal for the Israelis who possess both types of technology. The Palestinians' access to these technologies is likely to be quite limited because of Israeli security demands, and, in principle, some form of limited *in situ* inspection would be necessary. A measure of mutuality might go a long way in addressing this problem. At any rate, notification of the joint institution would be essential.

A final joint management task is the resolution of disputes over "facts or circumstances."[100] In the absence of dispute resolution mechanisms, the integrity of a water accord could be compromised altogether, and violations finally could threaten the water resources themselves. When the joint institution is made up of only two parties, as it would be in the Israeli-Palestinian case, there is no "democratic" procedure, in the sense of the acceptance of majority votes for resolving disputes (not that such a procedure is likely to be welcome even in a multiparty institution). The dispute resolution mechanism in the Taba Agreement (Annex III, Article 40. 12.f) confines the deliberations to the Joint Water Committee; disputes are not to be mediated by third parties. The arrangement, however, is inadequate and is in place only because Israel has not recognized Palestinian sovereignty. Under the arrangement, per-

99. Ibid., p. 691.
100. Ibid., p. 714, citing actual terms used in the Bellagio Draft Treaty.

sisting disputes either are not resolved or are likely to be resolved in favor of Israel because it has control on the ground.

Changing that arrangement in the upcoming talks necessitates the establishment of a hierarchical, open procedure. For example, resolution of a given dispute first would be attempted within the joint management body itself; if that failed after a specified time lapse, the governments themselves would take up the matter. If the governments fail to resolve their differences, they would resort to mediation, conciliation, or arbitration at the International Court of Justice or any other channel they deem appropriate. This is similar to the procedures recommended by the Bellagio Draft Treaty and by the Draft Articles of the ILC's forty-sixth session.[101]

Water Trade and Conveyance

Transboundary water trade is a management question and may be negotiated once the issue of water rights is settled. It is not a common practice in the world today. However, it has been discussed as a way to increase the use efficiency of the limited water resources in the region. In particular, two models have been constructed to estimate, among other things, the water use gains from water trade between Israel and the West Bank and Gaza.[102] The one that is of interest here was done at Harvard University's Kennedy School of Government.[103] It is more elaborate and makes wider claims than the second model by Zeituni et al. It was a joint project by American, Israeli, and Arab (including Palestinian) specialists, although the Arab participants did not necessarily endorse the findings. The Kennedy School model conflates two categories of transfer.[104] One category refers to trading through the creation of transboundary water markets, which are not, strictly speaking, transfers because water would be bought and sold, not given free. The other category essentially proposes the conveyance of the potential Palestinian water share in the western basin of the mountain aquifer from Israel's side of the border. To avoid confusion, I will refer to the first category as "transboundary water trade" or mar-

101. ILC, 1994, article 33, p. 359.
102. Zeituni et al., 1994; and Fisher et al., 1994.
103. The results of the model, which was a group project, have been summarized in Fisher et al., 1994.
104. Ibid.

keting and to the second as "conveyance." Each category has different economic and political ramifications, and either's inclusion in, or exclusion from, joint management tasks needs to be examined separately.

Trade

Theoretically, it would be economically advantageous for the two sides to engage in transboundary water marketing: the seller of water would be paid a higher price than the monetary value he would obtain from within-boundary use; and the buyer would obtain from use of the water a higher value than the price he paid for it. This theoretical construct is supported by the two models; the Zeituni et al. model indicates that an optimal allocation that maximizes aggregate efficiency would lead to the transfer of a considerable amount of water from Israel to the West Bank and Gaza: 320 mcmy above and beyond the *present* allocation regime (thus tacitly acknowledging the inefficiency of the current allocation regime).[105] A full investigation of the gains from trade, however, should take into account the strengths and weaknesses of markets and the numerous requirements for their establishment (see chapter 3), something this model does not do.[106]

Before examining the problems with transboundary marketing and the feasibility of their establishment, we need to have an idea of whether the size of economic benefits from Israeli-Palestinian water trade justifies the effort and costs of arranging it. The Kennedy School model puts the entire value of the disputed portion of the water of the mountain aquifer, which is assumed to be 400 mcmy in the year 2020, at $210 million.[107] If the value of the disputed water is small, why bother with complex international arrangements to increase efficiency? This question becomes even more pertinent if one considers the amounts of water that could be traded. By the year 2020, all the naturally available freshwater in geographic Palestine could be sufficient only to meet the municipal

105. This is the amount that would be allocated by a hypothetical "social planner," who would want to maximize aggregate efficiency. In a market, however, each side would seek to pursue its benefits, which results in a reduction of Palestinian allocations. See further Zeituni et al., 1994, p. 405.

106. None of the cited studies addresses these questions.

107. This figure is based on 1990 dollars calculated in terms of the *in situ* price, under particular and very detailed assumptions.

Israeli and Palestinian demand. If the allocation of water rights to Israelis and Palestinians were based on such needs, there would be little water to trade. Thus, gains from any traded water at the margins would not be significant. Desalinated water, which the Kennedy School model finds uneconomical, could be traded, especially for supplying Gaza (discussed later in this chapter). In that case, the motivation would not be boosting efficiency but providing municipal water needs. Moreover, any efficiency gains ought to be assessed in light of the costs of establishing transboundary markets.

Two considerations stand out with regard to the costs of establishing transboundary markets. The first consideration is that transboundary marketing would be difficult to undertake without the mechanisms of within-boundary marketing in place. In order for one side to know how much it wants to buy or sell, it would need to get information from, and the consent of, the users and property rights owners. Thus, the question that will have to be answered is: Will the benefits from trade justify the creation of the physical and institutional structures for water markets?

The second consideration is the level of cooperation that transboundary marketing calls for. That level would be a function of the tasks involved, including such activities as ensuring the efficient allocation of water, managing the externalities, transferring funds, and using any profits for joint water projects. Water marketing hence could require a high level of cooperation and the creation of a fairly independent but powerful joint institution. However, if the economic gains from transboundary water trade were insubstantial, there may not be sufficient incentives for a complex cooperation regime. Nevertheless, should the two sides still wish to take advantage of even minor gains, and considering the history of the dispute, any agreement they enter into on water trade would have to stipulate at the outset that the traded water by no means prejudice the agreed-upon water rights or be used to establish future prior use claims.

Water Conveyance for the Palestinians

The Kennedy School model concludes that conveyance of water to Gaza from the Jordan River via the Israeli National Water Carrier is economically superior to transfer from the West Bank and to desalination from within Gaza's own boundaries.[108] Regarding the

108. Fisher et al., 1994.

mountain aquifer, it finds (without the benefit of a hydrological model) that the extraction of water from the western basin would be more efficient from the Israeli side than from the West Bank. Even if further investigations confirm those inferences, the economic benefits would have to be weighed against the vulnerability stemming from having the Palestinian water supply controlled by another country and against the desire for the integration of Gaza and the West Bank versus the integration of each with Israel.

In principle, there are two alternative methods of supplying Gaza with water other than from Israel: desalination and a conduit from the West Bank.[109] Desalination has the advantage of reducing vulnerability but is neutral as far as the integration of the West Bank and Gaza is concerned. Although Israel easily could bomb a desalination plant, it is easier and less visible to tamper with the spigot than to raid a water facility. At an rate, I am not concerned about vulnerability in time of war but rather as a result of the ups and downs of everyday relations or low-level hostilities. Under such circumstances, desalination is less risky than supply from Israel. Which of the two options is found superior will depend on whether the difference in the cost of supply from Israel and from desalination outweighs having the independent water source provided by desalination.

A conduit from the West Bank to Gaza carries the same risk as one from Israel because it would have to pass through Israeli territory. However, it would help in the integration of these two geographically discontinuous Palestinian regions rather than tying Gaza closer with Israel. Thus, the choice between them would have to be based on whether the economic gains of having water from Israel are viewed as less or more valuable than fostering greater integration of Gaza and the West Bank.

A third type of comparison would have to be made between desalination and a conduit from the West Bank. An assessment of which option is superior would have to factor in the economic merits of the two methods of supply, in addition to the vulnerability aspect. At the same time, the integrative effects of water supply from the West Bank have to be weighed against the more assured security of desalination.

109. The Nile has been suggested as a possible source, but decisions about it are not in the hands of either Israel or the Palestinians, and Egypt itself would have to contend with the rivers' eight other riparians before extending water to Gaza.

In the case of the West Bank, conveying the water from Israel would be tantamount to the inversion of the West Bank from an upstreamer to a vulnerable downstreamer of the mountain aquifer (in addition to its being naturally a downstreamer of the Jordan River). It also would have a "domino" effect on Gaza, linking it effectively to Israel even if it was supplied from the West Bank. In sum, any economic advantages that might be had from the conveyance of the West Bank's water from Israel would have to be compared with the costs of rendering the bulk of Palestinian water supply under Israeli control.

Political and Economic Constraints

Tension often arises between the ecological view of the management of international common water resources and that stemming from the perceived political and economic interests of the riparians. From an ecological point of view, sound management often dictates the inclusion of the basin as an integrated whole. Frequently, however, countries segment the management to suit their perceived interests rather than to protect the water sources. A chief challenge to devising joint management regimes thus is how to reconcile this tension or opposition. Doing so demands at the outset that the political and economic interests of the riparians be understood and acknowledged rather than belittled or treated as illegitimate.

Economic and political constraints that may conspire against sound management of the joint Israeli-Palestinian water resources have been mentioned in tandem with specific tasks in a fragmented fashion. They now will be synthesized and examined as issues in their own right. Economically, a main question would be: How are the costs of water protection to be estimated and divided between the two sides? Some of the costs involve large initial investments, such as building sewage systems and water treatment plants, that would have to be available for the Palestinian economy (Israel already has such systems in place). Although such undertakings would be necessary for health and other environmental reasons, water protection and reuse would have to be a primary objective. Other protection measures, such as limiting the release of industrial effluent and requiring liners for storage tanks and landfills to meet specific standards, would raise the costs of production. Still others, such as banning certain pesticides and converting to less chemically dependent agriculture, could lower crop yields. In either case, protection would have adverse repercussions on Palestinian economic competitiveness.

Another inference from the preceding remarks is that the costs would be ongoing and touch upon innumerable economic activities. Getting the two sides to agree on their value could prove difficult. Be that as it may, the costs very likely would be burdensome for the Palestinian economy and could act as disincentives against having them implement effective protection measures. Because Israel would be a co-beneficiary of protection measures, equity dictates that it shares the burden of protection. This is especially so regarding sewage systems and treatment plants that call for large initial outlays.

Sharing protection costs, which is the equivalent of sharing pollution quotas, is not a novel suggestion. For example, Michael Renner wrote that

> Countries suffering from "imported" pollution may want to consider offering technical or financial assistance for pollution control measures in the "exporting" country.[110]

He offered two water related examples from Europe where this happened. West Germany (before unification) considered co-financing a water treatment plant in East Germany to reduce the contamination of the badly polluted Elbe River. Another instance was West Germany and the Netherlands sharing in the French costs of pollution control for the Rhine River. If countries have been willing to share protection costs with upstreamers of like economic capabilities, it would be more incumbent upon Israel to pay the Palestinians to enable them to implement measures to protect the aquifers in which they are upstream. In a sense, Israel's willingness to pay for the protection of the aquifers would be an indicator of how much it values water.

Two political considerations are germane to the management of the common aquifers. One is the level of linkage the two sides wish to develop in their overall relationship. The second is sovereignty. The greater the number of tasks tackled jointly and the wider their scope, the more extensive the level of attendant cooperation. Such cooperation is not without repercussions. While a

110. Renner, 1989, p. 42.

water specialist may propose close cooperation in the water sphere, an economist may advocate a customs union between the two sides, and an energy specialist may promote linking the electrical grids. When such proposals are aggregated, they add up to a project of virtual economic union which, if the European experience of economic integration is an indicator, will have profound political repercussions.

It is true that such a union, albeit totally asymmetrical and forced on the Palestinians, has been in effect since the capture of the West Bank and Gaza by Israel in 1967. However, what is being addressed here is voluntary cooperation. Two central questions regarding such cooperation are: Would the most mortal of enemies wish to become the most intimate of neighbors; and Is this possible? At present, there is no clear consensus on either side that indicates what to expect. Nature, geography, and certain economic interests propel the Palestinians and Israelis toward close ties, whereas contemporary history, cultural differences, and unequal levels of development and capabilities push them in the opposite direction. Nor should it be assumed, as it sometimes is by well-meaning people on both sides and from the outside, that closer cooperation is automatically beneficial for the Palestinians, for the Israelis, or for co-existence.

The second political consideration is sovereignty. As numerous observers have noted, the contemporary trend has been for state sovereignty to erode as a result of the increase of flows of technology, information, capital, and goods from outside the state boundaries. On the face of it, sovereignty may not appear as a salient constraint that prevents the two sides from agreeing to cooperate closely. Yet, in the Israeli-Palestinian case, the question of sovereignty may have a special twist.

It may seem ironic to speak about Palestinian sovereignty as being a potential constraint on cooperation when it has been non-existent, to say the least, and that any loosening of the Israeli grip might be viewed by the Palestinians as an improvement over the past. Yet, it could be precisely because of Israeli domination that the Palestinians would become particularly sensitive to what might be construed as intervention in their affairs. On the Israeli side, the question is whether Israel would accept having as equal partners the same people over whom it has ruled for many years. Equality between Israelis and Palestinians would mean cooperation in activities that some Israelis might view as infringing on Israel's sovereignty. These are hard questions, and to try to answer them here would take us far beyond the scope of the present work. What can be said is that the answers to these questions will influence the type and scope of joint management tasks, as well as the type of institutions set up to implement them. At any rate, the sensitivities regarding sovereignty can be attended to by some of the suggestions made in the present text, suggestions which revolve around avoiding infringement as much as possible, weighing the gains against the costs of infringement, and reciprocity.

Conclusion

The natural, freshwater resources of geographic Palestine are scarce in a technical, not just, an economic sense. Virtually all of them are under Israeli control, maldistributed in favor of Israel, under threat of creeping pollution, and inefficiently allocated in the irrigation sector. Under these circumstances, the Palestinian water supply, both quantitatively and qualitatively, is in a particularly critical condition, lagging far behind that of Israel. As part of the accommodation effort, the Israelis and Palestinians have signed a series of agreements with provisions for both the interim period of Palestinian self-government, which is supposed to extend to the middle of 1999, and for the bilateral talks that are supposed to determine the final status of the West Bank and Gaza (and, tacitly, Israel). For the transitional period, the accords gave to the Palestinians a limited amount of additional water and a restricted role in the management of the water sector. These concessions were part of a larger economic and political package intended to improve the living conditions of the Palestinians and thus advance the peace process. For the final status talks, the accords laid out a partial agenda in the form of general principles such as equitable utilization of water rights, joint management, protection of water resources, and enhancement of the water supply. At the same time, the international community has stepped in with financial and technical assistance for the PA to build the infrastructure and institutions that would improve the water supply and sanitation conditions of the Palestinians. The questions that need to be addressed are whether the general principles agreed to by the Palestinians and Israelis will be translated into a physical and institutional reality during the final status talks and whether the work of the international donors and the PA will lay the foundations for a viable, well-managed water system.

* * *

The West Bank, Gaza, and Israel have a high degree of hydrological interdependence in the sense that most of the fresh, renewable resources in geographic Palestine are common to both sides. These resources belong to two basins, the Mediterranean Sea and Jordan River. They consist of groundwater and surface water. The two key aquifers are the mountain aquifer, which is replenished primarily from the West Bank and drains into the above-mentioned two basins, and the coastal aquifer, which chiefly is recharged from Israel and drains into the Mediterranean. There are additional aquifers that are replenished entirely from Israel, including the Galilee aquifer, which, like the mountain aquifer with which it shares the same watershed, drains both into the Jordan River system and the Mediterranean.

Analysts generally have considered only the mountain aquifer and, to a limited extent, the coastal aquifer as common resources. This identification is incomplete because a common international resource, according to international law, is one that is located in the territory of both sides. Consequently, the mountain, coastal, and eastern Galilee aquifers are common resources. It may be that for practical reasons the Palestinians would end up obtaining their groundwater allocations from the mountain and coastal (beneath Gaza) aquifers; but hydrologically and legally the common resources include more than the mountain aquifer.

Little runoff originates from within geographic Palestine because the central hills, its topographical and hydrological backbone, are highly absorbent limestone, and because the country's narrowness does not allow for floodwater to accumulate in significant quantities in the lateral watercourses. The principal surface water source is the Jordan River system, common to Israel, Jordan, Lebanon, Syria, and the West Bank. The system is fed predominantly from Syria, Lebanon, and Jordan; Israel and the West Bank contribute only a small fraction of the flow. That Israel contributes little to the Jordan River system is at odds with the prevalent opinion that puts Israel's contribution at about one-fifth of the total. The standard opinion considers the Dan River as an "Israeli" river when, in fact, only its aboveground channel appears in Israel; the flow itself originates from Mount Hermon in Lebanon and Syria.

In addition to these renewable resources, there is a tremendous fossil aquifer (70 billion m³) underlying the Negev—all within Israeli territory. It seldom is mentioned by official, or even nonofficial, specialists except for those who advocate its planned depletion to supply the Negev and even the coastal plain.

A second defining feature of the common, renewable water resources (in addition to the heavy dependence of both parties on them) is that their yield is relatively modest and aberrant. Their potentially safe yield is about 1,790 mcmy, of which, roughly speaking, more than one-third comes from the Jordan basin, a similar portion from the mountain aquifer, and the rest from the assortment of other sources. In addition, the rainfed land utilizes about 200 mcmy of IWE. The IWE is distributed nearly equally between the two sides and, because it is so distributed, will not be considered in the rest of the discussion. For the combined Israeli and Palestinian populations the 1,790 mcmy is the smallest per capita supply in the Middle East, except for Jordan, Libya, and the countries of the Arabian Peninsula. Further, the average is highly variable due to the wide seasonal and interannual oscillation of rainfall.

The downside of the oscillation of rainfall are the frequent droughts, which have a double, negative effect on water use: They reduce the supply and simultaneously increase the demand owing to higher soil water deficit in the irrigated land. On numerous occasions, droughts have tempted the water authorities in Israel to overpump from the groundwater, often with injurious consequences for the affected aquifers. Although measures, such as artificial recharge of the aquifers, can attenuate the impact of short duration droughts, their effectiveness is compromised when droughts are protracted. Ironically perhaps, the scarcity is particularly felt during the nonwinter periods when water ebbs. During these times, the soil moisture deficit rises, and plants require more water. In the summer, municipal demand peaks due to the heat and influx of tourists and visitors (especially Palestinian expatriates).

The scarcity is aggravated by contamination from untreated wastewater, return irrigation, industrial chemicals, sea intrusion, and leakage from saline rock formations in the aquifers themselves as a result of overpumping. Contamination also comes from point sources such as garbage dumps. The aquifers themselves, with their karstic outcroppings and, in the coastal areas, sand and sandstone formations, are highly absorbent and hence prone to pollution. In Gaza, the salinity and nitrate contamination have become pervasive, and the aquifer beneath it can be resuscitated only by a palpable reduction of pumping. Although it has the severest contamination problem, Gaza is not alone. Salinity is at serious levels in the Palestinian wells in the Jordan Valley, and the appearance of nitrates may be a matter of time because of the dumping of sewage from Jerusalem and other hill towns. Nitrates also have found their way to many of the West Bank springs. Although not enough is known at present about contamination from pesticides and other chemicals, Gaza can be expected to fair badly because of its relatively large irrigated area. The Israeli settlements in both Gaza and the West Bank add to the water pollution, whether from raw sewage or agricultural and industrial chemicals. Moreover, because many of these settlements are perched on hilltops, Palestinian fields become their sinks. So far, the quality of groundwater in many areas in the West Bank seems to be acceptable, but it may be a matter of time before contaminants become manifest due to the slow travel time of groundwater.

In Israel, the extent of pollution from all the foregoing sources is unknown because often the test results are not made public and the tests themselves have not covered many possible pollutants. According to the spotty information from independent environmental groups, years of sewage and garbage dumping, intensive use of pesticides, industrial effluents, and overexploitation have heavily contaminated groundwater, notably along the coast. It may be that in time, after all the pertinent tests have been conducted and their results disclosed, the extent of contamination will be found to be more profound than has been thought. The threat of pollution on both sides of the border only can increase as a result of population growth, rising incomes, industrialization, and urban expansion. Unless measures to protect the water sources are sped up, the availability of good quality water might dwindle.

* * *

Scarcity and high dependence on common resources are a sure recipe for conflict. Although the Israeli-Palestinian and Arab-Israeli conflicts have centered on the land, water also has been a perennial issue. In step with territorial expansion, the Zionist movement and subsequently Israel extended control over the water resources. Since 1967, Israel has had a firm grip over virtually all the groundwater resources of geographic Palestine and the Jordan River's headwaters. In contrast, the Palestinians, who early in the twentieth century had access to all the water resources of the country and on the eve of the 1948 war had tapped more of these resources than had the Jewish community, now find their access to water confined to quantities from the mountain aquifer in the West Bank and coastal aquifer under Gaza, amounts that are subject to Israeli approval. Israel has acted as if it were a full sovereign over the resources under its control, as exemplified in (among other things) its unilateral management of the water sector in the West Bank and Gaza since 1967. It thus has been able to exploit the water resources to its own advantage, while at the same time curbing the access of the Palestinians and, in the case of the Jordan River basin, other Arab riparians as well. Israel takes nearly 80–90 percent of the freshwater resources of geographic Palestine. Included in this figure are the shares of Israel and the West Bank under the Johnston Plan.

The disparity in extraction between the two sides has translated into a conspicuous water gap in all sectors. The Palestinian per capita municipal use, irrigation use, and aggregate use are less than 30 percent of the Israelis'. In all, the water supply in the West Bank and Gaza is substandard and intermittent. The pipe distribution network is dilapidated and its complements, the sewage system and water treatment plants, are critically lacking. Likewise in agriculture, the portion of the cultivated Palestinian land under irrigation is 10 percent, whereas in Israel it is more than 50 percent. The irrigation gap is summarized by the fact that the West Bank and Gaza have a per capita nonprocessed food import bill four times as large as Israel's, as well as by the significant food trade deficit they have with it.

The gap is even more conspicuous between the Palestinians and the Israeli settlers who consume five to six times as much per capita as do the Palestinians and are profligate irrigation water users. In the West Bank, their water supply compromised the Palestinians' opportunity to enhance their extraction from the eastern groundwater basin, the only basin of the mountain aquifer that was not fully exploited by Israel. The wells that supply the settlements with water occasionally had detrimental effects on Palestinian springs and wells because, among other things, they were dug adjacent to those water sources. Similar patterns are observable with respect to the settlers' water situation in Gaza, where the settlements, by chance or by design, are located on the segment of Gaza's aquifer with the freshest water.

Israel, without ever producing supportive economic analysis, often has imputed the substandard Palestinian municipal use to low income. Economic reasoning and comparative international data, however, suggest that although income plays a role in determining the level of water use, it fails to explain why Palestinian use is *as* low as it has been. The culprits here are the poor supply conditions and the stringent restrictions that Israel has instituted since the early days of the occupation. In fact, in Israel itself the level of household water supply is based not on income but on what is believed to be conducive to a good quality of life. This quantity has been steady under different income levels. Without a doubt, a latent or suppressed demand exists for municipal water in the West Bank and Gaza that might be equal to their present manifest demand.

Similarly, irrigation consumption stagnated under Israeli rule as a result of the combination of restrictions on land use and on well-drilling and pumping. There is enough class-1 land in the West Bank to double its irrigated area, and plans had been drafted on the eve of the June 1967 war to expand the irrigated area by 40 percent. Israel, on the other hand, increased its irrigation water supply which, together with improved technical water use efficiency, enabled it to extend its irrigated acreage.

Furthermore, although it has assigned agriculture the role of drought shock absorber, Israel devotes relatively large amounts of subsidized water to export crops for Europe and the United States, a policy that is tantamount to out-of-basin water transfer and a subsidy for consumers in developed countries. Moreover, it inefficiently uses substantial amounts of water to irrigate crops, such as cotton and wheat, with MVPWs that are much less than the water costs and MVPWs for a large portion of Palestinian horticultural crops and, certainly, for municipal water. Cotton, for example, consumes large quantities of water; it is planted chiefly in the hot Negev Desert and southern coastal plain. It is true that cotton is irrigated with treated wastewater, but water, like money, is fungible, and wastewater can be used for crops other than cotton, notably fruits, and equivalent amounts could be released for alternative uses. The water earmarked for cotton alone is greater than the entire irrigation water used in the Palestinian territories.

It is noteworthy that Israeli consumers would pay less for fruits and vegetables if Palestinians were to use the water to grow produce and sell it to Israel. This is because Palestinian wages are much lower than their Israeli counterparts, and the Israeli consumer would not have to pay agricultural subsidies. Indeed, letting the Palestinians grow the produce would not be exceptional; it would merely enable them to join the ranks of third world countries that export primary products to the metropolis.

* * *

The persistence of the poor water supply conditions and stark asymmetries regarding the control of water resources and water use cannot help to move the Israelis and Palestinians from a state of protracted conflict to that of a sustainable peace. The transitional agreements between the two sides accorded the Palestinians a limited additional water supply and a constrained management role of the water sector. They also committed both sides, albeit in general terms, to measures for the protection of the water supply from contamination and depletion. In concert, the international community in 1994 formed a consortium of donors largely from the developed countries, Arab oil-producing states, and international organizations—notably the United Nations and the World Bank—to help the PA augment the water supply, build sewage systems and water treatment plants, and boost the technical and institutional water management capabilities. Although cooperation between the PA and the donors had a rocky start, since 1995 their relations appear to be progressing more smoothly.

It is too early to assess the prospects of the projects that barely have begun. It is possible that the multiplicity of the donors, the emergency atmosphere, the high costs of the projects, and the bottlenecks in local expertise carry a risk of lessening the efficacy of international aid. Still, if the planned projects are implemented, they could have a tangible impact on sewage collection and wastewater treatment. Their contribution to the water supply will be constrained by the quantities allowed in the Taba Agreement. The development of viable institutions for water management, however, is a complex, lengthy process and will depend on the Palestinians themselves and the economic and political conditions under which they live.

More significantly, the accords laid down two broad principles for the final status negotiations: equitable utilization of water rights and joint management. If turned into commensurate actions, equitable utilization and joint management could redress the current asymmetry in water control and supply. Moreover, the accords included a recognition by both sides of the necessity to increase the available water supply; irrespective of how water rights are divided, the existing resources will not be sufficient to meet the future basic needs for a modern mode of life. Arguably, such needs amount to 220 m^3 per capita: 120 m^3 for municipal and industrial water at current Israeli levels, and 100 m^3 to provide an individual's demand for fresh fruits and vegetables and 25 percent of the demand for dairy products. However, the Palestinians get less than 50 percent of this amount, while the Israelis get more than 150 percent.

By the year 2040, and perhaps earlier, securing 220 m^3 per person for the population of geographic Palestine will require an increase of water supply from alternative resources equal to 1,790 mcmy. In the absence of technological breakthroughs in energy or crop production, the water for the production of the rest of the foodstuffs, perhaps 700 m^3 per capita, will have to be substituted by requisite or virtual water, or water imported indirectly through foodstuffs. Israel, which the World Bank classifies as a high-income economy, is likely to be able to absorb without much difficulty the costs of food imports, assuming their availability on the world market. For the Palestinians, whose economy falls in the lower middle-income economy category, the only way to compensate for the lack of water is through economic growth.

What constitutes equitable utilization is arguable. The Israeli-Palestinian agreements themselves have not identified criteria for translating the principle into actual shares. Nonetheless, equitable utilization and joint management are the central tenets of international water law with respect to common international water resources. The equitable utilization criteria must be found in international law. More specifically, the criteria are those "factors" or "rules" of the doctrine of equitable utilization. They pertain, *inter alia*, to the natural attributes of the resources, prior use, social and economic needs, avoidance of appreciable harm, and relative capability to harness alternative resources. Along with absolute sovereignty and prior use, the equitable utilization doctrine, at least theoretically, is the most widely accepted doctrine of international water law.

International law easily can be criticized, if not dismissed, as being nonbinding and lacking an enforcement mechanism. The rules of equitable utilization also can be faulted for being too numerous, unwieldy, and stated in broad terms without weighing preferences or operationalization procedures. This elasticity of the rules opens the door for agreements informed more by power relations than by equity. On the other hand, grounding a riparian's claims in international law confers legitimacy on those claims and at the same time constrains them, two prerequisites for a stable water-sharing regime. In this regard, it may not have been a coincidence that the Israelis and Palestinians used the term "equitable utilization" in the DOP, the same term used in international water law. Finally, both the official and academic discourse of the two sides invokes, often selectively, criteria for reallocation from the rules of equitable utilization. Thus, at a minimum, examination of the rules may not produce a magic number acceptable to the two sides, but it could make transparent their respective claims and arguments.

All factors considered, the Palestinians would be entitled to a share of the water equal to several times the present amount. The only factor in which the Israelis have an edge is prior use, although most of this use was obtained under conditions of war and would be hard to defend in terms of international law. In the Jordan basin during the 1950s and early 1960s, Israel drained Lake Hula and its marshlands and diverted water from Lake Tiberias out of the basin despite Arab protests. In the aftermath of the June 1967 war, Israel unilaterally boosted its diversion beyond its quota under the Johnston Plan on which utilization before the war had been based. Likewise, it failed to notify Jordan when it increased its pumping from the downstream of the mountain aquifer before 1967 and altered the physical properties of the aquifers as a result of supplanting water springs with artesian wells. Finally, by virtue of its control of the West Bank, Israel allowed the Palestinians only a minuscule increase of supply from the mountain aquifer and banned them altogether from access to the Jordan River.

Nonetheless, it is proposed here that bargaining could be simplified by avoiding those rules that lead to labyrinthine legal arguments and by assessing equitable utilization according to the social and economic needs of both sides and their capabilities to produce alternative water resources. In this way, the water can be seen for its utility and be subject to rational calculation, as was done during the Johnston negotiations over the Jordan when water quotas were assigned according to the irrigation needs within the basin. Consideration of social and economic needs also preempts the question of appreciable harm, which, at any rate, has been downgraded by the ILC as a principle for water apportionment in favor of equitable utilization. Although disagreements on the definition of needs and capabilities can be anticipated, the demand projections made by both sides are *not* irreconcilable.

The social and economic needs are those of the long-term, as water resources need planning. The year 2040, for example, could be taken as a maximum horizon for calculating the needs. By that time, the Israeli population may reach 12.8 million and the Palestinian 7.4 million. If the 1,790 mcmy were divided on equal per capita basis, the Palestinians would get 660 mcmy and Israelis 1,130 mcmy. Israel still would come out with an edge because it can harness much larger quantities from alternative resources than can the Palestinians. It has a broad seafront, a tremendous fossil brackish water aquifer, and the economic and technological resources for water desalination. Its population also is concentrated along the coast, a factor that reduces the cost of water conveyance. (By way of comparison, the island state of Malta, which has only one-half of Israel's personal income per capita, desalinates more than 70 percent of its water needs.) In contrast to Israel, the West Bank is landlocked and has only a minor amount of inland brackish water that could be desalinated. Gaza has a short sea coast, which has competing uses, including recreation, fishing, and a commercial port. Nevertheless, the shore may be able to support one major desalination plant. The facility could be built in phases, by adding more modules, commensurate with the ability of Gaza's economy to finance it and of its consumers to pay the price for desalinated water.

A significant desalination program is on Israel's agenda; the top officials in charge of water affairs, the ministers of agriculture and infrastructure, are known as advocates of desalination. In addition, desalination has a kind of multiplier effect in the sense that it increases the amount of water available for recycling. It also has the added advantage of being steady, unlike the supply from natural resources. In essence, the party that can produce more desalinated water also would have more wastewater to recycle. Thus, if both needs and capabilities are taken into account, an equitable solution would give the Palestinians perhaps as much as 800 mcmy.

As to the sources of these quantities, the Israelis and Palestinians would take their quotas of 400 mcmy and 215 mcmy, respectively, under the Johnston Plan from the Jordan basin. The Palestinians would draw the rest of their share from the mountain and Gaza aquifers. The Johnston Plan is not passé, as has been suggested by some analysts. Israel's population has remained proportionally similar (i.e., relative to the other riparians) to what it was at the time of the plan. It may be argued, moreover, that, although it was not ratified, the Johnston Plan acquired the status of customary law, at least for Jordan and Israel. Both the Palestinians and Lebanese rest their claims in the Jordan basin on the Johnston Plan as well. Syria has not stated its position regarding the Johnston Plan, although its initial reaction in the 1950s was not favorable. From a legal point of view, Syria has in its favor the 1920 Anglo-French Convention, which accorded it (and Lebanon) priority use and relegated Mandate Palestine to the status of a residual user. Syria may demand a larger share than its quota under the Johnston Plan, a share commensurate with its contribution to the Jordan River system.

The Johnston Plan was not drafted in a detailed form at the time Johnston terminated his mission; without breaching the basic quotas, it could benefit from technical modifications, such as breaking down the annual allocations on a seasonal basis and stating the quotas in percentages to allow for rainfall fluctuation. Renegotiating the plan, however, is likely to come at the expense of the Jordanians and the Palestinians, the two vulnerable downstream riparians.

The second principle for resolving the water conflict is joint management. International water law advocates that cooperation in management should rest on mutuality, equality, and respect for sovereignty. However, the present management regime of the common water resources lacks all of these attributes. Under the Taba Agreement, only the water resources in the areas under Palestinian jurisdiction are managed jointly, while the Jordan River is largely under Israeli control. This political arrangement would have to give way to a joint regime that covers the common water resources on both sides of the border.

It is recognized today that ecologically sound management should be integrated, treating the water sources as unitary basins or watersheds. Tensions often arise, however, between the ecological imperative and the real or perceived political and economic interests of riparians. A main challenge to devising joint management regimes thus becomes how to reconcile such tension. It requires at the outset that the economic and political interests of the riparians be understood and acknowledged rather than belittled or treated as illegitimate.

A joint management regime includes tasks to be undertaken by the riparians, as well as by a joint management body. The structure and composition of the latter would be too speculative without an agreement on the tasks. The joint tasks can range from minimal to all-encompassing, but the greater their number and the wider their scope, the higher the attendant level of cooperation between the parties. It is in light of a wider framework that the level of desired cooperation must be evaluated.

Discussions of a joint management regime also should factor in other water-related political and economic considerations, notably sovereignty and cost sharing. Palestinian sovereignty in particular could be profoundly infringed upon because hydrological interdependence is most pronounced in the northern and northeastern basins of the mountain aquifer that underlie an extensive area of the West Bank. The encroachment on sovereignty can be minimized, for example, by substituting technical means for the presence of Israeli personnel and restraining the powers of the joint management body, particularly regarding water quality protection measures that necessarily would touch upon virtually every activity in the aquifer area, from wastewater disposal to designing a landfill. Mutuality of arrangements also would go a long way toward attenuating sensitivities about sovereignty. Finally, a joint management agreement would have to resolve the economic question of how both sides would share the costs of water protection.

In the Jordan basin, a multilateral unified management regime eventually will have to be established among its five riparians. Such a regime depends on the Israel-Syria talks, which were suspended in March 1996. In the meantime, trilateral arrangements among Israel, Jordan, and the Palestinians can be made by adapting the provisions of the 1994 Jordan-Israel water agreement to the new situation. In addition to water rights allocation and joint management, the following issues are likely to figure, tacitly or explicitly, in any negotiations over water: adequate water for Gaza, the land-water nexus, and water-related compensation for the Palestinians.

Water for Gaza could be an issue if the Palestinians decide that they wish to supply water to Gaza from the West Bank or Israel. In the past, the Palestinians have raised the question of financial compensation for damages resulting from Israel's insufficient water allocations. If they want to raise this issue in the final status negotiations, they need to assess the legal basis and monetary value of compensation. Regarding the land-water nexus, Israel is unlikely to demand retention of West Bank border areas for hydrological purposes, although this has been a recurrent theme among Israeli strategists. It is likely to appeal to the "more credible," time-tested rationale of "security." From a Palestinian point of view, the loss of water is not the most compelling reason to oppose the annexation of territory by Israel. Nonetheless, when Israel presents boundary maps at the negotiations table, Palestinian negotiators need to scrutinize their water consequences carefully. A final issue is the water supply to the Israeli settlements. The questions that could arise regarding this matter are tied to the future status of the settlements and would be too conjectural to raise here.

* * *

Whether a water agreement, and especially an equitable one, will be concluded depends on several factors, some of which are related directly to water and others that are not. A water agreement is possible only within an overall peace accord. In fact, a water agreement would be a necessary component of such an accord. However, the deck is stacked in favor of Israel, which, especially under a Likud-led government, is unlikely to embrace compromise and equity. On its side is arrayed economic and military power. Moreover, the PA has weighty matters to negotiate with Israel—settlements, Jerusalem, refugees—and thus may find itself having to balance achievements in those areas against gains in the less visible water sector.

However, Israel can be hydrostrategically vulnerable if it decides to withdraw from the Golan Heights and the West Bank. Israel is downstream from Lebanon and Syria in the Jordan basin and from the West Bank in the mountain aquifer. This stream position helps explain why Israel was able, and could continue, to tap the bulk of these resources only either through direct control or by the use or the threat of force. By the same token, Israel needs to reach agreements with the Palestinians and the Syrians if it is to guarantee its water supply from these sources. In this connection, the fortunes of the Palestinians in the Jordan basin clearly would depend not just on Israel's stance but on that of Syria as well, assuming that Syria regains the Golan Heights.

The outcome of the negotiations could be influenced, too, by the manner in which they are conducted, that is, whether they are conducted bilaterally, through mediation, or through arbitration. Bilateral negotiations are more likely to be conducted according to the adage "international negotiations are nonprincipled solutions." Mediation by a third party, such as the World Bank, which could offer ideas as well as financial inducements, may facilitate an agreement and even ameliorate the effect of the power factor. If neither bilateralism nor mediation bears fruit, there is the negotiation of last resort, arbitration. Although arbitration carries risks for (and must be agreed to by) both sides, it is less susceptible to the vagaries of power than either bilateral negotiations or mediation.

* * *

It often is said that it would be difficult for Israel to compromise over water issues because water carries an ideological baggage by virtue of its association with agriculture, itself viewed ideologically by an influential segment of the Zionist movement, Labor Zionism. According to this ideology, agriculture, in addition to its economic utility, was to be a means for redemption of the land from its supposedly neglected state and refashioning a new Jewish man rooted in the land. However, this ideology has lost much of its salience due to the changes in the material foundations of Israeli society. Today, Israel's population is 90 percent urban, and agriculture contributes less than 3 percent of the GDP and a similar percentage of employment. Agricultural operations are highly mechanized, and a significant fraction of the agricultural labor force is Palestinian and foreign. It is difficult to sustain a water-agriculture ideology amidst such a social and economic milieu. Significantly, the Likud Party itself is the successor of Zionist factions that were not particularly impressed by the agricultural ideology of Labor Zionism.

The ruling ideology in contemporary Israel seems to transcend, but entails repercussions for, water. Holders of this ideology view Gaza and, in particular, the West Bank (which they commonly refer to by the biblical name, "Judea and Samaria") as part of *Eretz Yisrael*, or the land of Israel. They tend to consider the Palestinians of the West Bank and Gaza as mere residents with no rights to land and water. Although the interim accords went beyond this view and recognized Palestinian water and land rights, the Likud leadership is on record as wanting to renegotiate and alter those accords. In this context, a statement by Water Commissioner Meir Ben Meir is significant: "We have to talk about the right to water of the peoples of the region, and not about water rights, as regrettably set down in the peace agreements."[1] In short, the historical water-specific ideology has been supplanted, insofar as water is concerned, by a water nationalism derived from a more inclusive ideology—not a favorable development for compromise.

* * *

The Israeli-Palestinian water conflict is but one of several in the Middle East over the region's much coveted water resources, especially those of the Nile and Tigris-Euphrates basins. It is more intricate and involves more questions than the other water disputes due to the peculiarities of the overarching political conflict between the two sides. However, it has two similar core issues: the apportionment of water rights and, increasingly, the joint management of the resources. Much has been written about these disputes, but systematic efforts to put side by side the water-related conditions of the riparians of each of those basins and propose solutions have yet to be made. I hope that this book serves to change this situation. Readers can decide whether my efforts to draw extended water budgets to account for rainfall in the rainfed areas and requisite or virtual water, my economic analysis of water use, my anticipating the water needs of, and resources available to, the disputants, or my interpretation of international water law and proposals regarding the rules of equitable utilization and joint management can serve as models for studies in other basins.

Ben Meir has been quoted as saying that he dreamed of desalinating 800 mcmy of water, of which amount Israel would give Jordan, the Palestinians, and "perhaps even the Syrians" 600 mcmy.[2] Ben Meir's dream may be necessary, but why not start with the existing resources? For Israel, an equitable resolution is affordable. Moreover, an equitable resolution would advance Israel's interests by giving the upstream Palestinian and other Arab riparians the incentive to care for the water that flows down to Israel from their territory. An equitable resolution also would present

1. Cited in Globes (Internet), 7 February 1997.
2. Ibid.

Israel with an opportunity to deploy its superior economic and technological capabilities for resolving the water conflict and bolstering a peace that for so long it has asserted it sought. For the Palestinians, an equitable resolution is necessary and would put in reverse the historical process of dispossession.

Appendix

Water-related Excerpts from the Declaration of Principles (DOP) and the Cairo and Taba Agreements

ISRAEL-PLO DECLARATION OF PRINCIPLES WASHINGTON, D.C., 13 SEPTEMBER 1993

Annex III

Protocol on Israeli-Palestinian Cooperation in Economic and Development Program

The two sides agree to establish an Israeli-Palestinian Continuing Committee for Economic Cooperation, focusing, among other things, on the following:

1. Cooperation in the field of water, including a Water Development Program prepared by experts from both sides, which will also specify the mode of cooperation in the management of water resources in the West Bank and Gaza Strip, and will include proposals for studies and plans on water rights of each party, as well as on the equitable utilization of joint water resources for implementation in and beyond the interim period.

Source: *Journal of Palestine Studies*, vol. 23 (autumn) 1993, p. 119.

AGREEMENT ON THE GAZA STRIP AND THE JERICHO AREA
CAIRO, 4 MAY 1994

The Government of the State of Israel and the Palestine Liberation Organization (hereinafter "the PLO"), the representative of the Palestinian people. . . .

Annex II
Protocol Concerning Civil Affairs

Article II
Transfer of Powers and Responsibilities of the Civil Administration

31. Water and Sewage

a. All water and sewage (hereinafter referred to as "water") systems and resources in the Gaza Strip and the Jericho Area shall be operated, managed and developed (including drilling) by the Palestinian Authority, in a manner that shall prevent harm to the water resources.

b. As an exception to subparagraph a., the existing water systems supplying water to the Settlements and Military Installation Area, and the water systems and resources inside them [shall] continue to be operated and managed by Mekoroth Water Co.

c. All pumping from water resources in the Settlements and the Military Installation Area shall be in accordance with existing quantities of drinking water and agricultural water.

Without derogating from the powers and responsibilities of the Palestinian Authority, the Palestinian Authority shall not adversely affect these quantities.

Israel shall provide the Palestinian Authority with all data concerning the number of wells in the Settlements and the quantities and quality of the water pumped from each well, on a monthly basis.

d. Without derogating from the powers and responsibilities of the Palestinian Authority, the Palestinian Authority shall enable the supply of water to the Gush Katif settlement area and the Kfar Darom settlement by Mekoroth, as well as the maintenance by Mekoroth of the water systems supplying these locations and of water lines crossing the Jericho Area.

e. The Palestinian Authority shall pay Mekoroth for the cost of water supplied from Israel and for the real expenses incurred in supplying water to the Palestinian Authority.

f. All relations between the Palestinian Authority and Mekoroth shall be dealt with in a commercial agreement.

g. The Palestinian Authority shall take the necessary measures to ensure the protection of all water systems in the Gaza Strip and the Jericho area.

h. Upon the signing of this agreement, the two Parties shall establish a subcommittee to deal with all issues of mutual interest including the exchange of all data relevant to the management and operation of the water resources and systems and mutual prevention of harm to water resources.

i. The subcommittee shall agree upon its agenda and upon procedures and manner of its meetings, and may invite experts or advisers as it sees fit.

Source: United States Department of State.

ISRAELI-PALESTINIAN INTERIM AGREEMENT ON THE WEST BANK AND THE GAZA STRIP

WASHINGTON, D.C., 28 SEPTEMBER 1995

The Government of the State of Israel and the Palestine Liberation Organization (hereinafter "the PLO)," the representative of the Palestinian people. . . .

Annex III
Protocol Concerning Civil Affairs

Article 40
Water and Sewage

On the basis of good-will both sides have reached the following agreement in the sphere of Water and Sewage:

Principles

1. Israel recognizes the Palestinian water rights in the West Bank. These will be negotiated in the permanent status negotiations and settled in the Permanent Status Agreement relating to the various water resources.

2. Both sides recognize the necessity to develop additional water for various uses.

3. While respecting each side's powers and responsibilities in the sphere of water and sewage in their respective areas both sides agree to coordinate the management of water and sewage resources and systems in the West Bank during the interim period in accordance with the following principles:

    a. Maintaining existing quantities of utilization from the resources taking into consideration the quantities of additional water for the Palestinians from the Eastern Aquifer and other agreed sources in the West Bank as detailed in this Article.

    b. Preventing the deterioration of water quality in water resources.

    c. Using the water resources in a manner which will ensure sustainable use in the future in quantity and quality.

    d. Adjusting the utilization of the resources according to variable climatological and hydrological conditions.

e. Taking all necessary measures to prevent any harm to water resources including those utilized by the other side.

f. Treating, reusing or properly disposing of all domestic urban industrial and agricultural sewage.

g. Existing water and sewage systems shall be operated, maintained and developed in a coordinated manner as set out in this Article.

h. Each side shall take all necessary measures to prevent any harm to the water and sewage systems in their respective areas.

i. Each side shall ensure that the provisions of this Article are applied to all resources and systems including those privately owned or operated in their respective areas.

Transfer of Authority

4. The Israeli side shall transfer to the Palestinian side and the Palestinian side shall assume powers and responsibilities in the sphere of water and sewage in the West Bank related solely to Palestinians that are currently held by the military government and its Civil Administration except for the issues that will be negotiated in the permanent status negotiations in accordance with the provisions of this Article.

5. The issue of ownership of water and sewage related infrastructure in the West Bank will be addressed in the permanent status negotiations.

Additional Water

6. Both sides have agreed that the future needs of the Palestinians in the West Bank are estimated to be between 70–80 mcm/year.

7. In this framework and in order to meet the immediate needs of the Palestinians in fresh water for domestic use both sides recognize the necessity to make available to the Palestinians during the interim period a total quantity of 28.6 mcm/year as detailed below:

a. Israeli Commitment:

(1) Additional supply to Hebron and the Bethlehem area including the construction of the required pipeline—1 mcm/year.

(2) Additional supply to Ramallah area—0.5 mcm/year.

(3) Additional supply to an agreed take-off point in the Salfit area—0.6 mcm/year.

(4) Additional supply to the Nablus area—1 mcm/year.

(5) The drilling of an additional well in the Jenin area—1.4 mcm/year.

(6) Additional supply to the Gaza Strip—5 mcm/year.

(7) The capital cost of items (1) and (5) above shall be borne by Israel.

b. Palestinian Responsibility:

(1) An additional well in the Nablus area—2.1 mcm/year.

(2) Additional supply to the Hebron, Bethlehem and Ramallah areas from the Eastern Aquifer or other agreed sources in the West Bank—17 mcm/year.

(3) A new pipeline to convey the 5 mcm/year from the existing Israeli water system to the Gaza Strip. In the future this quantity will come from desalination in Israel.

(4) The connecting pipeline from the Salfit take-off point to Salfit.

(5) The connection of the additional well in the Jenin area to the consumers.

(6) The remainder of the estimated quantity of the Palestinian needs mentioned in paragraph 6 above over the quantities mentioned in this paragraph (41.4–51.4 mcm/year) shall be developed by the Palestinians from the Eastern Aquifer and other agreed sources in the West Bank. The Palestinians will have the right to utilize this amount for their needs (domestic and agricultural).

8. The provisions of paragraphs 6–7 above shall not prejudice the provisions of paragraph 1 to this Article.

9. Israel shall assist the Council in the implementation of the provisions of paragraph 7 above including the following:

a. Making available all relevant data.

b. Determining the appropriate occasions for drilling of wells.

10. In order to enable the implementation of paragraph 7 above both sides shall negotiate and finalize as soon as possible a Protocol concerning the above projects in accordance with paragraphs 18–19 below.

The Joint Water Committee

11. In order to implement their undertakings under this Article the two sides will establish upon the signing of this Agreement a

permanent Joint Water Committee (JWC) for the interim period under the auspices of the CAC.

12. The function of the JWC shall be to deal with all water and sewage related issues in the West Bank including inter alia:

    a. Coordinated management of water resources.

    b. Coordinated management of water and sewage systems.

    c. Protection of water resources and water and sewage systems.

    d. Exchange of information relating to water and sewage laws and regulations.

    e. Overseeing the operation of the joint supervision and enforcement mechanism.

    f. Resolution of water and sewage related disputes.

    g. Cooperation in the field of water and sewage as detailed in this Article.

    h. Arrangements for water supply from one side to the other.

    i. Monitoring systems. The existing regulations concerning measurement and monitoring shall remain in force until the JWC decides otherwise.

    j. Other issues of mutual interest in the sphere of water and sewage.

13. The JWC shall be comprised of an equal number of representatives from each side.

14. All decisions of the JWC shall be reached by consensus including the agenda, its procedures and other matters.

15. Detailed responsibilities and obligations of the JWC for the implementation of its functions are set out in Schedule 8.

Supervision and Enforcement Mechanism

16. Both sides recognize the necessity to establish a joint mechanism for supervision over and enforcement of their agreements in the field of water and sewage in the West Bank.

17. For this purpose both sides shall establish upon the signing of this Agreement Joint Supervision and Enforcement Teams (JSET) whose structure, role and mode of operation is detailed in Schedule 9.

Water Purchases

18. Both sides have agreed that in the case of purchase of water by one side from the other the purchaser shall pay the full real cost incurred by the supplier including the cost of production at the source and the conveyance all the way to the point of delivery. Relevant provisions will be included in the Protocol referred to in paragraph 19 below.

19. The JWC will develop a Protocol relating to all aspects of the supply of water from one side to the other including inter alia reliability of supply, quality of supplied water, schedule of delivery and off-set of debts.

Mutual Cooperation

20. Both sides will cooperate in the field of water and sewage including inter alia:

a. Cooperation in the framework of the Israeli-Palestinian Continuing Committee for Economic Cooperation in accordance with the provisions of Article XI and Annex III of the Declaration of Principles.

b. Cooperation concerning regional development programs in accordance with the provisions of Article XI and Annex IV of the Declaration of Principles.

c. Cooperation within the framework of the joint Israeli-Palestinian-American Committee on water production and development related projects agreed upon by the JWC.

d. Cooperation in the promotion and development of other agreed water-related and sewage-related joint projects in existing or future multi-lateral forums.

e. Cooperation in water-related technology transfer research and development training and setting of standards.

f. Cooperation in the development of mechanisms for dealing with water-related and sewage related natural and man-made emergencies and extreme conditions.

g. Cooperation in the exchange of available relevant water and sewage data including:

(1) Measurements and maps related to water resources and uses.

(2) Reports, plans, studies, researches and project documents related to water and sewage.

(3) Data concerning the existing extractions, utilization and estimated potential of the Eastern, North-Eastern and Western Aquifers (attached as Schedule 10).

Protection of Water Resources and Water and Sewage Systems

21. Each side shall take all necessary measures to prevent any harm, pollution or deterioration of water quality of the water resources.

22. Each side shall take all necessary measures for the physical protection of the water and sewage systems in their respective areas.

23. Each side shall take all necessary measures to prevent any pollution or contamination of the water and sewage systems including those of the other side.

24. Each side shall reimburse the other for any unauthorized use of or sabotage to water and sewage systems situated in the areas under its responsibility which serve the other side.

The Gaza Strip

25. The existing agreements and arrangements between the sides concerning water resources and water and sewage systems in the Gaza Strip shall remain unchanged as detailed in Schedule 11.

Schedule 8
Joint Water Committee

Pursuant to Article 40, paragraph 15 of this Appendix, the obligations and responsibilities of the JWC shall include:

1. Coordinated management of the water resources as detailed hereunder while maintaining the existing utilization from the aquifers as detailed in Schedule 10 and taking into consideration the quantities of additional water for the Palestinians as detailed in Article 40. It is understood that the above-mentioned Schedule 10 contains average annual quantities which shall constitute the basis and guidelines for the operation and decisions of the JWC:

a. All licensing and drilling of new wells and the increase of extraction from any water source by either side shall require the prior approval of the JWC.

b. All development of water resources and systems by either side shall require the prior approval of the JWC.

c. Notwithstanding the provisions of a. and b. above it is understood that the projects for additional water detailed in paragraph 7 of Article 40 are agreed in principle between the two sides. Accordingly only the geo-hydrological and technical details and specifications of these projects shall be brought before the JWC for approval prior to the commencement of the final design and implementation process.

d. When conditions such as climatological or hydrological variability dictate a reduction or enable an increase in the extraction from a resource, the JWC shall determine the changes in the extractions and in the resultant supply. These changes will be allocated between the two sides by the JWC in accordance with methods and procedures determined by it.

e. The JWC shall prepare within three months of the signing of this Agreement a Schedule to be attached to this Agreement of extraction quotas from the water resources based on the existing licenses and permits.

The JWC shall update this Schedule on a yearly basis and as otherwise required.

2. Coordinated management of water and sewage systems in the West Bank as follows:

a. Existing water and sewage systems which serve the Palestinian population solely shall be operated and maintained by the Palestinian side solely without interference or obstructions in accordance with the provisions of Article 40.

b. Existing water and sewage systems serving Israelis shall continue to be operated and maintained by the Israeli side solely without interference or obstructions in accordance with the provisions of Article 40.

c. The systems referred to in a and b above shall be defined on Maps to be agreed upon by the JWC within three months from the signing of this Agreement.

d. Plans for construction of new water and sewage systems or modification of existing systems require the prior approval of the JWC.

Schedule 9
Supervision and Enforcement Mechanism

Pursuant to Article 40, Paragraph 17, of this Appendix:

1. Both sides shall establish upon the signing of this Agreement no less than five Joint Supervision and Enforcement Teams (JSETs) for the West Bank under the control and supervision of the JWC which shall commence operation immediately.

2. Each JSET shall be comprised of no less than two representatives from each side in its own vehicle unless otherwise agreed. The JWC may agree on changes in the number of JSETs and their structure.

3. Each side will pay its own costs as required to carry out all tasks detailed in this Schedule. Common costs will be shared equally.

4. The JSETs shall operate in the field to monitor, supervise and enforce the implementation of Article 40 and this Schedule and to rectify the situation whenever an infringement has been detected concerning the following:

   a. Extraction from water resources in accordance with the decisions of the JWC and the Schedule to be prepared by it in accordance with sub-paragraph 1.e of Schedule 8.

   b. Unauthorized connections to the supply systems and unauthorized water uses;

   c. Drilling of wells and development of new projects for water supply from all sources;

   d. Prevention of contamination and pollution of water resources and systems;

   e. Ensuring the execution of the instructions of the JWC on the operation of monitoring and measurement systems;

   f. Operation and maintenance of systems for collection, treatment, disposal and reuse of domestic and industrial sewage of urban and agricultural runoff and of urban and agricultural drainage systems;

   g. The electric and energy systems which provide power to all the above systems;

   h. The Supervisory Control and Data Acquisition (SCADA) systems for all the above systems;

i. Water and sewage quality analyses carried out in approved laboratories to ascertain that these laboratories operate according to accepted standards and practices as agreed by the JWC. A list of the approved laboratories will be developed by the JWC;

j. Any other task as instructed by the JWC.

5. Activities of the JSETs shall be in accordance with the following:

a. The JSETs shall be entitled upon coordination with the relevant DCO to free, unrestricted and secure access to all water and sewage facilities and systems including those privately owned or operated as required for the fulfillment of their function.

b. All members of the JSET shall be issued identification cards in Arabic, Hebrew and English containing their full names and a photograph.

c. Each JSET will operate in accordance with a regular schedule of site visits to wells, springs and other water sources, water works and sewage systems as developed by the JWC.

d. In addition either side may require that a JSET visit a particular water or sewage facility or system in order to ensure that no infringements have occurred. When such a requirement has been issued the JSET shall visit the site in question as soon as possible and no later than within 24 hours.

e. Upon arrival at a water or sewage facility or system the JSET shall collect and record all relevant data including photographs as required and ascertain whether an infringement has occurred. In such cases the JSET shall take all necessary measures to rectify it and reinstate the status quo ante in accordance with the provisions of this Agreement. If the JSET cannot agree on the actions to be taken the matter will be referred immediately to the two Chairmen of the JWC for decision.

f. The JSET shall be assisted by the DCOs and other security mechanisms established under this Agreement to enable the JSET to implement its functions.

g. The JSET shall report its findings and operations to the JWC using forms which will be developed by the JWC.

Schedule 10
Data Concerning Aquifers

Pursuant to Article 40, paragraph 20, and Schedule 8, paragraph 1 of this Appendix:

The existing extractions, utilization and estimated potential of the Eastern, North-Eastern and Western Aquifers are as follows:

Eastern Aquifer:
—In the Jordan Valley 40 mcm to Israeli users from wells;
—24 mcm to Palestinians from wells;
—30 mcm to Palestinians from springs;
—78 mcm remaining quantities to be developed from the Eastern Aquifer;
—Total = 172 mcm.

North-Eastern Aquifer:
—103 mcm to Israeli users from the Gilboa and Beisan springs including from wells;
—25 mcm to Palestinian users around Jenin;
—17 mcm to Palestinian users from East Nablus springs;
—Total = 145 mcm.

Western Aquifer:
—340 mcm used within Israel;
—20 mcm to Palestinians;
—2 mcm to Palestinians from springs near Nablus;
—Total = 362 mcm.
All figures are average annual estimates.
The total annual recharge is 679 mcm.

Schedule 11
The Gaza Strip

Pursuant to Article 40, Paragraph 25:

1. All water and sewage (hereinafter referred to as "water") systems and resources in the Gaza Strip shall be operated, managed and developed (including drilling) by the Council in a manner that shall prevent any harm to the water resources.

2. As an exception to paragraph 1, the existing water systems supplying water to the Settlements and the Military Installation Area and the water systems and resources inside them shall continue to be operated and managed by Mekoroth Water Co.

3. All pumping from water resources in the Settlements and the Military Installation Area shall be in accordance with existing quantities of drinking water and agricultural water.

Without derogating from the powers and responsibilities of the Council the Council shall not adversely affect these quantities. Israel shall provide the Council with all data concerning the number of wells in the Settlements and the quantities and quality of the water pumped from each well on a monthly basis.

4. Without derogating from the powers and responsibilities of the Council the Council shall enable the supply of water to the Gush Katif settlement area and Kfar Darom settlement by Mekoroth as well as the maintenance by Mekoroth of the water systems supplying these locations.

5. The Council shall pay Mekoroth for the cost of water supplied from Israel and for the real expenses incurred in supplying water to the Council.

6. All relations between the Council and Mekoroth shall be dealt with in a commercial agreement.

7. The Council shall take the necessary measures to ensure the protection of all water systems in the Gaza Strip.

8. The two sides shall establish a subcommittee to deal with all issues of mutual interest including the exchange of all relevant data to the management and operation of the water resources and systems and mutual prevention of harm to water resources.

9. The subcommittee shall agree upon its agenda and upon the procedures and manner of its meetings and may invite experts or advisers as it sees fit.

Source: Information Division of the Israeli Foreign Ministry.

Note: *This is the text of the agreement as initialled in Taba, Egypt, on 24 September 1995 and approved by the Israeli government on 27 September. It may differ slightly from the final text signed in Washington on 28 September.

References

Abd al-Salam, Adil. 1990. "Water in Palestine" (in Arabic). *Encyclopaedia Palaestina*, Vol 2: 163–267. Special Topics Series. Beirut: Council of Encyclopaedia Palaestina.

Abd Rabbu, Alfred. 1990. "Drinking Water in the Bethlehem Area" (in Arabic). Pages 55–68 in *Water and Health in the West Bank and Gaza Strip*, edited by Save the Children. Proceedings of the Second Symposium. Ramallah: al-Sharika al-wataniyya.

Abd al-Razzaq, Omar, and Mahir Abu Salih. 1991. *The Agricultural Pools in the Jordan Valley Region* (in Arabic). Center for Rural Research, Special Paper Series 25. Nablus: al- Najah National Univ.

Abdeen, Ziad, and Hasan Abu-Libdeh. 1993. *Palestinian Population Handbook*. East Jerusalem: Planning and Research Center.

Abid, Abd al-Qadir. 1990. "Palestine: Location and Status" (in Arabic). *Encyclopaedia Palaestina*, Vol 2: 1–56. Special Topics Series. Beirut: Council of Encyclopaedia Palaestina.

Abu Arafeh, Abdel Rahman, et al. 1992. "Developmental Needs of the Palestinian Agricultural Sector." Paper submitted to UNDP. East Jerusalem.

Abu Mayla, Yusuf. 1990. "An Introduction to the Water Problem in Gaza Strip" (in Arabic). Pages 25–44 in *Water and Health in the West Bank and Gaza Strip*, edited by Save the Children. Proceedings of the Second Symposium. Ramallah: al-Sharika al- wataniyya.

———. 1992. "The Future of the Water Situation in the West Bank, Gaza and Israel" (in Arabic). Department of Geography, Islamic University, Gaza. Photocopy.

Abu Taleb, Maher, et al. 1991. "The Jordan Basin." Paper presented at the International Workshop on Comprehensive Water Resources Management Policies, 24–28 June, World Bank, Washington.

Adler (Cohen), Raya. 1988. "The Tenants of Wadi Hawarith: Another View of the Land Question in Palestine." *International Journal of Middle East Studies* 20:197–220.

Agriculture Unit. 1989. Report. Gaza: Author. Photocopy.

Aharoni, Yair. 1991. *The Israeli Economy*. New York: Routledge.

Al Alawi, Jamil, and Mohammed Abdulrazzak. 1994. "Water in the Arabian Peninsula: Problems and Perspectives." Pages 171–202 in *Water in the Arab World. Perspectives and Progress*, edited by Peter Rogers and Peter Lydon. Cambridge: Harvard University Division of Applied Sciences.

Aliewi, Amjad, et al. 1995. *Design, Construction and Chemical Analysis of Deir Sharaf Well No. 2a and Assessment of the Properties of the Upper Beit Kahil Aquifer in the Nablus Area*. East Jersualem: Palestinian Hydrology Group in association with Department of Civil Engineering, Univ. of New Castle upon Tyne.

Allan, J.A. 1994. "A Transition of the Political Economy of Water and the Environment in Israel-Palestine." Pages 31–44 in *Joint Management of Shared Aquifers*, edited by Eran Feitelson and Marwan Haddad. Second Workshop. Jerusalem: Palestine Consultancy Group in association with the Harry S. Truman Institute for the Advancement of Peace at Hebrew Univ.

American Friends of the Middle East. 1964. *The Jordan Water Problem*. Washington: Author.

Applied Research Institute of Jerusalem. 1994. *Dryland Farming in Palestine*. Bethlehem: Author.

Applied Research Institute of Jerusalem and Harvard University Institute for International Development. 1994. "Water Supply and Demand in Palestine: 1990 Baseline Estimates and Projections for 2000, 2010, and 2020." Bethlehem. Photocopy.

Arad, A., and A. Michaeli. 1967. "Hydrological Investigations in the Western Catchment of the Dead Sea," *Israel Journal of Earth Sciences* 16:181–196.

Aronson, Geoffrey. 1990. *Israel, Palestinians and the Intifada: Creating Facts on the West Bank*. New York: Kegan Paul in association with the Institute for Palestine Studies.

———. 1996. *Settlements and the Israel-Palestinian Negotiations: An Overview*. An IPS Final Status Issues Study. Washington: Institute for Palestine Studies.

ASIR (al-mu'assasa al-'ilmiyy al-Arabiyya li-al-abhath wa naql al-technolojia). 1986. "The Water Situation in the West Bank and Gaza." Symposium on Water Resources and Use in the Arab World, 17–20 February, Kuwait.

Assaf, K. et al. "A Proposal for Development of a Regional Water Master Plan." Jerusalem: Israeli/Palestinian Center for Research and Information, 1993.

Associates for Middle East Research Water Project. 1987. *Israel: Political, Economic and Strategic Analysis*. Series on Water: The Middle East Imperative. Philadelphia: Univ. of Pennsylvania.

Atlas of Israel. 1985. New York: Macmillan.

Attur, Ibrahim, and John Pike. 1966. *Water Resources in Jordan* (in Arabic). Amman: Central Water Authority.

Awartani, Hisham. 1991a. "Artesian Wells in the Occupied Palestinian Territories: Reality and Ambition" (in Arabic). Nablus: al-Najah National Univ., Department of Economics.

———. 1991b. "A Projection of the Demand for Water in the West Bank and Gaza Strip" (in Arabic). Nablus: al-Najah National Univ., Department of Economics.

Awartani, Hisham, and Shakir Juda. 1991. "Irrigated Agriculture in the Occupied Palestinian Territories" (in Arabic). Nablus: al- Najah National Univ., Rural Research Center.

Bachmat, Y. 1974. "Seawater Encroachment in the Coastal Plain of Israel during the Period 1958–1971." Report. Jerusalem: Israel Hydrological Service.

Bar-Am, Aviva. 1992. "Whatta Wadi." *Jerusalem Post Magazine*, 24 March.

Barberis, Julio. 1991. "The Development of International Law of Transboundary Groundwater," *Natural Resources Journal* 31 (winter):167–86.

Barghouthi, Mustafa, Ibrahim Daibes, et al. 1993. *Infrastructure and Health Services in the West Bank: Guidelines for Health Planning. The West Bank Rural P.H.C Survey.* 3 vol. East Jerusalem: Health Development Information Project in cooperation with the United Nations World Health Organization.

Bar-On, Mordechai. 1996. "Conquering the Wasteland: Zionist Perceptions of the Arab-Israeli Conflict." *Palestine-Israel* 3:13–23.

Baskin, Gershon, ed. 1993. *Water: Conflict or Cooperation.* East Jerusalem: Israel-Palestine Center for Research and Information.

Bellisari, Anna. 1994. "Public Health and the Water Crisis in the Occupied Palestinian Territories", *Journal of Palestine Studies*, 23, no. 2 (winter):52–63.

Ben Gurion University of the Negev with Tahal Consulting Engineering [BUNT]. 1994. *Israel Water Study for the World Bank.* Report R-94-36 (1). Washington: World Bank.

Benvenisti, Eyal. 1990. *Legal Dualism: The Absorption of the Occupied Territories into Israel.* Boulder, Colorado: Westview Press for the West Bank Data Base Project.

Benvenisti, Eyal, and Haim Gvirtzman. 1993. "Harnessing International Law to Determine Israeli-Palestinian Water Rights: The Mountain Aquifer," *Natural Resources Journal* 33 (summer):543–66.

Benvenisti, Meron. 1984. *The West Bank Data Base Project: A Survey of Israel's Policies.* Washington: American Enterprise Institute for The West Bank Data Base Project.

———. 1987. *The West Bank Data Base Project 1987 Report: Demographic, Economic, Legal, Social and Political Developments in the West Bank.* Jerusalem: *Jerusalem Post* for the West Bank Data Base Project.

Benvenisti, Meron and Shlomo Khayat. 1988. *The Atlas of the West Bank and Gaza.* Jerusalem: *Jerusalem Post* for The West Bank Data Base Project.

Benvenisti, Meron, et al. 1986. *The West Bank Handbook: A Political Lexicon.* Jerusalem: *Jerusalem Post* for The West Bank Data Base Project.

al-Bilbasi, Mu'taz, and M. Bani Hani. 1990. "Water Resources and Use in Jordan" (in Arabic). In *Conference on Water Resources and their Strategic Importance in the Arabic Countries,* edited by Muhammad al-Bakhit and Elias Salameh. Amman: Jordan Univ.

Bingham, Gail, et al. 1994. "Resolving Water Disputes: Conflict and Co-operation in the United States, the Near East, and Asia." Paper prepared by the Irrigation Support Project for Asia and the Near East for the U.S. Agency for International Development, Bureau for Asia and the Near East, Washington.

Birzeit Community Health Unit. 1987. "Report." Ramallah: Birzeit University.

Biswas, Asit K., ed. 1994. *International Waters of the Middle East: From Euphrates-Tigris to Nile.* World Resources Management Series, No. 2. Bombay: Oxford University Press for the United Nations University and the International Water Resources Association.

Blake, G. S. 1947. *Geology and Water Resources of Palestine.* Jerusalem: Government of Palestine.

Boneh, Yohanan, and Uri Baida. 1977–78. "Water Sources in Judea and Samaria and Their Exploitation" (in Hebrew). In *Yehuda Veshomron,* edited by Absalom Shmueli, et al. Jerusalem: Kenaan.

Bowen, R. L., and R. A. Young. 1985. "Financial and Economic Irrigation Net Benefit Functions for Egypt's Northern Delta." *Water Resources Research* 21, no. 9:1329–35.

Brajer, Victor, et al. 1989. "The Strengths and Weaknesses of Water Markets as They Affect Water Scarcity and Sovereignty Interests in the West." *Natural Resources Journal* 29 (spring):489–509.

Brawer, Moshe. 1968. "The Geographical Background of the Jordan Water Dispute." In *Essays in Political Geography,* edited by Charles A. Fisher. London: Methuen.

———. 1994. "The Boundaries of Peace." Pages 41–63 in *Peace in the Middle East: The Challenge for Israel,* edited by Efraim Karsh. London: Frank Cass.

Bruins, H. J., and A. Tuinhof. 1991. *Identification of Water Resources and Water Use—Recommendations for Netherlands Assistance.* Phase I Desk Study, Directorate General for International Cooperation. Amsterdam: Government of The Netherlands, Ministry of Foreign Affairs.

Brynen, Rex. 1996. "Buying Peace? A Critical Assessment of International Aid to the West Bank and Gaza." *Journal of Palestine Studies* 25, no. 3 (winter):79–92.

al-Buhayri, Salah al-Din. 1991. *The Geography of Jordan* (in Arabic). Amman: Maktabat al-jam'i al-Husayni.

Caponera, Dante. 1994. "The Legal-Institutional Issues Involved in the Solution of Water Conflicts in the Middle East: The Jordan Basin." Pages 163–80 in *Water and Peace in the Middle East,* ed. by Jad Isaac and H. Shuval. Studies in Environmental Science 58, Proceedings of the First Israeli-Palestinian International Academic Conference on Water, Zurich, 10–13 December 1992. Amsterdam: Elsevier.

Center for Engineering Analysis. 1992a. *Masterplanning: The State of Palestine.* Ramallah: Palestine Studies Project.

———. 1992b. "A Summary of Wadi al-Fari'a Project" (in Arabic). Ramallah. Photocopy.

Center for Rural Research. 1989. "Report." Nablus: An-Najah National University.

———. 1990. "Report." Nablus: An-Najah University.

CES Consulting Engineers Salzgitter GmbH with Deutsche Gesellschaft für Technische Zusammenarbeit. 1996. *Middle East Regional Study on Water Supply and Demand Development. Phase I.* Study submitted to Multilateral Working Group on Water. Eschbom, Germany.

Chan, Arthur. 1989. "To Market or not to Market." *Natural Resources Journal* 29 (summer):629–43.

Childers, Erskine B. 1971. "The Worldless Wish: From Citizens to Refugees." Pages 165–202 in *The Transformation of Palestine: Essays on the Origin and Development of the Arab-Israeli Conflict,* edited by Ibrahim Abu-Lughod. Evanston: Northwestern Univ. Press.

Cohen, Saul. 1986. *The Geopolitics of Israel's Border Questions.* Boulder, Colorado: Westview Press in association with Jaffee Center for Strategic Studies of Tel Aviv Univ.

Colby, Bonnie G. 1989. "Estimating the Value of Water in Alternative Uses." *Natural Resources Journal* 29 (spring):511–27.

Conservation Foundation. 1987. *Groundwater Protection: The Final Report of the National Groundwater Policy Forum.* Washington: Author.

Cooley, John K. 1984. "The War over Water." *Foreign Policy* 54 (spring):3–26.

al-Dabbagh, Mustafa Murad. 1973. *Biladuna Filastin* (Our country, Palestine). Vol. 1, part 1. Hebron: Matbu'at rabitat al-jamii'iyyin bi-muhafazat al-Khalil.

———. 1976. *Biladuna Filastin* (Our country, Palestine). Vol. 10, part 2. Hebron: Matbu'at rabitat al-jamii'iyyin bi-muhafazat al-Khalil.

Dar al-Jalil. 1981. "Water" (in Arabic). Report 362. Amman: Dar al-Jalil lil-nashr wa al-abhath al-Filastiniyya.

———. 1988. "Water Resources in the West Bank and Gaza" (in Arabic). Report 20. Amman: Dar al-Jalil lil-nashr wa al-abhath al-Filastiniyya.

Davidson, E. S., and B. Hirzallah. 1966. "Hydrology of the Jericho Area." Amman: Central Water Authority.

Dellapenna, Joseph W. 1990. "Water in the Jordan Valley: The Potential and Limits of Law." Pages 15–47 in *The Palestine Yearbook of*

International Law, vol. 5, 1989. Nicosia, Cyprus: al-Shaybani Society of International Law.

———. 1995. "Designing the Legal Structures of Water Management Needed to Fulfill the Israeli-Palestinian Declaration of Principles." Pages 63–103 in *The Palestine Yearbook of International Law, vol. 7, 1992–94*. Nicosia, Cyprus: al-Shaybani Society of International Law.

Department of State. N.d. *Department of State Administrative History*. Vol. 1, Chapter 4.H.2, The Johnson Administration. Case no. NLJ 83-223. Austin: The LBJ Library.

Dillman, Jeffery D. 1989. "Water Rights in the Occupied Territories." *Journal of Palestine Studies* 19, no. 1 (autumn):46–71.

Doorenbos, J., A. H. Kassam, et al. 1986. *Yield Response to Water*. Irrigation and Drainage Paper no. 33. Rome: United Nations Food and Agriculture Organization.

Dudley, Norman J. 1992. "Water Allocation by Markets, Common Property and Capacity Sharing: Companions or Competitors." *Natural Resources Journal* 32 (autumn):657–78.

Dumper, Michael. 1993. "Forty Years without Slumbering: Wafq Politics and Administration in the Gaza Strip, 1948–87." *British Journal of Middle East Studies*, 20, no. 2.

Duna, Cem. 1988. "Turkey's Peace Pipeline." In *The Politics of Scarcity: Water in the Middle East*, edited by Joyce Starr and Daniel Stoll. Boulder, Colorado: Westview Press.

Eisenhower, Dwight David. 1958. Papers, 28 March, Case no. 80-331, Document no. 1.

Elmusa, Sharif S. 1994a. *A Harvest of Technology: The Super-Green Revolution in the Jordan Valley*. Georgetown Studies on the Modern Arab World Series. Washington: Center for Contemporary Arab Studies, Georgetown Univ.

———. 1994b. "Towards an Equitable Distribution of the Common Palestinian-Israeli Waters: An International Law Framework." Pages 205–18 in *Water and Peace in the Middle East*, edited by J. Isaac and H. Shuval. Studies in Environmental Science 58, Proceedings of the First Israeli-Palestinian International Academic Conference on Water, Zurich, 10–13 December 1992. Amsterdam: Elsevier.

———. 1995a. "Dividing Common Water Resources According to International Water Law: The Case of the Israeli-Palestinian Waters." *Natural Resources Journal* 35 (spring):231–42.

———. 1995b. "The Jordan-Israel Water Agreement: A Model or an Exception?" *Journal of Palestine Studies* 24 (spring):63–73.

———. 1996. *Negotiating Water: Israel and the Palestinians*. Israeli-Palestinian Final Status Negotiations Series. Washington: Institute for Palestine Studies.

Elmusa, Sharif S., and Mahmud El-Jaafari. 1995. "Power and Trade: The Israeli-Palestinian Economic Protocol." Pages 173–95 in *The Arab-Israeli Accords: Legal Perspectives*, edited by Eugene Cotran and Chibli Mallat. The Hague: Kluwer Law International in association with the School of Oriental and African Studies, Univ. of London.

Encyclopaedia Judaica. 1971. Various volumes. Jerusalem: Keter Publishing House.

Encyclopaedia Palaestina. 1984. Volumes 1–4 (in Arabic). Damascus: Hay'at al-mawsu'a al-Filastiniyya.

European Community. 1993. *Prospects for Brackish Water Desalination in Gaza.* Report presented to the MWGW, Geneva, April. Brussels: the Commission of the European Communities, Directorate General of External Relations.

Falah, Ghazi. 1990. "Arabs versus Jews in Galilee: Competition for Regional Resources." *GeoJournal* 21, no. 4:325–36.

Falkenmark, Malin. 1984. "New Ecological Approach to the Water Cycle: Ticket to the Future." *Ambio* 13:152–60.

———. 1986. "Fresh Water: Time for a Modified Approach." *Ambio* 15:192–200.

———. 1996. "Meeting Water Requirements of an Expanding World Population." Paper presented at Land Resources: On the Edge of the Malthusian Precipice, 4–5 December, Royal Society, London.

Al-Fataftah, Abd Al-Rahman and Maher Abu Taleb. 1992. "Jordan's Water Plan." Pages 153–72 in *Canadian Journal of Development Studies.* Special issue on Sustainable Water Resources Management in Arid Countries.

FBIS [Foreign Broadcast Information Service]. 1994. "Daily Report. Near East and South Asia, 28 June." Washington.

———. 1996. "Daily Report. Near East and South Asia, 4 April." Washington.

Feachem, Richard G. 1977. "Infectious Disease Related to Water Supply and Disposal Facilities." *Ambio* 6:55–58.

Feitelson, Eran. 1994. "Joint Management of Groundwater Resources: Its Need and Implications." Pages 213–20 in *The Arab-Israeli Accords: Legal Perspectives,* edited by E. Cotran and C. Mallat. The Hague: Kluwer Law International in association with School of Oriental and African Studies, Univ. of London.

Feitelson, Eran, and Marwan Haddad. 1994 and 1995. *Joint Management of Shared Aquifers.* 3 vol. Jerusalem: Palestine Consultancy Group and Harry S. Truman Institute for the Advancement of Peace at Hebrew Univ.

Fetter, C. W. 1988. *Applied Hydrology.* 2nd ed. Columbus, Ohio: Merrill Publishing.

Fishelson, Gideon. 1994. "The Allocation and Marginal Value Product of Water in Israeli Agriculture." Pages 427–40 in *Water and Peace in the Middle East,* edited by Jad Isaac and Hillel Shuval. Studies in Environmental Science 58, Proceedings of the First Israeli-Palestinian International Academic Conference on Water, Zurich, 10–13 December 1992. Amsterdam: Elsevier.

Fisher, Frank, et al. 1994. "The Harvard Middle East Water Project: Overview, Results and Conclusions." Interim Report, December. John F. Kennedy School of Government, Institute for Social and Economic Policy in the Middle East, Harvard University, Cambridge. Photocopy.

Fletcher, E. R. 1991. "Fouling Their Own Waters." *Jerusalem Report* (August):20–21.

Flint, Courtney G. 1995. "Recent Developments of the International Law Commission Regarding International Watercourses and the Implications for the Nile River," *Water International* 20, no. 4:197–204.

Frey, Frederick. 1992. "The Political Context of Conflict and Cooperation over International River Basins." Paper presented at Middle East Water Crisis: Creative Perspectives and Solutions, 7–9 May, Univ. of Waterloo, Waterloo, Ontario.

Frischwasser-Ra'anan, H.F. 1955. *The Frontiers of a Nation*. London: Batchworth Press.

Galnoor, Itzhak, 1980. "Water Planning: Who Gets the Last Drop?" In *Can Planning Replace Politics? The Israeli Experience*, edited by R. Bilski. The Hague: Martinus Nijhoff.

Garfinkle, Adam. 1994. *War, Water and Negotiation in the Middle East: The Case of the Palestine-Syria Border, 1916–1923*. Occasional Papers, 115. Tel Aviv: Moshe Dayan Center for Middle Eastern and African Studies, Tel Aviv Univ.

Garreston, A.H., et al., eds. 1967. *The Law of International Drainage Basins*. Dobbs Ferry, N.Y.: Oceana Publications for the Institute of International Law, New York Univ. Law School.

"The Gaza-Jericho Agreement." 1994. *Journal of Palestine Studies* 23, No. 4 (summer):103–118.

Gaza Water Unit. 1989. "Report." Photocopy.

Ghezawi, Ali Z., and Mohammad M. Khasawneh. 1993. *Irrigation Water and Agriculture in the Jordan Valley and Southern Ghor: The Possibility of Cultivating Substitute Crops*. Amman: Royal Scientific Society, Center for International Studies.

Giacaman, Rita. 1988. *Life and Health in Three Palestinian Villages*. London: Ithaca Press.

Gilbert, Martin. 1993. *Atlas of the Arab-Israeli Conflict*. New York: Oxford Univ. Press.

Goldberg, David. 1992. "Projects on International Waterways: Legal Aspects of the Bank's Policy." In *Country Experiences with Water Resources Management: Economic, Institutional, Technological and Environmental Issues*, edited by Guy Le Moigne, et al. Washington: World Bank.

Goldraich, Yair. 1977–78. "The Climatic Regions of Judea and Samaria: Categorization According to the Thornwaite Method" (in Hebrew). In *Yehuda Veshomron*, edited by Absalom Shmueli, et al. Jerusalem: Keenan.

Goldschmidt, M. J., et al. 1967. "The Mechanism of the Saline Springs in the Lake Tiberias Depression." Hydrological Paper 11, Bulletin No. 45. Jerusalem: Israel Hydrological Service.

Government of Palestine. 1946. *A Survey of Palestine*, 2 vol. Reprint ed. Washington: Institute for Palestine Studies.

Gustafson, Ronald, et al. 1978. "The Future for Livestock, Poultry Production." *Feedstuffs* 50, no. 24 (June):22–25.

Gvirtzman, Haim. 1994. "Groundwater Allocation in Judea and Samaria." Pages 205–18 in *Water and Peace in the Middle East*, edited by Jad Isaac and H. Shuval. Studies in Environmental Science 58, Proceedings of the First Israeli-Palestinian International Academic Conference on Water, Zurich, 10–13 December 1992. Amsterdam: Elsevier.

Haddad, Marwan, and Samir Abu Ghusha. 1992. "Consumption of Water in the West Bank: Past, Present and Future" (in Arabic). Nablus: Department of Civil Engineering, al-Najah National Univ. Photocopy.

Haddadin, Munther. 1992. "Water and the Peace Process: A View from Jordan." *Policy Focus*, 20 September. Washington: Washington Institute for Near East Policy.

al-Hamidi, Muhammad S. 1990. "Water Quality in the West Bank." Pages 17–24 in *Water and Health in the West Bank and Gaza Strip*, edited by Save the Children. Ramallah: al-Sharika al-wataniyya.

Hayton, Robert, and Albert Utton. 1989. "Transboundary Groundwaters: The Bellagio Draft Treaty." *Natural Resources Journal* 29 (summer):663–722.

Heiberg, Marianne, and Geir Øvensen, et al. 1993. *Palestinian Society in Gaza, West Bank and Arab Jerusalem: A Survey of Living Conditions*. Report 151. Oslo: FAFO; distributed in U.S. by Institute for Palestine Studies.

Hillel, Daniel. 1991. *Out of the Earth: Civilization and the Life of the Soil*. New York: Free Press.

———. 1994. *Rivers of Eden: The Struggle for Water and the Quest for Peace in the Middle East*. New York: Oxford Univ. Press.

El-Hindi, Jamal. 1990. "Note: The West Bank Aquifer and Conventions Regarding Laws of Belligerent Occupation." *Michigan Journal of International Law* 11, no. 4:1400–1416.

Hitti, Philip. 1951. *History of Syria, Including Lebanon and Palestine*. New York: Macmillan.

Hof, Fredric C. 1995. "The Yarmouk and Jordan Rivers in the Israel-Jordan Peace Treaty." *Middle East Policy*, no. 4 (spring):1–9.

Homer-Dixon, T.F. 1991. *Environmental Change and Acute Conflict: A Research Agenda*. New York: Global Environmental Change Committee, Social Science Research Council.

Howe, Charles W., et al. 1986. "Innovative Approaches to Water Allocation: The Potential for Water Markets," *Water Resources Research* 22, no. 4:439–45.

Huerta, Carlos. 1991. "Running Silent, Running Deep." *Scopus* (Hebrew Univ.), no. 41:18–25.

El-Hurani, M. Haitham, and Mahmud Duwayri. 1986. "The Problems of Rain-fed Agriculture." Pages 55–72 in *Agricultural Policy in Jordan*, edited by Alison Burrell. London: Ithaca Press for the Abdul Hameed Shoman Foundation.

Husary, Samar, et al. 1995. *Analysis of Secondary Source Rainfall Data from the Northern West Bank*. East Jerusalem: Palestinian Hydrology Group in association with Department of Civil Engineering, Univ. of New Castle upon Tyne.

Hyatt, Eran, et al. 1992. "Peace Now Settlement Watch: Excerpts from Comprehensive Report on Settlements, January 22, 1992." *New Outlook* (Israel), March–April:15–17.

Inbar, Moshe and Jacob Maos. 1984. "Water Resources Planning and Development in the Northern Jordan Valley." *Water International*, 9, no. 1:18–25.

Institute for Palestine Studies. 1975. *United Nations Resolutions On Palestine and the Arab-Israeli Conflict, 1947–1974*. 3rd ed. Washington: Author.

International Law Commission. 1994. "The Law of Non-Navigational Uses of International Watercourse." *Environmental Policy and Law* 24, no. 6:335–68.

Ionides, M. G. 1946. "The Perspective of Water Development in Palestine and Transjordan." *Journal of the Royal Central Asian Society* 33, part 3–4:271–80.

Israel, Central Bureau of Statistics. *Statistical Abstract*, various years. Jerusalem: Author.

Israel Environmental Bulletin. 1991.

Israel, Ministry of Foreign Affairs, 1995. *Israeli-Palestinian Interim Agreement on the West Bank and the Gaza Strip*. Washington: Embassy of Israel.

Israel, Ministry of Foreign Affairs. 1982a. "Israel's Water Policy in Judea and Samaria." Information briefing, 14 February. Jerusalem.

———. 1982b. "Transfer of Water Systems in Judea-Samaria to Mekorot Water Company." Information briefing, 14 February. Jerusalem.

Israel, Morris, and Jay R. Lund. 1995. "Recent California Water Transfers: Implications for Water Management." *Natural Resources Journal* 35 (winter):1–32.

Israel Palestine Center for Research and Information. 1991–92. "Roundtable Forum of Israeli-Palestinian Water Scientists Meetings." Minutes nos. 1–14. Jerusalem.

Israel, State Comptroller Report. 1990. "Report on the Management of the Water Resources in Israel" (in Hebrew). Jerusalem. Photocopy.

Issar, Arie, et al. 1972. "On the Ancient Water of the Upper Nubian Sandstone Aquifer in Central Sinai and Southern Israel." *Journal of Hydrology* 17:353–74.

Issar, Arie and Ronit Nativ. 1988. "Water Beneath Deserts: Keys to the Past, a Resource for the Present," *Episodes* 11, no. 4:256–62.

———. 1990. *Water Shall Flow from the Rock: Hydrogeology and Climate in the Lands of the Bible.* New York: Springer-Verlag.

El-Jaafari, Mahmud. 1994. *An Econometric Analysis of the Agricultural Sector of the Palestinian Territories.* Sustaining Middle East Peace through Regional Cooperation Series, no. 4. Bethlehem: DATA.

El-Jaafari, Mahmud, and Radwan Shaaban. 1995. *Foreign Commodity Trade of the West Bank and Gaza: Capabilities and Horizon* (in Arabic). East Jerusalem: Palestine Center for Economic Policy Research.

al-Jabiri, Abd al-Qadir. 1983. *The Two-Seas Canal* (in Arabic). Amman: Jordan Univ.

Jaffee Center for Strategic Studies. 1989. *The West Bank and Gaza: Israel's Options for Peace.* Jersualem: Tel Aviv Univ.

al-Jarbawi, Ali, and Rami Abd al-Hadi. 1990."The Waters of the Palestinian State: From Taking Away to Restoration" (in Arabic). *Majallat al-dirasat al-Filastiniyya* (Beirut) 4 (autumn):84–108.

———. 1993. "Special Document File: The Peace Process," 23, No. 1 (autumn):115–21.

Jerusalem Water Undertaking-Ramallah District. 1991. "Report." Photocopy.

Jordan, Jordan Valley Authority. 1981. "Report." Amman: Author [JVA Archives are part of Ministry of Water and Irrigation].

Jordan, Ministry of Water and Irrigation. 1992. "Report." Amman: Author. Photocopy.

Kahan, David. 1987. *Agriculture and Water Resources in the West Bank and Gaza (1967–1987).* Jerusalem: *Jerusalem Post* for West Bank Data Project.

Kahhaleh, Subhi. 1981. *The Water Problem in Israel and Its Repercussions on the Arab-Israeli Conflict.* Washington: Institute for Palestine Studies.

Kally, Elisha. 1991–2. "Options for Solving the Palestinian Water Problem in the Context of Regional Peace." Israeli Palestinian Peace Research Project, Working Paper Series 19. Jerusalem: Harry S. Truman Institute for the Advancement of Peace, Hebrew Univ.

Kally, Elisha with Gideon Fishelson. 1993. *Water and Peace: Water Resources and the Arab-Israeli Peace Process.* Westport, Connecticut: Praeger, in cooperation with the Armand Hammer Fund for Economic Cooperation in the Middle East at Tel Aviv Univ.

Karmon, Yehuda. 1971. *Israel: A Regional Geography.* New York: Wiley-Interscience.

Kassim, Anis. 1984. "Legal Systems and Development in Palestine." Pages 19–35 in *The Palestine Yearbook of International Law.* Nicosia, Cyprus: Al-Shaybani Society of International Law.

Katsnelson, Jacob. 1985. "Sheet 13: Annual Rainfall, 1932/33–1975/76." In *Atlas of Israel.* New York: Macmillan.

Katz, D. 1994. "A Model for Evaluating Conflict over Shared Water Resources: the Arab-Israeli Conflict as a Case Study." Ph. D. diss., Univ. of Washington.

Kawash, Fadil. 1992. Interview, 11 December. Washington.

Khalidi, Walid, ed. 1971. *From Haven to Conquest: Readings in Zionism and the Palestine Problem Until 1948.* 2nd ed. Washington: Institute for Palestine Studies.

Khalidi, Walid, et al., eds. 1992. *All That Remains: The Palestinian Villages Occupied and Depopulated by Israel in 1948.* Washington: Institute for Palestine Studies.

Khassawneh, Awn. 1995. "The International Law Commission and Middle East Waters." Pages 21–28 in *Water in the Middle East: Legal, Political and Commercial Implications*, edited by J.A. Allan and Chibli Mallat. New York: Tauris Academic Studies.

al-Khatib, Nader. 1993. Telephone interview, 14 September.

al-Khatib, Nader, and Karen Assaf. 1992. "Palestinian Water Supplies and Demands." Paper presented at First Israeli-Palestinian International Academic Conference on Water, 10–13 December, Zurich, Switzerland.

al-Khudari, Riyad. 1992. Interview, 22 March. Gaza.

Kimmerling, Baruch. 1983a. *Zionism and Economy.* Cambridge, Mass.: Schenkman Publishing Company.

———. 1983b. *Zionism and Territory: The Socio-Territorial Dimensions of Zionist Politics.* Berkeley: Institute of International Studies.

Kislev, Yoav, 1990. "Structure and Reforms in Agriculture in Israel." Paper presented at Agricultural Reform in Eastern Europe and the USSR, Budapest.

Kleiman, Ephraim. 1991. *The Future of Palestinian-Arab and Israeli Economic Relations.* Working Paper Series No. 1. Jerusalem: Harry S. Truman Research Institute for the Advancement of Peace, Hebrew University, in association with Israeli-Palestinian Peace Research Project.

Kliot, Nurit. 1992. "The Application of Helsinki and ILC Rules to the Jordan-Yarmuk Drainage Basin." Photocopy.

Kolars, John. 1992. "Water Resources of the Middle East." Pages 103–29 in *Canadian Journal of Development Studies*, Special Issue on Sustainable Water Resources Management in Arid Countries.

Krafft, R. J. 1985. *Field Services in Gaza.* Health Division Department, 29 October, Reference EH/030/85). Gaza: UNRWA.

Kutcher, G. P. 1980. *An Agro-economic Model for Egypt.* Washington: World Bank.

Kuttab, Ata Allah. 1990. "Drinking Water and Health in the West Bank and Gaza." Pages 77–84 in *Water and Health in the West Bank and Gaza Strip*, edited by Save the Children. Proceedings of the Second Symposium. Ramallah: al-Sharika al-wataniyya.

al-Labadi, Ali M. 1990. "Israeli Policies and Practices Concerning Water and Land in the Arab and Palestinian Occupied Territories" (in Arabic). Baghdad: United Nations Economic and Social Commission for West Asia.

Laqueur, Walter. 1989. *A History of Zionism.* New York: Schocken Books.

Lesch, Ann, et al. 1992. *Transition to Palestinian Self-government: Practical Steps Toward Israeli-Palestinian Peace.* Cambridge, Mass.: American Academy of Arts and Sciences in association with Indiana Univ. Press.

Lipper, Jerome. 1967. "Equitable Utilization." In *The Law of International Drainage Basins,* edited by A. H. Garretson, et al. Dobbs Ferry, N.Y.: Oceana Publications.

Local Aid Coordination Committee for Development Assistance in the West Bank and Gaza. 1996. "Partners in Peace." Joint Report prepared by the United Nations and the World Bank. Washington: World Bank.

Lonergan, C. Stephen, and David B. Brooks. 1994. *Watersheds: The Role of Fresh Water in the Israeli-Palestinian Conflict.* Ottawa: International Development Research Center.

Lowi, Miriam L. 1993. *Water and Power: The Politics of a Scarce Resource in the Jordan River Basin.* London: Cambridge Univ. Press.

————. 1994. "Conflict and Cooperation in Resource Development." In *Peace Building in the Middle East: Challenges for States and Civil Society,* ed. by Elise Boulding. Boulder: Lynn Rienner.

Lustick, Ian. 1980. *Arabs in the Jewish State: Israel's Control of a National Minority.* Austin: Univ. of Texas Press.

McGinnies, William G. 1983. "Semi-arid Regions in the World." In *Natural Resources and Development in Arid Regions,* edited by Enrique Campos-López and Robert Anderson. Boulder, Colorado: Westview Press.

Main, Charles T., Inc. 1953. *The Unified Development of the Water Resources of the Jordan Valley Region.* Boston: Author.

Mansour, Camille. 1993. *The Palestinian-Israeli Peace Negotiations: An Overview and Assessment, October 1991-January 1993.* Washington: Institute for Palestine Studies.

al-Maw'id, Hamad Said. 1990. *Water War in the Middle East* (in Arabic). Damascus: Dar Kan'an li al-dirasa wa al-nashr.

Miller, Ylana. 1985. *Government and Society in Rural Palestine, 1920–1948.* Austin: Univ. of Texas Press.

Miro, P., and A. Ben Zvi. 1969. *Water Balance of Lake Tiberias for the Years 1949/50–1967/68* (in Hebrew). Tel Aviv: Tahal Consulting Engineers.

Moore, James. 1994. "An Israeli-Palestinian Water Sharing Regime." In *Water and Peace in the Middle East,* edited by Jad Isaac and Hillel Shuval. Studies in Environmental Science 58, Proceedings of the First Israeli-Palestinian International Academic Conference on Water, Zurich, 10–13 December 1992. Amsterdam: Elsevier.

Movement for Preservation of Israel's Water. 1994. (In Hebrew). Pamphlet.

Mudallal, Usama. 1975. "Water Resources and Water Needs in Jordan" (in Arabic). Amman: Natural Resources Authority.

Naff, Thomas. 1991a. "The Jordan Basin: Political, Economic, and Institutional Issues." Paper presented at the World Bank International Workshop on Comprehensive Water Resources Management Policies, 24–28 June, Washington.

———. 1991b. "Jordan River: Average Flows, 1985–1990." Philadelphia: Univ. of Pennsylvania. Photocopy.

Naff, Thomas, and R.C. Matson. 1984. *Water in the Middle East: Conflict or Cooperation?* Boulder, Colorado: Westview Press.

Al-Nahar, 1990. 7 September.

Nakhleh, Khalil. 1994. *Indigenous Organizations in Palestine: Towards a Purposeful Societal Development.* East Jerusalem: Arab Thought Forum.

Nashashib, Karim and Oussama Kanaan. 1994. "Which Trade Agreements for the West Bank and Gaza?" *Finance and Development*, 31: 10–13.

Nativ, Ronit, and Arie Issar. 1987. "Problems of an Over-Developed Water System." *Water Quality Bulletin* 13, no. 4:126–31.

Netanyahu, Sinaia, et. al. 1995. "Possibilities and Limitations in Sharing the Mountain Aquifer between Israel and the Palestinians." Pages 200–215 in *Joint Management of Shared Aquifers, vol. 2.* Jerusalem: Palestine Consultancy Group and the Harry S. Truman Institute for the Advancement of Peace at Hebrew University.

Newman, David. 1995. "Boundaries in Flux: The 'Green Line' Boundary between Israel and the West Bank—Past, Present and Future." *Boundary and Territory Briefing* 1, no. 7. Durham, UK: Univ. of Durham.

Nijim, Bashir K. 1990. "Water Resources in the History of the Palestine-Israel Conflict." *GeoJournal* 21 no. 4: 317–24.

Nir, N. 1991. "City of Gaza—Water Supply: Preliminary Study of Desalination of Brackish Water by Reverse Osmosis System." Report 1-1-91. Tel Aviv: Consulting Engineer.

Nuseibeh, Mustafa, and Taher Nasser Eddin. 1995. *Palestinian Fresh Water Springs: Springs Description, Flow and Water Quality Data 1970–1994.* East Jerusalem: Palestine Consultancy Group.

Office of Technology Assessment. 1988. "Water Supply: The Hydrologic Cycle." Pages 37–65 in *Perspectives on Water: Uses and Abuses*, edited by Avid H. Speidel, et al. New York: Oxford Univ. Press.

Orni, Efraim, and Elisha Efrat. 1973. *Geography of Israel.* 3rd ed. Philadelphia: Jewish Publication Society of America.

Palestine Delegation. 1992. "Policy Statement." Presented to the MWGW, September, Washington.

Palestinian Hydrology Group and Palestine Advocacy Group. 1992. "Case Document for International Water Tribunal." East Jerusalem. Photocopy.

Palestine Liberation Organization. 1992. "Water" (in Arabic). Tunis. Photocopy.

Patai, Raphael. 1971. "Labor Zionism." Pages 695–97 in *Encyclopaedia of Zionism and Israel*. New York: McGraw-Hill.

Pearce, Fred, 1991. "Wells of Conflict on the West Bank." *New Scientist* (UK), 1, June:36–40.

Policy Research Incorporated. 1992. *Development Opportunities in the Occupied Territories: Agriculture*. Report to USAID. Clarksville, Md.: Author.

Postel, Sandra. 1992. *Last Oasis: Facing Water Scarcity*. The World Watch Environment Alert Series. New York: W. W. Norton for World Watch Institute.

———. 1996. *Dividing the Waters: Food Security, Ecosystem Health, and the New Politics of Scarcity*. Worldwatch Paper No. 132. Washington: Worldwatch Institute.

Project in Development and the Environment. 1992. *Water Management Study for Jordan*. Report for USAID/Jordan, August. Washington: Chemonics.

al-Rabi, Ayman, and Abd al-Rahman al-Tamimi. 1989. *Hydrology of and Guide to Water Springs in the West Bank*. East Jerusalem: Palestinian Hydrology Group.

Rajab, Mu'in. 1991. *Agricultural Conditions in Gaza Strip* (in Arabic). East Jerusalem: Arab Thought Forum.

Renner, Michael. 1989. "National Security: The Economic and Environmental Dimensions." Worldwatch paper no. 89. Washington: Worldwatch Institute.

Rofe and Raffety Consulting Engineers. 1965a. *Nablus District Water Resources Survey*. Study for the Central Water Authority, Amman. Westminster, UK.: Author.

———. 1965b. *West Bank Hydrology, 1963–1965*. Study for the Central Water Authority, Amman. Westminster, UK.: Author.

Rogers, Peter, and Peter Lydon, eds. 1994. *Water in the Arab World*. Proceedings of conference sponsored by the Arab Fund for Economic and Social Development and the Division of Applied Sciences of the Center for Middle Eastern Studies at Harvard Univ. Cambridge: Harvard Univ. Press.

Rosenthal, A. and J. Kronfeld. 1982. "234U–238U Disequilibria as an Aid to the Hydrological Study of the Judea Group Aquifer in Eastern Judea and Samaria, Israel," *Journal of Hydrology*, 58:149–54.

Rowley, Gwyn. 1990. "The West Bank: Native Water-Resources Systems and Competition." *Political Geography Quarterly* 9, no. 1:39–52.

Roy, Sara. 1995. *The Gaza Strip: The Political Economy of De-development*. Washington: Institute for Palestine Studies.

Salameh, Elias, and Helen Bannayan. 1991. *Water Resources of Jordan: Present Status and Future Potentials*. Amman: Friedreich Ebert Stiftung and Royal Society for the Conservation of Nature.

Saliba, Samir. 1968. *The Jordan River Dispute*. The Hague: Martinus Nijhof.

Saliba, Bonnie Colby, and David B. Bush. 1987. *Water Markets in Theory and Practice*. Studies in Water Policy and Management Series, no. 12. Boulder, Colorado: Westview Press.

Sanad, Musa. 1992. "Solomon Pools: A National Treasure." al-Quds (East Jerusalem), 1 February.

Save the Children. 1990a. "Gaza Strip: Basic Agricultural Statistics." Gaza. Photocopy.

Sbeih, Mohammad Y. 1996. "Recycling of Treated Water in Palestine: Urgency, Obstacles, and Experience to Date." *Desalination* (Amsterdam) 106:165–78.

Scarpa, David J. 1994. "Eastward Groundwater Flow from the Mountain Aquifer." Pages 399–412 in *Water and Peace in the Middle East*, edited by Jad Isaac and H. Shuval. Studies in Environmental Science 58, Proceedings of the First Israeli-Palestinian International Academic Conference on Water, Zurich, 10–13 December 1992. Amsterdam: Elsevier.

Schama, Simon. 1995. *Landscape and Memory*. New York: Alfred A. Knopf.

Schiff, Ze'ev. 1989. *Security for Peace: Israel's Minimal Security Requirements in Negotiations with the Palestinians*. Policy Papers No. 15. Washington: Washington Institute for Near East Policy.

Schwarz, Joshua. 1993. Letter to author. 23 February.

———. 1982. "Water Resources in Judaea and Samaria and the Gaza Strip." In *Judaea, Samaria and Gaza*, ed. by J.D. Elazer. Washington: American Enterprise Institute.

Scobbie, Iain. 1996. "H₂O after Oslo: Legal Aspects of Water in the Occupied Territories." Pages 79–110 in *The Palestine Yearbook of International Law*. The Hague: Kluwer Law International in association with Al-Shaybani Society of International Law.

Shata and Salim. 1965. "Geology of the Undergroundwater Supply in Gaza." Cairo: Desert Institute.

Shawwa, Isam. 1993a. Personal correspondence, 13 July.

———. 1993b. Personal correspondence, 17 July.

Shehadeh, Raja. 1988. *Occupier's Law: Israel and the West Bank*. Rev. ed. Washington: Institute for Palestine Studies, 1988.

Shehadeh, Raja, and Jonathan Kuttab. 1982. *The West Bank and the Rule of Law*. Geneva: International Commission of Jurists and Law in the Service of Man.

Shu'un Tanmawiyya. 1988. "Water in Palestine." Series on Development in the West Bank and Gaza. East Jerusalem: The Arab Thought Forum.

Sirhan, Nimir. 1989. *Encyclopedia of Palestinian Folklore* (in Arabic). Vol. 2. 2nd ed. Amman: Matba'at al-dustur al-tijariyya.

Smith, C. G. 1966. "The Disputed Waters of the Jordan," *Transactions of the Institute of British Geographers*, no. 40:111–28.

Smith, Chris. 1990. "Geohelminth—Ascaris—in the West Bank." Pages 97–108 in *Water and Health in the West Bank and Gaza Strip*, edited by Save the Children. Proceedings of the Second Symposium. Ramallah: al-Sharika al-wataniyya.

Society for Austro-Arab Relations. 1992. *Development Perspectives for Agriculture in the Occupied Palestinian Territories*. East Jerusalem and Vienna: Society for Austro-Arab Relations.

Soffer, Arnon. 1994. "The Relevance of Johnston Plan to the Reality of 1993 and Beyond." Pages 107–22 in *Water and Peace in the Middle East*, edited by Jad Isaac and H. Shuval. Studies in Environmental Science 58, Proceedings of the First Israeli-Palestinian International Academic Conference on Water, Zurich, 10–13 December 1992. Amsterdam: Elsevier.

"State of the Environment." 1991. *Tanmiyya* (quarterly newsletter Welfare Association, Geneva), no. 25 (December)

Stauffer, Thomas. 1984. "The Benefits of War and the Costs of Peace." In *Israel and Arab Water*, edited by Abdel Majid Farid and Hussein Sirriyeh. Proceedings of symposium in Amman, 25–26 February. London: Ithaca Press for the Arab Research Center.

Steinberg, Gerald. 1987. "Large-scale National Projects as Political Symbols: The Case of Israel." *Comparative Politics* 19, no. 3: 331–46.

Stevens, Georgiana. 1965. *Jordan River Partition*. Stanford, Calif.: Stanford Univ. Press and Hoover Institution on War, Revolution and Peace.

Stork, Joe. 1983. "Water and Israel's Occupation Strategy." MERIP Reports, no. 16 (July–August):19–24.

Tahal Consulting Engineers. 1990. *Israel Water Sector Review: Past Achievements, Current Problems and Future Options*. Report for the World Bank. Tel Aviv and Washington: Author.

al-Tamimi, Abd al-Rahman. 1988. "Water Security in the West Bank: A Study of the Hydrology of the West Bank," *al-Katib* (West Bank), no. 94 (February):17–31.

Taylor, Alan. 1971. "Vision and Intent in Zionist Thought." Pages 9–26 in *The Transformation of Palestine: Essays on the Origin and Development of the Arab-Israeli Conflict*, edited by Ibrahim Abu-Lughod. Evanston: Northwestern Univ. Press.

Tessler, Mark. 1994. *A History of the Israeli-Palestinian Conflict*. Bloomington: Indiana Univ. Press.

Toye, Patricia, ed. 1989. *Palestine Boundaries*. 4 vol. London: Archive Editions in association with the International Boundaries Research Unit, Univ. of Durham.

United Nations. 1980a. *Israel's Policy on the West Bank Water Resources*. Report 16322-July. New York: Author.

———. 1980b. *Efficiency and Distributional Equity in the Use and Treatment of Water: Guidelines for Pricing and Regulations*. Natural resources/water series no. 8, E.80.II.A.11. New York: Author.

————. 1992. *Water Resources of the Occupied Territory*. Report A/AC.183/-. New York: Committee on the Exercise of the Inalienable Rights of the Palestinian People.

————. 1993. *Environmental Data Report, 1993–94*. Cambridge, Mass: Blackwell Publishers for UN Environmental Programme.

United States, Army Corps of Engineers. 1991. *Water in the Sand: A Survey of Middle East Water Issues (Draft)*. Washington: Department of the Army.

United States, Department of Agriculture. 1981. *Agricultural Statistics*. Washington: Government Printing Office.

————. 1991. *Agricultural Statistics*. Washington: Government Printing Office.

United States, Department of State. N.d. *West Bank Water Resources Are Being Exploited*. Washington. Photocopy.

Vardi, Yacov. 1980. "National Water Resources Planning and Development in Israel—the Endangered Resource." In *Water Quality Management Under Conditions of Scarcity: Israel as a Case Study*, edited by Hillel Shuval. New York: Academic Press.

Virshubski, Mordechai. 1961. "Water Administration and Legislation in Israel." Prepared by Water Commission of Israel. Photocopy.

Waterbury, John. 1979. *Hydropolitics of the Nile*. Syracuse: Syracuse Univ. Press.

Water Resources Action Program Task Force. 1994. *Palestinian Water Resources: A Rapid Interdisciplinary Sector Review and Issues Paper*. East Jerusalem: Author

Weshah, Abdel Aziz, and Ziad K. Elias. 1993. "The Jordan Valley: An Integrated Development Experience." Pages 9–26 in *Water Resources in the Middle East: Policy and Institutional Aspects*, edited by International Water Resources Association. Proceedings of International Symposium. Urbana: Univ. of Illinois Press.

Whittington, Dale, and K.E. Haynes. 1980. "Valuing Water in the Agricultural Environment of Egypt: Some Estimation and Policy Consideration," *Regional Science Perspectives* 10, no. 1:109–26.

Wolf, Aaron. 1992. "The Impact of Scarce Water Resources on the Arab-Israeli Conflict: An Interdisciplinary Case Study of Water Conflict Analysis and Proposals for Conflict Resolution." Ph.D. diss., Univ. of Wisconsin, Madison.

World Bank. 1988. *Jordan Water Resources Sector Study*. Report no. 7099–30. Washington: Author.

————. 1993a. *Developing the Occupied Territories: An Investment in Peace*. 6 vols. Washington: Author.

————. 1993b. *Water Resources Management*. Washington: Author.

————. 1994. *A Strategy for Managing Water in the Middle East and North Africa*. Washington: Author.

————. 1995. *From Scarcity to Security: Averting a Water Crisis in the Middle East and North Africa*. Washington: Author.

World Resources Report. Various years. Washington: World Resources Institute.

Young, Robert A., and S. Lee Gray. 1985. "Input-Output Models, Economic Surplus, and the Evaluation of State or Regional Water Plans." *Water Resources Research* 21, no. 12: 1819–23.

al-Za'im, Shurhabil. 1993. "Military Orders Regarding Water in the Gaza." Photocopy.

Zarour, Hisham, and Jad Isaac. 1994. "A Novel Approach to the Allocation of International Water Resources." Pages 389–98 in *Water and Peace in the Middle East,* edited by Jad Isaac and H. Shuval. Studies in Environmental Science 58, Proceedings of the First Israeli-Palestinian International Academic Conference on Water, Zurich, 10–13 December 1992. Amsterdam: Elsevier.

Zarour, Hisham, et al. 1993. "Hydrochemical Indicators of the Severe Water Crisis in the Gaza Strip." Pages 9–26 in *Water Resources in the Middle East,* edited by International Water Resources Association.

Zeituni, Naomi, et al. 1994. "Water Sharing Through Trade in Markets for Water Rights: An Illustrative Application to the Middle East." Pages 399–412 in *Water and Peace in the Middle East,* edited by Jad Isaac and H. Shuval. Studies in Environmental Science 58, Proceedings of the First Israeli-Palestinian International Academic Conference on Water, Zurich, 10–13 December 1992. Amsterdam: Elsevier.

Zerubavel, Yael. 1996. "The Forest as a National Icon: Literature, Politics, and the Archaeology of Memory." *Israel Studies,* 1, no. 1:60–99.

Index